LEGAL GUIDE FOR THE

VISUAL ARTIST

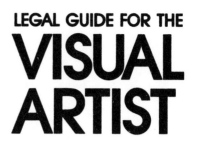

LEGAL GUIDE FOR THE
VISUAL ARTIST

REVISED EDITION

Tad Crawford

Allworth Press

New York

Acknowledgments

In writing the first edition of *Legal Guide for the Visual Artist,* I received invaluable encouragement and assistance from Bill Beckley; Jeffrey Cooper, Esquire; Professor Jack Crawford, Jr.; Eileen Farley; James L. Garrity, Esquire; Simon Gluckman, C.P.A.; Rubin L. Gorewitz, C.P.A.; Paul Jacobs, Esquire; Elsie Mills; Professor Joseph M. Perillo; the School of Visual Arts; the School of Visual Arts Alumni Association; Carolyn Trager; Roger Welch; and Carl Zanger, Esquire. I would particularly like to express my appreciation to Phyllis Rowley for her unstinting support and enthusiasm.

For their help in making this revised edition a reality, I would like to thank Hilda Brown; Arthur Eisman, C.P.A.; Tim Jensen, Esquire; Arie Kopelman, Esquire; Caryn Leland, Esquire; Marybeth Peters, Esquire; and Ellen Saks for their concern and careful advice. I would also like to thank Bill Beckley for co-authoring the discussion of uniqueness in Chapter 12; Brenda Ramirez and Zulema Rodriguez for their secretarial assistance; Warren Rogers for designing the book; Jill Bossert for her editorial encouragement and insight; and the National Endowment for the Arts for assistance that enabled me to interview Alberto Vargas and Alfred Crimi.

1989 Revised Edition

Published by Allworth Press, an imprint of Allworth Communications, Inc., 10 East 23rd Street, New York, NY 10010.

Distributor to the trade in the United States and Canada: North Light Books, an imprint of F&W Publications, Inc., 1507 Dana Avenue, Cincinnati, Ohio 45207. To order additional copies of this book, call toll-free 1-800-289-0963.

Library of Congress Catalog Card Number: 85-61351

ISBN: 0-927629-00-3

Contents

1 The Business of Art   1

2 Copyright: Gaining and Keeping Protection   3

3 Copyright: Registration   15

4 Copyright: The Issue of Work for Hire   23

5 Copyright: Infringement, Fair Use, Compulsory Licensing and Permissions   27

6 Moral Rights: State, Federal and Foreign   33

7 Moral Rights: Two Interviews   43

8 Risks in the Content and Creation of Art   53

9 Contracts: An Introduction   63

10 Original Art: Sales, Commissions and Rentals   73

11 Original Art: Ownership, Insurance, Submissions and Resale Proceeds   85

12 Unique Art and Limited Editions   91

13 Sales by Galleries and Agents   99

14 Sales of Reproduction Rights   111

15 Publishing Contracts   127

16 Video Art Works   137

17 Studios and Leases   145

18 Income Taxation   149

19 Income Taxation II   157

20 The Hobby Loss Challenge   163

21 The Artist's Estate   169

22 Artists and Museums   179

23 The Artist as a Collector   183

24 Grants and Public Support for the Arts   187

Appendices

    Artists Groups and Organizations for the Arts   193

    State Arts Agencies   195

    Joint Ethics Committee Code of Fair Practice   201

Selected Bibliography   205

Index   207

*Business art is the step that comes after
Art. I started as a commercial artist, and I
want to finish as a business artist. After I
did the thing called "art," or whatever it's
called, I went into business art. I wanted
to be an Art Businessman or a Business
Artist. Being good in business is the most
fascinating kind of art. During the hippie
era people put down the idea of business -
they'd say, "Money is bad," and "Working
is bad," but making money is art and
working is art and good business is the best
art.*

Andy Warhol
pop artist
from *The Philosophy of Andy Warhol:
From A to B and Back Again*

*The immediate cause of the sense of infinite
corruption, degradation and humiliation
that is the normal lot of the American artist
today is the art world...One has only to
observe what happens to the sense of
friendship, love, fraternity and comradeship
among artists as they are "picked up" by the
art world to see, instantly, that the rewards
of such "success" are death and
degradation. The art world is a poison in
the community of artists and must be
removed by obliteration. This happens the
instant artists withdraw from it.*

Carl Andre
minimal artist
from *Open Hearing*

UPDATE

The law is constantly changing. *Legal Guide for the Visual Artist* was completely revised in 1985 and updated in 1987. Fortunately, it is being reprinted in July of 1989 which allows the important changes that have taken place since 1987 to be covered. This Update follows the page numbers and headings of the book, including additions when necessary.

Lawyers for the Arts

Page 2. In California, the Bay Area Lawyers for the Arts have merged into California Lawyers for the Arts. The San Francisco office retains the same address and telephone. The Los Angeles office is located at 315 West 9th Street, Suite 1101, Los Angeles, California 90015. The telephone number is (213) 623 8311. In Illinois the address for the Lawyers for the Creative Arts has changed to 213 West Institute Place, Suite 411, Chicago, Illinois 60610. The telephone number is (312) 944 2787. In New York the address for the Volunteer Lawyers for the Arts has changed to 1285 Avenue of the Americas, Third Floor, New York, New York 10019. The telephone number is (212) 977 9270. For artists seeking legal advice, the art-law number is (212) 977 9271.

Gaining and keeping protection

Page 3. The Copyright Office hotline number for forms and circulars has been changed to (202) 707 9100. When requesting a Copyright Information Kit, specify that the kit is for a visual artist. The public information number for the Copyright Office is (202) 479 0700.

Who can benefit from copyright?

Pages 4-5. The United States joined the Berne Union on March 1, 1989. This Union has 79 countries as members, including 25 countries that are not members of the Universal Copyright Convention. It is no longer necessary for United States artists to publish simultaneously in a Berne Union country to gain protection under the Berne Convention. In fact, because the Berne Convention forbids member countries from imposing copyright formalities as a condition of copyright protection for the works of foreign authors, a number of changes have been made in the United States copyright law. These changes will be described in relation to the appropriate sections of the text. Copyright Office Circular 93, "Highlights of U.S. Adherence to the Berne Convention," and Circular 93a, "The United States Joins the Berne Union," offer an excellent overview.

Manufacturing requirement

Page 5. The manufacturing requirement expired on June 30, 1986. Bills introduced to extend this requirement did not gain the support necessary for passage.

Publication with copyright notice

Page 9. Due to joining the Berne Union, as of March 1, 1989, the United States copyright law no longer requires copyright notice to be placed on published works. In fact, however, most copyright proprietors will continue to use copyright notice. The notice warns potential infringers of the copyright. Use of the copyright notice prevents an infringer from being allowed to ask the court for mitigation of damages on the grounds that the infringement was innocent. And the Universal Copyright Convention still requires copyright notice and has as members some countries which are not members of the Berne Union.

Defective notice

Pages 11-12. Since copyright notice is permissive after March 1, 1989, works without notice are fully protected and the provisions on defective notice are not relevant. However, the changes in the copyright law are not retroactive, so works published without copyright notice prior to March 1, 1989, must still come within these provisions if the copyright is to be preserved.

Registration of copyright

Page 15. The Register of Copyrights has proposed that the application fee be doubled from $10 to $20 and legislation has been introduced to accomplish this.

Advantages of registration

Page 15. For artists in the United States, the advantages of registration remain the same and works must be registered prior to starting a lawsuit for infringement. However, works originating in a Berne Union country other than the United States will not have to be registered prior to commencing a lawsuit for infringement. Because of the other advantages of registering, presumably even such foreign works will be registered before the commencement of any infringement action.

Group registration

Page 16. For published contributions to periodicals and newspapers, the requirement that copyright notice accompany each contribution has been eliminated. However, the copyright claimant must be the same for all of the contributions.

Deposit

Pages 16-17. The deposit regulations referred to in the text have now been finalized and are in effect. Two helpful circulars from the Copyright Office are R40a, "Specifications for Visual Arts Identifying Material," and R40b, "Deposit Requirements for Registration of Claims to Copyright in Visual Arts Material."

Deposit for the Library of Congress

Page 18. After March 1, 1989, all works are required to be deposited with the Library of Congress, regardless of whether or not copyright notice appeared on these works. Regulations exempt certain categories of works from this requirement and, in any case, the failure to comply does not affect the validity of the copyright.

Employees

Page 23. The split between federal appellate courts over the issue of work for hire finally led to a decision by the United States Supreme Court. In an important victory for artists and other creators, the Court decided that whether someone is an employee must be decided under the law of agency. Under the law of agency one factor is "the hiring party's right to control the manner and means by which the product is accomplished." However, the Court went on to state, "Among other factors relevant to this inquiry are the skill required; the source of the instrumentalities and tools; the location of the work; the duration of the relationship between the parties; whether the hiring party has the right to assign additional projects to the hired party; the extent of the hired party's discretion over when and how long to work; the method of payment; the hired party's role in hiring and paying assistants; whether the work is part of the regular business of the hiring party; whether the hiring party is in business; the provision of employee benefits; and the tax treatment of the hired party." Based on these factors, it is unlikely that free-lance artists working on assignment will ever be found to be employees. For such free lancers to do work for hire, the assignment will have to fall into the categories enumerated on pages 23-24 and there will have to be a written work-for-hire contract signed by both parties. However, there is still the risk that a commissioning party that contributes to the work may contend that it is a joint work. For this reason, a written contract specifying the exact rights transferred remains a wise precaution. It might even include a provision stating, "This work is not a joint work or a work for hire under the copyright law of the United States."

Reform of Work for Hire

Page 24. The first hearings on work for hire since 1982 are scheduled before the Senate subcommittee on August 3, 1989. A work-for-hire reform bill was introduced by Senator Cochran in June, 1989, after the United States Supreme Court's decision on work for hire. This bill differs in a number of ways from the bill discussed in the text. First, it defines employee for the definition of work for hire as a "formal salaried employee." This would be even more restrictive than the agency test adopted by the Supreme Court, since employees would have to receive a salary and employee benefits. With respect to works commissioned from free lancers, the written work-for-hire contract would have to be obtained before the commencement of work and such a written contract would be necessary for each assignment. A shortcoming of the bill is that it would not reduce the categories in which assignments can be agreed to be work for hire. The bill would clarify the situation with joint works, since it would require that each author make an original contribution and, for commissioned works, would require the parties to agree in a written contract signed by both parties before the commencement of the assignment that the resulting work is to be work for hire.

Ownership of original art

Page 26. Senator Charles Mathias has retired and the new Chairman of the Subcommittee on Patents, Copyrights and Trademarks is Senator Dennis DeConcini.

Damages for infringement

Page 27-28. For infringements after March 1, 1989, statutory damages have been increased to an amount between $500 and $20,000, which can be reduced to $200 if the infringement was innocent, or increased to $100,000 if the infringement was willful. Also, the discussion of the value of copyright notice for collective works applies to infringements occurring prior to March 1, 1989. After that date, copyright notice in the name of the magazine will protect contributions in the sense that innocent infringers will not be eligible to ask for mitigation of damages due to reliance on the absence of copyright notice for a contribution. A surprising development has been that States have been held by the courts not to be liable for copyright infringements. This is because of the Sovereign Immunity of states under the Constitution. Since state institutions, such as schools, are also immunized, artists must be cautious when licensing copy-

rights in these situations. A bill has been introduced to make the states liable for copyright infringements which they commit.

Permissions

Page 29. After March 1, 1989, copyright notice is not required any longer and permission must be obtained for works published after that date regardless of whether or not they have notice. However, the change is not retroactive and any works that had already gone into the public domain because they lacked copyright notice will remain in the public domain.

United States legislation

Page 33. A Senate bill to provide moral rights by amending the copyright law was modified and reintroduced by Senator Edward Kennedy in 1989. Titled the Visual Artists Rights Act of 1989, the bill gives a narrow definition of a work of visual art as "a painting, drawing, print, sculpture, or still photographic image, produced for exhibition purposes only, existing in a single copy, in a limited edition of 200 copies or fewer, or, in the case of a sculpture, in multiple cast sculptures of 200 or fewer." Thus, unfortunately, the bill does not cover commercial art, nor does it cover art which is reproduced. The artist has the rights to claim authorship of his or her work, to prevent use of his or her name on the works of others, to prevent use of his or her name on mutilated or distorted versions of his or her own work, to prevent the mutilation or distortion itself if it will damage the artist's reputation, and to prevent the destruction of a work of recognized stature by any artist. The test for recognized stature is like that under the California law. However, the bill wisely gives artists rights in their own work regardless of stature and reserves the stature test for works which should be preserved for the culture. Other well-conceived provisions include a term of life plus 50 years and a restriction against waiver of these rights by the artist. The bill also provides rules with respect to art incorporated into buildings and commissions a study on resale royalties to be undertaken by the Register of Copyrights.

Moral rights: state, federal and foreign

Page 33. Eleven states now have moral rights laws. California, Massachusetts and New York have been joined by Connecticut, Louisiana, Maine, Nevada, New Jersey, New Mexico, Pennsylvania and Rhode Island. Utah has enacted moral rights for works commissioned under its percent-for-art law.

International copyright protection

Page 33. Although the text refers to the absence of moral rights as a "stumbling block" to the United States joining the Berne Union, this stumbling block was not insurmountable. Concluding that the United States law contains sufficient equivalents to moral rights under the Berne Convention, Congress did not choose to enact any explicit moral rights. This alleged equivalence is highly debatable, but it placated the film industry and many publishers who felt moral rights would hinder their operations. The Berne Convention is not self-executing, which means that United States law is not changed by the Berne Convention itself. The creation of moral rights will require United States legislation.

Future Directions

Page 39. The state moral rights laws have followed either the California or New York approach. Connecticut, Louisiana, Maine, Nevada, New Jersey and Rhode Island have taken the lead from New York; while Massachusetts, New Mexico and Pennsylvania use the model of California. The fact that so many states have enacted such laws suggests that national legislation would be advisable to ensure uniformity of treatment. Such uniformity is a goal of the copyright law, which preempts state laws that govern rights equivalent to rights of copyright.

Trademarks and tradenames

Page 40. An important revision of the trademark law has been signed into law and will take effect on November 16, 1989. Trademarks will be allowed to be registered before use, whereas previously they could only be registered

after use. The application must include a bona fide "intent to use" statement. Every six months an "intent to use" statement must be filed again and additional fees paid, and in no event can such a preregistration period exceed three years.

Right to publicity

Page 41. In 1984 California enacted a celebrity rights law. A number of other states have followed California's lead. The basic approach of these laws is to protect the publicity rights of deceased people for fifty years after their death. This applies to people whose name, voice, signature or likeness had commercial value at the time of death, whether or not that commercial value had been exploited during life. Prohibited uses cover commercial exploitation to sell merchandise or services, including advertising. Typical exemptions from the coverage of the law would include works in the public interest, material of political or newsworthy value, and single and original works of fine art. These laws impinge on the freedom of expression guaranteed to artists by the First Amendment. Since creative works are likely to be disseminated nationally, it may be that the most restrictive celebrity rights law will govern whether the artist must seek permission from the people to whom the decedent has transferred the celebrity rights or, if no transfer has been made, the heirs of the decedent.

Artists in the United States

Page 42. Connecticut, Louisiana, Maine, Nevada, New Jersey, New Mexico, Pennsylvania and Rhode Island have also enacted moral rights laws.

Crimi vs. Rutgers Presbyterian Church

Page 43. Alfred Crimi also discusses this case in his autobiography, *A Look Back – A Step Forward*, which was published in 1987 by The Center for Migration Studies, Staten Island, New York. I was surprised when the newsletter of the Rutgers Presbyterian Church requested permission to excerpt from one of my essays about its battle with Crimi. *Renewal*, the newsletter, ran a lengthy article about the dispute and lawsuit in its November, 1988 issue. The article, accompanied by photographs of the mural and Alfred Crimi, concluded, "Was it really only a 'tempest in a teapot' or a valid moral rights case? You be the judge."

Risks in the content and creation of art

Page 53. Since violation of the right to publicity is a risk faced by the artist, the discussion of the right to publicity on page 41 should also be reviewed.

Obscenity

Page 58. The United States Supreme Court has clarified that community standards apply to clauses (a) and (b) in the test for obscenity, but that a reasonable man standard is to be used for clause (c). The reasonable man standard, while still difficult to ascertain objectively, is a national standard which should not vary from one community to another. The Supreme Court has also made clear that even under racketeering laws there can be no seizure of art or books without an adversarial hearing. Because Congress has enacted The Child Protection and Obscenity Enforcement Act of 1988, artists should exercise special care if minors are to be portrayed nude. The law requires anyone producing images of sexual activity or a "lascivious exhibition of the pubic area" to maintain records giving the model's name (including stage names and nicknames), address and proof that the model is not a minor. Failure to keep such records will create a presumption such models are minors in the event of a criminal prosecution. Although the law is scheduled to take effect on August 17, 1989, its requirements are retroactive to February 5, 1978. Some parts of the Act may be found to violate the First Amendment; in the meantime, however, the law imposes a heavy burden and the risk of criminal penalties on artists who have used or wish to use nude models.

Ownership when selling rights

Page 85. Nevada has also enacted a statute to protect the artist's ownership of original art when reproduction rights are sold.

Fine prints

Page 93. Additional states with statutes governing fine prints or multiples include Georgia, Iowa, Michigan, Minnesota, Oregon and South Carolina.

California legislation

Page 93. The California law was amended in 1988 to require a certificate of authenticity (instead of a written instrument) when a multiple is sold by an art dealer into or from the state. A certificate of authenticity is defined as "a written or printed description of the multiple which is to be sold, exchanged or consigned by an art dealer." The law requires every certificate to contain the following statement: "This is to certify that all information and the statements contained herein are true and correct."

Consignment or sale

Page 99. Additional states which have enacted consignment laws include Alaska, Florida, Georgia, Idaho, Illinois, Iowa, Kentucky, Missouri, Montana, New Hampshire, North Carolina, Ohio, Pennsylvania and Tennessee.

Authorship credit and copyright notice

Page 113. The discussion of the value of copyright notice for collective works, such as magazines, applies to infringements occurring prior to March 1, 1989. After that date no copyright notice is required, so a copyright notice without a year date should not present any problems. Copyright notice in the name of the magazine will protect contributions in the sense that innocent infringers will not be eligible to ask for mitigation of damages due to reliance on the absence of copyright notice for a contribution.

Income taxation

Page 149. *Fear of Filing* is no longer being published each year by the Volunteer Lawyers for the Arts, but they are now distributing *The Art of Filing* which costs $9.95.

Accounting methods and periods

Page 150. Photographers and artists won a great victory in 1988 when they were exempted from having to capitalize their expenses. A provision of the Tax Reform Act of 1986 would have required that creators only deduct expenses over the period that income from their creative works would be received. After vigorous lobbying by creator's organizations, the Technical and Miscellaneous Revenue Act of 1988 allowed creators to deduct their expenses in the year incurred. Qualified works include photographs, paintings, sculptures, statues, etchings, drawings, cartoons, graphic designs and original print editions, as long as the work is created by the personal efforts of the artist. Congress enumerated certain types of art which are not qualified works and are subject to capitalization. These include "jewelry, silverware, pottery, furniture, and other similar household items..." This reflects a distinction between whether work is original, unique, and aesthetic or utilitarian. Utilitarian objects are likely to be subject to capitalization. Personal service corporations are also exempt from capitalization, as long as the expenses directly relate to the activities of the owner. The owner must be a qualified photographer or artist and own 95 percent or more of the corporation's stock.

Types of income

Pages 150-51. The Tax Reform Act of 1986 has changed the treatment of the different categories of income and created some new income categories. For tax years after 1986, long-term capital gains no longer receive the favorable tax treatment of being reduced by 60 percent before being taxed. Both short-term and long-term capital gains will be taxed at the same rate as ordinary income, except that in no event will the tax on capital gains exceed 28 percent. The Tax Reform Act has lowered individual tax rates with 28 percent as the highest rate (with some exceptions for those with high incomes).

Grants

Page 151. Grants to artists for schol-arships or fellowships may be excluded from income only by degree candidates and only to the extent that amounts are used for tuition and course-related fees, books, supplies and equipment at a qualified educational institution. Non-degree candidates no longer have any right to exclude scholarship or fellowship grants from income. These changes are effective for 1987 and thereafter. However, the old law will apply to scholarships and fellowships granted prior to August 17, 1986. For those granted between August 18, 1986 and December 31, 1986, amounts received in 1986 will be subject to the old law while amounts received in 1987 will be subject to the new law.

Prizes and awards

Page 151. All prizes and awards given to artists are now included in taxable income, unless the recipient assigns the prize or award to a governmental organization or a charitable institution. This applies to all prizes and awards made after December 31, 1986. Thus, the prior exclusion for prizes and awards given without being applied for to honor past achievement no longer exists. Under the new law, the person assigning a prize or award is treated as having received no income and having made no charitable contribution. For tax purposes it is as if the prize or award were never received.

Art supplies and other deductions

Page 152. Self-employed artists may deduct 25 percent of health insurance costs for themselves and their families from their adjusted gross income. If the artist employs people, they must also be covered for the artist to be eligible for the deduction. The deduction will not be allowed if the artist is eligible to participate in a health plan offered by the artist's employer or the artist's spouse's employer. Also, the deduction may not exceed net earnings from self-employment.

Work space

Pages 152-153. Starting with the 1987 tax year, the Tax Reform Act of 1986 more severely restricts the amount which may be deducted for an office at home. To avoid permitting the deduction for an office at home to reduce taxable income from the business to less than zero, the law only allows the home office deduction up to the amount of the net income from the business. Assuming art business expenses of $400, the example on page 153 would be recalculated as follows:

Gross income $1,500

Expenses of art business
    excluding home office expenses
    (such as supplies, postage, etc.)
    .... $400

Home office expenses allocated
to the business
    Interest and property
    taxes $900
    Electricity, heat, cleaning,
    depreciation $2,200
Total home office expenses...... $3,100

Total expenses $3,500

The new law allows the $3,100 of home office expenses to be deducted only up to the limitation amount of $1,100. This loss of $2,000 of deductions is a far less favorable treatment than that described in the example on page 153 in which only $1,600 of deductions were lost. The home office expenses which cannot be deducted under this test can be carried forward for use as a deduction in a future year when income is sufficient. Of course, mortgage interest and property taxes remain fully deductible on Schedule A for those who itemize deductions.

Professional equipment

Page 153. The 1986 tax reform moves cars from the 3-year property class to the 5-year property class. Office furniture and fixtures have been shifted to a new 7-year category. Houses have become 27.5 year property. The recovery period is specified and the percentages to be applied each year have generally increased. For the alternative ACRS, the recovery period for personal property with no class life is 12 years, for nonresidential and residential rental property is 40 years, and for all other property is the appropriate class life. The alternative ACRS System must be used to determine the depreciation for certain types of property, such as luxury cars, computers, and airplanes, if the property is not used more than 50 percent for business purposes. In addition, limits are placed

on the amount of annual depreciation allowable for luxury cars. Another important change modifies the rule which permits the expensing of $5,000 of equipment each year. Starting in 1987, $10,000 of such equipment may be expensed, but only if the amount to be expensed does not exceed taxable income from the business and the property itself is used in the active conduct of the business. Also, if the amount of such property placed in service exceeds $200,000 in any year, the $10,000 amount must be reduced.

Travel, transportation and entertainment

Page 155. Transportation costs will remain fully deductible. However, expenses for business meals and entertainment will only be 80 percent deductible. This reflects Congress' belief that such meals and entertainment inherently involve some personal living expenses. A meal which is merely conducive to discussing business will not be deductible. Nor will a meal not attended by the party taking the deduction (or an employee). Both meals and entertainment must involve a substantial business discussion. There are some exceptions which will probably not have great relevance to artists. This provision will take effect for 1987.

Income averaging

Page 157. The Tax Reform Act of 1986 has eliminated income averaging for tax years beginning on or after January 1, 1987, which may hurt artists whose incomes fluctuate a great deal.

Self-employment tax

Page 157. The effective rate for the self-employment tax is 13.02 percent for 1988 and 1989. The maximum amount of income subject to this tax is $45,000 for 1988 and $48,000 for 1989.

Retirement plans

Page 158. To qualify to make a deductible contribution to an IRA, an artist must either (1) not be covered by another retirement plan, or (2) if covered by another retirement plan, the artist must have no more than $25,000 of adjusted gross income ($40,000 for a married artist). If an artist were covered by a disqualifying retirement plan, it would still be possible to make a non-deductible contribution to an IRA (subject to the current limitations on the amount of the contribution). This has the tax deferral advantage of shielding from tax the earnings on the IRA contribution. IRS Publication 566 is no longer published.

Investment credit

Page 159. For property placed in service after December 31, 1985, the investment tax credit is generally repealed. For property placed in service prior to 1986, the investment tax credit carryover rules will continue to apply. The investment tax credit will also be available for certain transition property which results from 1985 transactions even if largely put in service in 1986.

American artists living abroad

Pages 160-61. For tax years after 1986, the exclusion for American citizens living abroad will be reduced to $70,000 per year. Also, this exclusion will be negatively affected if an artist travels in countries restricted to United States citizens under the Trading with the Enemy Act or the International Emergency Economic Powers Act.

Forms of doing business

Pages 161-62. The Tax Reform Act of 1986 lowered the highest corporate tax rate from 46 percent to 34 percent for tax years commencing on or after July 1, 1987. For taxable years which included July 1, 1987, transitional rates applied of 15 percent on the first $25,000 of taxable income, 16½ percent from $25,001 to $50,000, 27½ percent from $50,001 to $75,000, 37 percent from $75,001 to $100,000, and 40 percent over $100,000. The rates for tax years commencing on or after July 1, 1987 are 15 percent on the first $50,000 of taxable income, 25 percent from $50,001 to $75,000, and 34 percent over $100,000. Because the highest corporate rates will exceed the highest personal rates (34 percent opposed to 28 percent), tax experts

suggest that Subchapter S corporations may be advantageous. In general, the new tax law requires that a partnership, an S corporation, or a personal service corporation (which is a corporation whose principal activity is the performance of personal services by an employee-owner) use a calendar tax year for years commencing after December 31, 1986, unless there is a business purpose for using a fiscal year.

Gifts

Page 162. For tax years after 1986, transfers of income- producing property from adults to children under 14 will have a very limited tax advantage. Basically, the unearned income of the child will be taxed at the parents' top rates. Of course, the transfer of art to the child might still be a wise decision, since the art might appreciate in value without producing income until a sale at a much later date.

A test: three years out of five

Page 163. The Tax Reform Act has now made this test three years out of five. To be presumed to have a profit motive and therefore be engaged in a business rather than a hobby, the artist must have a profit in three years out of five. However, the nine factors to determine profit motive remain the same.

The will

Page 172. In the indented example of a bequest, the words "An example of a bequest to a class would be:" should be a separate paragraph.

Trusts

Page 173. The Tax Reform Act of 1986 requires that trusts (except for certain tax exempt and charitable trusts) adopt a calendar tax year. This will prevent deferral of income to beneficiaries of the trust who use a calendar tax year.

Basis

Page 178. Despite the fact that capital gains and ordinary income will basically be taxed at the same rates, it is still advantageous to receive stepped-up basis. One advantage is that the amount of the gain is simply less. In the example in which the daughter receives the art, the only change is that the $2,500 of gains would no longer be taxed at the favorable capital gains rate. However, the $5,000 of stepped-up basis would avoid any income tax whatsoever.

The value of art

Page 183. The value of art sold at auction has increased dramatically. Christie's and Sotheby Parke-Bernet sold $3.2 billion in 1988, a sharp increase from the $1.5 billion sold in 1986 and the $1 billion sold in 1984. Projected sales for 1989 exceed $4 billion.

Tax status of the collector

Pages 185-86. Of course, the rates for ordinary income and capital gains will now generally be the same. There has also been speculation that art used for office decoration may be more easily depreciated under the ACRS than had previously been the case. This is because the IRS has generally attacked such depreciation on the grounds that neither the useful life nor salvage value of art can be determined. However, neither of these factors enter into the ACRS calculation, so there is some possibility the viewpoint of the IRS may change.

Charitable contributions

Page 186. The collector remains able to donate art which has appreciated in value and receive a charitable deduction of full fair market value. This is in striking contrast to the artist, who remains unable to do this and will generally receive no deduction for contributions of his or her art to charity. The Tax Reform Act of 1986 does have an impact on collectors by providing that untaxed appreciation in donated art will be a preference item for calculation of the alternative minimum tax. As a simple rule, a taxpayer with no other preference items should be able to donate art with appreciation of up to 25 percent of regular income without being affected by the minimum tax.

NEA funding

Page 187. The reference for artists' grants should be page 191. For the 1989 fiscal year, the appropriation for the NEA was $169,090,000, compared with $167,731,000 for the 1988 fiscal year. The Administration has proposed an appropriation of $170,100,000 for the 1990 fiscal year.

State and local support

Page 188. In 1988, state arts agencies distributed $270,000,000, a sum far in excess of the budget for the NEA.

Artists groups and organizations for the arts

Page 193. The address for the Advertising Photographers of America has changed to 27 West 20th Street, New York, New York 10011. The address for the American Council for the Arts has changed to 1285 Avenue of the Americas, Third Floor, Area M, New York, New York 10019. The address for the American Craft Council has changed to 40 West 53rd Street, New York, New York 10019, for its administrative offices, and 45 West 45th Street, New York, New York 10036, for its library. The address for the American Society of Magazine Photographers has changed to 419 Park Avenue South, New York, New York 10016. The address for the Art Dealers Association of California has changed to 718 North La Cienega Boulevard, Los Angeles, California 90069. The entry for Artists Equity Association of New York should be deleted from page 193. A complete, current entry appears on page 194 under New York Artists Equity Association. The address for The Artists Foundation has changed to 8 Park Plaza, Boston, Massachusetts 02116. The address of the Association of Artist-Run Galleries has changed to 164 Mercer Street, New York, New York 10012. The address of the Boston Visual Artists Union has changed to c/o The Art Institute of Boston, 700 Beacon Street, Boston, Massachusetts 02215.

Page 194. The Center for Arts Information has been closed. Anyone interested in their services should contact the American Council for the Arts. The address of the Graphic Artists

Guild has changed to 11 West 20th Street, New York, New York 10011. The address for the Picture Agency Council of America has changed to c/o Bob Roberts, 4023 Locust Street, Philadelphia, Pennsylvania, 19104.

Page 195. The address of the Society of Publication Designers has changed to 60 East 42nd Street, Suite 1416, New York, New York 10165.

State arts agencies, etc.

Pages 195-199. These listings can be updated by requesting current information from the National Endowment for the Arts.

Selected Bibliography

Page 205. Additional books of interest to artists include: Advertising Photographers of America – New York Chapter, *Assigning Advertising Photography: A Buyer's Guide*. New York: Advertising Photographers of America, 1988; Borchard, William M., *Trademarks and the Arts*. New York: Center for Law and the Arts, 1989; Conner, Floyd, Karlen, Peter, Perwin, Jean S., and Spatt, David M., *The Artist's Friendly Legal Guide*. Cincinnati: North Light Books, 1988; Feldman, Franklin, Weil, Stephen E., and Duke Biederman, Susan, *Art Law: Rights and Liabilities of Creators and Collectors*. Boston: Little, Brown and Company, 1986, Supp. 1988. (This book is the successor to *Art Works: Law, Policy, Practice*.); Green, Laura R., *Money for Artists: A Guide to Grants and Awards for Individual Artists*. New York: ACA Books, 1987; Messman, Carla, *The Art of Filing*. Saint Paul, Minnesota: United Arts, 1988; Michels, Caroll, *How to Survive & Prosper as an Artist*. Revised edition. New York: Henry Holt and Company, 1988; Navaretta, Cynthia, *Whole Arts Directory*. New York: Midmarch Arts, 1987; Pinkerton, Linda F., and Guardalabene, John T., *The Art Law Primer*. New York: Nick Lyons Books, 1988. ASMP-The American Society of Magazine Photographers and the Graphic Artists Guild have also published revised editions of their books.

Chapter 1

The business of art

Artists should never feel intimidated, helpless or victimized. Legal and business considerations exist from the moment an artist conceives a work or receives an assignment. While no handbook can solve the unique problems of each artist, the artist's increased awareness of the general legal issues pertaining to art will aid in avoiding risks and gaining benefits that might otherwise pass unnoticed.

Art law, although drawn from many areas of the law, is developing more and more into a distinct entity. *Legal Guide for the Visual Artist* seeks to introduce artists to the legal problems of both art in commerce and artists' rights. It deals with each of the sequence of issues which begin as soon as the artist contemplates creating a work of art.

Action in the legal sphere may appear to be an anomaly for the artist involved with creative work. Perhaps, as Carl Andre suggests, the artist should seek to withdraw from the art world and the dangers of success. Yet the artist seeking to earn his or her living from an art career must focus on art as commerce, what Andy Warhol calls being "a business artist."

All artists, whether they agree with Carl Andre or Andy Warhol, must be capable of resolving business and legal issues. In this respect, a greater familiarity with art law and other sources of support will help the artist.

Artists' groups

Artists' groups provide a valuable support network. There are too many of these groups across the country to mention each by name, but those with a special interest in artists' rights, including legal and business issues, are listed in the Appendix on pages 193–195.

Many of the groups offer newsletters and other information services of value to their members. A few provide legal services, while others lobby for legislation favorable to artists. Health, life and even automobile insurance are frequently offered at group rates. Some of the groups promote art by sponsoring shows, publishing books or maintaining slide registries of art.

Within the boundaries of the antitrust laws, certain groups seek to establish minimum rates for pricing art sold by members. A number of the groups have codes of ethics, which dictate standards for both business and art practices in the profession. Among the other organizations of interest to artists which are listed in the Appendix is the Joint Ethics Committee. Its Code of Fair Practice appears on pages 201–204.

Joining an artists' group can be an important step in protecting rights and advancing professional prestige.

Lawyers for the arts

The search for a lawyer is often time-consuming and disheartening. Not only are fees high, but many lawyers are not knowledgeable about the issues encountered by artists. Standard techniques for finding a lawyer include asking a friend who consulted a lawyer for a similar problem, calling a local bar association's referral service or going to a legal clinic. All of these approaches have merits, but today the artist may be able to locate a knowledgeable lawyer with far greater precision.

By the way, the very definition of an area of the law as "art law" is an encouraging sign for the expertise lawyers will bring to the artist's problems. The literature and educational programs for lawyers have vastly increased in the last five years. Law schools are beginning to offer art law courses and bar associations are paying greater attention to art and the artist. The selected bibliography shows how many art law books are now available for lawyers.

Equally encouraging are the lawyers across the country volunteering to help needy artists. Both volunteer lawyers' groups and artists' groups are good resources to use when seeking a lawyer with art-law expertise. Such referrals may result in finding lawyers who either do not charge or work at more affordable rates. Up-to-date information on the volunteer lawyers closest to a specific location can be obtained from one of the following established groups:

CALIFORNIA
Bay Area Lawyers for the Arts
Fort Mason Center
Building C, Room 255
San Francisco, California 94123
(415) 775-7200

ILLINOIS
Lawyers for the Creative Arts
623 South Wabash Avenue, Suite 300-N
Chicago, Illinois 60605
(312) 427-1800

NEW YORK
Volunteer Lawyers for the Arts
1560 Broadway, Suite 711
New York, New York 10036
(212) 575-1150

Value of the *Legal Guide*

Legal Guide for the Visual Artist trains the artist to think in a new way. It alerts the artist to issues that are likely to trap the unwary. It opens doors to those who seek to better their business practices, increase their incomes and protect their art. Knowing when it is advisable to consult with a lawyer can itself be a great asset.

The artist who conducts his or her business affairs with clarity and confidence gains not only a better livelihood but also peace of mind. It is for those artists who seek self-reliance, confidence and success that *Legal Guide for the Visual Artist* will be most valuable.

Copyright:

gaining and keeping protection

On January 1, 1978, an entirely new copyright law replaced the law that had been in effect since 1909. Copyright is the source of all the reproduction rights that an artist sells in an artwork. While the changes in the law are generally favorable for the creator, each artist must be aware of the provisions of the new law to achieve maximum benefit from it and, particularly, avoid the "work for hire" pitfall explained later in this chapter. One helpful—and free—aid every artist should obtain is the Copyright Information Kit, which can simply be requested from the Copyright Office, Library of Congress, Washington, D.C. 20559. The Copyright Information Kit includes copies of the new law, the Copyright Office's regulations, the copyright application forms and circulars explaining a great deal about the operation of the Copyright Office. The Copyright Office will supply as many copies as requested of any application form free of charge. A hotline telephone number (202-287-9100) has been established by the Copyright Office to expedite requests for registration forms.

Effective date

January 1, 1978, marks the dividing line between the old and the new copyright laws. It is important to keep in mind that copyright transactions prior to January 1, 1978, will be governed by the old law. For example, if the copyright on a drawing has gone into the public domain (where it can freely be copied by anyone) under the old law, the new law will not revive this lost copyright—even if the copyright would not have gone into the public domain had the new law been in effect. However, the new law will govern the future treatment of copyrights that were in existence on January 1, 1978.

Single copyright system

Traditionally, copyright has existed in two quite distinct forms: common law copyright and statutory copyright. Common law copyright derived from precedent in the courts, while statutory copyright derived from federal legislation. Common law copyright protected works as soon as created without any copyright notice; statutory copyright protected works only when registered with the Copyright Office or published with copyright notice. Common law copyright lasted forever unless the work was published or registered; statutory copyright lasted for a 28-year term which could be renewed for an additional 28 years.

The new law almost entirely eliminates common law copyright, a reform that will substantially simplify the copyright system. All works will now be protected by statutory copyright as soon as created in tangible form. This immediate statutory copyright protection, regardless of registration or publication with copyright notice, is an important change in the law. It is not necessary to comply with any formalities to get a statutory copyright, because it comes into being as soon as an artist creates work. However, as explained in Chapter 3, the formalities of registration and deposit are neither difficult nor expensive to comply with and do offer advantages to the artist.

What is copyrightable?

Pictorial, graphic and sculptural works are copyrightable. Included in these categories are such items as two-dimensional and three-dimensional works of fine, graphic and applied art; photographs; photographic slides not intended to be shown as a related series of images; prints and art reproductions; maps; globes; charts; technical drawings; diagrams; and models. Audiovisual works form another category of copyrightable work and cover works that consist of a series of related images intended to be shown by the use of a machine such as a projector or a viewer, together with any accompanying sounds. The form of the audiovisual work, such as a tape, film or set of related slides intended to be shown together, doesn't matter as long as the work meets the definition just given. A motion picture is an audiovisual work that also imparts an impression of motion, something the other audiovisual works don't have to do. The law makes clear that the sound track is to be copyrighted as part of the audiovisual work and not as a separate sound recording.

Work must be original and creative to be copyrightable. Originality simply means that the artist created the work and did not copy it from someone else. If, by some incredible chance, two artists independently created an identical work, each work would be original and copyrightable. Creative means that the work has some minimal aesthetic qualities. A child's painting, for example, could meet this standard. All the work of a professional artist should definitely be copyrightable. Also, the fact that part of a work may infringe someone else's copyrighted work does not deny protection for the rest of what the artist creates. For example, if an artist publishes a group of drawings as a book and fails to get permission to use one copyrighted drawing, the rest of the book would still be copyrightable. On the other hand, if someone were simply copying one film from another copyrighted film without permission, the entire new film would be an infringement and it would not be copyrightable. If new elements are added to a work in the public domain, the new work would definitely be copyrightable. However, the copyright would only protect the new elements and not the original work that was in the public domain.

Ideas, titles, names and short phrases are usually not copyrightable because they lack a sufficient amount of expression. Ideas can be protected by contract as discussed on pages 69 – 70. Likewise style is not copyrightable, but specific pieces of art created as the expression of a style are copyrightable. Utilitarian objects are not copyrightable, but a utilitarian object incorporating an artistic motif—such as a lamp base in the form of a stat-ue—can be copyrighted to protect the artistic material. Basic geometric shapes, such as squares and circles, are not copyrightable, but artistic combinations of these shapes can be copyrighted. Typeface designs are also excluded from being copyrightable. Calligraphy is copyrightable in some cases, although the Copyright Office has not issued clear guidelines on this. It would appear to be copyrightable if expressed in art work, especially insofar as the characters are embellished, but not to be copyrightable if merely expressed in the form of a guide such as an alphabet. Applications from artists doing calligraphy should clarify this area of the law. Computer programs and the images created through the use of computers are both copyrightable.

Who can benefit from copyright?

If works are unpublished, the new law protects them without regard for the artist's nationality or where the artist lives. If works are published, the new law will protect them if: (1) the artist is a national or permanent resident of the United States; (2) the artist is a stateless person; or (3) the artist is a national or a permanent resident of a nation covered by a copyright treaty with the United States or by a presidential proclamation. The United States is a party of the Universal Copyright Convention, so publication in any nation that is a party to that Convention will also gain protection in the United States. The copyright notice for the Universal Copyright Convention must include the symbol ©, the artist's full name and the year of first publication. Thus, the short form notice © JA (discussed on page 10) should be avoided when protection is desired under the Universal Copyright Convention. For the Buenos Aires Convention—covering many Western Hemisphere countries—the phrase "All rights reserved" should be added to the notice. Protection under the Berne Copyright Convention, to which the United States is not a signatory, can be gained by simultaneously publishing a work in the United States and a country which is a member of that convention. Details of the international copyright relations of the United

States can be obtained from the Copyright Office in Publication R38a, "International Copyright Relations of the United States."

Manufacturing requirement

The pre-1978 law sometimes required books or pictorial or graphic works to be manufactured in the United States. The new law was to eliminate the manufacturing requirements as of July 1, 1982. However, Congress voted a four-year extension to July 1, 1986 (overriding a veto by President Reagan for the first time). In any case, pictorial or graphic works are no longer subject to the manufacturing provisions. Also, books consisting predominately of pictorial or graphic materials may be printed abroad and imported without compliance with the manufacturing requirements. A recent case offers the following test: "In the absence of any other standards, the Court holds that a book 'consists of preponderantly nondramatic literary material . . . in the English language' when more than half of its surface area, exclusive of margins, consists of English language text." (*Stonehill Communications, Inc.* v. *John Martuge,* 512 F. Supp. 349) Such predominately pictorial or graphic books should be registered on Form VA.

For a book consisting of both nondramatic text and pictorial or graphic materials, the text would have to be manufactured in either the United States or Canada if the text predominated in importance, but the pictorial or graphic works could be manufactured anywhere. If a book has the text predominating over the pictorial or graphic materials, it should be registered on Form TX for a nondramatic literary work so that question 7 on that form can be answered with respect to the place of manufacture. However, it is possible to import up to 2,000 copies of a predominately textual book, provided that an import statement is obtained from the Copyright Office. Form IS is used to apply for such an import statement.

Exclusive rights

The owner of a copyright has the exclusive rights to reproduce the work, sell and distribute the work, prepare derivative works, perform the work publicly and display the work publicly. A derivative work adapts or transforms an earlier work, such as using the image from a painting for a picture on the front of a tee-shirt, taking an old drawing and adding new elements to it so that the new drawing would be a substantial variation from the original drawing or making a novel into a film. The right to sell and distribute the work doesn't prevent someone who has purchased a lawfully made copy from reselling it.

The right to display the work doesn't prevent the owner of a copy of the work from displaying it directly or with the aid of a projector to people present at the place of display, such as exhibiting a fine print in a gallery. For an audiovisual work, including a motion picture, a display is defined as showing its images nonsequentially. The owner of a copy could do this publicly. Performing an audiovisual work—that is, showing its images sequentially—would be allowed only if the owner of the copy did it in private. To perform the work publicly—either in a public place or to an audience including a substantial number of people besides the family and its normal circle of friends, permission of the copyright owner would be needed. If a gallery or museum does not own copyright-protected art that it wishes to display, it will need the permission of the copyright owner.

By the way, copyright is completely separate from ownership of a physical art work. An artist can often sell the physical work verbally, but the copyright must always be transferred in writing and the artist or the artist's authorized agent must sign that transfer. Because prior to 1978 it appeared the sale of an art work might transfer the common law copyright to the purchaser, New York and California have enacted statutes reserving the common law copyright to the artist unless a written agreement transfers the common law copyright to the purchaser. The New York statute covers sales of paintings, sculptures, drawings and graphic works. The broader California statute covers commissions as well as sales of fine art (defined to include mosaics, photography, crafts, and mixed media) and also includes the categories covered under the New York statute. These statutes will continue to be of importance with respect to sales that took place prior to 1978. After 1978, the new copyright law provides the same protection and should preempt these laws.

It's also important to know that each of the exclusive rights belonging to the copyright owner can be subdivided. For example, the reproduction rights sold might be "first North American serial rights" instead of "all rights". All rights would be the entire copyright. First North American serial rights is a subdivided part of the exclusive right to authorize reproduction of the work. It is still an exclusive right, because it gives a magazine the right to be first to publish the work in a given geographical area. All copyrights and subdivided parts of copyrights must be transferred in writing, except for nonexclusive licenses. For example, a magazine could verbally be given "simultaneous rights" because such rights are not exclusive but specifically permit giving the same rights to other magazines at the same time and for the same area.

Since nonexclusive licenses can be transferred verbally, it's necessary to watch out for publishers or manufacturers who try to get more than a one-time use of art work through masthead notices or memoranda that might create an implied agreement. The additional uses would be nonexclusive, but the artist would not be paid again. For example, a store might purchase the right to use copies of a work in a window display, but later want to use the same work in printed advertising. The artist should know exactly what rights are being sold, preferably by having them detailed in a purchase order obtained prior to doing the work. If there is no express agreement when dealing with a magazine or other collective work, the new law provides a presumption as to what rights are transferred (discussed later in the section on selling to magazines and other collective works on pages 8 –9).

There are some limited exceptions to the exclusive rights of the copyright owner. Both fair use and compulsory licensing, discussed on pages 28–30, are limited rules under which someone else can use a copyrighted work without asking permission of the copyright owner. As a general rule, however, anyone using a work in violation of the copyright owner's exclusive rights is an infringer who must pay damages and can be restrained from continuing the infringement.

Term of copyright

The term of copyright under the new law is the artist's life plus fifty years. The old copyright law had an original twenty-eight year term and a renewal term of twenty-eight years, so the new term will be longer in almost every case. For works created anonymously, under a pseudonym or as a work for hire, the term shall be either seventy-five years from first publication of the work or a hundred years from its creation, whichever period is shorter. The Copyright Office will maintain records as to when an artist dies, but a presumption will exist that a copyright has expired if seventy-five years have passed and the records disclose no information indicating the copyright term might still be in effect. If the name of an artist who has created a work anonymously or using a pseudonym is recorded with the Copyright Office, the copyright term will then run for the artist's life plus fifty years. Also, the term of copyright for jointly created works is the life of the last surviving artist plus fifty years. A joint work is defined as a work prepared by two or more artists with the intention that their contributions be merged into inseparable or interdependent parts of a unitary whole.

Copyrights in their renewal term that would have expired on or after September 19, 1962, were extended due to the deliberations over the new copyright law. They fall under the general rule that the terms of statutory copyrights in existence on January 1, 1978, are extended to seventy-five years. However, any copyrights obtained prior to 1978 that are still in their first twenty-eight year term will have to be renewed in order to benefit from the extension to a total term of seventy-five years (request Form RE to renew copyrights). This renewal must take place between January 1st and December 31st of the year in which the first term of the copyright expires. As shown on Form RE, it may be possible to make a group renewal for a number of copyrights expiring in the same year.

Since common law copyright has basically been eliminated, all works protected by common law copyright as of January 1, 1978, will have a statutory copyright term of the artist's life plus fifty years. In no event, however, will such a copyright previously protected under the common law expire prior to December 31, 2002, and, if the work is published, the copyright will extend at least until December 31, 2027.

The new law provides that all copyright terms will run through December 31st of the year in which they are scheduled to expire. This will greatly simplify determining a copyright's term and, when necessary, renewing a copyright.

Transfer and termination

As mentioned before, all copyrights and subdivided parts of copyrights must be transferred in writing, except for nonexclusive licenses. This had not been the case for common law copyrights (except in California and New York), which could be transferred verbally, and is an important protection for the artist.

Another significant innovation is the artist's right to terminate transfers of either exclusive or nonexclusive rights. If, after January 1, 1978, an artist grants exclusive or nonexclusive rights in a copyright, the artist has the right to terminate this grant during a five-year period starting at the end of thirty-five years after the execution of the grant or, if the grant includes the right of publication, during a five-year period beginning at the end of thirty-five years from the date of publication or forty years from the date of execution of the grant, whichever term ends earlier. Similarly, if before January 1, 1978, the artist or the artist's surviving family members made a grant of the renewal right in one of the artist's copyrights, that grant can be terminated during a five-year period starting fifty-six years after the copyright was first obtained. However, the artist has no right of termination in transfers by will or in works for hire. The mechanics of termination involve giving notice two to ten years prior to the termination date and complying with regulations the Copyright Office can provide, but the important point is to remember that such a right exists. The purpose of the right of termination is to provide creators the opportunity to share in an unexpected appreciation in the value of what has been transferred.

Copies of documents recording transfers of copyright should be filed with the Copyright Office by the person receiving an interest in the copyright to protect that person's ownership rights. This filing should be done within one month if the transfer took place in the United States and within two months if the transfer took place outside of the United States.

A form for the assignment of all right, title and interest in a copyright is included here. In general, it should not be used to sell rights, since limited rights transfers are far better for the artist. However, this form can be used when the artist is reacquiring rights in a copyright—for example, if a right granted reverts back to the artist by contract.

Copyright assignment form

For valuable consideration, the receipt of which is hereby acknowledged, (name of party assigning the copyright), whose offices are located at (address), does hereby transfer and assign to (name of party receiving the copyright), whose offices are located at (address), his or her heirs, executors, administrators, and assigns, all its right, title, and interest in the copyrights in the works described as follows: (describe work, including registration number, if work has been registered) _____

_____

_____ ,

including any statutory copyright together with the right to secure renewals and extensions of such copyright throughout the world, for the full term of said copyright or statutory copyright and any renewal or extension of same that is or may be granted throughout the world.

IN WITNESS WHEREOF, (name of party assigning the copyright) has executed this instrument by the signature of its duly authorized corporate officer on the _____ day of _____ , 19 ____ .

ABC Corporation

By: _____

Authorized Signature

_____

Name Printed or Typed

_____

Title

Selling to magazines and collective works

Magazines, newspapers, anthologies, encyclopedias—anything in which a number of separate contributions are combined together—are defined as "collective works." The law specifically provides that the copyright in each contribution is separate from the copyright in the entire collective work. The copyright in a contribution belongs to the contributor who can give the owner of the copyright in the entire work whatever rights the contributor wishes in return for compensation.

However, especially where magazines are concerned, it is not uncommon for a contribution to be published without any express agreement ever being made as to what rights are being transferred to the magazine. The new law deals with this situation by providing that, in a case where there is no express agreement, the owner of copyright in the collective work gets the following rights: (1) the nonexclusive right to use the work in the issue of the collective work for which it was contributed; (2) the right to use the contribution in a revision of that collective work; and (3) the right to use the contribution in any later collective work in the same series.

For example, a drawing is contributed to a magazine without any agreement with respect to what rights are being transferred. The magazine can now use that drawing in one issue and again in later issues, but it cannot publish that drawing in a different magazine. Magazines aren't usually revised, but anthologies and encyclopedias are. In that case the drawing could be used in the original issue of the anthology or encyclopedia and any later revisions, but it couldn't be used for a new anthology or a different encyclopedia.

Of course, only nonexclusive rights are transferred to the magazine or other collective work, so the drawing could be contributed elsewhere at the same time. The artist will have to weigh whether this is practical in terms of keeping the good will of the various clients.

The best solution is simply to have a written agreement signed by the artist or his or her authorized agent transferring "first North America rights" in the contribution to the collective work. This transfers exclusive first-time rights in North America, but it has the advantage of restricting the magazine or other collective work from making subsequent uses of the contribution without payment. It also makes the sale governed by terms agreed to and understood by both parties, instead of by a law that may not satisfactorily achieve the end result desired by either party. The need for a signed written transfer can be satisfied by a simple letter stating: "This is to confirm that in return for your agreement to pay me $ _____ , I am transferring to you first North American rights in my work titled _____ described as follows: _____ for publication in your magazine titled: _____ ."

Publication with copyright notice

Since the artist has statutory copyright the moment a work is created, publication is not as important as it was under the old law. However, the artist risks losing a copyright if, upon authorized publication either in the United States or abroad, proper copyright notice has not been placed on the work.

In some cases, the time when publication occurs can be confusing. Publication in the new law basically means public distribution. This occurs when one or more copies of a work are distributed to people who are not restricted from disclosing the work's content to others. Distribution can take place by sale, rental, lease, lending or other transfer of copies to the public. Also, offering copies to a group of people for the purpose of further distribution, public performance or public display is a publication. In circulating copies of a work to publishers or other potential purchasers, it would be wise to indicate on the copies that the contents are not to be disclosed to the public without the artist's consent. Even if this is not done, however, it should be implicit that such public disclosure is not to be allowed.

The history of the law's enactment (in the form of a statement by Representative Kastenmeier in the *Congressional Record*) indicated that Congress did not intend for unique art works—those that are one of a kind—to be considered as published when sold or offered for sale in such traditional ways as through an art dealer, gallery or auction house. Works intended to be sold in multiple copies, however, would be considered as published if publicly distributed or offered for sale to the public—even if the offering for sale occurs at a time when only a single prototype copy exists. But unique works should, in any case, be registered since they can still be infringed on by someone who has access to them. Also, some experts believe that unique works are published when offered for sale by a dealer, gallery or auction house. To warn the public of the artist's copyright and to avoid taking any chances that a court in the future might decide that unique works can be published, copyright notice should be placed on such works as soon as they are created. This won't change the term of copyright protection, but it will avoid having to worry about possible ambiguities in the definition of publication.

For works created prior to 1978, it is worthwhile to discuss the meaning of "publication" under the old law. For both common law and statutory purposes, publication generally occurred when copies of the work were offered for sale, sold or publicly distributed by the copyright owner or under his or her authority. However, art works are frequently first exhibited or offered for sale not through copies but by use of an original work or works. The consensus was that the exhibition of an uncopyrighted art work would not be a publication if copying of the work, usually by photography, was prohibited and if this prohibition is enforced at the exhibition. On the other hand, such an exhibition would have been a publication if copies could be freely made or disseminated. Authority was also divided over whether the sale of an original uncopyrighted art work was a publication which would bring an end to common law copyright protection. Despite this, both New York and California enacted the statutes discussed earlier, which provided that the sale of an uncopyrighted art work did not transfer the right of reproduction to the buyer unless a written agreement was signed by the artist or the artist's agent expressly transferring such right of reproduction.

Form of copyright notice

The form of the copyright notice is as follows: Copyright or Copr. or ©, the artist's name or an abbreviation by which that name can be recognized or an alternative designation by which the artist is known, and the year date of publication (or the year date of creation, if the work is unpublished and the artist chooses to place notice on it). Valid notice could, therefore, be © JA 1985, if the artist's initials were JA. In general, the Copyright Office takes the position that an artist's initials are insufficient unless the artist is well known by his or her initials. If the artist is not well known by his or her initials, the Copyright Office will treat the notice as lacking any name. The year date can be omitted only from art work reproduced on or in greeting cards, postcards, stationery, jewelry, dolls, toys or any useful articles. If a work consists preponderantly of one or more works created by the United States Government, a statement indicating this must be included with the copyright notice. If this is not done, the work will be treated as if notice had been completely omitted.

Placement of copyright notice

The copyright notice must be placed so as to give reasonable notice to an ordinary user of the work of the copyright. The Copyright Office regulations are very liberal as to where notice can be placed, but, in fact, any reasonable placement of notice will be valid. Of course, it would be wise to follow the guidelines given in the regulations and explained here.

The notice requirements for pictorial, graphic and sculptural works insure that the use of copyright notice will not impair the aesthetic qualities of the art.

For a two-dimensional work, such as a fine print or poster, the copyright notice can go on the front or back of the work or on any backing, mounting, matting, framing or other material to which the work is durably attached so as to withstand normal use or in which it is permanently housed. The notice can be marked on directly or can be attached by means of a label that is cemented, sewn or otherwise permanently attached. A slide that is not part of a series of related slides would be a two-dimensional work and the copyright notice would go on the slide's mounting.

For a three-dimensional work, such as a sculpture, the copyright notice can be placed on any visible portion of the work or on any base, mounting, framing or other material to which the work is permanently attached or in which it is permanently housed. Again, the notice can be marked on directly or can be attached by means of a label that is cemented, sewn or otherwise durably attached so as to withstand normal use. If, in an unusual case, the size of the work or the special characteristics of the material composing the work make it impossible to mark notice on the work directly or by a durable label, the notice could be placed on a tag of durable material attached with sufficient permanency to remain with the work while passing through the normal channels of commerce.

If a work is reproduced on sheet-like or strip materials bearing continuous reproductions, such as wallpaper or textiles, the copyright notice may be placed in any of the following ways: (1) on the design itself; (2) on the margin, selvage or reverse side of the material at frequent and regular intervals; (3) if the material has neither selvage nor a reverse side, then on tags or labels attached to the materials and to any spools, reels or containers housing them so that the notice is visible during the entire time the materials pass through their normal channels of commerce.

If a work is permanently housed in a container, such as a game or puzzle, a notice reproduced on the permanent container will be acceptable.

For a contribution to a collective work, such as a magazine or anthology, the regulations state that copyright notice can be placed in any of the following ways: (1) if a contribution is on a single page, the copyright notice may be placed under the title of the contribution, next to the contribution or anywhere on the same page as long as it's clear that the copyright notice is to go with the contribution; (2) if the contribution takes up more than one page in the collective work, the copyright notice may be placed under the title at or near the beginning of the contribution, on the first page of the body of the contribution, immediately following the end of the contribution or on any of the pages containing the contribution as long as the contribution is less than twenty pages and it's clear the notice applies to the contribution; (3) as an alternative to numbers (1) or (2), the copyright notice may be placed on the page bearing the notice for the collective work as a whole or on a clearly identified and readily accessible table of contents or listing of acknowledgments appearing either at the front or back of the collective work as a whole. For (3), there must be a separate listing of the contribution by its title or, if it has no title, by an identifying description.

For motion pictures and other audiovisual works the copyright notice is acceptable if it is embodied in the copies by a photomechanical or electronic process so that it appears whenever the work is performed in its entirety and is located in any of the following positions: (1) with or near the title; (2) with the cast, credits, or similar information; (3) at or immediately following the beginning of the work; or (4) at or immediately preceding the end of the work. Since a series of related slides intended to be shown together is considered an audiovisual work, the notice would have to be visible when the work is performed in one of the positions just listed. There would be no requirement, however, that notice appear on the mounting of the slides as on the case of a slide that is not part of a related series. Also, a motion picture or other audiovisual work distributed to the public for private use (such as a video recording cassette) may have the notice on the container in which the work is permanently housed if that would be preferred to one of the four placements listed above.

Defective notice

But it's important to remember that a copyright isn't lost just because the copyright notice is incorrect. For example, if the wrong name appears in the copyright notice, the copyright is still valid. This means that if an artist contributes to a magazine or other collective work but there is no copy-

right notice in the artist's name with the contribution, the copyright will still be protected by the copyright notice in the front of the magazine even though the notice is in the publisher's name. Notice in the publisher's name would not, however, protect advertisements that appeared without separate notice (unless the publisher is also the advertiser). If an earlier date than the actual date of publication appears in a copyright notice, the term of copyright will simply be computed from the earlier date, but the copyright will remain valid. Computing the copyright from the earlier date won't make any difference, since the term of the copyright is measured by the artist's life plus fifty years (not a fixed time period which could be shortened by computing the term from the earlier date).

If the name or date is simply omitted from the notice, or if the date is more than one year later than the year in which publication actually occurred, the validity of the copyright is governed by the same provisions that apply to the complete omission of copyright notice. In such a case, the copyright will be valid and not go into the public domain if any one of the following three tests is met: (1) the notice is omitted only from a relatively small number of copies distributed to the public; (2) the notice is omitted from more than a relatively small number of copies, but registration is made within five years of publication and a reasonable effort is made to add notice to copies distributed in the United States that don't have notice (such a reasonable effort would at least require notifying all distributors of the omission and instructing that they add the proper notice; foreign distributors need not be notified); or (3) the notice was left off the copies against the artist's written instructions that such notice appear on the work. Before work leaves the studio, it is therefore wise to stamp the following notice on it:

Copyright © Jane Artist 19_____ . An express condition of any authorization to use this art is that copyright notice in the artist's name appear on all publicly distributed copies of the photograph as follows: © Jane Artist, year of first publication.

However, an innocent infringer who gives proof of having been misled by the type of incorrect or omitted notice discussed in the preceding paragraph will not be liable for damages for infringing acts committed prior to receiving actual notice of the registration. Also, the court in its discretion may allow the infringement to continue and require the infringer to pay a reasonable licensing fee.

Prior to 1978, a defective notice usually caused the loss of copyright protection because statutory copyright for published works was obtained by publication with copyright notice. If, for example, a year later than the year of first publication was placed in the notice, copyright protection was lost. There were exceptions, however. For example, the use in the notice of a year prior to that of first publication merely reduced the copyright term but did not invalidate the copyright. Also, if copyright notice was omitted from a relatively small number of copies, the copyright continued to be valid, but an innocent infringer would not be liable for the infringement.

A brief history of copyright

Copyright does not always appear to be a system well-suited to art, especially art which is not for reproduction. This is because copyright arose to protect authors' writings. In fact, creators were not always blessed with the benefits of copyright.

The Roman legal system, for example, had no copyright. This meant that as soon as a poem or play was created, anyone who could obtain a copy was free to reproduce it without even asking the author's permission. A wealthy man could use his retinue of educated slaves to have copies made of his favorite works. The profits from any sales of the copied manuscripts went to the property owner, not the author.

The concept that writing had a value beyond that of the parchment was not to develop for a millenium. In the middle ages the reproduction of manuscripts rested in the dominion of the Church, and it was only with the rise of the great Universities in the twelfth and thirteenth centuries that lay writers began producing works on secular subjects. Extensive copying by

trained scribes again became the norm, with only the publishers—or *stationarii* as they were called—gaining any profit. Even before the introduction of block printing into the west in the 15th century, the publishers had formed a Brotherhood of Manuscript Producers in 1357 and were soon given a charter by the Lord Mayor of London.

Printing created an even greater demand for books, and Richard III in 1483 lifted the restrictions against aliens if those aliens happened to be printers. Within fifty years, however, the supply of books had far exceeded the demand and Henry VIII passed a new law providing that no person in England could legally purchase a book bound in a foreign nation. At about this time the Brotherhood of Manuscript Producers, now known as the Stationers' Company, was given a charter—that is, a monopoly—over publishing in England. No author could publish except with a publisher belonging to the Stationers' Company. This served the dual purpose of preventing both writings seditious to the Crown and heretical to the Church. The right of ownership was not in the author's creation, but rather in the right to make copies of that creation. Secret presses came into existence, but the Stationers' Company sought to maintain its monopoly with the aid of repressive decrees from the notorious Star Chamber.

Due largely to the monopoly of the Stationers' Company, a recognition had come into being of a right to copy which might also be called a common law copyright—that is, a right supposedly existing from usages and customs of immemorial antiquity as interpreted by the courts. With this concept of property apart from the physical manuscript established, the Stationers' Company objected vehemently when their charter and powers expired in 1694 and Scotch printers began reprinting their titles. The stationers pushed for a new law, but this law—enacted in 1710 and called the Statute of Anne—was largely drafted by two authors, Joseph Addison and Jonathan Swift. The result was a law that protected authors as well as publishers by the creation of statutory copyright (that is, copyrights protected under a statute). At this point authors had something to sell on the open market—a copyright which had been created to encourage "learned men to compose and write useful books."

The Confederation of States in this country had no power to legislate with respect to copyright, but the Federal Constitution provided that "The Congress shall have the power . . . To promote the Progress of Science and useful Arts, by securing for limited Times to Authors and Inventors the exclusive Right to their respective Writings and Discoveries." In 1791 Congress enacted our first federal copyright statute providing copyright for an initial term of 14 years plus a renewal term of 14 years. It applied to the making of copies of books, maps and charts. This law was amended in 1802 to apply to engraving and etching of historical and other prints. In 1831 the initial term of copyright was lengthened to 28 years. In 1865 the law was amended to include photographs and negatives. In 1870 it was revised to cover paintings, drawings, statuaries and models or designs of works of the fine arts. From the artist's viewpoint, it is interesting that drawings and paintings were added as a postscript to the copyright law.

In 1909 the copyright law was revised again. The initial term of copyright remained 28 years and the renewal term was lengthened to 28 years for potential protection of 56 years. In fact, statutory copyrights that would have expired at the end of the renewal term on or after September 19, 1962, were extended to a term of 75 years from the date copyright was originally obtained. Any statutory copyright obtained more than 75 years ago has definitely expired and the art is in the public domain.

Radio, television, motion pictures, satellites and other technological innovations required revision of the 1909 law. After a long gestation, the new law took effect on January 1, 1978. No doubt future revisions lie ahead as new tools to make, store and deliver creative works shape the copyright needs of creators, users and society itself.

Chapter 3

Copyright:
registration of copyright

All works can be registered, whether or not they have been published. Form VA is the appropriate form to use for pictorial, graphic and sculptural works. When registering something with both text and art work, Form VA should be used if the art work predominates and Form TX if the text predominates. However, the classifications are for administrative purposes only, so protection will not be diminished simply because a mistake may be made in choosing the correct classification. Also, when registering a contribution to a magazine or other collective work, the class to be used is that for the contribution and not the class into which the entire collective work falls. For example, a cartoon or illustration contributed to a magazine should be registered on Form VA, not Form TX. An audiovisual work is registered on Form PA, which is for a work of the performing arts.

A copy of Form VA appears on pages 20–21. This is a simple two-page form with step-by-step directions explaining how to fill it out. Along with the appropriate form, the filing fee of $10 and copies of the work being registered must be sent to the Copyright Office. The application form, copies of the work and fee should be mailed in one package, unless the artist doesn't have to include the fee because he or she maintains a deposit account with the Copyright Office.

Advantages of registration

It is true, as stated earlier, that registration is not necessary to gain copyright protection—that protection exists the moment a work is created under the new law. But registration does have the following important advantages: (1) the certificate of regis-

tration, if issued either before or within five years of first publication, is presumptive proof of the validity of the copyright and the truth of the statements made in the copyright application; (2) registration must be made before an infringement commences in order to qualify to receive attorney's fees and "statutory" damages (a special kind of damages that an artist can elect to receive if actual damages are hard to prove), except that a published work registered within three months of publication would still qualify; (3) registration is necessary in order to bring a suit for infringement of copyright; and (4) by registering, certain defenses that an innocent infringer might be able to assert due to a defective copyright notice are cut off. The effective date of registration is the day on which an acceptable application, deposit, and fee have all reached the Copyright Office.

To correct a mistake or amplify information contained in a completed registration, Form CA for supplementary registration is used. Form CA may only be submitted after a registration number has been obtained for the work.

Group registration

It is important to note that a group registration of unpublished works can be made under a single title for a $10 registration fee. Registering an unpublished collection is a way to sharply reduce the cost of registering each work in the collection (and no copyright notice need be placed on unpublished work). To qualify for such a group deposit, the following conditions have to be met: (1) the deposit materials are assembled in an orderly form; (2) the collection bears a single title identifying the work as a whole, such as "Collected Drawings of Jane Artist, January, 1985"; (3) the person claiming copyright in each work forming part of the collection is also the person claiming copyright in the entire collection; and (4) all the works in the collection are by the same person or, if by different persons, at least one of them has contributed copyrightable material to each work in the collection. There is no limit on the number of works which can be included in a collection. Also, the law specifically states that a work registered when unpublished need not be registered again when published. Of course, if new material is added to the work or it is transposed into a new medium— creating a substantial variation from the registered work—it would be desirable to register the work again to protect the changed version.

But what if work has already been published in a number of magazines? The law specifically provides for group registration of contributions to periodicals and newspapers made by an artist during a twelve month period, as long as each contribution had its own copyright notice in the artist's name. In such case, Form GR/CP is used as an addition to the basic application on Form VA. A copy of Form GR/CP appears on page 22. It is likely that a regulation will be issued to permit group registration for some related published works that do not come under this rule. If promulgated, this can be requested from the Copyright Office as regulation 202.3(b)(4). The artist will want to register contributions, even if the periodical or newspaper is also registered by the owner of its copyright. The registration of the collective work by its owner will not confer the benefits of registration on the artist, since the artist's copyright in the contribution is separate from the copyright in the collective work. Also, if the artist is going to use Form GR/CP with Form VA, it would be wise to file every three months in order to be certain of qualifying for attorney's fees and statutory damages in the event of an infringement, as explained in the section on registration.

Deposit

With the registration form and fee, one complete copy of an unpublished work or two copies of an unpublished work should be sent to the Copyright Office. If editions of differing quality have been published, the Copyright Office regulations provide guidelines as to how to determine which edition is to be considered the best. For works first published outside of the United States, only one complete copy of the work need be deposited. The proposed amendments to the deposit

regulations discussed in the text are likely to be made final by the end of 1985. To check on whether the regulations have been finalized, contact the Copyright Office.

For registrations under the provision allowing group registrations for contributions to periodicals and newspapers, only one complete copy of each periodical or section of a newspaper in which the work appeared needed be deposited. When registering published greeting cards, picture postcards or stationery, only one complete copy need be deposited. Similarly, only one complete copy has to be deposited for commercial prints, labels, advertising catalogs and other advertising matter used in connection with the rental, lease, lending, licensing or sale of articles of merchandise, works of authorship or services. This would include, for example, the advertising used in connection with a motion picture. If the print, label, advertising catalogs or other advertising material appears in a larger work, the page or pages on which it appears can be submitted in place of the larger work. If it appears on a three-dimensional work, an alternate deposit must be made as explained in the next section.

A proposed amendment to the deposit regulations would allow photocopies of contributions to collective works, such as periodicals, newspapers and anthologies, to be deposited instead of requiring the deposit of a complete copy of the collective work (or complete section of a newspaper).

For a published motion picture, whether on film or videotape, only one complete copy need be deposited. For an unpublished motion picture, one complete copy must be deposited or, instead, the alternate deposit materials described in the next section may be submitted. It is possible, when submitting a copy of a published motion picture, to enter into a "Motion Picture Agreement" with the Librarian of Congress. This Agreement provides for the copy to be immediately returned to the artist subject to recall by the Library of Congress. There is no requirement to deposit photographs with either a published or an unpublished motion picture, but in either case the deposit must include a separate description with respect to the content of the work, such as a continuity, pressbook or synopsis.

For a published multimedia kit,

proposed Copyright Office regulations require that only one complete copy of the best edition need be deposited (whether or not the kit is used for systematic instructional activities, as the present regulations require). Such a kit might include an audiovisual work, such as a related series of slides. Likewise, the proposed regulations would require only one copy of a published work in the form of two-dimensional games, decals, fabric patches or emblems, calendars, instructions for needle work, needle work and craft kits. The proposed regulations would require only one copy to be deposited for a box, case, carton or other three-dimensional container.

Alternate deposit

In certain situations it is possible to make an alternate deposit in place of the actual work itself. This may allow saving a great deal of expense by depositing something in place of copies of a work. Regardless of whether a work is published or unpublished, generally only one set of alternate deposit materials need be sent in. Combining this with the group deposit provisions, all the benefits of registration may be gained without great cost.

Alternate deposit can be made for an unpublished motion picture or, in some cases, for a published or unpublished soundtrack that is an integral part of a motion picture. It can be made for pictorial or graphic works if: (1) the work is unpublished; (2) less than five copies of the work have been published; or (3) the work has been published and sold or offered for sale in a limited edition consisting of no more than three hundred numbered copies. If the work is too valuable to deposit, a special request may be made to the Copyright Office for permission to submit identifying material rather than copies of the actual work. Alternate deposit materials must be sent in for three-dimensional works and oversize works (which are those exceeding 96 inches in any dimension). If this mandatory requirement of alternate deposit would create a hardship due to expense or difficulty, a special request may be made to the Copyright Office to deposit actual copies of a work. The proposed regulations would allow the deposit of an

actual copy of small pieces of published jewelry made of inexpensive metal and published games consisting of multiple parts in boxes or containers no greater than 12 x 24 x 6 inches.

The alternate deposit for an unpublished motion picture can be either: (1) an audio cassette or other reproduction of the entire soundtrack of the motion picture and a description of the motion picture; or (2) a set consisting of one frame enlargement or similar visual reproduction from each ten minute segment of the motion picture and a description of the motion picture. The description can be a continuity, a pressbook or a synopsis, but it must in all cases include: (1) the title or continuing title of the work and the episode title, if any; (2) the nature and general content of the program; (3) the date when the work was created and whether or not it was simultaneously transmitted; (4) the date of the first transmission, if any; (5) the running time; and (6) the credits appearing on the work, if any. A motion picture's soundtrack can be registered separately if it has not been embodied in any form other than as a soundtrack that is integral to a motion picture. The alternate deposit for a soundtrack consists of a transcription of the entire work, or a reproduction of the entire work on a tape or record, accompanied by photographs or other reproductions from the motion picture showing the title of the picture, the soundtrack credits and the copyright notice for the soundtrack, if any. For both motion pictures and separate motion picture soundtracks, the reproductions for deposit can be photographic prints, transparencies, photostats, drawings or similar two-dimensional renderings that are visible without use of a machine.

A different set of rules for alternate deposit apply for works that are pictorial or graphic, three-dimensional or oversize. The materials used for alternate deposit can be photographic prints, transparencies, photostats, drawings or similar two-dimensional reproductions or renderings of the work in a form that can be looked at without the aid of a machine. The materials used for alternate deposit should all be of the same size, with photographic transparencies at least 35mm (mounted if 3 x 3 inches or less, and preferably mounted even if greater than 3 x 3 inches) and all other materials preferably 8 x 10 inches (but no less than 3 x 3 inches and no more than 9 x 12 inches). For pictorial and graphic work, the materials must reproduce the actual colors of the work. In all other cases, the materials may be either in color or in black and white. Also, except for transparencies, the image of the work must be lifesize or larger or, if it's less than lifesize, it must be large enough to show clearly the entire copyrightable content of the work. The title and an exact measurement of one or more dimensions of the work must appear on the front, back or mount of at least one piece of the identifying material, and the position and form of the copyright notice must be shown clearly on at least one piece of the identifying material if the work has been published. The piece showing the copyright notice does not have to be of uniform size with the material showing the work itself. For example, a 35mm transparency of the work could be accompanied by a drawing of up to 9 x 12 inches showing the exact appearance and contents of the notice, its dimensions, and its position on the work.

Deposit for the Library of Congress

In addition to depositing copies for copyright registration, copies may also have to be deposited for the Library of Congress when work is published with a copyright notice in the United States. For published work, the requirement of deposit for the Library of Congress can be satisfied by simply making the correct deposit for registration and sending in the application form and fee with the deposit. For work that has previously been registered as unpublished, within three months of publication two copies of the best edition of the work should be deposited for the Library of Congress. However, many works will be exempt from deposit, including three-dimensional sculptural works; contributions to collective works; greeting cards, picture postcards and stationery; prints, labels, advertising catalogs and other advertising matter published in connection with renting, leasing, lending, licensing or selling merchandise, works of authorship or services; and

any works published only on jewelry, dolls, toys, plaques, floor coverings, wallpaper, textiles and other fabrics, packaging or other useful articles. In addition, for published pictorial and graphic works, it is possible to deposit one complete copy or make an alternate deposit of identifying materials if either: (1) fewer than five copies of the work have been published, or (2) the work is published and offered for sale in a limited edition of three hundred or fewer numbered copies. This is of particular help to printmakers, who, under the old law, had to deposit two copies of fine prints.

The requirement of deposit for the Library of Congress does not in any way affect the copyright protection already in effect. If, for example, an artist registered work when unpublished and didn't bother to send in the required copies upon publication, the Register of Copyrights could request copies from the artist. Only if the artist didn't comply with such a request within three months would he or she become liable for fines and other penalties. However, the copyright would remain valid.

Filling out the copyright forms

The application forms have directions that are not difficult to follow. However, to simplify the process further, let's cover some of the types of answers an artist would be most likely to give. The assumption is that an individual artist, working under his or her own name, created a work and now wants to register it.

1. Unpublished pictorial, graphic, or sculptural works. Use Form VA. Space 1—Fill in the title of the work and the nature of the work, such as its being an oil painting or a charcoal drawing. If it was a contribution to a collective work such as a magazine, give the requested information about the collective work. Space 2—Give the artist's name and indicate that the work is not a work for hire. Give the date of the artist's birth, indicate the appropriate country of his or her citizenship or permanent residence, and indicate that the work is neither anonymous nor written under a pseudonym. Where it says "Author of," it is generally sufficient to repeat the infor-

mation written in space 1 under "Nature of this Work." Space 3—For an unpublished work give the year the work was finished; leave blank the date and nation of first publication. Space 4—The artist's name and address should be shown for the copyright claimant. Space 5—Answer no, as the artist will not have previously registered the work. A yes answer be appropriate if the artist were adding new material to work that had been previously registered. Space 6—If the artist has added new material to a previously registered work, explain what material the artist added to the old work to make a derivative work. The artist's registration would then protect the new elements of the derivative work. Space 7—Fill in the information about a deposit account if the artist has one. Also, give the artist's name and address for correspondence purposes. Space 8—Check the box for author, sign your name and then print or type his or her name. Space 9—Enter the artist's name and address so that the certificate of registration will be mailed to the artist.

2. Group registration for unpublished pictorial, graphic or sculptural works. Use form VA, filling it out exactly as for unpublished pictorial, graphic, sculptural work, except for the changes shown here. Space 1—The collection must have its own title, and it is that title which is used here. Space 3—The year in which creation of the work was completed is the year in which the most recently completed work contained in the collection was completed.

3. Published pictorial, graphic or sculptural works. Use Form VA, filling it out exactly as for an unpublished pictorial, graphic or sculptural work, except for the changes shown here. Space 3—In addition to giving the date of creation, give the date and nation of first publication of the work.

4. Group registration of published contributions to periodicals. Use Form VA if the contributions are pictorial or graphic, along with the adjunct Form GR/CP. To qualify, the contributions must meet the criteria listed on page 00. Form VA is filled out exactly as for a published pictorial or graphic work, except for the changes shown here. Space 1—In the space for the title, write "See Form GR/CP, attached" and leave the other parts of Space 1 blank. Space 3—Give the year of creation of the last work completed and leave blank the date and nation of first publication.

Then fill out Form GR/CP. Space A—Mark Form VA as the basic application and give the artist's name as both author and copyright claimant. Space B—For each box, fill in the requested information about the title of the contribution, the title of and other information about the periodical, and the date and nation of first publication. Mail Form GR/CP with form VA, the deposit copies, and the filing fee. As mentioned in the text, it may eventually be possible to make group registrations for published work other than those permitted on Form GR/CP.

5. Unpublished audiovisual works, including motion pictures. Use Form PA. This is filled out in essentially the same way as for unpublished pictorial, graphic or sculptural work.

6. Published audiovisual works, including motion pictures. Use Form PA. This is filled out essentially the same way as for published pictorial, graphic or sculptural work.

FORM VA
UNITED STATES COPYRIGHT OFFICE

REGISTRATION NUMBER

_____

VA   VAU

EFFECTIVE DATE OF REGISTRATION

_____

Month   Day   Year

DO NOT WRITE ABOVE THIS LINE. IF YOU NEED MORE SPACE, USE A SEPARATE CONTINUATION SHEET.

1

TITLE OF THIS WORK ▼   **NATURE OF THIS WORK ▼** See instructions

PREVIOUS OR ALTERNATIVE TITLES ▼

PUBLICATION AS A CONTRIBUTION If this work was published as a contribution to a periodical, serial, or collection, give information about the collective work in which the contribution appeared.   **Title of Collective Work ▼**

If published in a periodical or serial give: **Volume ▼**   **Number ▼**   **Issue Date ▼**   **On Pages ▼**

2

a

NAME OF AUTHOR ▼   **DATES OF BIRTH AND DEATH**
Year Born ▼   Year Died ▼

Was this contribution to the work a "work made for hire"?
☐ Yes
☐ No

AUTHOR'S NATIONALITY OR DOMICILE Name of Country
OR { Citizen of ▶ _____
Domiciled in ▶ _____

WAS THIS AUTHOR'S CONTRIBUTION TO THE WORK
Anonymous? ☐ Yes ☐ No
Pseudonymous? ☐ Yes ☐ No
If the answer to either of these questions is "Yes," see detailed instructions.

NATURE OF AUTHORSHIP Briefly describe nature of the material created by this author in which copyright is claimed. ▼

NOTE

Under the law, the "author" of a "work made for hire" is generally the employer, not the employee (see instructions). For any part of this work that was "made for hire" check "Yes" in the space provided, give the employer (or other person for whom the work was prepared) as "Author" of that part, and leave the space for dates of birth and death blank.

b

NAME OF AUTHOR ▼   **DATES OF BIRTH AND DEATH**
Year Born ▼   Year Died ▼

Was this contribution to the work a "work made for hire"?
☐ Yes
☐ No

AUTHOR'S NATIONALITY OR DOMICILE Name of country
OR { Citizen of ▶ _____
Domiciled in ▶ _____

WAS THIS AUTHOR'S CONTRIBUTION TO THE WORK
Anonymous? ☐ Yes ☐ No
Pseudonymous? ☐ Yes ☐ No
If the answer to either of these questions is "Yes," see detailed instructions.

NATURE OF AUTHORSHIP Briefly describe nature of the material created by this author in which copyright is claimed. ▼

c

NAME OF AUTHOR ▼   **DATES OF BIRTH AND DEATH**
Year Born ▼   Year Died ▼

Was this contribution to the work a "work made for hire"?
☐ Yes
☐ No

AUTHOR'S NATIONALITY OR DOMICILE Name of Country
OR { Citizen of ▶ _____
Domiciled in ▶ _____

WAS THIS AUTHOR'S CONTRIBUTION TO THE WORK
Anonymous? ☐ Yes ☐ No
Pseudonymous? ☐ Yes ☐ No
If the answer to either of these questions is "Yes," see detailed instructions.

NATURE OF AUTHORSHIP Briefly describe nature of the material created by this author in which copyright is claimed. ▼

3

YEAR IN WHICH CREATION OF THIS WORK WAS COMPLETED This information must be given in all cases.   ◀ Year

DATE AND NATION OF FIRST PUBLICATION OF THIS PARTICULAR WORK
Complete this information ONLY if this work has been published.   Month ▶ _____ Day ▶ _____ Year ▶ _____   ◀ Nation

4

See instructions before completing this space.

COPYRIGHT CLAIMANT(S) Name and address must be given even if the claimant is the same as the author given in space 2. ▼

TRANSFER If the claimant(s) named here in space 4 are different from the author(s) named in space 2, give a brief statement of how the claimant(s) obtained ownership of the copyright. ▼

APPLICATION RECEIVED

ONE DEPOSIT RECEIVED

TWO DEPOSITS RECEIVED

REMITTANCE NUMBER AND DATE

DO NOT WRITE HERE OFFICE USE ONLY

MORE ON BACK ▶
• Complete all applicable spaces (numbers 5-9) on the reverse side of this page.
• See detailed instructions.   • Sign the form at line 8.

DO NOT WRITE HERE

Page 1 of _____ pages

DO NOT WRITE ABOVE THIS LINE. IF YOU NEED MORE SPACE, USE A SEPARATE CONTINUATION SHEET.

PREVIOUS REGISTRATION Has registration for this work, or for an earlier version of this work, already been made in the Copyright Office?
☐ Yes ☐ No If your answer is "Yes," why is another registration being sought? (Check appropriate box) ▼
☐ This is the first published edition of a work previously registered in unpublished form.
☐ This is the first application submitted by this author as copyright claimant.
☐ This is a changed version of the work, as shown by space 6 on this application.
If your answer is "Yes," give: **Previous Registration Number** ▼   **Year of Registration** ▼

5

DERIVATIVE WORK OR COMPILATION   Complete both space 6a & 6b for a derivative work; complete only 6b for a compilation.
a. **Preexisting Material**   Identify any preexisting work or works that this work is based on or incorporates. ▼

b. **Material Added to This Work**   Give a brief, general statement of the material that has been added to this work and in which copyright is claimed.▼

6

See instructions
before completing
this space.

DEPOSIT ACCOUNT If the registration fee is to be charged to a Deposit Account established in the Copyright Office, give name and number of Account.
Name ▼   **Account Number** ▼

7

CORRESPONDENCE   Give name and address to which correspondence about this application should be sent.   Name/Address/Apt/City/State/Zip ▼

Area Code & Telephone Number ▶

Be sure to
give your
daytime phone
◀ number.

CERTIFICATION*   I, the undersigned, hereby certify that I am the
Check only one ▼
☐ author
☐ other copyright claimant
☐ owner of exclusive right(s)
☐ authorized agent of
Name of author or other copyright claimant, or owner of exclusive right(s) ▲

8

of the work identified in this application and that the statements made
by me in this application are correct to the best of my knowledge.

Typed or printed name and date ▼ If this is a published work, this date must be the same as or later than the date of publication given in space 3.

_____ date ▶ _____

Handwritten signature (X) ▼

* 17 U.S.C. § 506(e): Any person who knowingly makes a false representation of a material fact in the application for copyright registration provided for by section 409, or in any written statement filed in connection with the application. shall be fined not more than $2,500.
☆ U.S. GOVERNMENT PRINTING OFFICE: 1981: 355-312

Nov. 1981-600,000

21

ADJUNCT APPLICATION
for
Copyright Registration for a Group of Contributions to Periodicals

- Use this adjunct form only if you are making a single registration for a group of contributions to periodicals, and you are also filing a basic application on Form TX, Form PA, or Form VA. Follow the instructions, attached.
- Number each line in Part B consecutively. Use additional Forms GR/CP if you need more space.
- Submit this adjunct form with the basic application form. Clip (do not tape or staple) and fold all sheets together before submitting them.

REGISTRATION NUMBER		
TX	PA	VA

EFFECTIVE DATE OF REGISTRATION

....
(Month)   (Day)   (Year)

FORM GR/CP RECEIVED

Page _____ of _____ pages

DO NOT WRITE ABOVE THIS LINE. FOR COPYRIGHT OFFICE USE ONLY

(A)
Identification of Application

IDENTIFICATION OF BASIC APPLICATION:
- This application for copyright registration for a group of contributions to periodicals is submitted as an adjunct to an application filed on: (Check which)

☐ Form TX   ☐ Form PA   ☐ Form VA

IDENTIFICATION OF AUTHOR AND CLAIMANT: (Give the name of the author and the name of the copyright claimant in all of the contributions listed in Part B of this form. The names should be the same as the names given in spaces 2 and 4 of the basic application.)

Name of Author: ....

Name of Copyright Claimant: ....

(B)
Registration For Group of Contributions

COPYRIGHT REGISTRATION FOR A GROUP OF CONTRIBUTIONS TO PERIODICALS: (To make a single registration for a group of works by the same individual author, all first published as contributions to periodicals within a 12-month period (see instructions), give full information about each contribution. If more space is needed, use additional Forms GR/CP.)

☐ Title of Contribution: ....
Title of Periodical: .... Vol. ...... No. ...... Issue Date .... Pages ....
Date of First Publication: .... Nation of First Publication ....
(Month) (Day) (Year)   (Country)

☐ Title of Contribution: ....
Title of Periodical: .... Vol. ...... No. ...... Issue Date .... Pages ....
Date of First Publication: .... Nation of First Publication ....
(Month) (Day) (Year)   (Country)

☐ Title of Contribution: ....
Title of Periodical: .... Vol. ...... No. ...... Issue Date .... Pages ....
Date of First Publication: .... Nation of First Publication ....
(Month) (Day) (Year)   (Country)

☐ Title of Contribution: ....
Title of Periodical: .... Vol. ...... No. ...... Issue Date .... Pages ....
Date of First Publication: .... Nation of First Publication ....
(Month) (Day) (Year)   (Country)

☐ Title of Contribution: ....
Title of Periodical: .... Vol. ...... No. ...... Issue Date .... Pages ....
Date of First Publication: .... Nation of First Publication ....
(Month) (Day) (Year)   (Country)

☐ Title of Contribution: ....
Title of Periodical: .... Vol. ...... No. ...... Issue Date .... Pages ....
Date of First Publication: .... Nation of First Publication ....
(Month) (Day) (Year)   (Country)

☐ Title of Contribution: ....
Title of Periodical: .... Vol. ...... No. ...... Issue Date .... Pages ....
Date of First Publication: .... Nation of First Publication ....
(Month) (Day) (Year)   (Country)

Chapter 4

Copyright:

the issue of work for hire

This is the provision of the new law that most threatens the artist. The employer or other commissioning party owns the copyright in a "work for hire" as if they in fact created the work. This means that the artist won't even have the right to terminate their ownership of copyright after thirty-five years. Also, if an artist were to copy all or part of a work done as work for hire, the artist would be infringing his or her own work. If enough work for hire is done, the artist may discover that he or she has created an alter ego (in the form of a large supply of the artist's work that can be reused and modified) who may very well compete with the artist and damage the artist's livelihood.

A work for hire can come into being in two ways: (1) an employee creating copyrightable work in the course of his or her employment, or (2) certain specially commissioned or ordered work, if both parties sign a contract agreeing it is work for hire.

Employees

If an employee creates copyrightable art in the course of his or her employment, the employer will be treated as the creater of the art and our the copyright. But what is an employee? Someone who is paid a salary for working from 9 a.m. to 5 p.m. from Monday through Friday under the control and direction of the employer and at the employer's office is certainly an employee. This type of employee will have state and federal tax payments withheld from the weekly paycheck and receive any benefits to which employees are entitled.

What if the artist is a free lancer who receives an assignment from an art buyer and executes it in his or her own studio? This artist should not be considered an employee. However, a minority of cases have adopted the questionable rationale that if the commissioning party exercises sufficient control and direction, the free lancer shall be treated as an employee for copyright purposes. A different gambit for the employer is to claim one of its employees contributed to the work in such a way as to become a joint creator with the freelancer. If this unusual case were true, the employer and the free lancer would both own the copyright. To prevent these risks, it is beneficial to the free lancer to have a written contract prior to the commencement of work. This contract should specify what rights are being transferred.

Another trap for the unwary involves work without pay, such as volunteer work. If an artist acts like an employee, then the work may be work for hire despite the fact no payment was made for the work.

Free-lance assignments

Certain specially commissioned or ordered work can be work for hire, if both parties sign a contract agreeing it is work for hire. If such an agreement is made, the following specially ordered or commissioned works will be work for hire:

- a contribution to a collective work, such as a magazine, newspaper, encyclopedia or anthology;
- a contribution used as part of a motion picture or other audiovisual work;
- a translation;
- a compilation, which is a work formed by collecting and assembling preexisting materials or data;
- an instructional text;
- a test or answer material for a test;
- an atlas;
- and a supplementary work, defined as a work used to supplement a work by another author for such purposes as illustrating, explaining or assisting generally

in the use of the author's work. Examples of supplementary works are forewords, afterwords, pictorial illustrations, maps, charts, tables, editorial notes, appendixes and indexes.

The crucial point is that the artist must agree in writing that a work is a work-for-hire. If the artist doesn't agree in writing that a work is a work for hire, then it can't be (unless the artist is treated as an employee). Since it isn't clear whether other language can be used in place of the phrase "work for hire," artists should also refuse to sign anything with language in it that sounds similiar to "work for hire" or an employment-type relationship. Also, if an artist does a specially ordered or commissioned work that is outside of the categories shown above, it cannot be a work for hire (unless the artist is treated as an employee). For example, a portrait of someone done on a commission basis should not be a work for hire because it doesn't fit any of the categories. If work is created independently and submitted in final form to a potential buyer, the work-for-hire problem should not arise. But, even here, caution dictates that the artist not sign anything indicating the work to be work for hire in order to avoid any confusion.

Some clients seek all rights or work-for-hire contracts because they fear the artist will sell the work to a competitor. If this is the client's concern, a noncompetition provision is a far fairer solution. The artist would transfer limited rights, such as first North American serial rights, and agree not to sell the same drawing to a competitor of the client. Since the definition of a competitor may be an issue, the provision might read, "The artist agrees not to resell the work for uses competitive with the client's use. In the event of a resale, the artist agrees to obtain the written approval of the client, which approval shall not be unreasonably withheld." The artist should be careful that such a noncompetition clause apply only to the work being purchased and not other work the artist might do on commission.

Of course, in some cases an artist may be perfectly willing to work under an agreement specifying that work in one of the enumerated categories will be work for hire. In that case, it's im-portant that the artist be aware that he or she is not the author of the work—the party commissioning or ordering the work is. They will own the copyright completely, so that it cannot be terminated after thirty-five years. This complete ownership is, therefore, even more than the transfer of "all rights" in a copyright. With this in mind, the artist should consider carefully what to charge for such work. The greater the right of use the other party gets, the more they should pay for it.

Reform of work for hire

On October 1, 1982, an overflowing audience in a hearing room of the United States Senate listened to three panels discuss work for hire—creators on the first panel, publishers on the second and film industry composers and producers on the third. An illustrator-member of the Graphic Artists Guild testified to one example of the destructive effect of work for hire on creators' careers and income. She had signed a work-for-hire contract with Doubleday Books to provide twenty-eight drawings for use in the interior of a book. For a modest fee, she produced a series of drawings which the publisher found acceptable. In fact, the publisher liked the work so much that one of the drawings was slightly altered and used as the front jacket for the book. The illustrator received no additional payment for the use of her illustration on the jacket. Nor was she able to complain about the fact the drawing had been altered. Nor would she have been able to complain if the publisher had chosen not to give her credit as the illustrator who did the art.

Refuse to sign?

Why didn't the illustrator simply refuse to sign the work-for-hire contract when Doubleday offered it to her? The assignment had been offered on a take-it-or-leave-it basis. If she had asked for a limited transfer of rights, the publisher would have selected a different illustrator to do the assignment.

This superior bargaining power leaves many creators no choice but to do work for hire. Once a pattern is established, the creator finds it difficult to demand any contract other than a work-for-hire contract. But cutting the creator off from potential reuse fees, work for hire make it unlikely that the creator's bargaining position will be strengthened by future residual income. Moreover, when freelancers do work for hire, they are given none of the benefits that employees receive—such as sick leave, medical coverage, unemployment insurance, disability coverage, vacations, retirement benefits and the like. To prevent this discrimination, California enacted a law in 1982 requiring commissioning parties to give certain of the benefits of employee status to free-lancers when work-for-hire contracts are used.

Nonetheless, work for hire might be justifiable if substantially higher fees were paid. However, the fees paid for work for hire were generally found to be lower, not higher, than the fees paid for limited rights transfers. Once again, the client is able to use its superior bargaining strength to force an unsatisfactory agreement on the issue of price as well as the issue of ownership of the copyright.

Widespread use

The 1982 testimony revealed widespread use of work-for-hire. Surveys compiled by the Graphic Artists Guild and the American Society of Magazine Photographers showed use of work-for-hire by a substantial majority of the publishers with the largest gross revenues. The survey found use of work-for-hire by:

- 65 percent of the 25 largest mass market magazines
- 60 percent of the 13 largest book publishers
- 54 percent of the 13 largest mass market book publishers
- 70 percent of the 10 largest elementary and high school textbook publishers
- 73 percent of the 11 largest hard cover publishers

Nor have these percentages improved as this book goes to press.

Publishers' justification

The publishers sought to justify work for hire on the grounds that the initial idea for the assignment and the money to make the project into a reality come from the client. The creators countered these arguments with observations about how business is transacted. In fact, the creator has a substantial investment in his or her professional training, studio, equipment and related expenses. Not only does the creator put all this at risk, but he or she also must wait until acceptance for payment and may have a continuing liability if the publisher is sued on account of the art. In addition, while the idea may come from the commissioning party, the realization of that idea comes from the creator. It is a basic rule that the copyright law does not protect ideas as such, but only the expression of ideas.

A new legislative proposal

On behalf of the Graphic Artists Guild and the American Society of Magazine Photographers, I authored a bill to amend the work-for-hire law. Introduced in the United States Senate by Senator Cochran and in the House of Representatives by Representative Frank, it proposes a thorough solution to the work-for-hire problem.

Senator Cochran, in his introductory remarks for the bill, stated, "Because publishers enjoy a superior bargaining position, they are able to demand a work-for-hire contract as a condition of publication." Noting that California has enacted a state law to curb the work-for-hire abuse and that many city councils have passed resolutions calling on Congress to take action, Senator Cochran concluded:

Mr. President, our copyright laws were enacted to promote and protect the creation of literary, artistic, musical, and other works. Yet our work-for-hire laws are depriving all artists, not only the new, young creators, of much of the income generated by their work; and, in many cases, are forcing them to abandon their careers. Society will be deprived inevitably of the richness that diversity of style and interpretation bring to literary and artistic expression unless Congress acts.

Employee defined

First, the bill defines "employee" as someone who must have withholding of federal taxes from his or her pay. This would eliminate the possibility that a free-lance artist will be found to be an employee for copyright purposes because of the supervision and control exercised by a commissioning party over the work. If the artist is to be treated as an employee for copyright purposes, then the artist should certainly be treated as an employee for the purpose of the benefits employees receive.

Work-for-hire categories restricted

In the situation in which the free lancer is definitely not an employee, the bill removes certain categories from those types of assignments that can be done as work for hire by a free-lancer. The categories deleted include all those in which visual creators are most likely to work: (1) contributions to collective works; (2) parts of audiovisual works (but parts of motion pictures might still be done as work for hire); (3) instructional texts; and (4) supplementary works.

If no more were done than to remove these categories from those which can be work for hire, undoubtedly "all rights" contracts would immediately become standard for publishers now using work for hire. The bill provides safeguards against the indiscriminate use of all rights transfers in the categories being removed from work for hire. This saves the artist from being cut off from the future stream of residual income that each image potentially represents.

A fair division

Existing law has a presumption as to what rights are acquired in a contri-

bution to a collective work if no explicit agreement has been reached between the parties. The bill extends this presumption to cover parts of audiovisual works (excluding motion pictures), instructional texts and supplementary works. Under the presumption, a publisher acquires art in these categories only for use in a particular larger work such as a book, any revision of that larger work and any work in the same series as the original larger work unless an explicit agreement has been reached between the parties as to a different transfer of rights.

Ownership of original art

The bill also provides that the sale of a right of copyright does not transfer ownership of any original art unless such originals are transferred in writing. For work-for-hire, the bill would clarify any present ambiguity by making the actual creator the owner of any original materials.

Expressions of support from the creative community are a necessity if the work-for-hire provisions of the copyright law are to be reformed.

Letters to Senator Thad Cochran, Senator Charles Mathias, Representative Robert Kastenmeier, Representative Barney Frank and Representative Howard Berman are significant in keeping momentum to move this bill or its successors toward enactment.

Chapter 5

Copyright:
infringement, fair use, compulsory licensing and permissions

If someone uses work without the copyright owner's permission (subject to the various exemptions, such as fair use and compulsory licensing, discussed in the copyright chapters), that person is an infringer. To win an infringement suit, the artist must prove that he or she owned the copyright and the work was copied by the infringer. Copying is often inferred from the infringer's access to a work and the substantial similarity of the work alleged to be infringing.

Reference files

One of the most frequently asked questions is whether the use of another artist's imagery is an infringement of copyright. In particular, illustrators must maintain files of imagery to fulfill assignments with deadlines too short to permit contacting anyone for permissions. The names for these files—the sedate "reference" file, the offhand "scrap" file or the larcenous "swipe" file—suggest the ambiguity felt when using such imagery. After all, the people who made that imagery are also artists and copyright proprietors—like the illustrator who wants to use it.

The test for infringement

The reference file probably contains a lot of photography and some illustration and design. To start with an obvious case, let's assume that an illustrator is asked to do a large painting of people on a beach as a magazine illustration. Finding a perfect full-page illustration in a competitive mag-

azine, the illustrator copies it. Since the painting is far larger than the magazine page, the illustrator feels this won't be an infringement.

What is the test for copyright infringement? It is whether an ordinary observer, looking at the original work and the work allegedly copied from it, recognizes that a copying has taken place. In the example of the painting, the ordinary observer test will certainly yield a conclusion of infringement. The fact that the painting is larger is of no significance if it was copied. Similarly, a change of media—such as making an illustration from a photograph or, alternatively, photographing an illustration—does not change the fact that the copying is an infringement.

Altering some parts of the original work will not avoid an infringement if application of the ordinary observer test leads to the conclusion that more than a trivial amount of the original work has been copied. For example, the people could be eliminated from the beach and sand dunes added. But any creator or buyer of imagery must have certainty that no infringement will take place. So the new work must be changed to the point where it can be said without doubt that no ordinary observer would believe the new image has been copied from the original. At that point, of course, the reference file becomes a more difficult resource to use.

What if the original work were used as a part of a collage of many works? This would be an infringement as long as the original work were recognizable.

Damages for infringement

An infringer can be sued for the artist's actual damages, plus any profits made by the infringer that aren't included in the computation of actual damages. If an artist is going to have trouble proving actual damages, the court can be asked to award statutory damages (assuming the artist qualifies for statutory damages as explained in Chapter 4 on registration). Statutory damages are an amount between $250 and $10,000 awarded in the court's discretion for each work infringed. These damages may be lowered to $100 by the court if the infringer shows the infringement was innocent or increased to $50,000 if the copyright owner shows the infringement was willful. In addition to damages, the court can also issue injunctions to prevent additional infringements, impound and dispose of infringing items, award discretionary court costs and award attorney's fees (if the artist qualifies for attorney's fees as explained in Chapter 4 on registration).

In relation to infringements, one advantage of having copyright notice in the artist's own name appear with the contribution to a collective work is that such a notice prevents an innocent infringer—a person who reprinted the work because he or she obtained permission from the owner of copyright in the collective work—from being able to use the fact of having permission as a defense. Registration of the contribution, by the way, also cuts off this defense. Of course, even if the innocent infringer has a defense, the magazine or other collective work would have to pay back to the artist whatever they had received by wrongfully selling reprint rights in the contribution. Also, the copyright notice in the artist's name will alert third parties that they should come directly to the artist for reprint rights and not deal through the owner of the collective work.

The limited liability normally provided by corporations may not prove a shield against individual liability in a copyright infringement lawsuit. Particularly if a corporate officer participates in the infringement or uses the corporation for the purposes of carrying out infringements, he or she can have personal liability. Likewise an employee who, in exercising discretion, commits or causes the employer to commit an infringement can be liable.

Fair use

Not absolutely every unpermitted use of someone else's copyrighted work is a copyright infringement. For example, a magazine might use one drawing to illustrate an article about the artist who did the drawing. That would be considered a fair use. The 1978 law includes a fair use provision that is meant to be the same as the fair use cases decided under the prior law. It provides that fair use of a copyrighted work for "purposes such as criticism, comment, news reporting, teaching (including multiple copies for classroom use), scholarship, or research, is not an infringement of copyright." To determine whether a use is a fair use, four factors are given: (1) the purpose and character of the use, including whether or not it is for profit; (2) the character of the copyrighted work; (3) how much of the total work is used in the course of the use; and (4) what effect the use will have on the market for or value of the copyrighted work.

The guidelines for fair use can be difficult to apply to specific cases. For example, an artist may see a variation of one of his or her drawings and consider the copying an infringement rather than a fair use. Or an artist may be wondering whether to use someone else's work as a background for some figures. These issues are factual and almost impossible to resolve other than by use of common sense. Satire, for example, may be a comment on another work which legitimately uses part of the original work. Or it may cross the line by using so much of the original work that the value of the satiric piece is simply what has been copied rather than any fair comment (in which case a copyright infringement is likely to have occurred).

Remember that the test for infringement is as follows: Will an ordinary observer, looking at the two works, believe one has been copied from the other? But, in an appropriate situation such as a review or scholarly article, a work could be copied exactly and it still wouldn't amount to an infringement, so the guidelines for fair use really have to be referred to in every case to determine whether or not an artist can safely use someone else's copyrighted work.

One interesting example of fair use given by the House Judiciary Committee involves the practice of calligraphers who reproduce excerpts from copyrighted literary works in making their art work. The committee concluded that a calligrapher's making of a single copy for a single client would not be an infringement of the copyright in the literary work.

Educators, authors and publishers have agreed to special guidelines covering the fair use copying of books and periodicals for classroom use in nonprofit educational institutions. To give an overview, brief portions of copyrighted works may be used for a class if the teacher individually decides to do so, the copyright notice in the owner's name appears on the class materials and this kind of use is not repeated too extensively. It is also permissible for a pictorial, graphic or sculptural work to be displayed or an audiovisual work, including a motion picture, performed by instructors or pupils for educational purposes in the course of face-to-face teaching activities at a nonprofit educational institution.

Permissions

Our discussion has assumed that the work the artist wishes to use is protected by copyright. Some work, however, will be in the public domain. This means that copyright was never obtained for the work or has now expired. Unfortunately, it is difficult to learn this simply by examining work in a reference file. Tear sheets without copyright notice may be protected because they came from copyrighted publications. Especially for work published after January 1, 1978, it will be difficult to rely on the absence of notice as a basis for concluding a work is in the public domain. This is because the new law has several provisions that protect copyrights even if notice is omitted from a work. For copyrights in work published in the United States prior to 1978, the maximum term of copyright protection under our law is 75 years. So, it is safe to assume that any work published more than 75 years ago in the United States is now in the public domain as far as protection in the United States is concerned. Obviously this rule is of limited value to a creator who maintains a current reference file.

If the public domain provides little succor, what about simply obtaining permission to use the work from the creator or present copyright owner? This can be done by a simple letter setting forth the artist's project, what material the artist wants to copy, what rights the artist needs in the material, what credit line and copyright notice will be given, and what payment, if any, will be made. To make the letter binding, the words "CONSENTED AND AGREED TO" would be added at the bottom with a line underneath for the signature of the person owning the copyright. If the person is signing as the representative of a magazine or other organization, the name of the organization and the title of the person signing should be indicated. The sample release form appearing here can be used as a model to be adapted to particular situations. The permitted use would be sharply delineated to protect the party selling the rights from giving up too much and to guarantee the party obtaining rights that what is needed has been lawfully acquired. The fact that re-use fees normally increase with greater usage is another reason to give an accurate description of intended usage.

Permission form

Dear Sir/Madam:

I am preparing a book titled _____to be published by _____.
May I please have your permission to include the following material: (specify the material
and, for a published work, include the original place of publication, date and page numbers)
in my book and in future revisions and editions thereof, including nonexclusive world rights
in all languages. These rights will in no way restrict republication of your material in any
other form by you or others authorized by you. Should you not control these rights in
their entirety, would you kindly let me know to whom else I must write. Unless you indicate otherwise, I will use the following credit line (specify credit line) and copyright notice
(specify the form of the copyright notice which will protect the material the artist is asking
to use): _____
I would greatly appreciate your consent to this request. For your convenience a release
form is provided below and a copy of this letter is enclosed for your files.

Sincerely yours,

Jane Artist

I (We) grant permission for the use requested above.

_____   _____

(Specify name and title, if any)   Date

Locating copyright owners

The problem with permissions
arises when the copyright owner can't
be located. Some work is very difficult
to trace, especially if a tight deadline
is involved. The Copyright Office in
Washington, D.C. will search its records for a reasonable fee, but many
pieces of art and photography have
never been registered. Thus, although
they may be protected by copyright,
they cannot be found by a search of
the records in the Copyright Office.
Even works that have been registered
can be difficult to find, since titles may
not aid sufficiently in locating the work.

Stock houses and archives for
photography and illustration may very
well prove the best resource when it
is impossible to determine if a work is
in the public domain or to reach a
copyright owner to pay for a re-use.
Millions of images are quickly available
to use as reference and expert guidance is usually provided by the staff.
Again, the fee for such uses should be
included in the estimate for the assignment.

Compulsory licensing

The law provides for the compulsory licensing of published pictorial,
graphic and sculptural works for transmission by non-commerical educational
broadcast stations. A compulsory license means that the copyright owner
has no right to prevent the use of
copyrighted work. The Copyright
Royalty Tribunal has set very low
rates for royalties to be paid when
such works are used. It has also established rules under which records
must be kept of compulsory licens-
ings, but to date almost no fees have
been paid to visual artists.

This ill-conceived infringement on
the traditional rights of the copyright
owner has been such a complete failure that even the Copyright Royalty
Tribunal has recommended that Congress repeal the compulsory licensing
of pictorial, graphic and sculptural
works. If an artist could make a direct
agreement with a station, it would replace the compulsory licensing provisions. Compulsory licensing, however,
does not permit a program to be
drawn to a substantial extent from a
compliation of pictorial, graphic or
sculptural works, nor does it permit
any use whatsoever of audiovisual
works. The new law also provides for
the payment, under a system of compulsory licensing, of certain royalties
for the secondary transmission of
copyrighted works on cable television
systems. The amounts paid will be
distributed to the copyright owners by
the Copyright Royalty Tribunal.

A question of ethics

Infringements, reference files and compulsory licensing all raise ethical questions. It isn't merely that using another artist's work without permission is a copyright infringement. The purpose of copyright is to reward creativity. The Code of Fair Practice, which includes among its sponsors the Graphic Artists Guild and the American Society of Magazine Photographers, unequivocally states: "20. There should be no plagarisms of any creative artwork."

This sensitivity toward other creators is in its deepest sense self-protective. No artist wants his or her work copied without the opportunity to receive a fee, be credited as author of the original work and make certain the work is not to be unacceptably altered in its new usage. By understanding the ethical and copyright implications in these areas, artists can advance the professional status of all visual communicators.

Chapter 6

Moral rights:
state, federal and foreign

Many American artists may simply assume that even after a sale they still have a right to be credited as the creators of their art and should still have control over how their art is displayed. These are the most important components of what is called *droit moral:* moral rights widely recognized abroad. In fact, the protections for the American artist are limited and often unsatisfactory. Some legal commentators have argued that American laws relating to unfair competition, trademarks, right to privacy, protection against defamation, right to publicity, patents and copyright amount to a satisfactory equivalent of moral rights. This is discussed thoroughly at the end of this chapter, but the better view is that this melange does not at all approach the protections offered to creative people and their work under specially designed moral-rights provisions. Many artists' groups have recognized moral rights as an important issue and urged the enactment of legislation to guarantee this protection.

The states of California, Massachusetts and New York have enacted quite different laws to protect moral rights, but no federal legislation offers this protection which many other countries give to artists. The moral rights suggested, for example, under the Berne Copyright Convention, to which the United States is not a signatory, provide that "the author shall have the right to claim authorship of the work and to object to any distortion, mutilation or other modification of, or other derogatory action in relation to said work, which would be prejudical to his honor or reputation."

United States legislation

Congressman Barney Frank has sponsored a bill to amend the copyright law by providing for moral rights: "Independently of the author's copyright in a pictorial, graphic, or sculptural work, the author or the author's legal representative shall have the right, during the life of the author and fifty years after the author's death, to claim authorship of such work and to object to any distortion, mutilation, or other alteration thereof, and to enforce any other limitation recorded in the Copyright Office that would prevent prejudice to the author's honor or reputation."

Copyright, the power to control reproduction and other uses of a work, is a property right. Moral rights are best described as rights of personality. Even if the artist has sold a work and the accompanying copyright, the artist would still retain rights of personality. Thus moral rights connect an artist to a work even in the absence of property rights.

International copyright protection

The bill follows closely the language of the Berne Copyright Convention. The 1978 revision of our copyright law increased the likelihood that the United States could join this Convention and gain greater worldwide protection for the creative works of our citizens.

One stumbling block to our becoming a signatory, however, is the absence under our law of any moral rights provisions. To understand what the reality of the proposed bill might ultimately prove to be, it is helpful to examine a number of European and American cases illustrating the effects moral rights could have if enacted in the United States.

Right of paternity

The first moral right listed in the bill is that of the artist "to claim authorship of such work." Known as the right of paternity, this would change the holding of a famous American case involving the artist Alberto Vargas and *Esquire* magazine. Vargas created a distinctive series of drawings of women over which *Esquire* acquired complete ownership by contract. For more than five years, *Esquire* had given Vargas credit as creator of the illustrations, although the contract itself did not provide for him to receive any such credit. After Vargas and *Esquire* had a falling out in 1946, the magazine changed the title on the remaining drawings it owned to "Esquire Girls" and gave no credit line at all to Vargas. Vargas sued, but the court decided that Vargas could not claim an implied right to receive authorship credit, because the contract specifically transferred all rights to *Esquire*. It stated, "What plaintiff in reality seeks is a change in the law in this country to conform to that of certain other countries . . . we are not disposed to make any new law in this respect." (*Vargas* v. *Esquire*, 164 F. 2d 522) An interview with Alberto Vargas appears in the next chapter on pages 47–52.

The bill would also prevent enforcement of a contractual provision by which an artist agrees to create work under a pseudonym. In a French case decided in 1967, for example, a painter named Guille agreed to deliver to his dealer his entire output for ten years. These works would either be unsigned by Guille or signed under a pseudonym. The court held the contract invalid, since it violated the painter's right of paternity.

One limit to the right of paternity, however, is shown in a bizarre 1977 case involving the Surrealist Giorgio deChirico. He filed suit in France when a painting titled *The Ghost* and attributed to him was displayed at the Musée des Arts Décoratifs. He claimed that the attribution was false and demanded the painting be destroyed. The court insisted that he pay an expert's fee to examine the painting for authenticity. When deChirico refused to do this and failed to prove by other means that the painting was a fake, the court not only refused to grant the relief requested but also required de Chirico to pay 50,000 francs to the woman who owned the painting. The right of paternity would permit an artist to prevent false attribution of a painting, but it would not allow the artist to stop the exhibition of a painting that is correctly attributed.

Right of integrity

The next moral right in Frank's bill would guarantee the artist the right "to object to any distortion, mutilation, or other alteration there—of . . ." Known as the right of integrity, this is illustrated by a leading French case involving six panels of a refrigerator painted by Bernard Buffet. It was Buffet's intention that the refrigerator be exhibited as a whole. Accordingly, he only signed one of the six panels. Within six months of the first auction, however, one of the panels was offered for sale at a second auction under the description of a painting on metal by Buffet. He brought suit to prevent the sale of the panel separately and to have the entire work returned to him. In 1962 the court upheld him to the extent that it refused to allow the panels to be sold separately in either a public or private sale, but the private owner was allowed to keep the work. Buffet also received one franc as a symbolic vindication, the right to have the court's decision published in three art journals of his choice at the defendant's expense and the court costs.

On the other hand, artists in the United States have not been notably successful in preventing the circulation and display of their work in altered or distorted form. Carl Andre, for example, lent a work to the Whitney Museum in New York City for its 1976 exhibition, "Two Hundred Years of American Sculpture." Because the work was displayed near a bay window and a fire exit, Andre claimed these distractions distorted it and withdrew it from the exhibition. The Whitney Museum simply substituted another work by Andre from its permanent collection. Andre objected again, this time because the substitute work had been misinstalled by placing rubber backings under the copper floor pieces. He found, however, that he had no recourse against the owner of the work, whether the owner was a private person or an institution.

Destruction of art

In the United States nothing prevents the owner of an artwork from destroying it completely. For example, in 1937 the muralist Alfred Crimi was selected by competition to create a fresco mural painting 35′ x 26′ for the Rutgers Presbyterian Church in New York City. The contract stated that the mural would be permanently affixed to the wall and that the church would also own the copyright. In 1938 the mural was completed by the artist, but already some members of the congregation objected to it on the grounds that the degree to which Christ's chest was exposed emphasized his physical rather than his spiritual qualities. This protesting segment apparently increased so that in 1946 the mural was painted over in the course of redecorating the church.

Crimi sued, demanding that the mural either be restored, removed from the wall at the church's expense and given to him or that he receive an award of damages as compensation. The court held against Crimi, stating, "The time for the artist to have reserved any rights was when he and his attorney participated in the drawing of the contract with the church." (*Crimi* v. *Rutgers Presbyterian Church*, 194 Misc. 570, 89 N.Y.S. 2d 813) In the view of the court, the mural was merely property and could be destroyed at its owner's whim. An interview with Alfred Crimi appears in the next chapter on pages 43–47.

However, it is not clear that the right of integrity, if enacted, would prevent an owner from destroying a mural or other artwork. In 1973 French artist Jean Dubuffet contracted with Renault, the state-owned automobile company, to construct a 2,000 square yard abstract sculpture at the company's headquarters on the outskirts of Paris. Dubuffet constructed a model for a sculpture which would be placed in the company's courtyard and provide leisure and recreation for the more than 1,500 employees. The model was approved in September, 1974, by Pierre Dreyfus, then President of Renault, and construction began. However, Dreyfus retired in the middle of 1975, and his successor, Bernard Vernier-Palliez, decided that "the automobile business has nothing to do with art." The project, approximately halfway toward completion, was halted. Dubuffet, although he had been paid his full fee of $80,000, brought suit to force Renault to permit him to complete the work. He even offered to use his own funds to

finance the completion. The lower court found in favor of Renault, but in 1983 the appellate court found in favor of Dubuffet and ordered that the work in progress be resumed. However, it is unlikely that the right of integrity would protect a privately displayed work from destruction, although this will be unclear until cases are decided in this regard.

Protecting reputation

The bill would permit enforcement of "any other limitation recorded in the Copyright Office that would prevent prejudice to the author's honor or reputation." For example, if an artist indicated in the records of the Copyright Office that his or her art should never be exhibited with the work of Soviet artists or used in any other works favorably portraying the Soviet Union, the work could not be used in a film praising the accomplishments of Soviet rule. This would be true even if the copyright had gone into the public domain so that the work could be freely copied by anyone. This right will clearly need more definition, since too extensive limitations could prove unfair to the owner of the work or violate free speech privileges.

For example, the artist could not validly record in the Copyright Office a limitation that the work never be criticized publicly. Whenever art is exhibited to the public, critics have the protection of the First Amendment in giving their honest opinions about its merit. If the boundaries of fair comment are exceeded by a critic, such as by falsely attacking the artist's private life, an action for libel can be brought for injury to reputation.

Right of disclosure

The right of disclosure gives the artist sole power to determine when a work is completed and ready to be disclosed to the public. This has led to some interesting decisions in French courts. In the *Whistler* case in 1900, the artist was dissatisfied with a portrait he had done on commission. Lord Eden, who had commissioned the portrait, was satisfied and demanded delivery of the work. Application of the right of disclosure gave Whistler the right not to deliver the work until such time as he considered the work completed, despite the fact that the work had been publicly exhibited. The *Camoin* case in 1931 involved a painter who had slashed and discarded several canvases. The slashed canvases were found and restored by another person who sought to sell the works. The painter intervened, based upon his right of disclosure, and the French court seized and destroyed the canvases in accordance with the artist's original intent.

The *Rouault* case in 1947 was a dispute between the artist and the heirs of the artist's dealer. The artist had left 806 unfinished canvases in a studio in a gallery of the dealer. Rouault, who had a key to the room and would occasionally work on the paintings, had agreed to turn over all his work as created to the dealer. The dealer died and the heirs of the dealer claimed to own the 806 works. The court held that Rouault owned the works, because the right of disclosure required the artist himself determine the work to be completed before any disclosure of the work to the public by sale could occur. Any agreement to the contrary would be invalid. Finally, the *Bonnard* case ultimately resolved that paintings only become community property upon completion to the artist's satisfaction. The estate of an artist's wife would, therefore, have no right in works the artist had chosen not to disclose. The right of disclosure, like the other moral rights, was enacted as legislation in France on March 11, 1957.

The United States bill does not provide for the moral right of disclosure. The right of disclosure gives the artist the absolute right to decide when a work is finished and ready to be revealed to the public. While it may be argued that our copyright laws provide similar protection, it is not clear that copyright or other laws would, for example, protect unfinished artworks from the demands of a bankrupt artist's creditors or from a spouse in divorce proceedings in a community property state.

Duration, transfer, enforcement

The bill proposes moral rights that last for the artist's lifetime plus anoth-

er 50 years. This is the same term as copyright protection under the copyright revision act which took effect January 1, 1978. Moral rights in a country such as France, however, are perpetual. If the moral rights are perpetual, the question arises who will enforce such rights after the artist's death. In France, the right of disclosure is enforced by the artist's executors, descendants, spouse, other heirs, general legatees and finally by the courts. The rights of paternity and integrity can be transmitted to heirs or third parties under the artist's will for enforcement. In the bill the designation of the artist's "legal representative" as the party to enforce such rights after the artist's death may well be insufficient, since heirs and perhaps the courts should also be given rights.

Another important point is that the bill does not indicate whether moral rights can be transferred by the artist. If the artist could assign moral rights in such a way that he or she would be unable to exercise them, their value would be greatly lessened. The intention of the bill needs to be clarified here.

Remedies for violations

The issue of remedies for violations of moral rights will also have to be resolved. The present bill proposes an amendment to the copyright laws. The copyright law provides for damages, injunctions, court costs and attorney's fees if a copyright infringement claim is successfully prosecuted. Should the artist bringing suit on a moral-rights claim have similar rights? For example, should the artist claiming a work has been mutilated have a right to receive damages as well as a right to have the work restored? And should our moral rights provision give that ultimate relief which the French courts denied to Bernard Buffet: return of the artwork itself? If an artist is to claim the protection of moral rights, will he or she have to comply with any copyright formalities?

Many obstacles must be overcome before moral rights will be enacted into law for United States artists. The present bill must be refined and clarified in many important respects. After that, a political effort must be undertaken by artists across the country to rally support for moral rights. At present, the most remarkable developments have been the enactment of state moral rights laws in California, New York and Massachusetts.

Moral rights in California

Former State Senator Alan Sieroty acted as a great friend to artists in California. He sponsored almost all of the art legislation which has made California the preeminent state in protecting its artists. His sagacity and concern for the artist is evidenced by the Art Preservation Act which he guided to passage in 1979 and which took effect on January 1, 1980.

The law protects, ". . . an original painting, sculpture, or drawing, or an original work of art in glass, of recognized quality, but shall not include work prepared under contrast for commercial use by its purchaser." The fine artist is protected by this law, but the commercial artist is not. Even today in California, Alberto Vargas would not be able to win a case like the one he brought against *Esquire* magazine. Moreover, only art of recognized quality is protected. This means that artists are protected by the law only when their work is recognized to have quality based ". . . on the opinions of artists, art dealers, collectors of fine art, curators of art museums, and other persons involved with the creation or marketing of fine art."

So the California does not focus its protection on the artist. Rather it protects art of a certain quality. The law does not necessarily connect the artist to his or her art, but instead preserves for society certain pieces of art which have an agreed upon significance.

Only an artist may alter, deface or destroy his or her art (provided, of course, that not even the artist may do this unless he or she owns the art). The artist retains, ". . . at all times the right to claim authorship, or, for a just and valid reason, to disclaim authorship of his or her work of fine art."

However, the California law allows the artist to waive these moral rights by an express written instrument signed by the artist. Artists' frequent lack of bargaining power may in some cases make this an oppressive provision.

The protections in the law last for the artist's life plus 50 years, the same term of protection granted under our copyright law. After the artist's death, these rights may be enforced by the artist's heir, legatee or personal representative (such as an executor or administrator).

A special provision of the law deals with art affixed to buildings. If the owner of the building intends to remove art which can be removed without substantial harm, the artist has rights to the art if the owner intends to alter, deface or destroy it. In such a case, the owner would have to make a diligent effort to give notice or actually give written notice of the planned removal to the artist or the artist's successor-in-interest. If the artist fails within 90 days of receipt of notice to remove the art at the artist's own expense, the owner may alter, deface or destroy it. An artist who removes or pays to remove art from a building in this situation becomes the owner of the art. On the other hand, if substantial harm will of necessity be caused to the art by its removal, the artist must obtain a written instrument signed by the owner of the building and providing for the protection of the art. Otherwise the artist will have no rights in the art and it may be destroyed by the owner. Clearly "substantial harm" will be an issue that the courts will have to determine. If Alfred Crimi's case had been tried under this law, for example, would his mural have been removable from the Rutger's Presbyterian Church without causing substantial harm?

An action under the law must be brought within the longer of either three years from the act complained of or one year from the artist's discovering that act.

The artist's remedies include injunctive relief, actual damages, punitive damages, reasonable attorneys' and expert witness fees and such other relief as the court considers appropriate. Since punitive damages are awarded to punish wrongful acts rather than compensate the artist, any punitive damages awarded under the law are paid to an organization selected by the court to be used for charitable or educational activities involving the arts in California.

It is instructive to contrast the provisions of the California law with those of the New York law described in the next section. The law enacted in Massachussetts in 1985, by the way, is almost identical with the California law.

Moral rights in New York

On January 1, 1984 a landmark law benefitting artists took effect in New York State. Sponsored by Assembly Majority Leader Richard Gottfried and known as the Artists' Authorship Rights Act, this law entitles artists to name credit when their work is displayed or reproduced and protects artists against alterations or mutilations of their work (but not against complete destruction). Working closely together, the Assembly's Committee on Tourism, Arts and Sports Development, the Graphic Artists Guild and the American Society of Magazine Photographers brought about the passage of the law. As the main author (along with Wendy Feuer of the Committee's staff) of the original draft of the New York bill, I sought to broaden the scope of the California protection to include reproductions of art, photography and design, even if these reproductions were prepared under a contract for commercial use. After much lobbying and numerous revisions, the New York law protects "any original work of visual or graphic art of any medium"—including reproductions of such art. However, the law does not protect works prepared under contract for advertising or trade use. Thus, the art or photography for a point of purchase display or product packaging would not be protected. Art prepared for magazines, books and other public interest uses would be covered.

No one—other than the artist or a person acting with the artist's permission—may publish or display an original work or a reproduction in an altered or defaced form if damage to the artist's reputation is reasonably likely to occur. If a violation takes place, the artist has the right to have his or her name removed from the work. If a work is published without the artist's name, the artist has the right to insist that his or her name accompany the work.

By protecting the reputation of the artist, the law protects the integrity of the art itself. Cropping for publication will undoubtedly become an issue. Is the cropping done in such a way that damage to the artist's reputation is reasonably likely to result? This test is flexible, so that unobjectionable cropping can continue. However, if a user fears that cropping or other alteration might damage the artist's reputation, it would be best to obtain permission from the artist for the form of the image to be disseminated. Other changes in the art—such as additions or deletions to the image—may risk violating the law and require the precaution of obtaining the artist's consent.

The law's name credit provisions would affect the result of the famous *Esquire* v. *Vargas* case. Under the newly enacted law in New York, Vargas would have had a much better chance to win his case. The law does not appear to permit a waiver by the artist of the right to claim or disclaim authorship credit, since it states, ". . . the artist shall retain *at all times* the right to claim authorship or, for just and valid reasons, to disclaim authorship of his or her work of fine art."

A limitation in the law provides that, "a change that is an ordinary result of the medium of reproduction does not by itself create a violation . . ." For example, a reproduction of a painting that appears in a magazine will not be identical to the painting itself, but the law will not be violated if the alterations are those that ordinarily accompany such a change of medium. At what point changes are no longer "ordinary" will have to be decided on a case by case basis.

The law does not apply unless a work is "knowingly displayed in a place accessible to the public, published or reproduced in this state." The work must be made public before a violation occurs. A painting defaced in a private home or a mechanical with an altered image for reproduction are not violations until the work reaches the public. Also, a person who does not know an image has been altered will not be liable for making it public, since the violation would not have been done "knowingly".

The law applies to any work published or displayed in New York. However, the true impact of the law will be national. Since most published works eventually are sold in New York, the law will undoubtedly have an impact on publishers in other states. Compliance with the law will be a necessity for publishers who plan to market in New York.

For original art, conservation is not a violation of the law unless it is done negligently. Also, changes caused to originals by "the passage of time or the inherent nature of the materials" will not be a violation of the law, unless such changes were the result of gross negligence in protecting or maintaining the art. Gross negligence is an intentional failure to perform a required duty with utter disregard for the consequences.

The protection of the law lasts for the artist's lifetime. The right is personal to the artist who is the only person who may sue to rectify violations. Any lawsuit must be brought within three years after the violation occurs—or within one year after the artist should have found out about the violation if that would be a longer time period.

If an artist's rights have been violated under the law, he or she may sue for damages. The amount of the damages will be based on the nature of the injury suffered. Expert testimony about the significance of a good and growing reputation for success in the field will probably aid in establishing the amount of damages. The law allows for a suit to prevent a potential violation from taking place as well as to prevent any existing violation from continuing.

Future directions

That both California and New York now have moral rights laws suggests the wisdom of enacting federal legislation. In this way, artists across our nation will benefit from a uniform standard of protection for their art and their professional reputations.

The artist in the United States can also attempt to approximate the moral rights granted abroad by the use of avenues such as unfair competition, trademarks, the right to privacy, protection against defamation, the right to publicity and patents. Each of these is considered separately, but often these protections will overlap.

Unfair competition

"The essence of an unfair competition claim is that the defendant as-sembled a product which bears so striking a resemblance to the plaintiff's product that the public will be confused as to the identity of the products . . . The test is whether persons exercising 'reasonable intelligence and discrimination' would be taken in by the similarity." (*Shaw* v. *Time-Life Records,* 38 N.Y. 2d 201) The application of the theory of unfair competition can be even broader than this definition indicates. In proper factual situations, it can prevent the artist being presented as the creator of works the artist in fact did not create; prevent the artist being presented as the creator of distorted versions of the artist's own works; prevent another person from claiming to have created works in fact created by the artist; protect titles which, although not usually copyrightable, may become so well recognized that use of the title again (such as *Gone With The Wind*) would create confusion of the new work with the original work; and generally prevent the competitors of an artist from confusing the public to benefit unfairly from the reputation for quality of the artist's work. Thus, although copyright does not protect an artist's style, it may in some cases prove to be unfair competition if a style is imitated.

An example of the application of the theory of unfair competition involved the "Mutt and Jeff" comic strip, which the cartoonist first sold to a San Francisco newspaper and then to a New York City newspaper. When the cartoonist signed an exclusive agreement with the San Francisco newspaper, the newspaper in New York City hired another cartoonist for a competitive "Mutt and Jeff" strip. However, the court stated, "No person should be permitted to pass off as his own the thoughts and works of another," and granted an injunction to prevent the New York City newspaper from continuing to produce a "Mutt and Jeff" comic strip. (*Fisher* v. *Star Co.,* 231 N.Y. 414, 132 N.E. 133, *cert. denied* 257 U.S. 654)

The artist should realize, however, that the theory of unfair competition does not entitle the artist to authorship credit when the artist has transferred a copyright without reserving the right to such credit. Also, in the United States, it appears that a contract is likely to be valid even if an artist agrees either to work under a pseudonym or not to receive authorship credit. However, an agreement to pass off the work of one artist as if it were the work of another artist would probably be voidable as against public policy, even if both artists agreed to such a scheme.

The theory of unfair competition cannot, basically, replace a contract expressly protecting the artist's rights. The artist may well wish a contractual provision requiring the artist's approval for any changes, including destruction, with regard to the work. But, at the least, the contract must provide for authorship credit if the artist is to argue that distortions or alterations are prevented by the theory of unfair competition. An unfair competition claim would not be flexible enough to extend to distortions or alterations of a work created anonymously and sold without any reservations.

Trademarks and trade names

A trademark is a distinctive motto, symbol, emblem, device or mark which a manufacturer places on a product to distinguish in the public mind that product from the products of rival manufacturers. Trademarks are usually registered with the Patent Office for federal protection and with the appropriate state office for state protection, although even an unregistered mark can have protection under the common law. An artist who is exploiting work commerically—for example, posters, jewelry or clothing—might wish to seek trademark protection for a distinctive logo or motto. Also, the artist would wish to be certain that any chosen trademark did not infringe an already registered trademark in commerical use. A trademark can be licensed, as long as the artist giving the license ensures that the quality of goods created by the licensee will be of the same quality that the public associates with the trademark. Trademarks are entitled to protection in foreign countries under treaties executed by the United States. The effect of having a trademark is like unfair competition in that others are prevented from using the trademark where confusion to the public would result. While trademarks are used for products, or in some cases for services, the artist should at least be aware of the existence of this type of protection.

Trade names are closely related to trademarks. Such a name may not technically be a trademark (because it is not affixed to marketed goods or is not capable of exclusive use by anyone), but may designate a particular business establishment, the location of a business or a class of goods. Artists operating under a trade or fictitious name should register the name with the local authority in charge of registration (such as the county clerk). Partnerships will also be required to make such a registration. In this way, a record exists of the names under which a business is being conducted. The registration fee is not expensive, and failure to obtain a certificate of registration may make it impossible to open a bank account and, in some cases, may foreclose the exercise of certain legal rights. When a business operating under a dba (doing business as) name ceases, a certificate of discontinuance may be filed with the local authority.

Occasionally artists wish to include a trademark in an art work. For example, an artist may paint a street scene which includes a sign with a company logo. Use of the trademark in this way should not be a problem for the artist, except in the unlikely case in which the public might be confused by the painting and imagine it was created by or was a product of the company depicted in the painting.

Right to privacy

The right to privacy is the right to be free from unwanted and unnecessary publicity or interference which could injure the personal feelings of the artist or present the artist in a false light before the public. The right is recognized in varying forms by almost every state. New York's Civil Rights Law Section 50, for example, prohibits using "for advertising purposes, or for the purposes of trade, the name, portrait or picture of any living person without having first obtained the written consent of such person." Under Section 51, however, this right is specifically not applicable to use of "the name, portrait or picture of any . . . artist in connection with his . . . artistic productions which he has sold or disposed of with such name, portrait or picture used in connection therewith."

The right to privacy is personal, which means that only the living artist may use it—not assignees or heirs. The right to privacy diminishes as the artist gains stature as a public figure, particularly as to those areas of the artist's life in which the public has a legitimate interest. The New York statute limits violations to uses for "advertising purposes" or "purposes of trade", but exhibitions of work, especially if by a private collector or a museum, would not appear to be for such uses. An artist could recover for invasion of privacy where an unauthorized use of the artist's name accompanied sale of pillows designed in imitation of the artist's work. But after the artist's sale of all rights in a cartoon, a magazine was able to use the artist's name in manufacturing and selling dolls based on the cartoon without an invasion of the artist's privacy. While theoretically the right to privacy might be used to protect the artist against distortions of the artist's work, the practical effect of the right to privacy in this area would seem quite limited.

Protection against defamation

Defamation is an attack on the reputation of another person. Both libel and slander are forms of defamation, libel being expressed by print, writing, pictures or signs, and slander being expressed by spoken words. For an artist to bring an action for defamation, the defamatory material must have reached the public. Also, the defamatory material must be false, since the truth of the alleged defamatory material will be a defense to a lawsuit based on defamation.

The effect of showing or publishing an artist's work in a distorted form while attributing the work to the artist would be damaging to the artist's reputation. Protection against defamation is, therefore, a possible method for an artist to use in preventing violations of the integrity of the artist's work. Defamation is discussed in more detail on pages 53–54.

Right to publicity

The right to publicity is a relatively new right independent of the right to privacy. The right of publicity states that a person with a public reputation has the right to benefit from the commercial value associated with that person's name or picture. Sports figures, for example, have the right to financial benefits from the use of their names and pictures on baseball cards or in a baseball game. But the right to publicity will be of little value to the artist who is not famous.

The right to publicity does not prevent advertising uses of a well-known person's name and picture if such uses are incidental to a legitimate news article. Joe Namath was the subject of many newsworthy articles on football in *Sports Illustrated.* However, when *Sports Illustrated* used photographs from the articles to illustrate advertising, Namath contended that his right to publicity had been violated. The court concluded that the use of the name and photographs of Namath were only uses incidental to establishing the quality and news content of *Sports Illustrated.* To allow damages might well violate the First Amendment guarantees of freedom of speech and press, so Namath lost the case.

Also, valuable as this right of publicity may be to well-known artists, the right will at present neither protect artists from being denied authorship credit when a contract is silent as to such credit nor protect art works from distorting changes.

Patents

Art works protected by copyright can sometimes also be protected by patent. While a copyright can be obtained for original work, a patent requires a far more difficult test of invention. A utility patent, which might be relevant for some conceptual works, can be obtained for a work which is useful, new and unobvious to persons skilled in the discipline. A utility patent has a nonrenewable term of 17 years.

The more common patent protection for art works would be a design patent, which has a term of 14 years. Such a patent is granted on an article of manufacture, for example, a statue used as a lamp base, which has a design that is new, original, ornamental and unobvious. The test for a design patent is whether the object when viewed as a whole by an ordinary observer makes an impression of uniqueness of character.

Unlike copyright protection which attaches at the moment that the work is fixed in a tangible means of expression, patent protection does not attach until the United States Patent Office grants the patent. Patent protection is only granted after lengthy requirements are fulfilled. For this reason patent protection is difficult and expensive to obtain and, for the most part, can only be gotten with the aid of a patent attorney.

Patent protection prevents others from exploiting the patented article regardless of whether the copying necessary for copyright infringement can be shown. However, patents are not designed to provide protection similar to moral rights. For further information contact the United States Department of Commerce, Patent Trademark Office, Washington, D.C. 20231.

Artists in the United States

The enlightened approach often found abroad, which creates moral rights for artists, has yet to be adopted in the United States. Although state laws in California, New York and Massachussetts as well as many different doctrines protect the artist in the United States, there are still substantial risks that the artist may either go unacknowledged as a creator or have no recourse to prevent the alteration or destruction of the artist's work. Only by contracts can the artist in the United States attempt to create protections similar to the moral rights established by law in certain foreign nations. At some future time, federal legislation may give to all American artists the protections now enjoyed by many artists abroad.

Chapter 7

Moral rights:
two interviews

Laws granting moral rights may seem obscure to artists who have never experienced a denial of authorship credit or defacement of a work of art. What do such laws mean in terms of human emotions and the impulses governing creativity? Two cases from the 1940s are invariably cited as authority for the fact that artists in the United States lack moral rights and must protect their reputation and their art by contract. But how did these cases affect the artists Alfred Crimi and Alberto Vargas who dared seek legal recourse in vain attempts to gain moral rights? How might moral rights laws affect other artists who find themselves involved in such disputes in the future? To learn the answers to questions such as these, I interviewed both Crimi and Vargas.

Crimi v. Rutgers Presbyterian Church

My interview with Alfred Crimi took place in his studio in Greenwich Village on February 3, 1979. He had contacted me more than a year earlier because of an article I had written on the subject of moral rights for *American Artist*. I stated that, "It is clear that in the United States nothing prevents the owner of an artwork from destroying it completely. For example, in 1937 a mural painter named Alfred Crimi was selected by competition to create a fresco mural painting 35' x 26' for the Rutgers Presbyterian Church in New York City . . ." Crimi's letter chided me as follows: "I am Alfred Crimi who painted that fresco mural back in 1936, and so you touched a sore spot. [You say], 'for example, in 1936 *a mural painter named Alfred Crimi,* etc.'—you made it sound mythical and remote. I gather you are not acquainted with my status in the profession, except for what you have read in the law records. I can understand that. However, some research in the *Who's Who* might have been appropriate. It behooves me, therefore, to identify and update myself from the remote to the living . . ."

The case of *Crimi* v. *Rutgers Presbyterian Church* is one of the landmarks in the area of art and law. It stands for the proposition that the owner of an artwork is free to destroy it and the artist has no right to prevent this. The mural, completed and signed by Crimi, was dedicated at a service on November 30, 1938. At that time a leaflet was distributed to the congregation stating, "Whether the committee and the artist have done well is not for them to say. They have done their best. The verdict must be left to the present congregation, to the successive generations of the worshippers who will look upon the fresco, and to Him whose glory is all in all." The prophetic irony was that in 1946 the Rutgers Presbyterian Church would destroy this same mural. In Crimi's 1946 lawsuit against the Church, he sought to compel removal of the paint covering the mural. Failing that, he asked for the removal of the mural and its restoration at another location. Or, finally, he demanded damages if the mural could not be saved.

The Court found in favor of the Church. The decision stated, "The time for the artist to have reserved any rights was when he and his attorney participated in the drawing of the contract with the church. No rights in the fresco mural were reserved . . ." (*Crimi* v. *Rutgers Presbyterian Church*, 194 Misc. 570, 89 N.Y.S. 2d 813) This failure to gain contractual protection meant that Crimi had no power to prevent the destruction of his mural after receiving payment for it. It is not clear, by the way, that the result of the Crimi case would be reversed if moral rights laws were in effect. In Europe, where moral rights are recognized in many countries, the courts have split over the right of the owner of publicly exhibited artwork to destroy it completely.

On receiving Crimi's letter I was curious to learn the background of this case, the human involvements that had led one artist to challenge the property concepts fundamental to American law and to seek moral rights that existed only abroad. So I arranged our interview in order to learn the story behind the court decision that is reprinted in so many collections of materials on art and law.

Alfred Crimi looked far younger than his seventy-eight years. When we met he wore a white gown for painting and was neatly dressed in a black beret, grey flannel trousers, a pin-striped shirt, a sweater and a bow tie. His manner was vigorous and, in addition to continuing to paint, he was writing his autobiography. He explained that he had achieved substantial success as a muralist, but had withdrawn from the world of galleries and dealers in 1959 so that he would not have to be a "peddler" as he pursued his own innovative "multidimensional" style (explained in his book, *The Art of Abstract Dimensional Painting,* published by Grumbacher Library). This withdrawal interested me, since it placed Crimi in the situation of many artists today, whether by choice or not, of pursuing art without connecting it to commerce. Crimi still felt the injustice of what had happened to his mural, and the interview began without my having to ask a question. Both the Crimi and Vargas interviews are edited. Deletions are indicated by ellipsis points and paraphrases by brackets.

Interview with Alfred Crimi

Crimi: . . . Most of the traditionalist architects and archeologists believe that a fresco is not good in the United States—it won't hold out in the weather, in our climatic conditions. This was the challenge for me [in doing the mural at the Rutgers Presbyterian Church], and I challenged them right from the beginning . . . So I would go every three or four months to check [the mural]. This time I was on vacation, it was right after the war and I spent a whole summer out of town in the country. I came back . . . and met a friend of mine I hadn't seen in years . . .

He said, "By the way, do you know such and such a man?"—whose name I don't remember.

"Why, what about him?" I said, "I don't know him."

"Well, he's a member of the Board of Trustees of the Rutgers Church. He wants to know from me what kind of paints you used because they tried to wash it off and it won't come out."

So that put a bug in my head . . . I went up to 72nd Street [on his way to visit his friend, the sculptor Carl Schmitz, in whose building he hoped to find a studio]. When I got there I decided to get off and I went to the Rutgers Church. For the first time they wouldn't let me in.

Crawford: Who was there?

Crimi: The sexton.

"I'm sorry, Mr. Crimi," [he said], "We've been given orders not to allow anybody in the church."

I said, "Well, can I see Dr. Russell?"—who was the minister.

He said, "Dr. Russell had retired."

I said, "Well, who is the minister now?"

He said, "Dr. Key."

I said, "Can I see Dr. Key?"

"Well, I'll go upstairs and see."

Dr. Key naturally had to be gracious and receive me. He said, "I'm very sorry, Mr. Crimi, the mural has been painted over."

"What?" I said. I couldn't believe it. "Painted over. What for?"

He said, "Well, the main objection was the nakedness of the chest of Christ."

I said, "You mean to say in the twentieth century they are so prudish? Even if he were naked, you could have called me and advised me and I could have done something about it. But instead you destroyed the mural. It's an offense to me, because you are destroying my name which is there . . . May I see the mural?"

He said, "I'm sorry, Mr. Crimi, but we cannot allow anybody there until the decorations are over."

So naturally I went over to him and said "I want to see under what shroud you buried this corpse."

[Crimi went to see Carl Schmidt. They contacted Dr. Frankfurter, the editor for *Art News,* who suggested they obtain an injunction to prevent the Church from going ahead with its destruction of the mural. Press coverage was highly favorable to Crimi throughout his struggle to save the mural. Carl Schmitz helped Crimi find a lawyer—Milton Morrison—to take the case.]

Crawford: How did he take the case?

Crimi: Without any charge. He thought the case was a rare case, an unusual case, and he took it.

Crawford: What was his background as a lawyer? What kind of cases did he usually handle?

Crimi: I have no idea. I was green myself. I was a babe in the woods, you see. I was grown up but I didn't know anything about legality. And I wasn't looking for trouble so I was unprepared for anything like that. . . . He did a lot of research. He had a young man to do all the research—European, Swiss, French cases, everything . . . Within two days we went to the Church. They wouldn't let me in, but this time they had to. And I tried to look at it. Now Dr. Russell had said that the mural is under a curtain of canvas. [Dr. Russell said this in a letter to Crimi dated September 18, 1946. Crimi's visit to the Church took place in September, soon after Crimi's return from his vacation.] . . . I examined the mural and it was painted over. I understand that they tried to wash off the paint and, since it wouldn't come off, the architect suggested giving it a coat of aluminum bronze. That neutralizes the bleeding, in case they thought the paint would bleed. [Crimi says that, in fact, the paint would never bleed because it was made from earth colors.] . . . Then they gave it two coats of buff . . . On the buff they put a design. [Crimi described the design, an insipid pattern of lattice work and, at the intersections, a motif of what Crimi recalled as cabbage leaves. Below the central rose window, a curtain of red velvet dropped to the floor. As Crimi described this, his face flushed and he said that he was "reliving the whole thing."]

Crawford: If it was painted over, why did Dr. Russell say it was intact behind the canvas covering?

Crimi: They lied to him . . .

Crawford: After what has been done to the mural, can it be restored?

Crimi: I don't know. It might be possible with an oil detergent, but it would be a very delicate operation because of the coat of aluminum bronze.

[Crimi said that the mural itself was to be a last gesture by Dr. Russell as a surprise for the parish before he retired. In discussing the history of how he was chosen to paint the mural, Crimi explained that he won an open competition sponsored by the National Society of Mural Painters in 1936 for the commission to do the mural. After he won the competition he met all 20 or 25 of the Church's Board of Trustees and the five or six members of the Decorations Committee to discuss his sketches for the mural. He pointed to the photograph of the mural as he recapitulated to me his explanation of the mural's imagery.]

. . . I have a triangle here which is the Trinity. And the all-seeing eye, an old Egyptian symbol that was taken over by the Christians. And this is the Holy Ghost, the dove.

Now there was a lady there, one of the officer's wives. And she said, "Mr. Crimi, is this a Communist symbol?" [The woman pointed to the all-seeing eye. Crimi told them to look on the Church's baptismal fountain where the same symbol appeared. This demonstration that it was not a Communist symbol cleared the way for his work to begin. But it also showed a bias against the mural that certain of the officers felt from the start of the project. Nor did the mural turn out to be a surprise by Dr. Russell, since Crimi had to work in the Church. In any case, Dr. Russell, whom Crimi admired greatly, was prevailed on to stay at the Church and didn't retire for another three years when he had reached his seventies. The following anecdote about Dr. Russell is perhaps more revealing than it appears, since Dr. Russell's tastes in art may have run counter to those of his Board of Trustees. Crimi stressed that the Congregation never voted on whether the mural should be kept, as he believed the Church's rules required.]

. . . Dr. Russell was very sympathetic. I was told this by his wife. He was in Rome one time and he got very sick and they took him to a Catholic hospital. He was taken care of by the nuns. And he was so impressed that he surrounded himself with religious pictures of the Renaissance . . . he had some beautiful Renaissance prints. He was a gentleman and we got along beautifully.

[On September 18, 1946 Dr. Russell wrote to Crimi that, "I did everything in my power to prevent what has happened, but what I could do was practically nothing as the committee took council with no one and none save the committee know even now what is to go on the wall . . . I am sorry beyond words that you have been so hurt. I've been hurt quite a lot myself. I try to remember One who said: 'Father forgive them for they know not what they do.'" Dr. Russell died of a heart attack three months after writing this letter.]

. . . When I went back to the Church with my lawyer, we had a meeting with their lawyer. Their lawyer must have been an Irish Catholic. He didn't know anything about it. He said, "Mr. Crimi, what is the problem?" And I told him that I was told that because of the nakedness of the chest of Christ, they had destroyed the mural. He said, "Oh, no, Mr. Crimi, that isn't it. If you know the background of the Presbyterians, they don't believe in murals."

"The Presbyterians wanted the mural," [I replied], "Why don't they believe it now? This is a contradiction."

Then Mr. Etherington, the culprit [the President of the Board of Trustees], came to the rescue and he said, "Mr. Crimi, that isn't it. To be honest, Dr. Key said that the mural interfered with his work during services."

Crawford: How could it have done that?

Crimi: He was a poor speaker to begin with and the acoustics were not so very good . . . So that the people were looking at the mural instead of listening to his sermons.

. . . Now, when we sued, we didn't sue for money. We sued for moral rights . . . Eventually we also had to sue for money. That's as far as the Church controversy got until we went to court.

Crawford: There were no more negotiations? In other words, it has been painted over and after your meeting with the Church's lawyer you had to sue?

Crimi: That's right . . .

Crawford: Were you represented by a lawyer when you signed the contract to do the mural in 1936?

Crimi: I had no lawyer, the Church had a lawyer when the contract was signed. And he really manifested the prejudice that had already been created. [Crimi's statement contradicts the court's decision referring to Crimi "and his attorney." I checked this important point again with Crimi

who assured me that he did not have a lawyer represent him when he signed the contract.]

Crawford: What kind of prejudice?

Crimi: I don't know. Because I was young . . . thirty-five . . . [Crimi explains that the lawyer wanted him to paint the 23 heads of the figures separately before painting them again on the wall. Crimi felt this completely unreasonable for his fee of $5,500. The total area to be covered was 800 square feet and he couldn't be burdened by obtaining approval in this way. The lawyer questioned how the quality of Crimi's work could be judged and Crimi answered that he had been chosen from among 32 competing members of the National Society of Mural Painters in the open competition.]

Crawford: They were paying you $5,500. How long did you have to do the mural?

Crimi: There was no deadline really, except that I notified them when the time had come and the job in the Church would be three to four months.

Crawford: How did they pay you? Did they give you a third to start?

Crimi: They gave me a third to start. When I had the cartoons finished I got the second payment. And when I finished the mural I got the third payment. [The Decorations Committee initialed each cartoon or paper study before Crimi would paint it on the mural.] . . . This was during the Depression and I was lucky to get it. I worked as long as 21 hours.

Crawford: And the only expenses they paid were the scaffolding, not the paint or anything else?

Crimi: That's right. I paid for everything . . .

Crawford: How would you describe the nature of the congregation in 1936?

Crimi: Hypocritical . . .

Crawford: These were well-to-do people?

Crimi: Yes . . .

Crawford: Can you describe the trial?

Crimi: The judge was retired and they called him in for this case. The judge was very much interested in this case. And he was like a young boy. He got up from the bench and he came down and he fed the slides into the projector himself. I could see that his attitude was all for the artist. At the end . . . he asked the two lawyers to come into his chambers. In the chambers he told the lawyers to come to some settlement. If the judge said, "Come to some settlement," he must have seen that I had some rights to be settled, otherwise he wouldn't have said it. But the other lawyer stuck to the letter of the law. He didn't have any compassion for the artist at all. And I think this is a damnation throughout the history of art in America and will continue to be.

Crawford: So there were no settlement offers made at any time?

Crimi: None. Then I got disgusted. You see, we didn't believe it would ever go on the calendar at all, because my lawyer knew the law . . . Our intention was to create enough publicity that . . . it would get support . . . [After losing the case, Crimi said that he couldn't appeal because he had no money and didn't feel he could ask the lawyer to continue working for free.]

Crawford: But you wanted to present a bill in Washington?

Crimi: Yes, we wanted to do that . . . It was my own experience. I thought there should be a bill for the profession . . . And I believe there should be a bill for the profession on the inheritance tax . . . But I'm sort of a loner. I don't participate anymore. Since the 1950's. In 1959 I withdrew from the rat race on Madison Avenue. I haven't given a one-man show on Madison Avenue since 1959.

Crawford: What prompted you to make that decision?

Crimi: Because I know that they're a bunch of crooks. They are opportunists. They treat an artist like a peddler. An artist is not a peddler, he's someone who anticipates the future . . .

Crawford: When you withdrew from the art world, did you feel a kind of freedom?

Crimi: Yes, because I've been painting to please myself. I never paint a picture on commission, unless it's a mural. I never paint to sell. My paintings are good or bad or indifferent. They are an expression of myself. I believe it's a sincere expression. It's not for the public to judge . . .

Crawford: In 1946, when you found out what was going on, did other artists rally to support you?

Crimi: In the beginning, some of them did.

[Crimi relates that the Salmagundi Club membership wanted to support him, but were dissuaded by a lawyer member. Instead of taking a moral position, they followed the lawyer's strictly legalistic conclusion that Crimi had no chance to win in court. At the beginning, he received support from the National Society of Mural Painters, but they withdrew their backing from fear of preventing other churches from having murals painted. After this support ended, the National Sculptors Society and other artists' groups also fell silent. Only the editors of the arts magazines gave unstinting support to Crimi throughout his struggle.]

Crawford: What happened after the lawsuit was over and the publicity had quieted down?

Crimi: Every now and then there was an article . . . on artist's rights . . . But I was glad that I did sue them, because if I hadn't I would never touch a brush again. I was so frustrated . . .

Crawford: What do you feel is the lesson for people, artists today, who are thinking about moral rights and these kinds of issues to draw from your own experience?

Crimi: I blame the artists because they're not willing to fight for their rights.

Vargas v. Esquire

Alberto Vargas, well known for his portraits of women, became a pioneer in the field of creator's rights in a famous legal battle, *Vargas* v. *Esquire*, in which the federal courts decided that *Esquire Magazine* could publish Vargas's illustrations without giving him credit as the artist who created them. This shocking decision, rendered in 1946, is one of special interest today because of the proposed federal legislation to create moral rights for artists, including the right to receive such credit regardless of a contractual provision to the contrary. While the *Vargas* decision is known to many artists and lawyers with an interest in the field of creator's rights, the struggle between Vargas and *Esquire* is not known. It is a struggle that is repeated many times over as artists, without the benefit of legal counsel or the backing of a professional organization, deal with efficient businesses possessing extensive legal and financial resources.

No problems developed between Vargas and *Esquire* under his first contract with *Esquire* which lasted from June, 1940 through May, 1944. On May 23, 1944, however, Vargas entered into a new contract with *Esquire* that required fifty-two drawings each year for a period of ten and a half years. The contract provided, "The drawings also furnished, and also the name 'Varga', 'Varga Girl', 'Varga Esq.,' and any and all names, designs or materials used in connection therewith, shall forever belong exclusively to *Esquire,* and *Esquire* shall have all rights with respect thereto . . ."

In February, 1946, Vargas sued in federal court to have the contract cancelled. The court decided the contract had been fraudulently obtained and granted Vargas the cancellation, but *Esquire* later obtained a reversal in the appellate court. In March, 1946, after cancellation of the contract, *Esquire* began calling the *Varga Girl* drawings by the title of the *Esquire Girls*. Vargas's name did not appear with his drawings at all. Vargas then sued to prevent the reproduction of any more of his work by *Esquire* because *Esquire* was not giving him credit as the artist for the drawings. But the court refused to grant Vargas his right to receive credit for his work, stating instead, "What plaintiff in reality seeks is a change in the law in this country to conform to that of certain other countries . . . [W]e are not disposed to make any new law in this respect." (*Vargas* v. *Esquire,* 164 F.2d 522)

Behind the story of the litigation against *Esquire,* however, is Vargas himself, a man with the courage and integrity to fight for his rights. My interview with Vargas focused on the personal aspects of this struggle with *Esquire.* What did Vargas feel? What prompted him to sue? How did it affect his career and his life? These questions, left unanswered by the narrow decision of the court, fascinated me and prompted my desire to learn more from Vargas. In a way, Vargas's struggle symbolized the struggles of many other creators who, even today, must decide whether to stand up or cave in when challenged.

Vargas briefly related his background, speaking with a slight accent, in a conversation frequently punctuated by laughter. Born in Peru's second largest city, Arequipa, in 1896, Vargas's father was well known for his photographs of the Inca ruins. Vargas's mother wanted Vargas and his older brother to study in Europe, so they accompanied their father when he travelled to Europe in 1911 to receive a gold medal for his photography. Vargas was to study languages and photography and his brother was to become a banker because, "he loved those girls in the banks." On his way to Switzerland, Vargas stopped in the Louvre where he was transfixed for hours by the French portraitists such as Ingres. He decided then that he wanted to be a painter rather than a photographer. However, he didn't study art, but constantly practiced drawing the parts of the human body as a diversion while he studied languages. One reason for his lack of interest in taking art classes was the ease with which he found himself able to draw these exercises.

In 1916 he left Europe with the outbreak of the World War. Planning to return to Peru, he was held over in New York City waiting for an American ship on a route through the Panama Canal. He recalled walking through the City on a summer day with the bells tolling for noon and, "all of a sudden the doors opened and out poured these girls. Oh, my! I dropped my bags and dropped everything and said, 'This is unbelievable. My gosh, so many beautiful girls.' So right then and there I had to stay here."

Vargas stayed in New York and his brother returned to Peru in his place. He had no money from home, but obtained a position retouching negatives for a photographer. Next he drew hats and heads for Butterick Patterns, but quit when he started freelance artwork. This led to a position painting women as part of window-display promotion in the Corona Typewriter Building. This embarrassed Vargas, but also immediately brought him a commission of $50 for a portrait of one of the Ziegfield girls. After successfully completing the portrait for Ziegfield's manager, Vargas was sent to meet Florenz Ziegfield, creator of the fabulous Follies. Ziegfield offered him a commission to paint nearly twenty portraits for an exhibition at the Ziegfield opening in June, 1916. The fee would be $200 for each portrait; they sealed this agreement by shaking hands. Vargas remained with Ziegfield until the Follies closed in 1931. He called the experience, "the most fantastic thing in my life. From then I was on my way." In 1919, Vargas also met his future wife, Anna Mae Clift. She modeled for him, but because of his struggles to gain financial security he didn't propose to her for 10 years.

After the closing of the Follies, Vargas continued the editorial and advertising illustration that had supplemented his work for Ziegfield throughout the 1920s. It was a difficult time. In 1934, Vargas moved to Hollywood and worked for Fox, Warner Brothers and the other major studios. In 1939 he was black balled by all the studios for joining in a union walkout. In 1940, Vargas returned to New York City and began working for *Esquire Magazine*. After leaving *Esquire*, of course, he was to meet Hugh Hefner and go on to great success in the pages of *Playboy Magazine*.

An excellent recounting of Vargas's life and work is *Vargas* by Alberto Vargas and Reid Austin (published by Harmony House).

The following interview with Alberto Vargas took place by telephone on April 9, 1979. Mr. Vargas was at his home in West Los Angeles, California, and I was in New York City.

Interview with Alberto Vargas

Crawford: I would really like to tell the full story of what was behind the lawsuit and the role that you played in it, because that was a time when people were not so aware of the idea of moral rights. I know that you had a contract with *Esquire* when you first started working for them. Everything went smoothly under that contract, but why was the second contract so unfavorable to you?

Vargas: Then came the war . . . *Esquire* used that as an excuse because I was going to get double for renewing the contract. He didn't want me to get it. [Vargas is referring to the executive at *Esquire*, whose name he refused to give. This man was David Smart, *Esquire's* owner and publisher. Vargas laughingly characterized this opponent as "a peculiar one" who is now "playing golf with Beelzebub".]

So he kept me busy every day. I was making a picture a day almost.

And my wife said, "Why are you working so hard? We have no time to go anywhere."

I said, "Honey, this is my opportunity. I don't care what happens. When I am finished with him, I am made."

That's exactly what happened. So the second contract was made by him exactly the way he wanted it.

Crawford: He was concerned that you might be getting too much?

Vargas: Yes. Not only that, he was concerned that somebody was advising me, which wasn't the case.

Crawford: You didn't have a lawyer for the first or second contract?

Vargas: No, I never had a lawyer. Do you know who my lawyer was? My right hand . . .

Crawford: How did you come to work for *Esquire?*

Vargas: . . . It was in 1939. A friend told me to go over to *Esquire*, because *Esquire* was having a falling out with Petty [George Petty the illustrator]. "They're trying to find someone to follow him and then throw Petty out."

Petty was armed with three lawyers and he had *Esquire* by the neck.

"Oh no," I said, "I don't want to go over there at all. I don't have anything that would interest *Esquire*".

[When he had worked for Warner Brothers, the other artists kidded him about Petty's women in *Esquire*. Vargas had criticized Petty's portrayals of women and now felt reluctant to follow him at *Esquire*. Vargas's friend then told him of another possible job and wrote out a Madison Avenue address on a slip of paper.]

So I went over, pressed the button for the sixth floor, and when I came out I was in the entrance for *Esquire*. So I said, "My God, he tricked me."

I rushed back to press the button to go down when a girl comes and says, "Can I help you, Sir?"

I said, "I'm looking for Mr. So and So."

And she answered, "Yes, you are right at his office . . ."

So I waited and when they [Mr. Smart and his assistants] came out, I had my 12 drawings which I showed them. Boy, when they looked at those drawings, immediately they said, "Will you please wait for us?" So they both

49

left and when they came back they said, "We just talked to the chief in Chicago and he's so glad that you came that he's going to come over tomorrow to interview you . . ."

Well, when he saw the drawings the next day when he arrived, he asked me a million questions—"Why did you make this for? And what was your idea?" Just to size me up from the answers.

I said, "I do it because I love it. I like to do it." So he says, "Well, I cannot talk business here, so I will hire you now. After I get back to Chicago, in a couple of days, you come over and bring your drawings,"—I had a big box full of them—"bring them all and we'll sit down and cook up something. And that's how I got in."

Crawford: That's an incredible story.

Vargas: It's so incredible I didn't dare tell my Anna, because she would have beaten me over the head or thought, "Perhaps he's so hungry he's gone nuts."

Crawford: Tell me a little bit more about the lawsuit itself. You began to have some troubles with *Esquire* about the credit for the pictures?

Vargas: Yes, first of all, he [the *Esquire* executive] said, "You know, Alberto, I like the work you're doing, but we must do something about your name."

I said, "What's wrong with my name?"

He said, "It's not phonetic. The Vargas Girl is no good, you have to drop the s."

I didn't know why he was doing this. I learned it later to my discomfort. I did the worse thing in the world to let him change my name.

Crawford: But you were being agreeable and he kept pushing you?

Vargas: Oh my, yes. That was the beginning.

Crawford: What was his reason for asking you to change your name?

Vargas: I don't know what he had in mind. He had in mind to destroy Petty and to destroy me.

Crawford: Did he think you were getting too much money?

Vargas: Yes. He thought that he was spending too much and I was getting seventy-five dollars a picture.

Crawford: How often was that?

Vargas: It was not often.

Crawford: That was once every week? You did one picture a week?

Vargas: Yes.

Crawford: How long did this disagreement go on where he wanted you to change your name and then he wanted to take your name completely off the pictures?

Vargas: Yes, he was following a pattern to destroy me, because he said, "I learned my lesson from Petty. He is very arrogant, this Vargas, he may even become worse than Petty and more famous than Petty and then I'll have him on my back. So the first thing I'm going to do is destroy him now."

That was when he began to ask for nearly a picture a day. I said, "My God, not even a machine can do that." But anyway, he insisted, because he made me sign that second contract which was entirely different. Even the lawyers in the court, the judges, when they read that contract said, "What in the name of anything is this?"

Crawford: After you signed this second contract without being represented by a lawyer, you were doing a picture a day. How much did he pay you? He didn't pay you for every picture?

Vargas: No, he was paying me only seventy-five dollars.

Crawford: How long did you go along doing this?

Vargas: In 1946 he couldn't stand it anymore. He had a backlog of about 200 pictures, so he could go on for three or four years without me.

Crawford: So he fired you at that point?

Vargas: Yes.

Crawford: Was it then that they started changing the name from *Varga Girls* to *Esquire Girls*?

Vargas: Not only that. He began to cut the name in pieces. I couldn't sign this, I couldn't put the name *Esquire* in the circle of my name, the signature of my drawing. My wife and I were bewildered. We didn't know what he was up to . . .

Crawford: Then he took your name completely off the pictures?

Vargas: Yes. He took it off entirely and called it the *Esquire Girls*.

Crawford: At that point, did you go to a lawyer?

Vargas: Oh yes. Even when my wife and I stopped to pick up a check, a little clerk [at *Esquire*] said, "May I talk to you please?" So she sat down and I said, "Yes, what is it?" She said, "I advise you to go see a lawyer . . .

Just please do and don't tell that I told you because he'll kill me . . ."

[When my lawyer read the second contract] he said, "My God, you signed your death warrant."

I said, "What do we do now?"

"Well, you have to fight now," he answered, "You haven't any money, but I'll take it on the provision that if you get some, I get some. Otherwise I don't see how to rescue you."

Crawford: Did you think that generous on the lawyer's part?

Vargas: Yes, he was honest, this lawyer, because he said, "He has put something on you that no man on earth can ever comply with. It said you are going to give him fifty pictures and he only had five. So you broke the contract," that's what he said. That I broke the contract for not producing fifty, only five. That was the whole thing . . . He thought he had destroyed me then. But it wasn't so, because we went and fought him. The lawyer went to work and he said, "There's no way that I can do it, but I have to try at least." But he [*Esquire*] had a slew of lawyers defending himself . . .

Crawford: Did you actually testify in court?

Vargas: Sure, I had to go. I took all my drawings. Everything that had to do with *Vargas Girls* I took with me. When the judge asked me, "Mr. Vargas, will you tell us now why did it take so long and what you were doing for the money he paid you—seventy-five dollars apiece?"

I said, "My honor, if you allow me, I would like to show you the process for one drawing."

He was sitting on a dias looking down at me. He ordered, "Clerk, bring a long table."

And this man's lawyer says, "Your honor, I protest."

The judge said, "Sit down, Mr. So and So, I am the judge here."

Then I showed them. First, I make a little sketch which I can do fast and put in a little color and see if I am pleased with the effect. Then I make a tissue drawing of the whole thing, that takes time.

"How long will it take you?" [the judge asked]. "Oh, it takes me four or five days to actually have the drawing laid out in the tissue paper and ink. I have to transfer it to the board. Then I have to start just working on it. It's long, but [*Esquire*] thinks that I do it like a printing press. I put a piece of cardboard down and press a button and—bang, it comes out all done. It isn't so."

[The judge said,] "Oh, yes, I can see that process." So we won.

Crawford: In what way did you win? What did the judge decide?

Vargas: He decided that he [*Esquire*] had cheated me, that he had changed my name, that he had made up his mind to destroy me because no man on earth can have that—I don't care what artist he had work at top speed. And he had three lawyers. I had none. [This refers to the suit for cancellation of the contract.]

Crawford: But the decision that was finally published said that *Esquire* had won, because it said that in the United States there are no moral rights the way there are in Europe. Even though *Esquire* had taken your name off the work, they were not going to punish *Esquire* in any way . . .

Vargas: The judge said, "This is a contractual matter. This has nothing to do with law. Nothing unlawful has been done to him. It is a contract that he has to live up to . . ." He [*Esquire*] saw the interest the other magazines had in me and he said, "My God, they are going to have what I just threw away." Then he appealed . . . He licked me also in the second court.

So I asked my attorney, "What can I do now? I cannot use my name. I have no money . . ."

"Oh, well, I tell you, Alberto," [the lawyer answered], "you can go and dig ditches. That you can do without any name."

Crawford: He was being ironic?

Vargas: Yes, purely. Then [the lawyer] was driving me to his home because his wife and my wife were waiting there for lunch when the decision came. And he was driving me and in the big yellow envelope was the decision. When we were six or seven blocks from the house, I said, "Do me a favor please. You go and give the bad news to Anna and tell her that I'm coming later. I don't want to face her. I don't want to go and have to tell her, because this is awful."

"And what are you going to do?" [the lawyer asked.]

"I'm going to kill that s.o.b."

He said, "Are you kidding?"

I said, "Look in my eyes. Do you think I'm kidding?"

He said, "Don't do anything foolish."

I said, "That's not foolish, that's a pleasure. I got the idea just how to do it too . . ."

Crawford: After leaving *Esquire* and losing the lawsuit, did you go to *Playboy*?

Vargas: Yes, when *Playboy* was in Chicago . . . We heard that Mr. Hugh Hefner was going to publish a magazine. Now three other magazines had gone down in that same month. Hef had the idea to put the bunny in and all was going fine so I told my wife, "You know, how would you like to go to Chicago and see if I can get in touch with Mr. Hefner?"

"Oh, you're going to get into one of those again?" [she asked].

"No, Mr. Hefner, I don't know him, but certainly there isn't anyone in the world that can be that smart. That's why he is who he is."

So we went and I had twelve drawings in pencil and I showed him and he said, "Oh, very well, Alberto, this is really beautiful, fantastic. But your trouble is that I am just beginning myself, I am feeling the way. But I will keep you in mind and if I can find a place for you, that you can help me and I can help you, then we'll get together. It won't be long." So we waited a year. We came back here [to West Los Angeles] and waited a year and all of a sudden he said, "Come on down." He had a place open.

Crawford: The rest is history.

Vargas: Yes, boy, what a difference. From a cad to a gentleman is quite a jump . . .

Crawford: I'd like to thank you for this interview.

Vargas: Will you send me your article on "Moral Rights and the Artist"? That is wonderful. Anytime that you need me, I would walk to Chicago or New York to help the cause because it's my own . . . I want to help all the other artists. My time is passed already, but the newcomers are the ones that need a lot of help, believe me.

Crawford: Thank you again.

Vargas: The pleasure has been mine.

Chapter 8

Risks in the content and creation of art

The First Amendment of the United States Constitution provides guarantees of freedom of expression which apply to artists and their works, but such guarantees are not unlimited. Copyright, patent, trademark, the doctrine of unfair competition, the rights of privacy and publicity and protection from defamation safeguard not only the artist but the artist's competitors as well. Significantly, other private citizens also have rights protecting them from invasion of privacy or defamation, which the artist will have to consider when creating work. Additionally, the public at large, through law enforcement agencies, may seek to suppress works which are considered either obscene or a desecration of a governmental symbol.

Defamation

Defamation, as discussed on page 41, is an attack on a person's reputation by print, writing, pictures or signs, or spoken words. The defamatory material must reach the public, since damage to reputation is a requirement for an action for defamation. While the truth of an alleged defamation would be a defense to such an action, the burden of proving truthfulness is on the person who asserts truth as a defense. Generally, everyone who participates in publishing or exhibiting defamatory material will be liable to the defamed person.

The artist who attacks a person's reputation, for example, by representing a person as involved in unethical or criminal conduct, as physically deformed in an unnatural or obscene way, or as lacking manners or intelligence may face a libel suit. The person defamed need not be mentioned by name, as long as the depiction will be recognizable to those acquainted with the person's reputation.

In a recent case, a painting titled *The Mugging of the Muse* showed three knife-wielding men about to attack a woman scantily covered by a red garment. Two artists sued, stating they had been depicted as the assassins of the Muse. The court agreed that these two artists were indeed so depicted. However, it concluded that this was not the statement of a false fact, but rather the expression of an opinion protected by the First Amendment. The court's opinion stated:

> The picture could not be intended, viewed by any reasonable person, as an accusation by defendant that either plaintiff had actually participated in an assault or related crime such as attempted homicide, or had any intention of so doing. . . . In the context provided by the factual background and the use of the word "Muse", that figure could be representative only of the arts; therefore, the painting states that plaintiffs' artistic beliefs and activities are destructive of the arts. It says nothing more. Far worse commentary is written almost daily by newspaper and magazine critics of every aspect of the arts and is deemed to be no more than an expression of opinion. (*Silberman* v. *Georges,* 91 A.D.2d 520)

The artist must be aware of this important distinction made between defamation and criticism. An artist who places work before the public invites criticism of the work. That criticism, no matter how hostile or fantastic or extravagant, is not by itself defamatory. However, if untrue statements are made disparaging the work, or if the artist is attacked personally in some way unconnected with the work, the critic may well have crossed the border into the area of defamation.

Another case involving a dispute between two artists illustrates a personal attack which was defamatory. One of the leading sculptors of the Pacific Northwest had created a 13-foot work of art titled *Rock Totem* which was displayed at the Seattle World's Fair in 1962. A younger sculptor, who was studying for his master's degree in sculpturing and had seen *Rock Totem*, was commissioned to do a piece for a bank. His piece stood 8-feet high and was titled *Transcending*.

The older sculptor went to the architects who commissioned the work and called *Transcending* a copy of *Rock Totem*. At the bank he called the younger artist a thief. Prior to suing the younger artist for this alleged copying, the older artist wrote a letter in which he said, "When a thief robs openly from a creative spirit no bit of talk around a legal table can quietly settle the issue. Is it not more important that the art student recognize his desire for money has guided his hand in his path of plagiarism." (*Fitzgerald v. Hopkins*, 70 Wash.2d 924, 425 P.2d 920)

The court concluded no copying had taken place and dismissed the older artist's infringement claim. In defending the lawsuit, the younger artist counterclaimed for damages for defamation. The court determined that calling someone a thief and a plagiarist is neither criticism nor a protected form of opinion. They are personal attacks beyond the scope of fair comment and entitled the younger artist to collect damages.

Of course, a depiction may not in itself be defamatory, but may become so because of accompanying written material. For example, an unobjectionable picture of a man might be accompanied by a caption calling him a thief, which is actionable if not true. In such a case, the creator of the original picture should not be liable for defamation if he or she had nothing to do with adding the words which, in combination with the picture, became actionable.

The First Amendment does limit the extent to which actions for defamation can successfully be pursued. The right of a public figure, in particular, to sue for libel is limited to false statments made with actual malice or reckless disregard of the truth. The term public figure is itself subject to definition. For example, a woman successfully sued a magazine for unfavorably misreporting the grounds of her divorce decree. Although the woman was often mentioned in society columns and actually gave news conferences because of the widespread reporting of her divorce proceedings, the Supreme Court reasoned she was not a public figure because she had no major role in society's affairs and had not voluntarily joined in a public controversy with an intention to influence the outcome. Similarly, when a magazine accused a prominent lawyer of having framed a policeman as part of a Communist conspiracy to discredit the police, the attorney was determined not to be a public figure. The United States Supreme Court stated, "The communications media are entitled to act on the assumption that public officals and public figures have voluntarily exposed themselves to increased risk of injury from defamatory falsehoods concerning them. No such assumption is justified with respect to a private individual." (*Gertz v. Robert Welch*, 418 U.S. 323)

The Supreme Court determined that the states should have discretion to determine the standard of liability for defamation when a private individual is involved in a matter of public interest, as long as the states require some negligence or fault on the part of the person accused of the defamation. Thus, when a matter of public interest is involved, a public figure will have to show actual malice or reckless disregard for the truth to recover for defamation while a private individual will only have to show negligence. When a private person is defamed on a matter not of public interest, there is no requirement even to show an intent to defame. Recovery in such a case is allowed on the basis of the defamation alone and malice or reckless disregard for the truth are only relevant in fixing the extra damages known as punitive damages. Retraction or correction of a libel will often be a factor in reducing damages.

Privacy

The right to privacy, as discussed in relation to the artists, is the right to live free from unwanted or unnecessary publicity or interference which would injure a person's feelings or present the person in a false light before the public.

Onassis v. Galella

The First Amendment again operates to reduce the right of privacy protecting public figures. A dramatic example is the litigation involving Ronald Galella, a photographer, and Jacqueline Onassis. Galella's role as a *paparazzo* pursuing Jacqueline Onassis for photographs created a substantial and unwanted interference in her life. The Federal Court of Appeals described Galella jumping into the path of John Kennedy's bicycle to take a picture, and also stated:

> Galella on other occassions interrupted Caroline at tennis, and invaded the children's private schools. At one time he came uncomfortably close in a power boat to Mrs. Onassis swimming. He often jumped and postured around while taking pictures of her party. . . . He followed a practice of bribing apartment house, restaurant and nightclub doormen as well as romancing a family servant to keep him advised of the movements of the family. (*Galella* v. *Onassis,* 487 F.2d 986)

The court indicated that such activities could not be tolerated, whether as an invasion of privacy or as harrassment. But the final order of the court, mindful of Galella's First Amendment rights, merely restricted the photographer from approaching within twenty-five feet of Jacqueline Onassis, blocking her movement in public places, or harassing or endangering her.

However, in 1982, a new action was brought by Onassis against Galella on the grounds that he had violated the 1975 court order on at least twelve occasions. Although the First Amendment protected the photographer's right to take photographs of a public figure, the contempt citations might still have resulted in Galella being imprisoned and paying heavy fines. To avoid this, Galella agreed never to photograph Mrs. Onassis or her children again.

The Arrington case

The artist will often, however, deal with a person who is not a public figure. The right of privacy—such as that granted under the New York Civil Rights Law Sections 50 and 51, prohibiting the advertising or trade use of an individual's name, portrait or picture without consent—would apply in full force. One exception is that Section 51 specifically permits a photographer to display portraits at the photographer's place of business unless the person portrayed objects in writing. Also, a factual account or portrayal of a matter of current newsworthy or legitimate public interest will not be an invasion of privacy. For example, a professional musician who spontaneously performed before 400,000 people at the Woodstock Festival in 1969 could not object to the distribution without his consent of a film of his performance. This was because the Woodstock festival was an occurrence of great public interest and remained newsworthy long after the end of the festival.

Arrington v. *The New York Times* arose from more troubling facts. Clarence Arrington, a black, was photographed without his knowledge while walking along a street in New York City. This photograph was then used on the cover of *The New York Times Magazine* in connection with an article titled "The Black Middle Class: Making It". This widely circulated article probed the issue of whether middle-class blacks felt divorced from the problems affecting less fortunate blacks. Arrington, a financial analyst at the time the photograph was taken, was indeed a member of the middle class. However, he had never consented to the use of his image; indeed, he was never asked by *The New York Times* for his consent. Although he was not mentioned by name in the article, he felt the article degraded not only the black middle class but himself as its apparent exemplar. He did not share the views of the article and also said that his acquaintances assumed that he had a least partly changed his vocation to that of a professional model.

New York's highest court, the Court of Appeals, reiterated its other decisions that a picture illustrating an article on a matter of public interest is not considered used for the purposes of trade or advertising unless it has no real relationship to the article. If the picture had no real relationship to the article, it would not serve the public interest and is simply a disguised advertisement.

The Court of Appeals concluded that the photograph of Arrington was related to the article about the black middle class. In the struggle between freedom of the press and the individual's right to privacy, the press emerged victorious. However, *The New York Times* had not been the only defendant in the suit. Other defendants included Gianfranco Gorgoni, the free-lance photographer who took the photograph on assignment for *The New York Times;* Contact Press Images, Inc., the photographic agency which handled the sale from Gorgoni to *The New York Times* and Robert Pledge, the president of Contact. If liability were found, the corporate shield would not protect an officer from being personally at risk.

In a decision that caused great concern among visual communicators, the Court of Appeals stated that the case against *The New York Times* was properly dismissed but reasoned that the defendants might be found to have made a sale of the photograph without Arrington's consent. Not being publishers, the photographer and his agency might be liable despite the fact that *The New York Times* was protected by the First Amendment. When the case would be sent back to a lower court to determine the facts, that lower court might well find that the defendants, operating independently from the publisher, had commercialized the photograph by the transfers leading to the publication by *The New York Times.*

This ill-reasoned decision could have led to an absurd result. A free-lance photographer working for a publisher would be liable for an invasion of privacy in this situation when the publisher would not be. Likewise, a free-lance photographer might be liable for an invasion when an employee of a publisher taking the same photograph would have no liability. The employee-photographer would be protected by his or her employer's First Amendment freedom of the press. Not only would this decision place

free-lancers in a precarious position, it would constrict the flow of imagery to the media. Indirectly, it would inhibit freedom of the press.

Publishers and visual communicators joined forces to lobby for a bill to overturn this aspect of the *Arrington* decision. The American Society of Magazine Photographers and the Graphic Artists Guild played important roles as this coalition formulated draft legislation and a strategy for guiding the legislation through both houses of the New York legislature.

The Arrington bill

The bill took the form of an amendment to the privacy statute in New York State. The amendment provided that if a use protected by the First Amendment is the purpose of the sale or transfer of an image from a photographer to an agent or an agent to a publisher, all the parties in the chain of transfers will be protected by the First Amendment.

No opposition formed against the bill. In one year it passed both the Assembly and Senate and was signed into law by Governor Cuomo. So free-lance photographers and their agents now enjoy the same protection that publishers and employee-photographers enjoy with respect to the *Arrington* factual pattern.

Releases

The user of images must always keep in mind the individual's right to privacy. Publisher, advertising agency, corporation, graphic designer, illustrator, art director, photographer and agent all risk liability in a suit brought for an invasion of privacy. In common commercial situations, releases are used as a matter of course. However, the *Arrington* case points to the borderline area where distinctions blur between what is a use for private gain and what is a use for the public interest. In such situations, the only safe course to adopt is the securing of a release.

An appropriate form of personal release is set forth at page 57. A release should provide for the date, the consideration (usually some payment of money—even $1—to the model), the subject matter, the extent of the release, the persons other than the artist who may benefit from the release, the signature of the individual giving the release and the guardian's consent if the person giving the release is a minor. The artist who is provided with a release, perhaps by an agency, should request indemnification against lawsuits based on invasion of privacy if the release appears inadequate to protect the artist. Although some states allow oral releases, New York requires that a release be written. In any case, it's always best to have a written release. The release should also specify what use of the art is permitted. Actual usage should not exceed this. Retouching or distortions in using art may open the risk of an invasion of privacy lawsuit even if a release has been obtained.

The artist may wonder whether a release might be necessary to portray a building, an animal or some other type of property. This is not a privacy issue, since the right of privacy basically only protects living people. Normally no release would be necessary to use the image of a public building. Of course, the artist should not tres-

pass and should obtain any permits which are necessary from local authorities. Similarly, a private building used as a background in a public place or thoroughfare would not require a release. But a private building or a public building where admission is charged might require a release, particularly since a subsequent advertising use might create a question regarding unfair competition. In addition, many states have laws forbidding the photographing of performances without the permission of the management of the theatre.

In general, the reason to obtain a release when using images of someone's private property is to have the release act as a contract. No questions can then arise as to whether the artist offered to pay, what the amount of payment might be or what the intended usage is. For example, an image of a model's hands does not require a release unless the model is identifiable. However, a release would probably be obtained simply to clarify the contractual arrangement with the model. It is not, however, necessary from the standpoint of a right to privacy.

Model release form

In consideration of $ _____, receipt of which is acknowledged, I, _____ _____ , do hereby give _____, his (her) assigns, licensees and legal representatives the irrevocable right to use my name (or any fictional name), picture, portrait, or photograph in all forms and media and in all manners, including composite or distorted representations, for advertising, trade or any other lawful purposes, and I waive any right to inspect or approve the finished product, including written copy, that may be created in connection therewith. I am of full age.* I have read this release and am fully familiar with its contents.

Witness: _____   Signed: _____

Address: _____   Address: _____

                                      Date: _____ , 19 _____

Consent (if applicable)
I am the parent and guardian of the minor named above and have the legal authority to execute the above release. I approve the foregoing and waive any rights in the premises.

Witness: _____   Signed: _____

Address: _____   Address: _____

                                      Date: _____ , 19_____

*Delete this sentence if the subject is a minor. The parent or guardian must then sign the consent.

Child models

Laws regarding the employment of minors vary from state to state. Parental consent and work permits are often required. Depending on the age of the model, supervision of the modeling session may also be necessary. The quickest way to find out the relevant state law is to check with the state departments of labor, employment or education.

For example, the New York statute provides:

> 1. It shall be unlawful to employ, use, exhibit or cause to be exhibited a minor as a model unless: (a) A child model permit has been issued as hereinafter provided; and (b) Such employment, use or exhibition is in accordance with the rules and regulations promulgated by the commissioner of education as hereinafter provided. Violation of this provision is a misdemeanor.

Obscenity

The laws regulating obscenity have been the focus of much controversy and concern. What the artist creates for aesthetic reasons may not be perceived in the same way by viewers in the general public. Yet the United States Supreme Court states that the guidelines to determine what is obscene are:

> (a) whether 'the average person, applying contemporary community standards' would find that work, taken as a whole, appeals to the prurient interest . . . (b) whether the work depicts or describes, in a patently offensive way, sexual conduct specifically defined by applicable state law; and (c) whether the work, taken as a whole, lacks serious literary, artistic, political, or scientific value. (*Miller* v. *California*, 413 U.S. 15)

These guidelines hardly seem to offer more guidance than the subjective reaction of the ordinary citizen as to what may be obscene. Also, the guidelines specifically refer to community standards and state laws. This means that standards for judging what is obscene will vary not only from state to state depending on the state laws, but also from community to community depending on the local standards.

The artist can hardly be certain, therefore, when and where a work, upon exhibition or publication, may be found to be obscene. At the least, if the artist keeps the work in the privacy of the studio, no violation of the obscenity laws will occur. But the obscenity laws, if applicable, can cover such uses of the work as possession for sale or exhibition, sale, distribution, mailing and importation through customs. The manner in which the material is offered to the public may be important in a determination of obscenity. If there is an emphasis solely on the sexual aspects of the works, this factor will make more likely a determination that the work is obscene. If minors have access to the material, an even higher standard than that applicable to pornography may be applied by the states without violating the First Amendment.

The First Amendment, however, offers important procedural safeguards to the artist whose work risks being challenged as obscene. Law enforcement agencies cannot simply seize such materials upon their belief the materials are obscene. The exhibitor of work must be given notice of a hearing to determine whether the work may be seized as obscene. At the hearing the exhibitor can be represented by a lawyer to argue that the works are not obscene. The judge must consider all relevant evidence, such as the works, the manner of publicizing the exhibit and the degree to which the general public may view the works. Law enforcement officers who testify the works are obscene must actually have attended the exhibition. Only after such a hearing can the works be seized or the exhibition prohibited.

The artist or exhibitor may find that law enforcement agents have chosen to seize work without a prior adversary hearing. In such a case the law enforcement officials should not be resisted in any way, but merely advised that they are acting in violation of the First Amendment procedural safeguards and may be liable for damages for their actions. In no event should consent be given to the conduct of the law enforcement officials, since consent might be a waiver of the procedural safeguards necessitated by the First Amendment.

Obscenity is a complex legal area. The artist who either fears an obscenity issue may arise or faces such an issue must consult a lawyer for assistance in proving the work is not obscene and should not be suppressed.

Flag desecration

The United States Code provides: "Whoever knowingly casts contempt upon any flag of the United States by publicly mutilating, defacing, defiling, burning, or trampling upon it shall be fined not more than $1,000 or imprisoned for not more than one year, or both." The definition of United States flag includes "any picture or representation . . . made of any substance or represented on any substance . . . by which the average person seeing same without deliberation may believe the same to represent the flag . . . of the United States of America." The states have enacted statutes which protect both state and federal flags.

The First Amendment does offer protection to artists who use the flag in creating their work, particularly where the purpose of the work is political protest as opposed to a commercial use. For example, in 1966, an artist named Marc Morrel exhibited in the Radich Gallery in New York City "an object resembling a gun caisson wrapped in a flag, a flag stuffed into the shape of a six-foot human form hanging by the neck from a yellow noose, and a seven-foot cross with a bishop's mitre on the head-piece, the arms wrapped in ecclesiastical flags and an erect penis wrapped in an American flag protruding from the vertical standard," as well as other works which used a Vietcong flag, a Russian flag, a Nazi swastika and a gas mask. (*U.S. ex rel Radich* v. *Criminal Court of City of New York*, 385 F. Supp. 165) The gallery owner, Stephen Radich, was charged with desecration of the flag and began a seven-year odyssey through the courts. Radich was finally vindicated on the basis of a two-part judicial test.

First the court determined whether the activity, in this case the exhibition, had such elements of communication as to be protected by the First Amendment. If so, as with Morrel's work, the court then decided whether the state had interests which were more compelling than the individual's. The interests of New York State—such as preservation of the flag as a symbol, avoiding breaches of the peace and protecting the feelings of passerby—were found less important than the interest of the artist and gallery owner in freely expressing the political protest conveyed by the exhibition.

The divergent state laws and complexity of the area of flag desecration will make consultation with a lawyer a necessity for the artist who wishes to determine whether the First Amendment will provide adequate protection for given works of art using a motif of the state or federal flag.

Other governmental symbols

Flags are not the only symbols protected by the federal or state governments. Federal law places restrictions on symbols such as the great seal of the United States, military medals or decorations, the Swiss Confederation coat of arms, the "Smokey Bear" character or name and the "Woodsy Owl" character or name or slogan. While the prohibited uses vary, they often include advertising, product packaging or uses that might mislead the public. For an artist to use such an emblem, insignia or name may require legal advice or obtaining an opinion from the appropriate government agency as to whether the use is allowed.

Coins, bills and stamps

The artist may also wish to use either United States currency or stamps as part of a work. Certain uses, however, are prohibited by federal statutes. For example, advertising on either real or imitation currency is forbidden and punishable by fines up to $500. Mutilation of currency with an intent to make such currency unfit to be reissued is punishable by fines up to $100 or six months in jail, or both. Also, anyone who makes or possesses a likeness of a United States coin for use in any manner is subject to a fine up to $100, but the likeness must be such as to create some possibility that the coin could be mistaken as minted by the United States.

The federal laws on counterfeiting had, however, made specific provisions to allow paper money and stamps to be printed and published, "for philatelic, numismatic, educational, historical, or newsworthy purposes in articles, books, journals, newspapers, or albums." Advertising uses were restricted to legitimate coin or stamp dealers in trade publications. *Time Magazine* challenged this purposes limitation as part of a lawsuit to permit it to publish images of currency without being subject to either the purposes or size and color limitations. Because the United States Supreme Court struck down the purposes limitation, the Department of Treasury made the following announcement on February 22, 1985:

> The Treasury Department today announced a new enforcement policy concerning reproductions. The Department will henceforth permit the use of photographic or other likenesses of United States and foreign currencies for any purposes, provided the items are reproduced in black and white and are less than three-quarters or greater than one-and-one-half times the size, in linear dimension, of each part of the original item. Furthermore, negatives and plates used in making the likenesses must be destroyed after their use.
>
> The policy is consistent with the Supreme Court's decision of July, 1984, in the case of *Regan* v. *Time, Inc.,* and was made with the concurrence of the Department of Justice. This decision will, for the first time, permit the use of currency reproductions in commercial advertisements, provided they conform to these size and color restrictions.
>
> Under the new policy, the Treasury Department expects to increase enforcement efforts against color currency reproductions and against black-and-white reproductions that do not conform to the size restrictions.

As the announcement stated, the illustrations of paper money must be black and white and either less than ¾ or more than 1½ times the size of the original. The size requirements apply to stamps which are in color, but not to black-and-white or canceled colored stamps. The negatives and plates must be destroyed after being used for the illustrations. Also, paper money and stamps may be used in films, microfilm and slides as long as no prints or reproductions are made that violate the foregoing restrictions. These size and color requirements were also considered by the Supreme Court in the case brought by *Time Magazine,* but the Supreme Court upheld the validity of these restrictions.

Photographs or printed illustrations, slides or films of United States and foreign coins may be made in any size and color and used for any purpose, including advertising. This is because such reproductions of coins raise no dangers with respect to passing off counterfeit money.

The enforcement of counterfeiting laws falls under the United States Secret Service, which will give an opinion as to whether a particular use is a violation of any federal statute. However, such an opinion does not prevent a later prosecution by either the Department of Justice or any United States Attorney. To obtain an opinion, the address is: Office of the Director, United States Secret Service, Department of the Treasury, Washington, D.C. 20223.

Dangerous art

Neither the First Amendment nor the fact of creating art give an artist the right to endanger others or violate the law. When an artist placed a "bomb" on top of a tower of the Brooklyn Bridge, he was arrested and charged with criminal possession of a weapon—a felony for which sentences can be as long as seven years. Two years later the Manhattan District Attorney's Office finally requested that the charges be dropped. Explosives experts had testified that the device was not dangerous. From the artist's point of view, it had been an attempt to create an environmental sculpture to illuminate the city skies. If he had succeeded in detonating the fireworks in the explosive device, he would at most have created entertainment and not danger for the public.

In the craft area, the artist must be aware of the risk of lawsuits based on a defect in a product sold to the public. If a customary or foreseeable use of a defective product causes injury, the artist will be held responsible for resulting injuries and be liable for damages. Careful quality control, development of the product to be safe even if misused, giving clear instructions to prevent injurious uses and obtaining product liability insurance will mitigate the risks in this area.

The Consumer Product Safety Commission oversees the Consumer Product Safety Act, the Flammable Fabrics Act and other laws relating to consumer safety. The artist creating clothing, furnishings or other products may wish to contact the Commission and determine whether regulations or instructions exist for a particular item: Consumer Product Safety Commission, 1111 19th Street, N.W., Washington, D.C. 20207, 800-638-2772.

Labeling

Artists working with wool, fur and other textiles should be aware of labeling requirements under various laws. While these laws are not for consumer safety, they do safeguard the consumer by requiring that infor-mation be provided which may include the materials in, processes used to create and appropriate uses of covered items.

The Federal Trade Commission enforces these law and can provide further information: Federal Trade Commission, Public Reference Library, Washington, D.C. 20580.

Protecting animals and plants

It is forbidden to kill certain protected species or use or sell any parts of such species, although regulations may exist for certain exemptions and Native Americans may receive special treatment in certain cases. The United States Department of the Interior administers these programs through its Fish and Wildlife Office. Up-to-date lists of covered animals and plants and other information may be obtained by writing: Office of Endangered Species, United States Fish and Wildlife Service, 18th and C Streets, N.W., Washington, D.C. 20240.

Protected expression

In certain expressions of creativity and opinion, artists are protected by the First Amendment with respect to acts which might otherwise be grounds for a civil or criminal suit. Generally, however, artists are subject to the law in the same way as any citizen and should be careful not to violate public laws or private rights.

Chapter 9

Contracts:
an introduction

A contract is an agreement creating legally enforceable obligations between two or more parties. The artist is constantly entering into contracts with collectors, dealers, agents, exhibitors, publishers, landlords, and others. While a lawyer should usually be consulted when the artist is given a contract to sign, the artist's knowledge of the different negotiable points in each contract can assist a lawyer in reaching the contract best suited to the artist's individual needs. This chapter develops a background of the law relating to contracts in order to make subsequent chapters on specific types of contracts more helpful.

Negotiation skills

Negotiation is integral to the process of making a contract. The terms of the contract are those reached by the negotiation. A few basic observations will help the artist negotiate successfully.

The purpose of negotiation is not to defeat the other party. The purpose is for both parties to be benefitted and feel satisfied their needs have been met. Prior to beginning any negotiation, the artist should have his or her goals clearly in mind. These goals certainly include money, but reach beyond this to issues of artistic control, authorship credit and other factors that may also have importance for the artist.

Of course, the other party has its goals. The artist should gather as much information as possible about the other party, including its resources and goals. For example, what advances and royalty rates has a publisher given to other artists? What provisions did it strike out of its standard contract? What commission rate has a gallery agreed to with other artists? Did a magazine agree to buy first North American serial rights or insist on more? This kind of information shows what an artist may expect in a negotiation. It also indicates what the other party must have in order to be satisfied with the business arrangement.

It is wise to keep records of both negotiators' strategies, including preparing written notes on all discussions. This will enable the artist to keep current on the nuances of the negotiation. It will also prepare the way for future negotiations, since the artist may be able to predict the other party's patterns while avoiding falling into patterns that give the other party an advantage.

Offers should be put in writing. This avoids disputes as to what the offer was. Generally, the first offer is not the best. In this way there is room for give and take in the negotiation. The more time and effort invested in a negotiation, the more both parties will want a successful conclusion by reaching an agreement. After an agreement is signed, both parties should feel the contract will be mutually beneficial—not that one party or the other won.

The telephone is, of course, one of the chief instruments of negotiation. Since negotiations must be prepared in order to be successful, it follows that no phone call should be made without adequate preparation. The artist should be aware of which party talks the most, since listening often produces more information and therefore better results. The artist should be certain the call will not be interrupted and that no distractions will divert attention from the negotiation. If a call to the artist catches him or her off guard, the best approach is to call back after taking the time to prepare properly.

The artist must be willing to lose a deal in order to negotiate from strength. It's also wise for any negotiator to ask for all he or she wants and something extra that can be sacrificed. Not to make demands because the artist fears rejection can only be self-defeating. If the artist makes the demands of a professional, he or she is far more likely to be treated as a professional.

Governing laws

Every state except Louisana has enacted the Uniform Commerical Code, a statute governing the sale of goods. For example, the Uniform Commerical Code applies when an artist contracts to sell a finished work or to create a specific work for a purchaser. The Uniform Commerical Code does not apply, however, where the artist's services are employed in a project such as the creation of a mural. Such a contract for services is governed by the case law of the various states, although general principles of the case law can be described.

Offer and acceptance

An offer is a proposal to enter into a contract. It is a promise which invites acceptance in the form of a return promise or, less usually, an acceptance by performance based on the terms of the offer. If a collector says to an artist, "I want to buy your painting, Doves of Peace, for $250," an offer has been made. The collector has promised in definite terms which can be accepted by the artist's return promise to sell the painting. If the collector says, "This painting would look wonderful in my office," or, "This painting will be worth a fortune soon," or, "I want to borrow this painting to try for a few weeks," no offers have been made. If the collector says, "You paint my portrait and we'll agree later about the price," or, "You paint my portrait and I'll pay you as I see fit," no offers have been made because a material term—the price—has been omitted. However, if the collector says, "Paint my portrait and I will pay you $250 if satisfied," a valid offer has been made. The artist should beware of such an offer, because the collector may be able to reject the finished portrait. The courts generally rule that a satisfaction clause means that a dissatisfied collector may reject the work, even if the collector reasonably should have been satisfied. But the artist certainly does not want to deal with vagueness of this nature and should either avoid satisfaction clauses or require step-by-step approval from the collector as does the Commission Agreement shown on pages 79–81.

It is interesting that the exhibition of a painting with a price is not an offer. The reason for this is that advertising to the public at large does not create an offer. If a collector is willing to meet the asking price, it is the collector who makes the offer which the artist may then accept or refuse.

The person making an offer can usually revoke the offer at any time prior to acceptance. Another way in which an offer can be terminated is by limiting the time for acceptance. An example of this would be, "I will purchase your painting for $250 if you will sell it to me within the next ten days." This offer would terminate at the end of ten days. If no such time limit is set, the assumption is made that the offer ends after a reasonable amount of time has passed. An offer is also terminated by a counteroffer. For example, if the collector offers $250 for a painting and the artist demands $500, the original offer of $250 is no longer effective.

Acceptance is usually accomplished by agreeing to the offer. If the collector offers to pay $250 for a portrait, the artist can accept by stating, "I agree to paint your portrait for $250." The less usual method of acceptance would be by conduct indicating acceptance to the offer. The artist could simply begin painting the portrait, which would be implied acceptance of the collector's offer. The best way, however, is to accept by giving a promise in return instead of merely performing according to the terms of the offer.

The end result of the process of offer and acceptance is a meeting of the minds, a mutual understanding between the parties to the contract.

Consideration

Every contract, to be valid, must be based on consideration, which is the giving of value by each party to the other. The consideration each party to a contract receives is what induces entry into the contract. Where the collector promises to pay $250 for a portrait which the artist promises to paint, each party has received value from the other. The consideration must be bargained for at the time of entry into the contract. If a collector says, "I'm enjoying my portrait you painted so much, I'm going to pay you an extra $250 even though I don't have to," the collector is not obliged to pay. The artist has already painted the portrait and been paid in full, so the promise to pay an additional $250 is not supported by consideration.

The one situation in which consideration is not required occurs when a person relies on a promise in such a way that the promise must be enforced to avoid injustice. If a collector makes a promise which one reasonably should know an artist will rely on, such as offering $250 as a gift for the artist to buy art suplies, the collector cannot refuse to pay the money after the artist has in fact relied on the promise and purchased the supplies.

Competency of the parties

The law will not enforce a contract if the parties are not competent. The rationale is that there can be no meeting of the minds or mutual understanding in such a situation. A contract entered into by an insane person is not enforceable. Similarly, contracts entered into by minors will, depending on the law of the specific state, be either unenforceable or enforceable only at the choice of the minor. The age of reaching majority has traditionally been twenty-one, but many states such as New York and California have now lowered the age of majority to eighteen years of age.

Legality of purpose

A contract for a purpose which is illegal or against public policy is not binding. Thus a contract to smuggle pre-Columbian art into the United States would not be valid because a federal statue prohibits such importation without the permission of the country where the art is found. Similarly, a contract between an unethical art dealer and an art forger to create and sell old masters could not be enforced by either party in court.

Written and oral contracts

A common fallacy is that all contracts must be written to be enforced. While this is not always true, it is certainly wise to insist on having contracts in writing. The terms of a con-

tract may come into dispute several years after the creation of the contract. At that time reliance on memory to provide the terms of the contract can leave much to be desired, especially if no witnesses were present and the parties disagree as to what was said.

A written contract need not even be a formal document. An exchange of letters can create a binding contract. Often a letter agreement is signed by one party, and the party completes the contract by also signing at the bottom of the letter beneath the words "AGREED TO". Both parties may not have signed an agreement, but a memorandum signed by the party against whom enforcement is sought can be found to constitute a valid contract. Even where the parties merely show, from their conduct, an intention to agree, a contract—called an implied contract—can come into existence. But when part of a contract is in writing, the artist should not rely on an oral agreement to the effect that compliance with all the written provisions will not be insisted upon. Courts are reluctant to allow oral evidence to vary the terms of a written contract, except in cases where the written contract is procured by fraud or under mistake or is too indefinite to be understood without the additional oral statements.

The Uniform Commercial Code also requires written evidence whenever goods of a value of more than $500 are to be sold. This simple rule, however, is subject to several important exceptions. If the contract provides for goods to be specially created for purchasers—photographs of a specific place, for example—an oral contract for more than $500 will be valid if the artist has made a substantial start on the work. If the artist receives and accepts payment or if the purchaser receives and accepts the work, the oral contract will be valid despite being for more than $500. Also, merchants who have made an oral contract for more than $500 will have a valid contract if one merchant then writes a note binding against that merchant and the other merchant doesn't give written objection to the contents of the note within ten days of receipt. Merchant is a special term under the Uniform Commercial Code, defined to mean a person who deals in goods or practices involved in the transaction. A gallery or publisher would be a merchant, and at least some artists may also come within the definition.

There are provisions, however, in statues other than the Uniform Commercial Code which also require certain contracts to be in writing. For example, the original Statute of Frauds enacted in 1677 in England required contracts which could not be performed within one year to be in writing. This is still the law in almost every state. Unlike the Uniform Commercial Code, which only requires evidence for sales of goods, this provision applies to contracts for services as well and requires that the writing contain all of the essential terms of the contract. If an artist agrees to sell a collector two paintings each year for three years at $50 per painting, the contract cannot be performed within one year and must be in writing to be valid. Similarly for services, if a muralist is hired by a church to paint a mural during the next fifteen months, that contract will take longer than a year to perform and must be in writing. If completion of the mural were only to take eleven months but the church's payments would be over a two-year period, the contract would again not be performable within one year and would have to be in writing to be valid.

The wisest course is to use only written contracts, but, particularly if the contract is for the sale of goods worth more than $500 or will take more than one year to perform, the artist should generally insist on a written contract.

What about the sale of reproduction rights as opposed to the sale of physical art or a contract for services? As mentioned in the discussion of copyright, the copyright law requires that any transfer of a copyright or an exclusive right in a copyright must be evidenced by a writing. While this would cover many of an artist's transactions, it does not apply to nonexclusive licenses. It also would not apply to literary property which might not be copyrightable—for example, an idea. However, the Uniform Commercial Code might still apply (in every state except Louisiana), requiring written evidence—indicating price and subject matter and signed by the party against whom enforcement is sought—of a contract for the sale of

intangible personal property if the amount being paid exceeds five thousand dollars.

Warranties

Caveat emptor—let the purchaser beware—expressed the traditional attitude of the courts toward the protection of purchasers of goods. More and more, especially under the Uniform Commercial Code, warranties are created with contracts of sale for the purchaser's protection. Warranties can be created orally, even if the contract must be written, and can be made during negotiations, when entering into a contract, or, in some cases, after the contract is effective.

One implied warranty guarantees that the seller—for example, an artist—has title or the right to convey title in the art work to the purchaser. Another implied warranty is that the art work will be fit for the particular purpose for which sold, if the artist is aware of the particular purpose and the purchaser relies on the artist's skill or judgment in furnishing the work. If, for example, a sculpture, particularly purchased for a fountain, cracked because of the effect of water on the materials composing the sculpture, this warranty would be breached. This warranty would not apply when goods are put to a customary use, presumably including most forms of exhibition in the case of art works.

An express warranty is created when the artist asserts either facts or promises relating to the work or describes the work in such a way that the purchaser relies on the facts, promises or description as a basis for making the purchase. Describing the work as being constructed of certain materials, for example, would be an express warranty if the purchaser considered that a basis for purchasing the work. However, sales talk or opinions as to the value or merit of the work by the artist will not create warranties. If, for example, the artist speculates that the work will be worth a fortune in a few years, the purchaser cannot rely upon such an opinion and no warranty is created.

One express warranty which the artist may wish to make is that a work is either unique (one of a kind) or original (one of a limited number).

This is particularly true where the work could be easily duplicated, such as photographs, found objects, collages, much pop art, and the manufactured geometric shapes created by some of the minimal artists. While the beauty of the work would not seem diminished by identical pieces, the value for most collectors would be greatly impaired. Painters benefit from the myth that all paintings are unique, but artists whose work can be duplicated must inspire faith in the purchaser that a unique work is unique and that an original work exists in no more than a given number of copies. For example, a photographic work might exist in color in black and white, as well as having versions with a greater or small number of photographs. Although the artist and the purchaser may differ as to what uniqueness is in an art work, the artist can void the purchaser's having any cause for complaint by placing a warranty like the following on the back of the work:

Model warranty

This art work, titled *Doves of Peace,* and briefly described as *doves flying against a background of clouds,* is an original work consisting of *6* numbered panels of *30″ x 40″* in dimension with no more than *3* other identical originals and no more than *4* other originals in black and white consisting of *3* panels of the dimension of *15″ x 20″.*

Date: _____   Artist: _____

The artist would place this notice on the back of each panel, but sign only panel 1 to avoid the possibility of the work being split up. The notice can easily be adapted to suit the details of different art works. The purchaser will be pleased by this reassurance as to the scarcity of the work, and the artist will benefit from the increased trust created by such a demonstration of integrity. If the work were unique, the notice could simply be shortened to state the work's uniqueness. The artist who creates one work with several different parts, such as a sculpture in three separate pieces, might want the purchaser to expressly warrant that the pieces would always be exhibited and sold as a single work.

A fuller discussion of unique art and limited editions appears in Chapter 12.

Assignments of contracts

Sometimes one party to a contract can substitute another person to take over the burdens or rewards of the contract. This is not true, however, for contracts which are based upon the special skills of one party to the contract. When such personal ability is crucial to the contract—for example, in a contract for the creation of an art work—the artist may not delegate the contractual duties for performance by another artist. But even though the artist is unable to delegate the performance of the artist's duties, the artist will still be able to assign to another person the artist's right to receive money due or to become due under the contract. A well-drafted contract will state the intention of the parties as to the assignment of rights or delegation of duties under the contract.

Nonperformance excused

There are a variety of situations in which the artist's failure to perform contractual obligations will be excused. The most obvious case is that the death of the artist is not a breach of contract which would permit a lawsuit against the artist's estate. Similarly, because the artist's work is personal, unforeseen disabling physical or mental illness will excuse performance by the artist. Also, payment by the party contracting with the artist will be excused if the continued existence of a particular person is necessary to the contract being performed—for example, if a portrait was commissioned but the person to be portrayed died prior to commencement of the work.

Grounds other than the personal nature of the artist's work will also permit the artist to refuse to perform.

If the other party waives the artist's performance or if both parties have agreed to rescind the contract, no performance will be necessary. If the artist is prevented by the other party from performing, perhaps by a person refusing to sit for a portrait, performance will be excused and the artist will have an action for breach of contract. Similarly, no performance is required where performance would be impossible, as in the case of a muralist who cannot paint a mural because the building has burned. Also, performance is excused if it would be illegal due to a law passed after the parties entered into the contract.

Remedies for breach of contract

A party who refuses to perform a contract can be liable to pay damages. There must, however, be some detriment or loss caused by a breach of contract before the recovery of damages will be allowed. The damages will generally be the amount of the reasonably foreseeable losses (including out-of-pocket costs and lost profits) caused by the breach. Also, the injured party must usually take steps to minimize damages.

The artist may wonder what happens when performance under a contract is either nearly completed or is completed but varies slightly from what was agreed on. Unless the contract specifies that strict compliance is necessary if the artist is to be paid for performing pursuant to the contract, the artist will usually be able to recover the contract price less the costs necessary to pay for the defects in performance. For example, when an artist created stained-glass windows in substantial compliance with the designs except that less light came through the windows than one of the parties had apparently intended, the court stated:

> Where an artist is directed to produce a work of art in accordance with an approved design, the details of which are left to the artist, and the artist executes his commission in a substantial and satisfactory way, the mere fact that, when completed, it lacks some ele-

ment of utility desired by the buyer and not specifically contracted for, constitutes no breach of the artist's contract. (Wagner-Larshield Co. v. Fairview Mausoleum Co., 190 Wis. 357, 208 N.W. 241)

The question, however, of what constitutes substantial performance is an area in which litigation is likely. The reason for this is another rule: that part performance under a contract will not allow recovery based on the price specified in the contract for full performance. Moreover, such part performance will not, in most states, even be paid for on the basis of reasonable value unless the part performance is of substantial benefit to the other party who accepts and retains the benefits of such performance. This rule would not apply, of course, if one party prevented the other from performing. Also, if one part of a contract can be separated from another part, such as a number of payments for a number of different sets of photographs, recovery will usually be permitted for the partial contract price specified for each partial performance.

In some situations damages may be adequate to compensate for the loss caused by a breach of contract. If a famous artist is retained to paint a portrait of unique emotional value, the artist's refusal to honor the contract might be difficult to value in money damages. But since involuntary servitude is prohibited, the artist cannot be forced to create the portrait. On the other hand, if a painting with unique value is already in existence, a purchaser might well be able to require specific performance of a contract of sale. This would mean that a court would order the seller, whether an artist or a dealer or a collector, to transfer to the purchaser the specific painting for which the purchaser had contracted. Specific performance may only be used, however, when the payment of money would not be sufficient remedy.

Statutes of limitation

A statute of limitation sets forth the time within which an injured party must bring suit to have the injury remedied. After the limitation period has passed, no lawsuit can be maintained.

The limitation period for actions based on contracts for the sale of goods under the Uniform Commercial Code is four years from the time of breach. The limitation period for actions based on breach of contract for services varies from state to state (for example, six years in New York). The limitation period in many states is longer for written contracts than for contracts which are oral, partly in writing or implied. The artist contemplating legal action is well advised to seek redress promptly so that no question will arise regarding statutes of limitation.

Protection of ideas

Ideas are denied copyright protection but can still be protected by contract. The idea may be a format, a campaign, a style, a game and so on. The problem comes upon submission of the idea, since the artist must feel assured of payment if the idea is used.

At the outset, it should be noted that many potential purchasers of ideas will have release forms which must be signed by persons submitting ideas before any consideration will be given the submission. Such release forms bar any claims by the artist based upon a subsequent use of similar material by the potential purchaser. In addition, if the artist should be able to sue and recover despite the release form, the maximum reasonable value of the material is stipulated (for example, two hundred dollars) and the total recovery possible is limited to such an amount. These provisions are accompanied by a recital from the artist, such as "I recognize that there is always a likelihood that this material may be identical with, like or competitive to material which has or may come to you from other sources. Identity or similarity of material in the past has given rise to claims and disputes between various parties and has caused misunderstandings. You have advised me that you will refuse to examine or consider material unless you obtain for yourself complete protection from me against the possibility of any such claims." The artist can expect to be bound by such provisions, so caution should be exercised before signing a release form in order to submit an idea or manuscript.

The artist will be best served by an express contract providing for payment in the event the purchaser does use the idea. This is likely to be difficult to obtain, but the artist who simply volunteers an idea is basically at the mercy of the other party. The express contract should specify the consideration and other details of the transaction. If a standard price is paid for such material, it should be stated. Otherwise, a reasonable standard of value should be required as compensation. The submission agreement need not be complex, although it must suit the individual circumstances. For example, the writer might use a brief letter:

Model idea submission letter

Dear Sir/Madam:

I understand it is your practice to entertain or receive ideas or suggestions for (specify the market). I have developed such an (indicate what will be submitted) for submission and would like to disclose this to you. I understand that if you use it you will pay me a reasonable compensation based on current industry standards. Please advise me if I should send this to you.

Sincerely yours,

Jane Artist

It is not uncommon, however, for the artist to disclose ideas without having thought to obtain an express contract. Recovery may still be possible under a variety of doctrines which will only be mentioned here: implied contract (which occurs when the parties indicate by their conduct that a contract exists), confidential relationships (applicable to some cases in which the party with less bargaining power trusts in the other party's good faith and discloses the idea), and quasi contract (in which the law implies an obligation that the party receiving the idea pay for the benefits conferred). Especially for a confidential relationship or quasi contract, however, the courts may require that the idea be concrete, elaborated or novel before recovery will be allowed. A written, express contract is by far the best way for an artist to protect an idea.

Lecture agreements

Artists are frequently invited to lecture at schools and universities. The rewards of such appearances are both psychic and financial. However, the artist does run the risk that the host organization may not be set up to pay fees quickly. This can mean that expenses and time are invested by the artist, who must then wait before any compensation is received. A good way to deal with this problem is by having a written agreement that specifies when payment will be made, as well as detailing the exact nature of services the artist is to perform and what other reimbursements, such as for travel and other expenses, the artist will receive. An alternative to breaking down the expenses is to provide that the University will be responsible for all expenses, with a stipulated amount paid in advance and the balance paid while the Artist is at the University or as soon as the Artist can send in a statement detailing all the expenses. (model agreement 1, Paragraph 3).

If artwork is to accompany the artist's visit, insurance and risk of loss will also have to be resolved. And the artist may wish to retain the right to copyrights in any recordings or transcripts that are made in the course of the visit.

Two contracts are shown here. The first is a more formal document, while the second is simply a letter from the artist to the university. In fact, the exchange of letters between the artist and university can also serve as a contract as long as the terms of their understanding are clearly delineated.

Model lecture agreement (1)

Agreement, dated the _____ day of _____ , 19 _____ , between _____ (the Artist), residing at _____

_____ and

_____ (the

University), whose address is _____

_____ .

WHEREAS, the University is familiar with and admires the work of the Artist; and

WHEREAS, the University wishes the Artist to visit the University to enhance the opportunities for its students to have contact with working professional artists;

WHEREAS, the Artist wishes to lecture with respect to his work and perform such other services as this contract may call for;

NOW, THEREFORE, in consideration of the foregoing premises and the mutual covenants hereinafter set forth and other valuable considerations, the parties hereto agree as follows:

1. The Artist hereby agrees to come to the University on the following date(s): _____ and perform the following services: _____

_____ The

Artist shall use best efforts to make his or her services as productive as possible to the University. The Artist further agrees to bring examples of his or her own work in the form of (specify slides, original art, video, etc.).

2. The University agrees to pay as full compensation for the Artist's services rendered under Paragraph 1 the sum of $ _____ . This sum shall be payable to the Artist on completion of the (first or last) day of the Artist's residence at the University.

3. In addition to the payment provided under Paragraph 2, the University agrees to reimburse the Artist for the following expenses:

(A) Travel expenses in the amount of $ _____ .

(B) Food and lodging expenses in the amount of $ _____ .

(C) Other expenses: (specify) _____ in the amount of $ _____ .

The reimbursement for travel expenses shall be made fourteen (14) days prior to the earliest date specified in Paragraph 1. The reimbursement for food, lodging, and other expenses shall be made at the date of payment specified in Paragraph 2.

4. If the Artist is unable to appear on the dates scheduled in Paragraph 1 due to illness, the University shall have no obligation to make any payments under Paragraphs 2 and 3 but shall attempt to reschedule the Artist's appearance at a mutually acceptable future date. If the University is prevented from having the Artist appear by Acts of God, hurricane, flood, governmental order or other cause beyond its control, the University shall be responsible only for the payment of such expenses under Paragraph 3 as the Artist shall have actually incurred. The University agrees in such a case to attempt to reschedule the Artist's appearance at a mutually acceptable future date.

5. The University agrees that, in the event it is late in making payment of amounts due to the Artist under Paragraphs 2, 3 or 8, it will pay as additional liquidated damages __ % in interest on the amounts it is owing to the Artist, said interest to run from the date stipulated for payment in Paragraphs 2, 3 or 8 until such time as payment is made.

6. Both parties agree that the Artist shall retain all rights, including copyrights, in relation to recordings of any kind made of the appearance or any works shown in the course thereof. The term "recording" as used herein shall include any recording made by electrical transcription, tape recording, wire recording, film, videotape, or other similar or dissimilar method of recording, whether now known or hereinafter developed. No use of any such recording shall be made by the University without the written consent of the Artist and, if stipulated therein, additional compensation for such use.

7. The Univeristy agrees that it shall provide wall-to-wall insurance for the following artworks in the amounts specified:

Artwork	Insurance amount
1.	
2.	
3.	
4.	
etc.	

The University agrees that it shall be fully responsible for any loss or damage to the artwork from the time said artwork leaves the Artist's residence or studio until such time as it is returned there.

8. The University agrees that it shall fully bear any costs of packing and shipping necessary to deliver the artworks specified in Paragraph 7 to the University and return them to the Artist's residence or studio.

9. This contract contains the full understanding between the parties hereto and may only be modified in a written instrument signed by both parties.

10. This contract shall be governed by the laws of the State of _____ .

IN WITNESS WHEREOF the parties hereto have executed this Agreement on the day and year first above written.

The University

Artist _____   By: _____
                                          Name and official title

Model lecture agreement (2)

Dear Sir/Madam:

I am delighted by your invitation to address your group and would like this letter to serve as our contract with respect to the details of my visit. I will travel to (specify the location) on (specify the date or dates) and perform the following services:_____ _____ . In return you agree to pay my round-trip travel expenses in the amount of $ _____ fourteen days prior to the date of my visit, to pay me at the end of my first day of services an honorarium of $ _____, and to pay me additional expenses in the amount of $ _____ on or before _____ for food, lodging, and the following other expenses: _____ _____ . No recordings or transcripts of my visit or any art of mine shall be made without my express written consent, and all copyrights in such recordings or transcripts shall belong to me. If I provide examples of my art, you agree to bear any risk of loss or damage and to provide wall-to-wall insurance for said artwork in the amounts agreed to in a rider to this contract. You will also pay for any shipping and packing expenses necessary to bring the artwork to the University and return it to me. This contract is complete and can be modified only in writing. It will be governed by the laws of the State of _____.

Please sign both copies of this letter beneath the words CONSENTED AND AGREED TO to make this a binding contract between us, and return one copy to me for my files.

Sincerely yours,

_____
Artist

CONSENTED AND AGREED TO:
The University

By: _____
     Name and official title

Chapter 10

Original art:
sales, commissions and rentals

The last chapter developed a background of contractual law in order to prepare for a discussion of the particular contracts into which an artist may enter. The artist's sale of art work directly to a purchaser—whether of already completed work or of commissioned work—will be explored in this chapter along with the less common arrangement in which art is rented.

Basic contractual terms

If a purchaser decides to purchase a work, the artist should at least insist on a simple written contract in a form such as the Model Bill of Sale on page 00. It can be a very simple form stating no more than the artist's name, the purchaser's name, the date, the title and description of the piece sold, the price, the sales tax due, if any, and the total amount payable. By including this basic information, the bill of sale is useful as a record of the transaction in at least two ways. First, it helps keeps track of sales for income tax purposes, since all the prices paid are recorded. The artist need only transfer the amounts from the bills of sale to the ledger for income. Second, it can help in maintaining an overall inventory of work and keeping track of who owns the artist's work at any given moment. Again, the artist will want to transfer the information from the bill of sale to a ledger, file or slide book in which all the works created are recorded.

The bill of sale can also be expanded to deal with various contingencies that may occur in a given transaction. These may arise from the nature of the work, the manner of payment, or the artist's desire to enforce certain standards of treatment for the work after sale. Such additional clauses can be added under Terms of Sale.

For example, the artist is the owner of copyright from the moment of creation of a work. However, the artist may still wish to express this in the bill of sale so the purchaser has no misunderstanding about his or her right to make reproductions. At the same time, the artist might want to permit limited reproductions that fall into the category of "fair use." Such a provision might read as follows: "The Artist hereby expressly reserves all rights whatsoever to copy or reproduce the work to the Artist, his or her heirs, executors, administrators and assigns. The Artist has placed copyright notice in his or her name on the Work. The Artist shall not unreasonably refuse permission to reproduce the Work for catalogs and other publicity purposes incidental to public exhibition of the work, provided all such reproductions bear appropriately placed copyright notice in a form identical to that appearing on the work."

The risk of loss passes to the purchaser on delivery of the work as discussed on page 87 . If the purchaser is to pick up the work at the artist's studio, the risk of loss passes to the purchaser at such time as the purchaser could reasonably have been expected to have picked up the work. The bill of sale can alter the time that risk of loss will pass to the purchaser. Of course, the passage of the risk of loss from one party to another should, ideally, be determined in view of the insurance coverage that each party has. This clause might read: "The risk of loss shall pass to the Purchaser on the _____(specify when the risk of loss shall pass, such as 'on the date hereof')."

The bill of sale might include acknowledgement of receipt of the work by the purchaser and receipt of payment by the artist if these events occurred.

It is not uncommon for purchasers to make installment payments in order to purchase a work. Such a clause might provide: "The price shall be paid in _____ equal monthly installments, commencing on the _____ day of _____ , 19 _____ , and ending on the _____ day of _____, 19 _____."

If installment payments are used,

the artist should consider retaining a security interest in the work until full payment has been made. Such a security interest would require the filling out and filing of Uniform Commercial Code Form 1 with the Secretary of State or local agency for filing such as the County Clerk. This would protect the artist's interest in the work from other creditors of the buyer until such time as the artist has been paid in full. Form 1 is available at any stationery store that carries legal forms. It is easy to fill out, since it requires a limited amount of information. This includes the name and address of the debtor (the buyer is the debtor until all payments are made), the name and address of the secured party (who is the artist) and a description of the art which is covered. When signed by the artist and filed with the proper agency, the artist has precedence over any other creditor who might seek to assert a claim over the art or proceeds from the sale of the art. In general, the debtor must also sign Form 1 unless a separate security agreement has already been signed by the debtor.

Provisions relating to the integrity of the work, nondestruction, restoration, a right to exhibit and an art resale proceeds right are discussed in relation to the Projansky contract.

Instead of using a Bill of Sale, the terms of sale could also be set forth in a brief letter to the purchaser. The artist would sign the letter and the purchaser would sign beneath the words "AGREED TO".

Model bill of sale

Artist's Letterhead

Date:

Purchaser:

(Name)

(Address)

Description of work:
Price:
Sales tax (if applicable):
Balance due:
Terms of sale:

Artist

Purchaser

Projansky contract

The Projansky contract, or The Artist's Reserved Rights Transfer and Sale Agreement, was drafted by New York City lawyer Bob Projansky to rectify the artist's lack of control over and profit from art work after sale. It seeks to create, by contract, rights which are somewhat similar to moral rights and art resale proceeds legislation. In reading over the provisions of the contract, reproduced on page 76, the artist should remember that not all of the proposed provisions need to be used for every sale and some sales will require provisions not present in the contract. The actual terms will vary, depending on the bargaining power of the parties, but the Projansky contract will aid the artist in developing an awareness of what can be demanded.

Basic terms

The Projansky contract, like the bill of sale, starts by setting forth the names and addresses of the parties. The whereas clauses explain the motives of the parties and prepares a rationale for the duties and rights under contract. The first whereas clause states that the artist has created a work of art which is described by the title, dimensions, medium and year. The next whereas clause, the fundamental goal of the Projanksy contract, states that "the parties want the Artist to have certain rights in the future economics and integrity of the Work." An earlier edition of the Projanksy contract set forth a more detailed basis for such rights: (1) that the value of the art work sold would be affected by subsequent works created by the artist; (2) that the value of the work would, in fact, increase; (3) that the artist should share in any such increase in value; and (4) that the artist's intention in creating the work should be recognized by giving the artist a certain control over the work.

The artist's economic benefits

The Projansky contract requires that each work have a permanently affixed notice showing that future transfers are subject to the contract (Article 11; Specimen Notice and Notice). Exchanges, gifts, inheritances, receipt of insurance proceeds, and similar transfer transactions relating to the work are covered by the contract as well as sales (Article 2). Depending on the nature of the transaction, either price or value is entered under Article 1 and used to calculate gross art profit, which is simply the excess of the present transfer value or price over the previous transfer value or price (Article 2 (d)). The purchaser agrees to have anyone who purchases the work sign a Transfer Agreement and Record (abbreviated as TAR, as required by Article 2 (b) and shown with the contract) and each subseqeuent purchaser is bound by all the terms of the original agreement (Article 12). Each time the work is sold, the seller within thirty days must file a current TAR signed by the new purchaser (Article 2(b), (c)) and pay 15 percent of gross art profit to the artist (Article 2(a)). The artist also reserves all reproduction rights in the work (Article 10) and has a right to receive 50 percent of any rentals received by the purchaser (Article 9). The term of the economic benefits would be for the lives of the artist and spouse, plus an additional twenty-one years (Article 13).

The provisions can be illustrated by an example. In 1985 the artist sells a work for $1,000, subject to the Projansky contract. In 1988 the work is sold for $1,500. The owner who sells in 1988 must, within thirty days, file a current TAR and pay 15 percent of the $500 to the artist. If, in 1988, the artist had parted ownership with the work through gift or barter, the Projansky contract could still be used. Similarly, if in 1988 the owner transfers the work by a method other than sale, the 15 percent of gross art profit would still have to be paid to the artist. If the party who purchases in 1988 for $1,500 resells in 1992 for $2,500, the artist will be entitled to receive 15 percent of $1,000 and a new TAR must be filed with the artist.

The artist's control

The artist also gains substantial control over the work after sale under the Projansky contract. Of course, reproduction rights are reserved to the artist (Article 10), which offers asethetic control as well as economic benefits. The purchaser must give written notice to the artist of any intended exhibition (Article 4). The earlier edition of the contract had a much stronger provision which allowed the artist to either give advice or veto any proposed public exhibition. Upon showing satisfactory proof of insurance and prepaid transportation, the artist is entitled to borrow the work back from the purchaser for the sixty-day period every five years for exhibition at a nonprofit institution. The purchaser agrees not to "permit any intentional destruction, damage or modification of Work," (Article 7), rights which the artist would not have in most states in the absence of a specific contractual provision. If the work is damaged, the purchaser must consult with the artist prior to making repairs and, if possible, use the artist to do the repairs (Article 8). The term of the contract is limited to the life of the artist as to notice of the purchaser's exhibitions, the artist's right to possession once every five years, and the artist's right regarding restorations. Lastly, any party forced to bring suit for a breach of the contract may demand reasonable lawyer's fees as well as other remedies (Article 14).

AGREEMENT OF ORIGINAL TRANSFER OF WORK OF ART

Artist: _____ address: _____

Purchaser: _____ address: _____

WHEREAS Artist has created that certain Work of Art ("the Work"):

Title: _____ dimensions: _____

media: _____ year: _____ and

WHEREAS the parties want the Artist to have certain rights in the future economics and integrity of the Work, The parties mutually agree as follows:

1. **SALE**: Artist hereby sells the Work to Purchaser at the agreed value of $ _____

2. **RETRANSFER**: If Purchaser in any way whatsoever sells, gives or trades the Work, or if it is inherited from Purchaser, or if a third party pays compensation for its destruction, Purchaser (or the representative of his estate) must within 30 days

    (a) Pay Artist 15% of the "gross art profit", if any, on the transfer; and

    (b) Get the new owner to ratify this contract by signing a properly filled-out "Transfer Agreement and Record" (TAR); and

    (c) Deliver the signed TAR to the Artist.

    (d) "Gross art profit" for this contract means only: "Agreed value" on a TAR less the "agreed value" on the last prior TAR, or (if there hasn't been a prior resale) less the agreed value in Paragraph 1 of this contract.

    (e) "Agreed value" to be filled in on each TAR shall be the actual sale price if the Work is sold for money or the fair market value at the time if transferred any other way.

3. **NON-DELIVERY**: If the TAR isn't delivered in 30 days, Artist may compute "gross art profit" and Artist's 15% as if it had, using the fair market value at the time of the transfer or at the time Artist discovers the transfer.

4. **NOTICE OF EXHIBITION**: Before committing the Work to a show, Purchaser must give Artist notice of intent to do so, telling Artist all the details of the show that Purchaser then knows.

5. **PROVENANCE**: Upon request Artist will furnish Purchaser and his successors a written history and provenance of the Work, based on TAR's and Artist's best information as to shows.

6. **ARTISTS EXHIBITION**: Artist may show the Work for up to 60 days once every 5 years at a non-profit institution at no expense to Purchaser, upon written notice no later than 120 days before opening and upon satisfactory proof of insurance and prepaid transportation.

7. **NON-DESTRUCTION**: Purchaser will not permit any intentional destruction, damage or modification of the Work.

8. **RESTORATION**: If the Work is damaged, Purchaser will consult Artist before any restoration and must give Artist first opportunity to restore it, if practicable.

9. **RENTS**: If the Work is rented, Purchaser must pay Artist 50% of the rents within 30 days of receipt.

10. **REPRODUCTION**: Artist reserves all rights to reproduce the Work.

11. **NOTICE**: A Notice, in the form below, must be permanently affixed to the Work, warning that ownership, etc., are subject to this contract. If, however, a document represents the Work or is part of the Work, the Notice must instead be a permanent part of that document.

12. **TRANSFEREES BOUND**: If anyone becomes the owner of the Work with notice of this contract, that person shall be bound to all its terms as if he had signed a TAR when he acquired the Work.

13. **EXPIRATION**: This contract binds the parties, their heirs and all their successors in interest, and all Purchaser's obligations are attached to the Work and go with ownership of the Work, all for the life of the Artist and Artist's surviving spouse plus 21 years, except the obligations of Paragraphs 4, 6 and 8 shall last only for Artist's lifetime.

14. **ATTORNEYS' FEES**: In any proceeding to enforce any part of this contract, the aggrieved party shall be entitled to reasonable attorneys' fees in addition to any available remedy.

Date: _____

_____
Artist

_____
Purchaser

TRANSFER AGREEMENT AND RECORD

Title: _____ dimensions: _____

media: _____ year: _____

Ownership of the above Work of Art has been transferred between the undersigned persons, and the new owner

hereby expressly ratifies, assumes and agrees to be bound by the terms of the Contract dated _____ between:

Artist: _____ address: _____ and

Purchaser: _____ address: _____

Agreed value (as defined in said contract) at the time of this transfer: $ _____

Old owner: _____ address: _____

New owner: _____ address: _____

Date of this transfer: _____

SPECIMEN NOTICE

Ownership, transfer, exhibition and reproduction of this Work of Art are subject to a certain Contract dated _____ between:

Artist: _____

Address: _____ and

Purchaser: _____

Artist has a copy.

cut out, affix to Work

NOTICE

Ownership, transfer, exhibition and reproduction of this Work of Art are subject to a certain Contract dated _____ between:

Artist: _____

Address: _____ and

Purchaser: _____

Artist has a copy.

Benefits to the purchaser

The Projansky contract might seem to favor only the artist, raising the question whether any but the most successful artist would have the bargaining power to force a purchaser to use the contract. However, there are benefits to the purchasers, the most important of which is the right to receive the artist's written certification of the work's provenance and history (Article 5). Also, the purchasers can feel more assured that they are treating the work as the artist would wish.

Arguments against the Projansky contract

The merits of the Projansky contract have been warmly debated, although the contract has not come into wide use. Some argue that use of copyright by artists would provide much of the economic benefit sought by the Projansky contract. A difficult problem for the artist would be enforcement of the provisions requiring the filing of a current TAR and the payment of 15 percent of gross art profit. Since art works as an investment may not be easily salable, and the purchaser might be quite reluctant to accept a work which could only be resold if the new purchaser agreed to the substantial obligations of the Projansky contract. The purchaser may additionally be deterred by the prospect of work burdened by the Projansky contract passing through the purchaser's estate.

Also, there must be an increase in the value of the work for the artist to benefit economically. For many artists, who are fortunate simply to sell their work, this increase may not occur. The contract, therefore, will benefit artists whose work does not increase in value only by giving such artists some control over the work at the expense of negotiating a more complex contract. Since the artist will not have to pay purchasers if the work decreases in value, the contract is argued to be unfair. In any case, appreciation of a work may be caused by inflation, in which case the appreciated value is merely an illusion. But still the 15 percent must be paid back to the artist. Some collectors even argue that increases in the value of the artist's work are due to the collector giving the work prestige by the collector's ownership of the work. And if the artist's work sells for such high prices, why can't the artist create more pieces for a sale at the new price levels?

Arguments for the Projansky contract

The best argument for the Projansky contract may simply be that it is an equitable proposal. Artists should receive part of the appreciation in value of work and maintain certain controls over the work after sale. The purchaser who refuses to purchase a work under such conditions fails to respect the integrity of either the artist or the artist's work. Copyright laws are most beneficial for works which are intended for mass production and sale, not for unique or original works which may well not be reproduced during the artist's lifetime. Also, since the payment back to the artist need only be made if the work appreciates in value, the purchaser will necessarily have made a profit each time such a payment must be made. And frequently an artist's early works represent the crucial period during which the artist's sensibility developed. Such works will always have a special aesthetic value to both the artist and the public. Often that aesthetic value will be translated into a substantial discrepancy between the prices such work brings compared to prices for later work. This would certainly be the case, for example, with an artist like de Chirico whose early surrealist work was crucial to an entire movement while his later work received no acclaim.

A compromise

The use of the Projansky contract will depend on bargaining power. Any artist who can persuade a purchaser to use the contract would certainly be justified in doing so. Even greater restrictions could be required by the artist—for example, that the work not be resold by the purchaser for a certain period of time. However, many artists will wish to modify the Projansky contract in ways which are more favorable to the purchaser. Bob Projansky suggests, for example, placing a higher value for the work in Article 1 so the gross art profit is initially less. Another alternative Projansky proposes is to have the 15 percent of gross art profit be used as a credit against the purchase of additional works from the artist. But it is possible to go beyond Projansky's proposals for modification. For example, the 15 percent of gross art could be changed to a lower figure. Or the contract might require that only the first purchaser, but not subsequent purchasers, be bound to pay the 15 percent of appreciated value. The artist might be willing to go even further and completely omit any requirement for payment of a part of appreciated value, but keep the requirements giving the artist privileges of control after the work is sold.

The issues raised by the Projansky contract penetrate to a deeper level than mere contractual negotiations. In fact, the very concept that art is to be treated as a commodity at all like other commodities is brought into question. Each artist will find a personal answer to either the fairness or the practicality of the Projansky contract, but there can be no doubt of the value of this innovative contract in bringing such issues to the attention of both artists and the public.

Commission agreement

The crucial terms of a contract for a commissioned work must attempt to ensure that the purchaser will be satisfied with the finished work, while letting the artist be certain that the work in progress is, in fact, satisfactory. Of course, the artist should never agree to satisfy the purchaser, except perhaps to agree to create a work which reasonably should satisfy the purchaser. On the other hand, satisfaction must be the artist's goal. The more opportunities provided for consultation and approval in the process of creation, the better the likelihood of success in the regard.

The preliminary design provides the first opportunity to see whether the artist and purchaser mutually understand one another with regard to the intention and execution of the work (Paragraph 1). The approximate budget, size of the finished work, materials, construction, scope of the artist's work, and responsibilities of the purchaser, such as posing or providing work space, should all be specified (Paragraphs 1 and 2). The preliminary design fee must be paid upon signing the agreement. A completion date for the design is specified and the purchaser must notify the artist within two weeks of any proposed changes in the design. In the event of changes the artist is entitled to receive additional compensation on an hourly basis. If the purchaser decides not to have the work created, the artist retains the design fee and all rights in the designs remain the property of the artist (Paragraphs 5(A) and 6).

Having specified the rights of the parties at the earliest stage of their relationship, the commission agreement then looks to the satisfactory completion of the designs and the continuation of work (Paragraph 2). In order to be certain the parties are in agreement as to the satisfactory progress of the work, a sequence of three progress payments is used. The first payment is made upon the purchaser's giving written approval of the preliminary design, the second when the work is one-third completed and the final payment (with any sales tax) upon completion of the work (Paragraph 2).

The issue of satisfaction is resolved by giving the artist the power to determine when the work is completed. Since the artist is "a recognized professional artist" and the purchaser wants the art created "in artist's own unique style," it is reasonable to allow the artist to determine completion of the work and deviate from the preliminary design if necessary (Paragraph 2). If, at any stage, the purchaser is dissatisfied, the agreement may be terminated (Paragraph 5). If this happens, the artist is entitled to a fee based on the degree of completion and owns the work, but the purchaser is freed of any further obligations to pay for completion of the work (Paragraph 5 and 6). Of course, the purchaser might negotiate in the contract for the return of payments in the event of termination, but this will depend on the relative bargaining strengths of the parties.

A date is provided for completion and final delivery of the work, but the artist shall not be liable for damages in the event of delays (Paragraph 3, and 5(D)). If the artist cannot finish the work within ninety days of the delivery date, the artist must return all progress payments to the purchaser but retains all rights in the work (Paragraph 5(E)). The purchaser might well insist either that the specific reasons, such as illness or act of God, be given to excuse delays or that the purchaser have an option to accept the partially completed work rather than merely to receive back the payments to date. Also, it is wise to specify where the work is to be received, any installation which may be necessary, and who will pay for insurance and the costs of transportation (Paragraph 4). Since the artist is excused from any penalties other than return of payments if the work isn't completed, the purchaser might also object that it is harsh to charge interest on unpaid progress payments and at the same time to give the purchaser no rights in the work until the final payment is made (Paragraph 2).

Other provisions cover the artist's ownership of copyright, the purchaser's agreement not to destroy or alter the work, the purchaser's obligation to maintain the work properly and the artist's rights to make repairs if practical and borrow the work for exhibition (Paragraphs 7, 9, 10, 11). If the work is a portrait, the purchaser waives his or her right of privacy. This is important if the artist comes to own the work because of a termina-

tion or wishes to exploit the work in multiples. Obviously the artist should obtain the purchaser's approval of any plans to reproduce the work.

The commission agreement may be simpler or more sophisticated depending on the work. If the work will be of very long duration, more than three progress payments would be reasonable. The purchaser may require the artist to maintain insurance on the work in progress so that the work can be replaced at no cost to the purchaser in the event of damage or theft (Paragraph 4). Also, a provision should definitely be included governing the effect of the death of either the artist or the purchaser while the work is in progress. If the artist dies, a fair provision might be to have the work, in whatever stage of progress, belong to the purchaser, while the payments to the date of death remain in the artist's estate (Paragraphs 5(F) and 6). The same provision would be reasonable if the death of the purchaser makes further performance impossible—for example, a portrait. Otherwise the estate of the purchaser should be required to perform as if the purchaser were living (Paragraph 13).

These are not all the possible terms of an agreement for a commissioned work, but knowledge of the more important terms and general approach will enable the artist to negotiate fair and effective agreements for commissions.

Model commission agreement

AGREEMENT dated as of the _____ day of _____ , 19 _____ , between _____
_____ ("the Artist"), whose address is, _____
and _____ ("the Purchaser"), whose address is
_____ .

WHEREAS the Artist is a recognized professional artist; and

WHEREAS the Purchaser admires the work of the Artist and wishes to commission the Artist to create a work of art ("the Work") in the Artist's own unique style; and

WHEREAS the parties wish to have the creation of this work of art governed by the mutual obligations, covenants and conditions herein,

NOW, THEREFORE, in consideration of the foregoing premises and the mutual covenants hereinafter set forth and other valuable considerations, the parties hereto agree as follows:

1. PRELIMINARY DESIGN. The Artist hereby agrees to create the preliminary design for the Work in the form of studies, sketches, drawings or maquettes described as follows: _____
_____ in return for which the Purchaser agrees to

pay a fee of _____ upon the signing of this Agreement. The Artist agrees to develop the preliminary design according to the following description of the Work as interpreted by the Artist:

Title:
Materials:
Dimensions:
Description:
Price:

The Artist shall deliver the preliminary design to the Purchaser within _____ days of the date hereof. The Purchaser may, within two weeks of receipt of the preliminary design, demand changes, and the Artist shall make such changes for a fee of _____ per hour; provided, however, that the Artist shall not be obligated to work more than _____ hours making changes.

2. PROGRESS PAYMENTS. Upon the Purchaser's giving written approval of the preliminary design, the Artist agrees to proceed with construction of the Work, and the Purchaser agrees to pay the price of _____ for the Work as follows: one-third upon the giving of written approval of the preliminary design; one-third upon the completion of one-third of the construction of the Work; and one-third upon the completion of the Work. The Purchaser shall also promptly pay the following expenses to be incurred by the Artist in the course of creating the Work: _____ . The Purchaser shall pay the applicable sales tax, if any, with the final progress payment. Completion of the Work is to be determined by the Artist, who shall use the Artist's professional judgment to deviate from the preliminary design as the Artist in good faith believes necessary to create the Work. If, upon the Artist presenting the Purchaser with written notice of any payment being due, the Purchaser fails to make said payment within two weeks of receipt of notice, interest at the prime interest rate for banks in _____ shall accrue upon the balance due. The Purchaser shall have a right to inspect the Work in progress upon reasonable notice to the Artist.

3. DATE OF DELIVERY. The Artist agrees to complete the Work within _____ days of receiving the Purchaser's written approval of the preliminary design. This completion date shall be extended for such period of time as the Artist may be disabled by illness preventing progress of the Work. The completion date shall also be extended in the event of delays caused by events beyond the control of the Artist, including but not limited to fire, theft, strikes, shortages of materials and Acts of God. Time shall not be considered of the essence with respect to the completion of the Work.

4. INSURANCE, SHIPPING, AND INSTALLATION. The Artist agrees to keep the Work fully insured against fire and theft and bear any other risk of loss until delivery to the Purchaser. In the event of loss caused by fire or theft, the Artist shall use the insurance proceeds to recommence the making of the Work. Upon completion of the Work, it shall be shipped at the expense of _____to the following address specified by the Purchaser: _____. If any special installation is necessary, the Artist shall assist in said installation as follows: _____.

5. TERMINATION. This Agreement may be terminated on the following conditions:

(A) If the Purchaser does not approve the preliminary design pursuant to Paragraph 1, the Artist shall keep all payments made and this Agreement shall terminate.

(B) The Purchaser may, upon payment of any progress payment due pursuant to Paragraph 2 or upon payment of an amount agreed in writing by the Artist to represent the pro rata portion of the price in relation to the degree of completion of Work, terminate this Agreement. The Artist hereby agrees to give promptly a good faith estimate of the degree of completion of the Work if requested by the Purchaser to do so.

(C) The Artist shall have the right to terminate this Agreement in the event the Purchaser is more than sixty days late in making any payment due pursuant to Paragraph 2, provided, however, nothing herein shall prevent the Artist bringing suit based on the Purchaser's breach of contract.

(D) The Purchaser shall have the right to terminate this Agreement if the Artist fails without cause to complete the Work within ninety days of the completion date in Paragraph 3. In the event of termination pursuant to this subparagraph, the Artist shall return to the Purchaser all payments made pursuant to Paragraph 2, but shall not be liable for any additional expenses, damages or claims of any kind based on the failure to complete the Work.

(E) The Purchaser shall have a right to terminate this Agreement if, pursuant to Paragraph 3, the illness of the Artist causes a delay of more than six months in the completion date or if events beyond the Artist's control cause a delay of more than one year in the completion date, provided, however, that the Artist shall retain all payments made pursuant to Paragraphs 1 and 2.

(F) This Agreement shall automatically terminate on the death of the Artist, provided, however, that the Artist's estate shall retain all payments made pursuant to Paragraphs 1 and 2.

(G) The exercise of a right of termination under this Paragraph shall be written and set forth the grounds for termination.

6. OWNERSHIP. Title to the Work shall remain in the Artist until the Artist is paid in full. In the event of termination of this Agreement pursuant to Subparagraphs (A), (B), (C) or (D) of Paragraph 5, the Artist shall retain all rights of ownership in the Work and shall have the right to complete, exhibit and sell the Work if the Artist so chooses. In the event of termination of this Agreement pursuant to Paragraph 5 (E) or (F), the Purchaser shall own the Work in whatever degree of completion and shall have the right to complete, exhibit and sell the Work if the Purchaser so chooses. Notwithstanding anything to the contrary herein, the Artist shall retain all rights of ownership and have returned to the Artist the preliminary design, all incidental works made in the creation of the Work and all copies and reproductions thereof and of the Work itself, provided, however, that in the event of termination pursuant to Paragraph 5 (E) or (F) the Purchaser shall have a right to keep copies of the preliminary design for the sole purpose of completing the Work.

7. COPYRIGHT. The Artist reserves all rights of reproduction and all copyrights in the Work, the preliminary design and any incidental works made in the creation of the Work. Copyright notice in the name of the Artist shall appear on the Work, and the Artist shall also receive authorship credit in connection with the Work or any reproductions thereof.

8. PRIVACY. The Purchaser gives to the Artist permission to use the Purchaser's name, picture, portrait and photograph, in all forms and media and in all manners, including but not limited to exhibition, display, advertising, trade and editorial uses, without violation of the Purchaser's rights of privacy or any other personal or proprietary rights the Purchaser may possess in connection with reproduction and sale of the Work, the preliminary design or any incidental works made in the creation of the Work.

9. NON-DESTRUCTION, ALTERATION AND MAINTENANCE. The Purchaser agrees that the Purchaser will not intentionally destroy, damage, alter, modify or change the Work in any way whatsoever. If any alteration of any kind occurs after receipt by the Purchaser, whether intentional or accidental and whether done by the Purchaser or others, the Work shall no longer be represented to be the Work of the Artist without the Artist's written consent. The Purchaser agrees to see that the Work is properly maintained.

10. REPAIRS. All repairs and restorations which are made during the lifetime of the Artist shall have the Artist's approval. To the extent practical, the Artist shall be given the opportunity to accomplish said repairs and restorations at a reasonable fee.

11. POSSESSION. The Purchaser agrees that the Artist shall have the right to possession of the Work for a period not to exceed sixty days for the purpose of exhibition of the Work to the public, at no expense to the Purchaser. The Artist shall provide proof of sufficient insurance and prepaid transportation. The Artist shall have such right of possession for one period not to exceed sixty days every five years.

12. NON-ASSIGNABILITY. Neither party hereto shall have the right to assign this Agreement without the prior written consent of the other party. The Artist shall, however, retain the right to assign monies due to the Artist under the terms of this Agreement.

13. HEIRS AND ASSIGNS. This Agreement shall be binding upon the parties hereto, their heirs, successors, assigns and personal representatives, and references to the Artist and the Purchaser shall include their heirs, successors, assigns and personal representatives.

14. INTEGRATION. This Agreement constitutes the entire understanding between the parties. Its terms can be modified only by an instrument in writing signed by both parties.

15. WAIVERS. A waiver of any breach of any of the provisions of this Agreement shall not be construed as a continuing waiver of other breaches of the same or other provisions hereof.

16. NOTICES AND CHANGES OF ADDRESS. All notices shall be sent to the Artist at the following address: _____ and to the Purchaser at the following address: _____ . Each party shall give written notification of any change of address prior to the date of said change.

17. GOVERNING LAW. This Agreement shall be governed by the laws of the State of _____ .

Artist: _____

Purchaser: _____

Rental agreement

Under this agreement, the purchaser has the right to purchase the artwork and apply rental payments to the purchase price (Paragraph 12). The agreement is not meant to be adopted as is, but to be modified and adapted to the artist's needs. The artist will have to decide, for example, how much to charge (museums frequently charge about 5% of the sales price per month, but the artist might want to charge a little more) and how long the artist wishes the renter to be able to lease the work. The artist will also have to set a policy on who must pay for shipping and insurance while the work is in transit. Although it's obviously to the artist's advantage to have the renter pay these costs, the artist may be willing to absorb them if there's a good chance the rental will result in a sale. In Paragraph 4 a blank has been left for the amount for which the artwork is to be insured.

Since the artist continues to own the rented work, it is particularly important that it be protected. The use is limited to personal use by the renter and any reproductions must be approved by the artist (Paragraphs 6 and 9). Maintenance of the work is determined by the artist (Paragraph 7). The location of the works is also restricted and the artist is given a right of access to the works (Paragraph 8). In the event of sale, the artist has continuing rights to borrow the work and repair the work while the purchaser agrees not to destroy or damage the work (Paragraph 12). A security interest retained by the artist allows the artist to file Uniform Commercial Code Form 1 with the Secretary of State or a local agency such as the County Clerk to gain priority over any creditors of the Renter that might try to seize the rented work (Paragraph 13 and see pages 73–74). Since the artist is far more likely to have to sue than the renter, a provision regarding attorney's fees is included (Paragraph 14).

Model rental agreement

Agreement dated as of the _____day of _____, 19 _____, between _____ _____(the "Artist"), whose address is _____, and _____(the "Renter"), whose address is _____.

WHEREAS the Artist is a recognized professional artist who creates artworks for rental and sale; and

WHEREAS the Renter admires the work of the Artist; and

WHEREAS the Renter wishes to rent and have the option to purchase certain works by the Artist; and

WHEREAS the parties wish to have the rentals and any purchases governed by the mutual obligations, covenants and conditions herein,

NOW THEREFORE, in consideration of the foregoing premises and the mutual covenants hereinafter set forth and other valuable considerations, the parties hereto agree as follows:

1. CREATION AND TITLE. The Artist hereby warrants that the Artist created and possesses unencumbered title to the works of art listed and described on the attached Schedule of Art Works ("the Schedule").

2. RENTAL AND PAYMENTS. The Artist hereby agrees to rent the works listed on the Schedule at the rental fees shown thereon and the Renter agrees to pay said rental fees as follows: _____ .

3. DELIVERY AND CONDITION. The artist shall be responsible for delivery of the works listed on the Schedule to the Renter by the following date: _____. All costs of delivery (including transportation and insurance) shall be paid by _____. The Renter agrees to make an immediate written objection if the works upon delivery are not in good condition or appear in any way in need of repair. Further, the Renter agrees to return the works in the same good condition as received, subject to the provisions of Paragraph 4.

4. LOSS OR DAMAGE AND INSURANCE. The Renter shall be responsible for loss of or damage to the rented works from the date of delivery to the Renter until the date of delivery back to the Artist. The Renter shall insure each work for the benefit of the Artist up to _____ percent of the Sale Price shown in the Schedule.

5. TERM. The term of this Agreement shall be for a period of _____ months, commencing as of the date of the signing of the Agreement.

6. USE OF WORK. The Renter hereby agrees that the rental under this Agreement is solely for personal use and that no other uses shall be made of the work, such other use including but not being limited to public exhibition, entry in contests and commercial exploitation.

7. FRAMING, CLEANING, REPAIRS. The Artist agrees to deliver each work ready for display. The Renter agrees not to remove any work from its frame or other mounting or in any way alter the framing or mounting. The Renter agrees that the Artist shall have sole authority to determine when cleaning or repairs are necessary and to choose who shall perform such cleaning or repairs.

8. LOCATION AND ACCESS. The Renter hereby agrees to keep the works listed on the Schedule at the following address: _____, which may be changed only with the Artist's written consent, and to permit the Artist to have reasonable access to said works for the purpose of taking photographs of same.

9. COPYRIGHT AND REPRODUCTION. The Artist reserves all reproduction rights, including the right to claim statutory copyright, on all works listed on the Schedule. No work may be photographed, sketched, painted or reproduced in any manner whatsoever without the express, written consent of the Artist. All approved reproductions shall bear the following copyright notice: © by (Artist's name) 19 _____ .

10. TERMINATION. Either party may terminate this Agreement upon fifteen (15) days written notice to the other party. This Agreement shall automatically terminate in the event of the Renter's insolvency or bankruptcy. Upon termination, the Artist shall refund to the Renter a pro rata portion of any prepaid rental fees allocable to the unexpired rental term, said refund to be made after the works have been returned to the Artist in good condition.

11. RETURN OF WORKS. The Renter shall be responsible for the return of all works upon termination of this Agreement. All costs of return (including transportation and insurance) shall be paid by _____ .

12. OPTION TO PURCHASE. The Artist hereby agrees not to sell any works listed on the Schedule during the term of this Agreement. During the term the Renter shall have the option to purchase any work listed on the Schedule at the Sale Price shown thereon. This option to purchase shall be deemed waived by Renter if he or she fails to make timely payments pursuant to Paragraph 2. If the Renter chooses to purchase any work, all rental fees paid to rent that work shall be applied to reduce the Sale Price. Any purchase under this paragraph shall be subject to the following restrictions:

(A) The Artist shall have the right to borrow any work purchased for up to sixty (60) days once every five years for exhibition at a nonprofit institution at no expense to the Renter-Purchaser, provided that the Artist gives 120 days advance notice in writing prior to the opening and offers satisfactory proof of insurance and prepaid transportation.

(B) The Renter-Purchaser agrees not to permit any intentional destruction, damage or modification of any work.

(C) If any work is damaged, The Renter-Purchaser agrees to consult with the Artist before restoration is undertaken and must give the Artist the first opportunity to restore the work, if practicable.

(D) The Renter-Purchaser agrees to pay the Artist any sales or other transfer tax due on the full Sale Price.

(E) The Renter agrees to make full payments of all sums due on account of the purchase within fiften days after notifying the Artist of the Renter's intention to purchase.

13. SECURITY INTEREST. Title to, and a security interest in, any works rented or sold under this Agreement is reserved in the Artist. In the event of any default by the Renter, the Artist shall have all the rights of a secured party under the Uniform Commercial Code and the works shall not be subject to claims by the Renter's creditors. In the event of purchase of any work pursuant to Paragraph 12, title shall pass to the Renter only upon full payment to the Artist of all sums due hereunder. The Renter agrees not to pledge or encumber any works in his or her possession, nor to incur any charge or obligation in connection therewith for which the Artist may be liable.

14. ATTORNEY'S FEES. In any proceeding to enforce any part of this Agreement, the aggrieved party shall be entitled to reasonable attorney's fees in addition to any available remedy.

15. NON-ASSIGNABILITY. Neither party hereto shall have the right to assign this Agreement without the prior written consent of the other party. The Artist shall, however, retain the right to assign monies due to him or her under the terms of this Agreement.

16. HEIRS AND ASSIGNS. This Agreement shall be binding upon the parties hereto, their heirs, successors, assigns and personal representatives, and references to the Artist and the Renter shall include their heirs, successors, assigns and personal representatives.

17. INTEGRATION. This Agreement constitutes the entire understanding between the parties. Its terms can be modified only by an instrument in writing signed by both parties.

18. WAIVERS. A waiver of any breach of any of the provisions of this Agreement shall not be construed as a continuing waiver of other breaches of the same or other provisions hereof.

19. NOTICES AND CHANGES OF ADDRESS. All notices shall be sent to the Artist at the following address: _____
and to the Renter at the following address: _____
Each party shall give written notification of any change of address prior to the date of said change.

20. GOVERNING LAW. This Agreement shall be governed by the laws of the State of _____ .

Artist: _____   Renter: _____

Schedule of art works

Title	Medium	Size	Rental Fee	Sale Price
1.				
2.				
3.				
4.				
5. (etc.)				

Chapter 11

Original art:

ownership, insurance, submissions and resale proceeds

Of course the artist owns whatever original art he or she creates, subject to the discussion of work for hire on pages 23–26. This art owned by the artist must be protected against unintentional transfers when reproduction rights are sold as well as against loss, damage or theft. When submitted either for the purpose of selling the original art or reproduction rights in that art, the submission form must provide for the safe return of the art.

As discussed in Chapters 6 and 7, moral rights connect the artist to original art after sale. Likewise France and other countries give the artist a right to share in the proceeds from certain sales of art. California has used this concept as the basis to enact an art resale proceeds right which gives artists a right to share in profitable resales of the art.

Needless to say, issues pertaining to original art are discussed throughout this book. However, this chapter focuses on certain unique or novel issues of significance to the artist.

Ownership when selling rights

California, New York and Oregon have now enacted statutes to protect the artist's ownership of original art when reproduction rights are being sold. This addresses the problem of a client who buys reproduction rights but also believes the original art is being sold without an additional fee. In such situations the requirement that any sale of the original art must be written means that the parties will have to discuss this issue and reach agreement about it. This is especially important in view of the fact that the client making reproductions is in possession of the art. In states without such laws, the artist might be found to have sold the art by an oral or implied contract.

The California and Oregon laws also resolve any ambiguity as to what reproduction rights are transferred in favor of the artist. I originally drafted this bill for presentation to the National Conference of State Legislatures. The support of the Graphic Artists Guild and the American Society of Magazine Photographers was crucial to the enactment of the laws. The California law reads as follows:

> 988. Ownership of physical work of art; reservation upon conveyance of other ownership rights; resolution of ambiguity (a) For the purpose of this section: (1) The term "artist" means the creator of a work of art. (2) The term "work of art" means any work of visual or graphic art of any media including, but not limited to, a painting, print, drawing, sculpture, craft, photograph, or film. (b) Whenever an exclusive or nonexclusive conveyance of any right to reproduce, prepare derivative works based on, distribute copies of, publicly perform, or publicly display a work of art is made by or on behalf of the artist who created it or the owner at the time of the conveyance, ownership of the physical work of art shall remain with and be reserved to the artist or owner, as the case may be, unless such right of ownership is expressly transferred by an instrument, note, memorandum, or other writing, signed by the artist, the owner, or their duly authorized agent. (c) Whenever an exclusive or nonexclusive conveyance of any right to reproduce, prepare derivative works based on, distribute copies of, publicly perform, or publicly display a work of art is made by or on behalf of the artist who created it or the owner at the time of the con-

veyance, any ambiguity with respect to the nature or extent of the rights conveyed shall be resolved in favor of the reservation of rights by the artist or owner, unless in any given case the federal copyright law provides to the contrary.

This law, which bolsters the protection for the artist provided by the copyright law, may well serve as a model for enactment in other states.

Ownership of negatives

Photographers will want to know about an unusual feature of the law relating to negatives. If the photographer works independently, of course, all rights in the works will belong to the photographer. If the photographer works for hire, the person hiring the photographer will own the copyright. This means that the photographer cannot sell or distribute any copies of those photographs without the permission of the copyright owner. But the photographer may be deemed to own the negatives, unless the photographer agrees otherwise. The photographer becomes, in essence, a warehouse, storing negatives to meet later requests for photographs from those who originally hired the photographer.

The rule may have ramifications for fine artists who employ photographers to make a photographic record of work. For example, the photographer Paul Juley was hired by portrait artist Everett Raymond Kinstler to photographer Kinstler's paintings. After Juley's death, an issue arose as to the ownership of the negatives which Juley had retained. Kinstler said Juley had orally agreed that the negatives belonged to Kinstler and Juley kept the negatives only for convenience. Juley, however, had bequeathed the negatives with the rest of his work to the Smithsonian Institution. Kinstler, presumably barred by rules of evidence from giving self-serving testimony regarding a contract with a man no longer living, found that the general rule applied giving ownership of the negatives to the photographer. So the negatives today belong to the Smithsonian Institution. Part of the moral is, again, to use written agreements.

Insurance and risks of loss

The artist may wish to insure original art in order to receive insurance proceeds in the event of its loss or destruction. The artist should seek an agent who is familiar with insuring art works. Such insurance may cover only works in the artist's studio or may extend to cover works in transit. Valuation can be difficult with art works, and the artist might even have to incur the extra expenses of an appraisal. The fact that an insurance company has the artist pay premiums based on a certain valuation of the art does not necessarily mean the company will not dispute the value in the event of a claim. Inquiry should be made of the agent regarding this issue. It should be ascertained whether certain risks are excluded from coverage, such as losses caused by war, film processing or mysterious disappearances. Also, once the artist has insurance, exact records as to the art subject to the insurance become crucial in order to document claims. If the artist's premises or work may be dangerous, the artist should consider liability coverage to pay for accidents on the premises or caused by the work.

If the artist has no insurance and the work is damaged or stolen while in the artist's studio, the artist will simply have lost the work. But if the artist has sold the work, when does the risk of loss pass to the purchaser? The general rule is that if a work must be shipped, the risk of loss passes to a purchaser upon delivery. Thus the artist would normally bear the risk of loss while the work was being shipped to a purchaser. However, if the purchaser buys the work at the artist's studio and leaves the work to be picked up later, the risk of loss will have passed to the purchaser. This is because a sale by a nonmerchant seller under the Uniform Commercial Code passed the risk of loss to the purchaser after such notification as would allow the purchaser a reasonable opportunity to pick up the work. For example, when a bronze sculpture was sold along with the contents of a house, it was not reasonable to expect the purchaser to take possession of the sculpture within twenty-four hours of being given the keys. The risk of loss remained on the seller, but might have shifted to the purchaser if the purchaser had a longer period in which to pick up the sculpture. The contract of sale offers the artist an opportunity either to shift any risk of loss to the purchaser or to provide for insurance on the works sold.

Bailments

A bailment is a situation in which one person gives his or her lawfully owned property to be held by another person. For example, an artist might lend a work to a museum, leave a painting for framing, drop off a portfolio at an advertising agency or leave film to be developed at a film lab. In all of these relationships, when both parties benefit from the bailment, the bailee (the person who takes the artist's property) must exercise reasonable care in safeguarding the work. If that person is negligent and the work is damaged or lost, the artist (as the bailor) will recover damages. Even if the work has no easily ascertainable market value, damages would still be awarded based on the intrinsic value of the work to the artist.

However, the reasonable standard of care required in a bailment can be changed by contract. Often, for example, film labs will require an artist to sign a receipt which limits the liability of the lab to the cost of replacing film which is ruined. This is so despite the great value which may exist in the images recorded on the film. Similarly, a museum, a framemaker, an advertising agency and so on might seek to limit liability, perhaps to the extent of requiring the artist to sign a contract under which the artist would assume all risks of injury to the work. The artist should seek just the opposite—that is, to have the other party agree to act as an insurer of the work. This would mean that the other party would be liable if the work were damaged for any reason, even though reasonable care might have been exercised in safeguarding the work. Even if the artist signs a limitation on the liability of a lab or other bailee, the artist should document how any loss occurs. If the bailee is extraordinarily negligent, it may be that the limitation will be invalid. At least, the language of the limitation should be closely examined before the artist de-

cides whether or not to make a claim.

A technical issue which arises is whether all of the artist's bailments are for mutual benefit or whether certain bailments would either be for the sole benefit of the bailor or the sole benefit of the bailee. If the bailment is for the sole benefit of the bailor, the bailee will only be liable for gross negligence. If the bailment is for the sole benefit of the bailee, the bailee can be liable even though reasonable care is taken with the goods. A bailment for mutual benefit will usually be found when the bailee takes possession of the goods as an incident to the bailee's business, even if no consideration is received.

Submission/holding forms

Rather than relying on the law pertaining to bailments, artists may wish to protect their art by use of a submission/holding form.

ASMP, for example, has developed a delivery memo for its members to have signed by the recipient of photographic positives or transparencies. The contract provides for the recipient to have the liability of an insurer as to submitted materials while either in the recipient's possession or in transit. Other provisions require the recipient: to make any objections to the terms of the delivery memo within ten days; to pay a fee for the recipient's keeping materials beyond fourteen days; not to use the materials without an invoice transferring rights in the work; to pay a specified amount per transparency in the event of loss or damage (often set at $1,500 per transparency); not to project any transparencies; and to submit to arbitration. The setting of damages in advance is a frequent practice to avoid the necessity of extensive proofs to establish proper damages at trial. The courts will normally enforce such provisions for damages, known as liquidated damages, as long as damages would be difficult to establish and the amount specified is not unreasonable or a penalty. Rather than using $1,500 as a standard minimum figure, it might be wise to list a value for each photograph. This will avoid any risk that a court might conclude the $1,500 figure to be excessive as to some transparencies.

In any case, other artists might well wish to follow the lead of ASMP whenever work leaves their hands. Certainly, however, the artist entering into a bailment relationship should avoid a contract which lowers the reasonable care usually required to safeguard the artist's work.

Model submission/ holding form

This model form can be adopted by any artist for use when work is to be submitted to and held by a client.

Model holding/submission form

Artist's Letterhead
Date:

Client's name:
    address:
Art enclosed   Value
(Describe by subject and type of art)
1.
2.
3.
4.
5.
6.
7.
8.
9.
10.
Subject to all terms and conditions on reverse side

(Model Holding/Submission Form—reverse side)

Terms and Conditions

The submitted art is original and protected under the copyright law of the United States. This art is submitted to the client in confidence and subject to the following terms and conditions:

1. ACCEPTANCE. Client accepts the listing and value of art submitted as accurate if not objected to in writing by immediate return mail. Any terms of this form not objected in writing within 10 days shall be deemed accepted.

2. COPYRIGHT. Client agrees not to copy or modify directly or indirectly any of the art submitted, nor will client permit any third party to do any of the foregoing. Reproduction shall be allowed only upon Artist's written permission specifying usage and fees.

3. RETURN OF ART. Client agrees to assume responsibility for loss, theft or damage to the art while held by Client. Client further agrees to return all art by bonded messenger, air freight or registered mail. Reimbursement for loss, theft or damage to each piece of art shall be in the amount of the value entered for that piece. Both Client and Artist agree the specified values represent the value of the art.

4. HOLDING FEES. Art held beyond _____ days incurs the following daily holding fees: (Enter the holding fees for each piece art of for the categories of art submitted.)

5. Client and Artist agree to submit all disputes hereunder in excess of $ _____ (Enter the maximum amount which can be sued on in Small Claims Court, since this is usually the quickest remedy.) to arbitration in _____ (Enter the Artist's city and state.) under the rule of the American Arbitration Association. The arbitrator's award shall be final and judgment may be entered on it in any court having jurisdiction thereof.

ACCEPTED FOR CLIENT

Company Name
By: _____
    Authorized Signature

    Name and Title

Droit de suite

The artist who sells original art seldom benefits from appreciation of the art in the future. Because of this, in 1920, France created the *droit de suite,* a right of artists to share in the proceeds from sales of their work. The legislation was prompted in part by a Forain drawing showing two children dressed in rags looking into an expensive auction salesroom and saying, "Look! They're selling one of daddy's paintings."

The measure, later incorporated in the copyright provisions under the law of March 11, 1957, was a response to the stereotyped image of the artist living in penury while works created earlier sold for higher and higher prices. The *droit de suite* lasts for a term of the life of the artist plus another fifty years, during which time the proceeds benefit the artist's spouse and heirs. The *droit de suite* applies to original works when sold either at public auction or through a dealer, although the extension of the *droit de suite* to dealers by the law of March 11, 1957, appears not to have been followed or enforced. The *droit de suite* is collected when the price is over 10,000 francs. The rate is 3 percent upon the total sales price, not merely the profit of the seller. Artists utilize *S.P.A.D.E.M. (Société de la Propriété Artistique, des Dessins et Modèles),* an organization like ASCAP, to collect proceeds due under the *droit de suite.* *S.P.A.D.E.M.,* by reciprocal agreements with similar organizations, also receives proceeds due its artists from sales of work in Belgium and West Germany.

The *droit de suite* is payable to a foreign artist if a French artist could collect a similar payment in the country of the foreign artist. Despite some commentary to suggest that United States artists should be able to collect the *droit de suite* in France because the United States has signed the Universal Copyright convention, it appears that United States artists are not entitled to the *droit de suite* because the United States offers no such right to foreign artists. Foreign artists can collect the French *droit de suite* in any case if such artists have resided in France for five years, not necessarily consecutively, and have contributed to the French life of the arts. This survey covers only the French law, of course, and the laws of other countries with rights similar to the *droit de suite* can vary significantly. A right to such proceeds exists in some form in countries as diverse as Belgium, Italy, Poland, Uruguay, Turkey, West Germany, Portugal, Tunisia, Chile and Luxembourg.

Resale proceeds right

The French *droit de suite* has at least been discussed for the United States under the designation of a resale proceeds right. Such a right would require the payment back to the artist of a certain percentage of either proceeds or profits from subsequent sales of the artist's work.

California has taken the lead in this area by enacting a 5 percent resale proceeds right for artists. Whenever an original painting, sculpture, drawing or original work of art on glass is sold in California or sold anywhere by a seller who resides in California, the artist must be paid 5 percent of the gross sale price within ninety days of the sale. This right may not be waived by the artist, although a percentage higher than 5 percent may be used. For this provision to apply, however, the sale must be for a profit and the price must be more than $1,000. Also, the artist must be either a citizen of the United States or a two-year resident of California at the time of the resale. The sale must take place during the artist's life or within twenty years after the artist's death if the artist dies after January 1, 1983. The law excludes from coverage a resale by an art dealer to a purchaser for a period of 10 years after the initial sale by the artist to the dealer. This would also exclude intervening resales between dealers. Also, stained glass incorporated in a building is not considered resold when the building is sold.

Monies due the artist for resale proceeds are protected from the dealer's creditors. If the seller cannot locate the artist within ninety days to make payment, the proceeds are deposited with the California Arts Council. After seven years, if the council has been unable to locate the artist, the proceeds are used to acquire fine art for the Art in Public Buildings program. The law took effect on January 1, 1977, and applies to works sold after that date regardless of when the works were created or first sold. If the seller does not make payment, the artist has the right to bring suit for damages within three years after the date of sale or one year after discovery of the sale, whichever period is longer. The winning party in any suit is entitled to reasonable attorney's fees as determined by the court.

Challenge to resale rights

When the California law was enacted, many people wondered if it might be unconstitutional. A number of theories were put forward by those opposed to the law as to why it might be invalid. A dealer sold two paintings subject to the provisions of the law and then brought a lawsuit challenging the law's constitutionality. He argued that the law: (1) is pre-empted by the copyright law; (2) violates due process; and (3) violates the contracts clause of the Constitution.

The federal district court rejected these assertions and found the law to be valid, stating:

> Not only does the California law not significantly impair any federal interest, but it is the very type of innovative lawmaking that our federalist system is designed to encourage. The California legislature has evidently felt that a need exists to offer further encouragement to and economic protection of artists. That is a decision which the courts shall not lightly reverse. An important index of the moral and cultural strength of a people is their official attitude towards, and nurturing of, a free and vital community of artists. The California Resale Royalties Act may be a small positive step in such a direction. (*Morseburg v. Balyon,* 201 U.S.P.Q.518, *aff'd* 621 F.2d 972, *cert. denied* 449 U.S. 983)

Resale rights contracts

The other approach to an art proceeds right has been by private contract. If an artist and collector agree for a payment back to the artist upon subsequent resales, the artist would be able to gain by private bargaining what French artists possess by national legislation. But the Projansky contract, which provides for such an art proceeds right as well as attempting to create moral rights for United States artists, is not yet widely used. The Projansky contract appears on page 76.

Chapter 12

Unique art and limited editions

The pricing of art has none of the abstract purity of supply and demand curves intersecting on a graph. Factors such as aesthetic impact, the reputations of the artist and art dealer, vogue and general market conditions, all influence an often mystifying process of which price is the end product. Even when artists have evolved apparently unmarketable art, dealers have adeptly priced this art (or art object surrogates, such as conceptualist documentation) for sale to equally receptive collectors. From Marcel Duchamp's readymades to Lawrence Weiner's words which have no specific tangible form, the market has absorbed every manner of art object and even the absence of such an object. When Ian Wilson's discussions are sold, the collector is given a paper indicating that a discussion in fact took place on a certain date. And a word piece by Weiner will, at the collector's request, be accompanied by a letter placing the piece within the collector's responsibility.

Scarcity and price

Scarcity, however, is a crucial determinant of price and affects even a marketplace open to innovation. Scarcity, in the present context, is the limited quantity of a work offered for sale. A unique work (one of a kind) is the ultimate in scarcity and, in terms of salability, is preferable to a work that is not unique (even if it is one of a very small number). Traditionally, editions of fine prints and sculpture castings have resolved issues relating to scarcity with a simple and accepted marking system - 1/8, 2/8, 3/8 and so on. These markings are a device of the law, a method of promising the collector that only a limited number of prints or castings have been made. But this system is inadequate to deal with the issues relating to uniqueness posed by much contemporary art.

Ideally, one might imagine an equation that would elucidate all issues relating to price:

$$A^2 + U = V$$
A = assimilation
   into the art context
U = uniqueness
V = value

This equation implies that A is of greater importance than U in determining V. But, in fact, recent art movements have made uniqueness an especially problematic marketing factor. Andy Warhol can exactly duplicate a Brillo box or Campbell Soup can. Dan Flavin can repeat an arrangement of standard, commercially produced florescent lights as many times as he wishes. Dennis Oppenheim's photographic documentation of *Cancelled Crop* or his other earthwork projects can be reproduced in unlimited quantity.

Yet, for the collector, limitation is an important factor in valuing work for purchase. It is intriguing to speculate whether collectors would care about scarcity if art could not be bought and sold, since uniqueness should have no bearing on esthetic appreciation. If, for example, five collectors owned an identical work which each collector believed unique, would enjoyment of the work diminish upon learning of the existence of the other copies? In fact, even collectors who knew their work existed in a small number of copies were upset when faced with another collector's copy of the work. The relationship between a collector and his art can be as intense, and irrational, as sexual jealousy.

Of course, duplication of art has always been possible in varying degrees, although the idea that paint on canvas necessarily produces uniqueness is still a popular myth. Robert Rauschenberg's *Factum I* and *Factum II*, two nearly identical abstract paintings, were probably prompted in part by a desire to demythify and deromanticize (as to Abstract Expressionism specifically) the uniqueness of paint on canvas. The Photo Realists could, if they wished to take the time, reproduce work in paint on canvas as closely as one photograph can duplicate another.

The issue of uniqueness

Uniqueness is not a new issue, therefore, but rather one which has assumed far greater importance and subtlety with recent art developments. Sol LeWitt, for example, can produce two unique works that appear identical. His intention in creating the work resides in his choice of materials, wood for one work and metal for the other. As LeWitt states in *Sentences on Conceptual Art,* "If an artist uses the same form in a group of works and changes the material, one would assume the artist's concept involved the material."

But a variation in materials would not create unique works if the artist's intention were directed toward a different kind of content. Lawrence Weiner is concerned with the communicative content expressed by his word pieces, so for him a unique object is unimportant. Regardless of variation in the materials, size or even the medium of expression, there is no unique object - only a single unique content. But the artist's intention toward the work may not always involve the issue of uniqueness. An artist working with narrative, for example, Peter Hutchinson whose work includes the *Alphabet* series, is concerned with appearence as well as written content. Is a new visual content, such as taking a color photograph and reproducing it in a smaller black and white version, going to create a new unique work when the written content remains unchanged? Endless variations of media, material, size, color, arrangement and the number of objects composing a piece are possible. Especially when photographs or other easily duplicated materials are used, and when content is the central issue, both the artist and collector may wonder whether a version changed in form is unique. This is directly in conflict with formalistic painting, in which a change in a single brush stroke or color makes a new unique work.

The artist's intent

Nor can the artist's concept of what is unique solely govern the matter. It might be contended that any legal definition of uniqueness should conform to the artist's intent or the opinion of experts such as art historians and critics. But a court determining the uniqueness of a work would consider statements by an artist or experts as merely factors in reaching a decision. Constantin Brancusi's statement that his *Bird in Space* was an art work (which could be brought duty free into the United States) did not dispose of that lawsuit, although an enlightened decision ultimately did find the *Bird in Space* a "pleasing to look at and highly ornamental" art work rather than dutiable scrap metal. A legal determination of an art issue can vary considerably from the consensus of art opinion, even in those cases in which a consensus could be obtained. As Hilton Kramer stated, after testifying as an expert in a flag desecration case involving art protesting the Vietnam war, "Suddenly complicated questions of aesthetic intention and artistic realization . . . were cast into an alien legalistic vocabulary that precluded the very possibility of a serious answer."

Warranty of uniqueness

Trust between the artist, dealer and collector usually will make uniqueness the art issue which it should be. If the work is one of several identical pieces, the artist will indicate this by the traditional designation - 1/3, 2/3, 3/3. This numbering, in legal terms, is a warranty as discussed on pages 66 – 67. In any sale, a warranty is an express or implied fact upon which a purchaser can rely. The artist can create a warranty by a marking such as 1/5, a writing or even a verbal statement. If a collector requests reassurance that a work is unique, the artist's statement is a warranty upon which the collector can rely. Dan Flavin puts warranties to a significant use by signing a certificate which must accompany the components to make them into a work of art (a drawing showing the arrangement of the components is also provided). This protects collectors, since it removes any incentive for copying of Flavin's work by persons who might simply purchase and arrange the components after seeing an exhibition. Jan Dibbets warrants that the negatives for his work will be held at the Stedelijk Museum so that print replacements can be made in the event of any fading of color.

The uniqueness warranty is a valuable device if the nature of the work would easily permit duplication. It reaffirms the trust which the collector must give the artist. But the warranty is perhaps most useful if a changed version might be argued by the collector to be merely a copy, despite the artist's belief each version is unique. The artist should not have to risk legal penalties if a court at some future time were to disagree with the artist's aesthetic evaluation as to uniqueness. Here the artist can, simultaneously with the giving of the warranty, disclose the basis of one work's uniqueness (for example, a change in materials) in relation to other unique works. This essentially offers the artist the opportunity to fix his or her aesthetic evaluation into the legal matrix of the transaction.

Uniqueness in art is hardly a new issue, but it is an issue which has assumed greater significance with the reproducible nature of the art of recent movements. Ideally, the sensibility and intention of the artist should control the issue of whether a work is unique. Thus, the collector must have a clear understanding of the artist's intention. The artist's warranty, coupled with a disclosure of similar works which the artist considers unique, will enable a collector to make an informed decision in an atmosphere of mutual trust. And, by a legal mechanism, uniqueness will remain the art issue which it should be, instead of becoming the legal issue which it should not be.

Fine prints

Fine prints have offered an opportunity for people of moderate means to enjoy art which is original but not unique. The growing enthusiasm for fine prints has been remarkable. To avoid unethical selling practices as a wider public began to purchase fine prints, California, New York, Illinois, Arkansas, Hawaii and Maryland each enacted legislation governing the sale of fine prints. In addition to having familiarity with this legislation, the artist must also be able to negotiate the contracts necessary for the publication of fine prints.

California legislation

In 1971 California became the first state to enact legislation regulating the sale of fine prints. This statute was extensively amended in 1982, including extending its coverage to multiples other than fine prints. The statute starts by defining fine art multiple, fine print, master, artist, signed, unsigned, art dealer, limited edition, proofs, written instrument and person. A fine art multiple is ". . . any fine print, photograph (positive or negative), sculpture cast, collage or similar art object produced in more than one copy."

The statute limits its application to any sale of a multiple for a price of $100 or more, exclusive of the cost of framing. When an art dealer sells such a multiple in California, a written instrument must be provided to the purchaser (or intermediate seller, in the case of a consignment) which sets forth certain information regarding the multiple. An artist, although not otherwise considered an art dealer, must also provide this information whether selling or consigning a multiple. If the artist does this, he or she will not be liable to the final purchaser of the multiple. This information includes the name of the artist, whether the artist signed the multiple, a description of the process by which the multiple was produced, whether the artist was deceased at the time the master image was created or the multiple was produced, whether there have been prior editions and in what quantity, the date of production, the total size of a limited edition (including how many multiples are signed, unsigned, numbered or unnumbered and whether proofs exist) and whether the master has been cancelled after the current edition. The requirements vary depending on whether the multiple was produced before 1900, from 1900 to 1949 or from 1950 to the present. In giving the name of the artist (for years after 1949) and the other information, the art merchant is held to have created express warranties on which the purchaser may rely.

An art dealer regularly engaged in the sale of multiples must conspicuously post the following sign: "California law provides for the disclosure in writing of certain information concerning prints, photographs, and sculpture costs. This information is available to you, and you may request to receive it prior to purchase." A dealer may disclaim knowledge of any required information, but such a disclaimer must be specific as to what is being disclaimed. Also, the dealer may still be liable if reasonable inquiries would have produced the required information. A charitable organization selling multiples may post a sign disclaiming knowledge of the required information (and include such a disclaimer in any catalog for the sale or auction). In such a case, the charitable organization would not have to provide the required information, unless it used an art dealer as its selling agent.

The penalties for violating the law may include refunding the cost of the multiple plus interest (if the multiple is returned to the dealer), damages of triple the cost of the multiple if the violition is willful and damages or other available remedies. If the purchaser wins, he or she may receive court costs together with reasonable attorney's and expert witnesses' fees. However, if the court determines the purchaser started the lawsuit in bad faith, it may award expenses to the dealer. Injunctions may be obtained by private purchasers or law enforcement officials to prevent violations of the multiples law.

New York legislation

New York originally enacted legislation in 1975 to prevent deceptive acts in the sale of fine prints and posters. The legislation took a different structure, however, from that previously enacted by California and Illinois. The New York law defines a fine print as "an impression produced by a printing method in more than one copy from an image or design created by an artist and includes impressions produced by or from such printing methods as engraving, etching, woodcutting, lithography, serigraphy and similar printing methods." Artist and plate are defined. Signed print is defined as "a fine print which has been signed by the artist's own hand, and not by any mechanical means of reproduction, after it has been printed." The law applies to all prints sold after January 1, 1976, regardless of when printed.

The law provides that no fine print

shall be described in writing as signed unless the print meets the law's definition of signed. Also, it is unlawful to sell prints altered from the image originally on the plate, unless such alteration is conspicuously disclosed. A purchaser does not have to show a knowing violation of the law to recover, but the seller can prove lack of knowledge as a defense. The purchaser is entitled to have the transaction rescinded and is not stopped from seeking any other damages which can be recovered.

In 1982 New York enacted an additional law governing visual art multiples which include "prints, photographs (positive or negative) and similar art objects produced in more than one copy and sold, offered for sale or consigned in, into or from this state for an amount in excess of one hundred dollars exclusive of any frame." In structure, this new law is similar to California's. Certain information must be disclosed or specifically disclaimed by art merchants selling multiples. The purchaser may generally rely on these disclosures as express warranties. Violations may be enjoined or be the basis for damages (including triple damages) and the award of court costs and reasonable fees for attorneys and expert witnesses.

Contracts for Fine Prints

Contracts for fine prints can vary greatly with the particular situation of the artist. First, the fine prints must be printed. The artist may undertake this, either personally or by contracting with a printer, and then either sell the fine prints directly to purchasers or enter into a distribution agreement with a gallery. Alternatively, the gallery, as a publisher, may agree with the artist for the creation of one or more editions of the prints, which the gallery would finance and distribute.

If the artist must use a printer, the artist should ensure that the printer's work will satisfy the artist. The best way to accomplish this is to specify materials and methods for the printing as well as to require the artist's approval at various stages of the printing process. Once the artist has the fine prints, sales can be made either directly to purchasers or through a gallery. If sales are made directly, the artist should review Chapter 10 on sales of art works, since the same considerations apply. If a gallery is to act as the artist's agent, the artist should consult Chapter 13 as to sales by galleries.

The gallery might, however, act as publisher as well as distributor of the edition or editions of fine prints, as in the sample agreement shown on page 96. Now the gallery is paying the costs of producing the fine prints and will want certain concessions from the artist. The degree to which the artist meets the gallery's demands will of course depend on the bargaining strength of the two parties.

The gallery's most extreme demand would be to own all rights in the fine prints. This would include ownership of the fine prints, ownership of the plate or other image used for the printing and ownership of the copyright. The artist would receive a flat fee and artist's proofs, but would not receive income from sales of the fine prints by the gallery.

The artist should bargain for an arrangement in which the artist owns the prints which are held by the gallery on consignment. Because the gallery has paid the costs of making the prints, however, the gallery might demand that these costs be deducted from sales receipts prior to any payments to the artist. If the gallery and the artist split sales receipts on an equal basis, the artist would receive 50 percent of sales receipts after subtraction of production costs. The artist might not agree to the subtraction of such costs or might demand a higher percentage than 50 percent. Any advance of money to the artist against future receipts from sales should be stated to be nonrefundable.

Both the gallery and the artist will want to agree regarding the size limits of each edition, the number of prints to be kept by the artist, the number to be consigned to the gallery, and whether the prints will be signed. The artist should usually seek a short term for the contract, perhaps one year, with a provision for the equal division of all unsold prints consigned to the gallery at the end of the contract's term. If the gallery defaults under the contract, all the prints should be returned to the artist. The artist should remain the owner of all prints, and title should pass directly from the artist to any purchaser.

The price at which the gallery will sell the prints should be specified, but the artist should resist any effort to set the same price for sales of the prints owned by the artist. If the contract will cover more than one edition, a schedule can be annexed at the end of the contract to provide the additional creations. The artist should, however, remain free to create competing prints without offering the gallery any option rights to such prints. If the gallery insists on such exclusivity, of course, the artist may have to make concessions to this regard.

The artist should be willing to warrant the originality of the prints. By this same token, the artist should have full artistic control over production. If the gallery is to choose the printer, the artist should insist on the right to approve the gallery's choice. The artist should not agree to any provisions subjecting the prints to the approval or satisfaction of the gallery. The artist should retain the copyright, and copyright notice in the artist's name should be placed on the prints. The printer should be required to give the artist certification of the cancellation of the plate or other image.

The remaining considerations in sales of prints through galleries are basically the same as with sales of any art work. Provision must be made for periodic accountings and payments, inspection of the gallery's books, insurance, responsibility for loss, termination and the other terms fully discussed in Chapter 13.

Print documentation

The artist will desire - and may be required by state law - to provide documentation regarding the process by which the prints were created. The excellent Print Documentation given by Gemini G.E.L. is shown on pages 97 – 98. The Gemini Print Terminology appears on the back of the print documentation form. This form, when properly completed, satisfies the disclosure of informational details required under the present California law discussed on pages 93 – 94. It is published here by permission of Gemini G.E.L., Los Angeles.

Print contract with gallery

Dear Artist:

   This letter is to be the agreement between you and Pisces Gallery regarding the publication of a suite of six of your woodcuts of fish in paper size 9 ½" x 13". The works selected are as follows: sunfish, trout, eel, bass, carp and whale. You shall create one hundred (100) impressions of each woodcut, which are to be signed and numbered accordingly by you. You may print ten (10) additional proofs for your personal use, and these are to be signed as artist's proofs. You shall affix copyright notice in your name to all prints and all copyrights and rights of reproduction shall be retained by you upon sales to purchasers. You shall provide Pisces Gallery with certification of the cancellation of the blocks after completion of the printing.

   Pisces Gallery shall be solely responsible for and pay all costs of the printing. Pisces Gallery shall prepare the title page, descriptive material and justification page.

   Nonrefundable advances of $1,000 shall be paid to you upon delivery of each one hundred (100) prints. The minimum selling price of each suite shall be $500. Pisces Gallery shall exercise best efforts to sell the suites and shall receive 50 percent of all sales revenues as its commission. The balance due you, after subtraction of any advances paid to you, shall be remitted on the first day of each month along with an accounting showing the sale price and number of prints sold and the inventory of prints remaining. Title to all work shall remain in you and pass directly to purchasers. Pisces Gallery shall insure all work for at least the minimum sale price and any insurance proceeds shall be equally divided.

   The term of this agreement shall be one (1) year. After one (1) year, this agreement shall continue unless terminated upon either party giving sixty (60) days written notice of termination to the other party. Upon termination the inventory remaining shall be equally divided between Pisces Gallery and you. Your share shall be promptly delivered to you by Pisces Gallery. If, however, termination is based upon a breach or default by Pisces Gallery under this agreement, all inventory remaining shall be promptly delivered to you. You agree to sign such papers as may be necessary to effectuate this agreement.

   Kindly return one copy of this letter with your signature below.

Sincerely yours,

John Smith
President, Pisces Gallery

Consented and agreed to:

_____

Artist

GEMINI G.E.L.   PRINT DOCUMENTATION

8365 Melrose Avenue
Los Angeles California 90069
213 651-0513

Ⅱ

Artist ___ Jasper Johns
Title ___ Periscope II

Period of collaboration ___ October 1978 to September 1979
Standard date ___ October 26, 1978
Cancellation date ___
Date signed ___ September 10, 1979
Medium ___ 7 color lithograph
Size: H ___ 56¼" ___ W ___ 41" ___ Edge: ___ cut
Signature location ___ lower right
Processing and proofing ___ Serge Lozingot and Edward Henderson
Edition printing ___ Serge Lozingot and Chris Sukimoto

Collaboration and supervision ___ Serge Lozingot

Printing Sequence		Process or Printing Element		Additional Information
1	black	aluminum plate		tusche wash
2	black	"	"	" "
3	black	"	"	" "
4	transparent black	"	"	tusche
5	transparent black	"	"	"
6	transparent black	"	"	"
7	transparent black	"	"	"
8				
9				
10				
11				
12				

	No.	Paper
Edition	28	Arches 88
Artist's Proofs	4	" "
Trial Proofs	5	A (2) Kurotani
		B Arches 88
		C (2) Arches 88
Standard		
Right to Print Proof	1	Arches 88
Printer's Proof II	1	" "
Gemini Impressions	3	" "
Cancellation Proof		
Other Proofs		

We declare the above information is correct:

Artist _____ Date ___ September 18, 1979

Gemini G.E.L. _____ Date ___ Sept 17, 1979

GEMINI PRINT TERMINOLOGY

STANDARD

The first impression achieved in the proofing period which meets the aesthetic and technical approval of the artist and Gemini. The *Standard* is used as a guide for the production of the *Edition*. Sometimes the artist affects last minute changes during the final proofing stage, causing the *Standard* to differ slightly from the *Edition*. In this case, if this proof is no longer considered desirable by the artist, it is destroyed.

EDITION

The body of prints completed by using the *Standard* as guide. Two numbers are used in the signing procedure: the upper one is numbered consecutively beginning with 1 and indicates the number of that print within the *Edition;* the lower number indicates the total number of prints in the *Edition*.

ARTIST'S PROOF

A proof of good quality which closely matches or equals the standards of the *Edition* prints.

TRIAL PROOF

Generally, a proof which varies from the *Edition* in imagery, printing sequence, has added or deleted elements, or in some way the printing has differed from the *Edition*.

COLOR TRIAL PROOF

Generally, these proofs have the same printing elements as those in the *Edition*, but there may be a sequence which differs, or has been added or deleted as in the *Trial Proof,* or there may simply be a color variance. Both a *Trial Proof* and *Color Trial Proof* may have been pulled at any time during the proofing period or while the *Edition* is being printed. They are signed if the artist feels they have a desirable quality of uniqueness which gives them special merit. Occasionally, there is an overlap in intent between the *Trial Proof* and the *Color Trial Proof*.

WORKING PROOF

A print which has at least one printing element and upon which the artist has added work by hand.

PROGRESSIVE PROOF

A series of proofs primarily intended to illustrate the development of the image of the finished print. One set of *Progressives* shows each color or element singly. The other set shows the actual development of the completed print as each color or element is added, one by one.

STATE

The result of an artist developing a variance in a previously resolved print resulting in a complete *Edition* with accompanying proofs. The variance may involve a change in color, elements or printing sequence.

GEMINI IMPRESSIONS

Prints identical to the *Edition* pulled for exhibition purposes.

RIGHT TO PRINT

The presentation proof received by the printer with whom the artist collaborated on the project.

PRINTER'S PROOF II

The presentation proof received by the printer who completed the *Edition*.

CANCELLATION PROOF

To assure that no further proofs can be pulled from the printing element after the *Edition* has been printed, the printing element is cancelled by either the artist or printer. In the case of the lithograph, the printed image is fully inked and then defaced by the use of a sharp instrument or a stone hone. In the case of the screen print, a chemical substance is added to the stencil to effect the *Cancellation* mark, thereby preventing future use of that image. In both cases, one impression is pulled of the defaced element to document the act. This impression is signed and dated by the artist. When a print has more than one color, the most complicated and involved color plate is chosen for cancellation. The *Cancellation Proof* may or may not have the complete color printings. If the artist decides to print a particular image in an additional *State,* the *Cancellation Proof* would be pulled after all States have been printed.

SIGNING PROCEDURE

At the completion of the printing of the *Edition* and its proofs, the approved prints are then signed and numbered by the artist. In some cases, the artist may also inscribe the title and the date.

CHOP

Each signed print bears an embossed, dry stamped or printed form of the Gemini *Chop*. It is generally placed adjacent to the artist's signature and is accompanied by a copyright mark. Each *Edition* and its accompanying proofs has its own identifying number which is inscribed in pencil on the reverse side of the print adjacent to the *Chop*.

Chapter 13

Sales by galleries and agents

The artist will often seek professional assistance in selling work. Relationships with galleries and other agents can take numerous forms. Arrangements are often oral, although the artist should insist on written agreements whenever possible. This chapter details many of the considerations involved in such agreements, but the artist should, as always, consult a lawyer for individual advice when such agreements are being negotiated.

Consignment or sale

The usual agreements in the United States involve work consigned to a gallery which has either a limited agency to represent only that particular work or an exclusive agency to represent all the artist's work. The artist remains owner of the work, and the gallery receives a commission on sale or rental.

If agreements are informal and unwritten, questions can arise whether a work has been consigned or sold to a gallery. New York, California and a number of other states have enacted statutes providing that any fine art left with an art gallery or dealer is held on consignment in trust for the artist. Generally, any money from sales of such work is also held by the gallery in trust for the artist. Even if a consigned work is subsequently purchased by the gallery, the work remains trust property held for the artist until full payment has been made. Creditors of the gallery have no right to make claims against the work or funds held in trust for the artist, even if the artist's rights to the work or funds have not been protected from creditors by filings of the financing statements required under the Uniform Commerical Code. Any waiver of these favorable rights by the artist will be invalid. The New York statue does allow the artist to give up his or her rights to have sale proceeds considered trust funds. This applies only to sales proceeds greater than $2,500 per year. The waiver must be written and, in any case, will not apply to works initially on consignment which are purchased by the gallery. The California statue requires first payment of the trust funds to the artist unless the artist agrees otherwise in writing.

Other states with statutes governing consignments are Arizona, Arkansas, Colorado, Connecticut, Maryland, Massachusetts, Michigan, Minnesota, New Mexico, Oregon, Texas, Washington and Wisconsin. The artist must consider the wide variations in the specific coverage and provisions of these statutes. What types of art are covered, whether the art or funds created by the sale of the art are trust funds, whether any rights can be waived by the artist and whether the art and proceeds from sales are protected against the claims of creditors of the gallery are among the many issues on which the statues vary. To take one example, California defines the fine art protected under the law as including "a painting, sculpture, drawing, work of graphic art (including an etching, lithograph, offset print, silk screen, or a work of graphic art of like nature), a work of calligraphy, or a work in mixed media (including a college, assemblage, or any combination of the foregoing art media)" while the New York law protects "a printing, sculpture, drawing, work of graphic art, photograph or craft work in materials including, but not limited to clay, textile, paper, fiber, wood, tile, metal, plastic or glass." The best way to find out if a certain state has enacted such a law and, if so, the provisions of the law is to contact the state legislature or an attorney in that state.

Artists should take warning if their states do not have such statutes. Written consignment agreements are a necessity to protect the artist by showing the artist's ownership of the work. A simple consignment agreement, where the gallery's agency is only for the sale of a given work or works, would specify the gallery's receipt on consignment of certain works which would be listed by title, medium size, retail selling price and the gallery's commission percentage on each work. The agreement would also state when payment must be made to the artist and indicate that the artist remains owner of the work until title passes to a purchaser. The agreement should provide for the return of the work upon the artist's request. Also, it would be specified that the agreement was not a general agency and the artist would have no responsibility to pay commissions on works other than those consigned.

A simple consignment agreement appears on this page, but this agreement could encompass many more aspects of the relationship between the artist and dealer. The chapter will focus on agreements under which the gallery represents all or most of an artist's output over a period specified in the contract. But many of the provisions relevant to such representation agreements can be used in the simple consignment as dictated by the given transaction.

Model consignment agreement

Artist's Letterhead

Date:

Dear Sir:

You hereby confirm receipt on consignment of my art works as follows:

TITLE	MEDIUM	SIZE	RETAIL PRICE	COMMISSION
1.				
2.				
3.				
4.				
5.				

I reserve title to the works until sale, at which time title shall pass directly to the purchaser. You shall remit to me the retail price of each work less your commission within 30 days after sale. This consignment applies only to works consigned under this agreement and does not make you a general agent for any works not so consigned.

At any time before sale of the works you will return the works to me immediately upon my request.

Sincerely yours,

Artist

CONSENTED AND AGREED TO:

_____

XYZ Gallery

By: _____

The less common arrangement of outright purchase by the gallery might involve a situation in which the gallery would wish to be the exclusive seller of the artist's work. Alternatively, the gallery might require either a given portion of the artist's output or a right of first refusal on all work. The gallery might also want to fix the prices at which the artist could make private sales. The outright purchase arrangement is rare, however, and this chapter will concentrate on representation agreements where work is consigned in an ongoing relationship of representation between the artist and the gallery.

A model form of artist-gallery agreement appears on pages 106–107 and its provisions are referred to in order to illustrate points covered in the text. Several other model contracts exist that are of special interest to artists. These are the Model Form of Artist-Gallery Agreement drafted by the Lawyers for the Arts Committee, Young Lawyers Section, Philadelphia Bar Association, 423 City Hall Annex, Philadelphia, Pennsylvania 19107; the Minimum Artist-Dealer

Agreement drafted by Artists Equity Association, Inc., in Washington, D.C.; the Artist-Gallery Agreement drafted by the Bay Area Lawyers for the Arts, in San Francisco; and the Artist-Gallery Consignment Arrangement Agreement drafted by Artists Equity Association of New York, Inc., in New York City. Addresses for these organizations appear on page 2 and pages 193–195.

Parties to the agreement

When a gallery serves as agent for an artist, the representation agreement creates a bond of trust and an obligation of good faith dealing on the part of the gallery. Often the gallery will be required to exercise best efforts to sell the artist's work, although this clause is difficult to enforce. In addition to assurance of certainty that the gallery deals only for the artist's interest, the artist can also expect the gallery to maintain as confidential information about transactions executed for artist.

The artist will be especially reassured that the gallery will live up to this fiduciary role, however, when the artist personally knows and trusts the gallery personnel. The artist might well wish to provide for termination of the agreement in the event of the death of a trusted dealer, a change of personnel, a transfer of ownership of the gallery or even a change in the legal form of the gallery (see model agreement, Article 2). The model agreement also deals with this by prohibiting assignment by the gallery of the agreement (Article 12). The artist might also want to be certain that the location of the gallery would remain the same and, perhaps, that all art work consigned would be kept at that location.

The gallery may in turn request certain assurances of fair dealing by the artist. These might be in the form of warranties that the artist is the creator of the work and has title to the work.

Scope of the agency

The artist may choose, in a number of ways, to circumscribe the gallery's authority as agent.

The geographic extent of the agency could be limited to a single city or country instead of the entire world (model agreement, Article 1).

The duration of the contract should be limited and provision made for the return of work and costs of return at the end of the term (model agreement, Article 2). The artist should probably hesitate to enter into an agreement for more than two years, unless the contract provides the artist with a right of termination—for example, on 30 or 60 days notice (model agreement, Article 2). A shorter term could also be extended by options to renew.

The kinds of work which the agreement will cover is an important provision (model agreement, Article 1). The gallery may want to receive a commission even on work which the artist sells (model agreement, Article 4). If the gallery sells only the artist's paintings, it must be resolved whether the gallery will receive commissions on the artist's sales of work in other media, such as drawings or graphics. Also, will the gallery be entitled to a percentage when the artist is commissioned for a work (model agreement, Article 4), gives away a work either to a family member or to a charity or barters a work to pay dentist's or accountant's bills? The gallery may demand a right to a percentage when the artist sells work created before the agency relationship was established or after the agency terminates. One possible resolution would be to exempt a certain number of works or dollar value of sales by the artist from the requirement of the gallery's commission. This approach is particularly feasible where the artist is not located closely enough to the gallery to be competitive. Or the artist might simply wish to limit the proportion of output which the gallery would have a right to demand. This raises a related issue of the gallery's right to inspect the artist's studio to see work, but, in fact, the artist would normally welcome such interest on the part of the gallery.

Textile designers might seek the following special restrictions on the scope of the agency and the agent's right to employ or represent other designers:

The Agent agrees to represent no more than ___ designers.

The Agent agrees not to represent conflicting hands, such hands being designers who work in a similar style to that of the Designer.

The Agent agrees to have no designers as salaried employees.

The Agent agrees not to sell designs from his or her own collection of designs in competition with the Designer's work.

The Agent agrees to employ _____ full time and _____ part time salespeople.

Few contracts will provide for all the possible contingencies discussed, yet the artist must be aware of the different limitations which can be placed upon the gallery's authority as agent.

Exhibitions

The artist will want to be guaranteed an exhibition each year (model agreement, Article 3). The dates (during the exhibition season), duration, space and location of the exhibition should all be specified. Also, the costs of the opening, advertisements, catalogs, announcements, frames (and ownership of the frames after the exhibition), photographs of the work, shipping either to purchasers or for return to the artist, storage and any other costs should all be detailed as either the gallery's or the artist's responsibility (model agreement, Article 3). The artist may demand a specific budget, especially for publicity and advertising. The artist should avoid any situation where the gallery might later seek to place a lien on the work, perhaps refusing to return it, for costs incurred under the agreement. The artist may also wish a specific provision ensuring the confidentiality of the artist's personal mailing list. However, consent will usually have to be made to use the artist's name, biography and picture in the publicizing of the exhibition. The artist might also wish the gallery to use best efforts in seeking museum exhibitions for the artist. In return, the gallery might request complimentary credit on any loan by

the artist to museums or in any magazine articles displaying the artist's work.

Another important consideration in exhibitions is artistic control (model agreement, Article 3). The artist will wish to avoid inclusion in a group exhibition without the power to prevent inappropriate work being shown in the same exhibition. Also, the artist should control the choice of work in either a solo or group exhibition. At the same time, the protection of the artist's reputation may require control over the publicity and advertising relating to the exhibition. An extreme form of control would be the power to prevent any given purchaser from buying a work. Or the artist might simply insist by an appropriate clause in the representation agreement that a contract specified by the artist (such as the Projansky contract) be used for all sales.

Gallery's commission

There are two ways in which a gallery may take compensation upon the sale of consigned work. The net price method specifies an amount—for example, $1,000—which will be paid to the artist in the event of sale. The gallery may then sell the work at any price, $1,500 or $4,000, and pay the artist the $1,000 originally agreed upon. The net price method is not common, especially if the artist lacks control over the gallery's selling price, because of its possible unfairness.

The commission method, in which the gallery takes a percentage of the sale price, is much more common (model agreement, Article 4). The percentage varies greatly, but 25 percent to 50 percent would be the usual limits of the range. A relatively high commission rate may be justified by the gallery's expenses and effort on behalf of an artist, such as extensive promotion, travel abroad to sell work and expensive gallery installations. Each situation must be evaluated on its own special facts.

If the gallery's commission is 33 percent, a sale of a $3,000 work will yield the artist $2,000. One risk the artist faces here is the computation of the value to be assigned a given work where a global invoice—that is, an invoice including many works—is used. If ten paintings are sold for $20,000, the artist who owned one of the works may find the value assigned that work—$1,000 or $2,000 or $3,000—is arbitrary. The artist can prevent this problem from arising by specifying a sale price in advance.

The artist whose work is expensive to construct might request that the cost of materials be subtracted from the sale price before commission of the gallery is taken. Or the artist might request different commission rates for works done in different media. A sliding scale based on the amount of sales would be another possible commission arrangement. Also, the problem of double commissions, where one gallery consigns a work to a second gallery, must be resolved.

The right of the gallery to rent work will be determined by the agreement. If this is permitted, a commission rate against such rental income must be specified. Also, the agreement will then need certain additional articles detailing rental rates, copying restrictions and, especially, insurance. The representation agreement should also indicate whether the gallery will receive commission on lecture fees, copyright royalties or other similar income received by the artist.

Pricing

Both gallery and artist will generally wish to control prices (see model agreement, Article 5). The gallery may wish to sell more cheaply to maintain a volume of sales, while the artist may wish to keep prices higher for the enhancement of reputation which accompanies steadily rising values for an artist's work. Usually, prices are set by consultation between the artist and the gallery. The agreed-upon prices may then be set forth in a schedule attached to the agreement (model agreement, Record of Consignment). The agreement may well give the gallery the power to vary prices slightly—for example, 10 percent—for flexibility. Also, the agreement will have to provide for the discounts which are customarily given certain purchasers, such as museums. If the gallery has complete power to set prices, the artist should beware of sales at low prices to dummies—persons who seem to buy the work when, in reality, they are holding the work for the gallery to sell later at higher prices.

The artist may want to restrict the gallery as to the prices placed on works of the artist to be sold by the gallery for its own account or for other galleries or collectors. Also, if the gallery has the right to sell works at auction, the artist may wish the gallery to guarantee receipt of an acceptable fair market price at auction. If the gallery sells through other galleries, the artist should require that the other galleries maintain the prices set in the agreement with the original gallery.

Accounting

The artist will want the gallery to record on a regular basis all business transactions in books which the artist may inspect. Periodically, perhaps every three or six months, statements of account indicating sales, commissions and proceeds due the artist should be sent out by the gallery (model agreement, Article 7). The artist will wish to receive the names and addresses of all purchasers, which most galleries will be willing to provide. If the gallery objects, a compromise might be to have a list of purchasers held by a third party so the artist will not be cut off from the work, but the gallery will have its market protected.

Payments

The artist must feel confident that the gallery will meet payment obligations with reasonable promptness (model agreement, Article 6). The gallery may want corresponding assurances as to payments of commissions based on sales made by the artist. If credit is extended to a purchaser, the risk of loss should be the gallery's. The artist should be paid even if the purchaser defaults or, at least, have a right to the first proceeds received by the gallery from the purchaser (model agreement, Article 6). If the gallery has the right to accept works in payment for the artist's works sold, a fair method of valuation must be agreed upon. The respective percentages of the artist and gallery would then be applied to this valuation instead of a sales price. When work may be sold in foreign countries, the artist would be well advised to require payment in American dollars. A provision regarding losses due to delays in converting foreign currencies might also be included in the agreement.

Payments are sometimes made to artists in the form of a monthly stipend. This is an advance given by the gallery regardless of whether or not sales have been made. The artist should insist that such advances are nonrefundable. Often the gallery will have the right, if the advance is nonrefundable, to purchase at year end that amount of the artist's work which will pay off the artist's debt to the gallery. The artist must be certain that the work will be purchased at fair prices, such as the prices set forth in the model agreement's Record of Consignment. The gallery would receive a discount, of course, equal to its normal commission. But purchases of a substantial amount of an artist's work by a gallery can create an unfortunate tension in the relationship of trust between gallery and artist. While the gallery is an agent, bound to deal in good faith for the interest of the artist, the gallery may promote and sell its own inventory instead of those works the artist has given on consignment. The artist may find the gallery has become an alter ego, competing with the artist instead of remaining a loyal agent. But this risk will have to be balanced in each case with the advantages of the regular income provided by a monthly stipend.

Copyright

The artist should require that the gallery reserve all copyrights to the artist upon sale and also take steps to protect the artist's copyrights (model agreement, Article 11).

Creditors of the gallery

The statutes of New York, California and a number of other states (see page 99) protect the artist from claims by creditors of the gallery against works on consignment. Title to art is transferred directly from the artist to any purchaser. The funds received by the galley become trust funds and must be paid first to the artist regardless of creditors' claims.

The absence of such provisions in the laws of many states should alert artists to the complex legal entanglements that may occur if a gallery's creditors claim rights to consigned works after the gallery has become bankrupt. For this reason, the artist should try to establish the financial stability of any gallery prior to consigning works. However, an agreement might also provide for termination in the event the gallery's financial condition becomes untenable, as shown by bankruptcy, insolvency, as assignment of assets for the benefits of creditors, a lien or attachment against the gallery not vacated within reasonable time or appointment of a receiver or trustee for the gallery or its assets (model agreement, Article 2). The gallery would be required in such circumstances to return immediately all work as well as money held for the artist. The agreement might also specify that the work and any proceeds from sales would be held in trust for the artist and not subject to the claims of creditors of the gallery, but the legal efficacy of these provisions is questionable.

The Uniform Commercial Code provides that creditors have rights against consigned goods. These rights can be cut off if the person consigning the goods, such as an artist, complies with certain filing provisions to gain a secured interest in the consigned work. The filing of Uniform Commercial Code Form 1, discussed on page 74, is not difficult. Compliance with these provisions, however, is a problem for the artist who finds galleries rarely willing to agree to such a filing. This approach should certainly be considered, however, as the safest alternative where works of great value are being consigned. The creditor's rights are also cut off if the artist's interest as the person consigning the goods is shown by a sign hung in the gallery—a procedure hardly ever followed. Or the creditor's rights could be cut off if the artist could prove the gallery was known to its creditors as being substantially engaged in the sale of goods of others. This raises a burden of proof which may be difficult for the artist to satisfy. For artists in states which lack special consignment protection laws, the safest course may be simply to make a close examination of the financial stability of the gallery before consigning any work.

Damage, loss, theft, insurance

The Uniform Commercial Code requires return of consigned work to be at the gallery's "risk and expense." This imposes a far higher standard on the gallery than a bailment would. The artist should still require a provision stating that the gallery is responsible for the safekeeping of the work and, in the event of loss, damage or theft, will pay the artist as if the work had been sold (model agreement, Article 9). In case of damage the artist might seek either the right to compensation for any restoration done by the artist or control over restoration done by any other party.

The gallery should be required to insure the work so there will definitely be money to pay the artist in the event of loss, damage or theft (model agreement, Article 10). The artist should, if possible, be named as a beneficiary of the insurance policy. The insurance may not be for the retail value of the work, but must be sufficient to pay what the artist would normally receive upon sale. The artist might wish to take a separate policy to increase coverage on the work to 100 percent of retail value. Also, the work should be insured while in the artist's possession or in transit to the gallery if not covered by the gallery policy. The artist whose works may be dangerous to either people or property may want insurance for injuries or damages caused by the work itself. The artist and gallery should agree as to the payment of the premiums in such a case.

Customs

If the gallery will be selling work abroad, the artist will want to be certain the gallery complies with customs regulations. Many countries place no duty on original works of art but require a bond to be posted upon entry to the country in case the work is sold. Upon sale the bond will guarantee payment of a value added tax, but otherwise the bond is returned when the works are taken from the country. Where countries do place duties on original works, the work may have to be declared valueless and shipped without insurance to avoid paying du-

ties. In such case the artist would want the gallery to take responsibility for loss, damage or theft of the work. The consulates of each country can provide assistance to both the gallery and the artist seeking to comply with customs regulations.

Arbitration

The parties will often agree to arbitrate disagreements (model agreement, Article 14). The arbitration provision in the model agreement allows the parties to select a suitable arbitrator who has familiarity with the art world. The model agreement also provides that either party may refuse to arbitrate if the dispute is less than a specified dollar amount. This amount should be the maximum acceptable in the local small claims court, since this may be an even easier forum for setting disputes than arbitration. The disadvantage of small claims court might be a lack of knowledge regarding the special trade customs in the visual arts field.

Other provisions

The artist will have to decide whether the artist's death should terminate the agreement or whether the gallery should continue to sell the consigned work and pay the proceeds to the artist's estate (model agreement, Article 2). This provision will have to correspond to the plan developed for the artist's overall estate. If a crucial person at the gallery dies or the gallery goes out of business, the agreement should require an accounting, payment to the artist for all funds due and a return of all works (model agreement, Articles 2 and 7).

The agreement will provide for modification to be in writing (model agreement, Article 14), that a waiver of a right is not permanent and affects no other rights under the agreement, that if one provision of the contract is invalid the rest of the agreement will remain in effect and that the law of a specific state will govern the agreement (model agreement, Article 15).

No agreement between an artist and a gallery is likely to contain all these possible provisions, but the artist's familiarity with the potential scope and details of such an agreement will enable the artist to forge more effectively the artist's relationship to a gallery.

Model artist-gallery agreement

Agreement entered into this _____ day of _____, 19 _____, between

_____ (hereinafter referred to as the "Artist"), residing at _____, and

_____ (hereinafter referred to as the "Gallery"), located at _____

WHEREAS, the Artist is a professional artist of good standing; and

WHEREAS, the Artist wishes to have certain artworks represented by the Gallery, and

WHEREAS, the Gallery wishes to represent the Artist under the terms and conditions of this Agreement,

NOW, THEREFORE, in consideration of the foregoing premises and the mutual covenants hereinafter set forth and other valuable consideration, the parties hereto agree as follows:

1. SCOPE OF AGENCY. The Artist appoints the Gallery to act as Artist's exclusive agent in the following geographic area: _____ for the exhibition and sales of artworks in the following media: _____ . This agency shall cover only artwork completed by the Artist while this Agreement is in force. The Gallery shall document receipt of all works consigned hereunder by signing and returning to the Artist a Record of Consignment in the form annexed to this contract as Appendix A.

2. TERM AND TERMINATION. This Agreement shall have a term of two years and may be terminated by either party giving sixty days written notice to the other party. The Agreement shall automatically terminate with the death of the Artist; the death or termination of employment of _____ with the Gallery; if The Gallery moves outside of the area of _____ ; or if the Gallery becomes bankrupt or insolvent. On termination, all works consigned hereunder shall immediately be returned to the Artist at the expense of the Gallery.

3. EXHIBITIONS. The gallery shall provide a solo exhibition for the Artist of _____ days between September and May in the exhibition space located at _____ which shall be exclusively devoted to the Artist's exhibition for the specified time period. The Artist shall have artistic control over the exhibition of his or her work and the quality of reproduction of such work for promotional or advertising purposes. The expenses of the exhibition shall be paid for in the respective percentages shown below:

EXHIBITION EXPENSES	ARTIST	GALLERY
Transport work to gallery (including insurance and packing)	_____	_____
Advertising	_____	_____
Catalogs	_____	_____
Announcements	_____	_____
Frames	_____	_____
Special installations	_____	_____
Photographing work	_____	_____
Party for opening	_____	_____
Shipping to purchasers	_____	_____
Transporting work back to artist (including insurance and packing)	_____	_____
All other expenses arising from the exhibition	_____	_____

After the exhibition, the frames, photographs, negatives and any other tangible property created in the course of the exhibition shall be the property of _____ .

4. COMMISSIONS. The Gallery shall receive a commission of _____ percent of the retail price of each work sold. In the case of discount sales, the discount shall be deducted from the Gallery's commission. In the event of studio sales by the Artist that fall within the scope of the Gallery's exclusive agency, the Gallery shall receive a commission of _____ percent of the retail price for each work sold. Works done on a commissioned basis by the Artist shall/shall not be considered studio sales on which the Gallery may be entitled to a commission.

5. PRICES. The Gallery shall sell the works at the retail prices shown on the Record

of Consignment, subject to the Gallery's right to make customary trade discounts to such purchasers as museums and designers.

6. PAYMENTS. The Gallery shall pay the Artist all proceeds due to the Artist within thirty days of sale. No sales on approval or credit shall be made without the written consent of the Artist and, in such cases, the first proceeds received by the Gallery shall be paid to the Artist until the Artist has been paid all proceeds due.

7. ACCOUNTING. The Gallery shall furnish the Artist with an accounting every six months, the first such accounting to be given on the _____ day of _____ , 19 _____ . Each accounting shall state for each work sold during the accounting period the following information: the title of the work, the date of sale, the sale price, the name and address of the purchaser, the amounts due the Gallery and the Artist and the location of all works consigned to the Gallery that have not been sold. An accounting shall be provided in the event of termination of this Agreement.

8. INSPECTION OF BOOKS. The Gallery shall maintain accurate books and documentation with respect to all transactions entered into for the Artist. On the Artist's written request, the Gallery will permit the Artist or the Artist's authorized representative to examine these books and documentation during normal business hours of the Gallery.

9. LOSS OR DAMAGE. The Gallery shall be responsible for loss or damage to any consigned artwork from the date of delivery to the Gallery until the work is returned to the Artist or delivered to a purchaser. In the event of loss or damage that cannot be restored, the Artist shall receive the same amount as if the work had been sold at the retail price listed in the Record of Consignment. If restoration is undertaken, the Artist shall have a veto power over the choice of the restorer.

10. INSURANCE. The Gallery shall insure the work for _____ percent of the retail price shown in the Record of Consignment.

11. COPYRIGHT. The Gallery shall take all steps necessary to insure that the Artist's copyright in the consigned works is projected, including but not limited to requiring copyright notices on all reproductions of the works used for any purpose whatsoever.

12. ASSIGNMENT. This Agreement shall not be assignable by either party hereto, provided, however, that the Artist shall have the right to assign money due him or her hereunder.

13. ARBITRATION. All disputes arising under this Agreement shall be submitted to binding arbitration before _____ (specify a suitable arbitrator) and the arbitration award may be entered for judgement in any court having jurisdiction thereof. Notwithstanding the foregoing, either party may refuse to arbitrate when the dispute is for a sum of less than _____ Dollars. (Note: Insert the jurisdictional amount of the local small claims court. This will provide an even easier forum than arbitration for settling disputes.)

14. MODIFICATIONS. All modifications of this Agreement must be in writing and signed by both parties. This Agreement constitutes the entire understanding between the parties hereto.

15. GOVERNING LAW. This Agreement shall be governed by the laws of the State of _____ .

IN WITNESS WHEREOF, the parties hereto have executed this Agreement on the day and year above set forth.

Gallery

By: _____
      (Name and Title)

_____
Artist

RECORD OF CONSIGNMENT (Appendix A)

This is to acknowledge receipt of the following works of art on consignment:

TITLE	MEDIUM	DESCRIPTION	RETAIL PRICE
1.			
2.			
3.			
4.			
5.			
6.			

Gallery

By: _____
      Name and Title

Cooperative galleries

Cooperative galleries often provide a welcome outlet for the artist who has difficulty in establishing a relationship with a commerical gallery. A group of artists normally contribute funds to establish and maintain the gallery in which their own work will be shown. Some cooperative galleries have sought status as federal tax-exempt organizations by making their primary function the service of the public through educational activities such as lectures, workshops, employment information and exhibitions of the work of both members and non-members without offering the work for sale. If the work of members was offered for sale, however, the cooperative gallery would probably not qualify for tax exemption. Such exemption was denied where "the cooperative gallery . . . engaged in showing and selling only the works of its own members and is a vehicle for advancing their careers and promoting the sale of their work. It serves the private purpose of its members, even though the exhibition and sale of paintings may be an educational activity in other respects." (Rev. Rul. 71-395, 1971-2 Cum. Bull. 228; Rev. Rul. 76-152, I.R.B.4 1976-17) But, regardless of tax status, many artists would value the promotion.

It is important, however, to remember that the cooperative gallery is a legal entity separate from the artists who compose its membership. Thus, the artist should anticipate that nearly all the problems of dealing with commerical galleries may arise when the artist joins a cooperative gallery.

Agents

Photographers and illustrators may use agents for sales of work. Most illustrators' agents represent the illustrator individually in selling work and selling assignments. Photographers may be represented individually and also use a stock agency which maintains exclusive sales rights over the photographs submitted to the agency by many photographers. Conceptually, the concerns of the illustrator or photographer with respect to agents are much the same as those of the fine artist. The parties to the agreement,

scope of the agency, promotion of the work, commission rates for the agent, prices, accountings, payment, risks of loss or theft or damage, insurance and responsibilities for expenses incurred will have to be considered and specified in the agreement. A good sample agreement to consult is the Graphic Artists Guild's Artist-Agent Agreement which appears on pages 109-110. Both the American Society of Magazine Photographers and the Society of Photographer and Artist Representatives (abbreviated as "SPAR") also have model agreements which are worth comparing to the Guild's version. One good source for finding an agent for both illustrators and photographers is the list of agent-members of SPAR. SPAR's address appears on page 195. Along with the list of agents who are members, artists might also request SPAR's "Policy Statement to Clarify Urgent Problems and Stem Growing Abuses." In most cases artist and agent are on the same side in seeking fair industry practices for the creators of artwork that will be reproduced. The model contract shown here favors the artist, but is not unreasonable in view of current practices between agents and artists.

The gallery is selling a finished work of art, while the agent is usually obtaining an assignment for the illustrator or photographer to undertake. The Guild's agreement requires the agent to use best efforts to secure assignments, but allows the artist to reject assignments with unacceptable terms (Article 1). The artist and agent share the cost of promotions (Article 2). This is often shared equally or in proportion to how proceeds are divided, but varies with the specific situation. Since the agent probably has reproductions for samples, loss or damage is not as serious as in the case of original art. The agreement provides that the agent will only be liable if he or she causes loss or damage by negligence. If valuable original art or transparencies are to be in the hands of the agent, this provision should be reconsidered. In such an event it would be wise to provide a valuation for the original work and require insurance coverage sufficient to protect the artist.

The standard commission rate is 25 percent (Article 4). Some agents charge a slightly higher rate for out-of-town assignments. House accounts are those the artist brings to the agent. The house accounts should be listed, as in Schedule A, to avoid confusion. The commission rate on house accounts is 10 percent. The agreement provides that the commission shall be payable on the artist's actual profit from the assignment, so expenses are excluded for that computation. The agent usually handles billing, but in some cases the artist may do so (Article 5). In any case, payment should be made immediately on receipt of payments from the client (Article 6). Accountings and the inspection of books and records should also be covered (Articles 7 and 8).

The term and termination provisions are among the most important in the agreement (Articles 3 and 9). The artist doesn't want to be bound to an agent who isn't selling; the agent doesn't want to build an artist's career only to have the artist find another agent. The result is that the agent will want commissions for assignments obtained by the artist after termination from clients originally secured by the agent. The duration of this after-termination right to commissions, the commission percentage and whether house accounts are included are all subject to negotiation. If the after-termination right continues for too long a period, it will be both costly to the artist and make finding a new agent more difficult.

Each party relies on the other party to render personal services so the agreement is not assignable. However, sums of money due under the contract would be assignable.

In the New York metropolitan area, the Joint Ethics Committee (discussed on page 201) might make an excellent choice to be specified in the agreement to arbitrate disputes.

The following contract is used by permission of the Graphic Artists Guild.

Model artist-agent agreement

AGREEMENT, this _____day of _____, 19 _____, between _____

(hereinafter referred to as the "Artist"), residing at _____, and ____

(hereinafter referred to as the "Agent"), residing at _____ .

WHEREAS, the Artist is an established artist of proven talents; and

WHEREAS, the Artist wishes to have an agent represent him or her in marketing certain rights enumerated herein; and

WHEREAS, the Agent is capable of marketing the artwork produced by the Artist; and

WHEREAS, the Agent wishes to represent the Artist;

NOW, THEREFORE, in consideration of the foregoing premises and the mutual covenants hereinafter set forth and other valuable consideration, the parties hereto agree as follows:

1. AGENCY. The Artist appoints the Agent to act as his or her exclusive representative: (A) in the following geographical area: _____(B) _____ for the markets listed here (specify publishing, advertising, etc.): _____

The Agent agrees to use his or her best efforts in submitting the Artist's work for the purpose of securing assignments for the Artist. The Agent shall negotiate the terms of any assignment that is offered, but the Artist shall have the right to reject any assignment if he or she finds the terms thereof unacceptable.

2. PROMOTION. The Artist shall provide the Agent with such samples of work as are from time to time necessary for the purpose of securing assignments. These samples shall remain the property of the Artist and be returned on termination of this Agreement. The Agent shall take reasonable efforts to protect the work from loss or damage, but shall be liable for such loss or damage only if caused by the Agent's negligence. Promotional expenses, including but not limited to promotional mailings and paid advertising, shall be paid _____percent by the Agent and _____percent by the Artist. The Agent shall bear the expenses of shipping, insurance and similar marketing expenses.

3. TERM. This Agreement shall take effect on the _____day of _____, 19 _____, and remain in full force and effect for a term of one year, unless terminated as provided in Paragraph 9.

4. COMMISSIONS. The Agent shall be entitled to the following commissions: (A) On assignments obtained by the Agent during the term of this Agreement, twenty-five (25%) percent of the billing. (B) On house accounts, ten (10%) percent of the billing. For purposes of this Agreement, house accounts are defined as accounts obtained by the Artist at any time or obtained by another agent representing the Artist prior to the commencement

of this Agreement and are listed in Schedule A attached to this Agreement.

It is understood by both parties that no commissions shall be paid on assignments rejected by the Artist or for which the Artist fails to receive payment, regardless of the reason payment is not made. Further, no commissions shall be payable in either (A) or (B) above for any part of the billing that is due to expenses incurred by the Artist in performing the assignment, whether or not such expenses are reimbursed by the client. In the event that a flat fee is paid by the client, it shall be reduced by the amount of expenses incurred by the Artist in performing the assignment, and the Agent's commission shall be payable only on the fee as reduced for expenses.

5. BILLING. The _____ Artist _____ Agent shall be responsible for all billings.

6. PAYMENTS. The Party responsible for billing shall make all payments due within ten (10) days of receipt of any fees covered by this Agreement. Late payments shall be accompanied by interest calculated at the rate of _____ percent per month thereafter.

7. ACCOUNTINGS. The party responsible for billing shall send copies of invoices to the other party when rendered. If requested, that party shall also provide the other party with semi-annual accountings showing all assignments for the period, the clients' names, the fees paid, expenses incurred by the Artist, the dates of payment, the amounts on which the Agent's commissions are to be calculated and the sums due less those amounts already paid.

8. INSPECTION OF THE BOOKS AND RECORDS. The party responsible for the billing shall keep the books and records with repect to commissions due at his or her place of business and permit the other party to inspect these books and records during normal business hours on the giving of reasonable notice.

9. TERMINATION. This Agreement may be terminated by either party by giving thirty (30) days written notice to the other party. If the Artist receives assignments after the termination date from clients originally obtained by the Agent during the term of this Agreement, the commission specified in Paragraph 4(A) shall be payable to the Agent under the following circumstances. If the Agent has represented the Artist for six months or less, the Agent shall receive a commission on such assignments received by the Artist within ninety (90) days of the date of termination. This period shall increase by thirty (30) days for each additional six months that the Agent has represented the Artist, but in no event shall such period exceed one hundred eighty (180) days.

10. ASSIGNMENT. This Agreement shall not be assigned by either the parties hereto. It shall be binding on and inure to the benefit of the successors, admininstrators, executors or heirs of the Agent and Artist.

11. ARBITRATION. Any disputes arising under this Agreement shall be settled by arbitration under the rules of the American Arbitration Association in the City of _____ _____. Any award rendered by the arbitrator may be entered in any court having jurisdiction thereof.

12. NOTICES. All notices shall be given to the parties at their respective addresses set forth above.

13. INDEPENDENT CONTRACTOR STATUS. Both parties agree that the Agent is acting as an independent contractor. This Agreement is not an employment agreement, nor does it constitute a joint venture or partnership between the Artist and Agent.

14. AMENDMENTS AND MERGER. All amendments to this Agreement must be written. This Agreement incorporates the entire understanding of the parties.

15. GOVERNING LAW. This Agreement shall be governed by the laws of the State of _____.

IN WITNESS WHEREOF, the parties have signed this Agreement as of the date set forth above.

_____
ARTIST

_____
AGENT

HOUSE ACCOUNTS (SCHEDULE A)

DATE:

1. _____
(name and address of client)

2. _____

3. _____

4. _____

5. _____

6. _____

7. _____

8. _____

9. _____

Chapter 14

Sales of reproduction rights

Commercial artists earn their livelihood by selling reproduction rights to clients. The art is often created on assignment for the client. Nonetheless, the artist will own the copyright (unless the assignment is work-for-hire) and the original art. What rights will the artist transfer to the client and what contractual protections will the artist require?

The artists' professional organizations have created model forms for use in selling reproduction rights. This chapter includes model forms for photographers, illustrators, graphic designers and textile designers that can be adapted to sell art to any market. In addition, syndication and other forms of commercial exploitation are covered. Sophisticated contracts for the sale of reproduction rights include the book publishing contract discussed in Chapter 15 and the video broadcast agreement discussed in Chapter 16.

Battle of the forms

One pitfall to be avoided is the often encountered battle of the forms. An art director sends a purchase order that has one set of terms. The artist sends back a confirming letter (or form) with different terms, but starts work immediately because the assignment is on a deadline. When the assignment is billed, the artist's invoice follows the terms of the confirming letter. But the client sends a check which has terms stamped on its back that conform to the terms of the client's original purchase order. When all is said and done, neither party knows the actual terms of the transaction.

As the chapter on contracts pointed out, agreement must be two-sided. The moment a potential disagreement arises, it must be confronted by the artist. If a purchase order has unacceptable terms, it becomes especially important to obtain a signed contract with terms acceptable to both parties (or a client's response accepting the terms of the confirmation form). If deadlines are tight, mailgrams or overnight mail can be used to speed the reaching of agreement. To continue working when agreement has not been reached is to invite disputes.

Such disputes can be avoided by using the model contracts at the end of the chapter, all of which cover certain basic terms.

Assignment description and due date

There must be a description of the assignment and a due date. If the client is to provide reference material or take other steps that are necessary for the artist to perform, any delay caused by the client should extend the artist's time for performance.

Fee

A basic fee should be specified for the assignment. For photography this might be a day rate or shot rate, in which case any minimum guarantee as to the number of days or shots should be specified. For sales to magazines the day rate will normally be an advance against the space rate in the magazine. For an advertising assignment, usage fees may be paid in addition to the day rate if a number of images are used, and sometimes even if a single image is used.

If work beyond the original assignment is required, such as overtime on a shoot for which the fee is modest or many additional sketches on an illustration, an hourly rate or per sketch fee may sometimes be agreed to. Days spent on travel and preparation should be compensated as should days on which it is impossible to work due to the weather if that is relevant. Travel and weather days may be paid for at half the regular day rate, although this is negotiable. Payment for extensive amounts of preparation time are also becoming common.

The textile design order-acknowledgement form provides a breakdown of estimated prices for different categories of work.

Cancellations

If an assignment is cancelled, a cancellation fee should be paid. By the way, cancellation fee and kill fee have the same meaning. Some artists consider the use of the phrase kill fee to be pejorative, since it may reflect on the artist's work. Of course some assignments are cancelled prior to work even commencing. In this case it is unusual to receive a cancellation fee, except that photographers may negotiate for such a fee if reasonable notice (such as 48 hours) of the cancellation is not given prior to the time the assignment was to start.

The contract for graphic designers requires payment for cancellation based on the contract price in relation to the degree of completion of the work, while the illustrators' contract allows the filling in of percentages to be paid if cancellation is after sketches (perhaps 25 to 50 percent of the fee) or finishes (perhaps 50 to 100 percent of the fee). If the cancellation is due to dissatisfaction with the art, the fee will usually be lower than if the cancellation is for reasons unrelated to the art (such as a decision not to do the project).

In the event of cancellation, the artist would seek to retain the rights in the art which has been created. Cancellation implies that the client has no use for that art, so retention of the rights by the artist appears reasonable.

Usage

The fee is often based on usage. This makes it important to specify what use of the art is anticipated. The photographer's contract does this by specifying category, media and title. The contractual terms then give the following definitions: "'Category' means advertising, corporate, editorial, etc.; 'Media' means brochure, magazine, hardcover book, billboard, etc.; 'Title' means publication or product name." By carefully limiting usage to the client's needs at the time of entering into the contract, the fee can

then be based on that usage. If the client later wishes to make greater usage, reuse fees can be agreed on (if such fees are not specified in the original contract).

The illustrators' contract limits usage in the same way, as does the graphic designers' contract. However, these contracts contain additional limitations since the geographic area of use, the time period of use, number of uses or the edition of a book can also be specified.

Most magazines purchase only first North American serial rights (sometimes called first rights), the right to be the first magazine to publish the work in North America. After such publication, the artist is free to sell the work elsewhere. A variation of first serial rights would be first North American serial rights, whereby the artist conveys to the client the right to be the first magazine publisher of the work in North America. Another grant of rights would be second serial rights—the right to publish art work which has appeared elsewhere. A different grant of rights would be one-time rights—the right to use the work once but not necessarily first and certainly not exclusively. Another way of expressing this could be the grant of simultaneous rights: granting the right to publish to several magazines at once. The artist should keep in mind the possibility of limiting the grant of rights with regard to exclusivity, types of uses, duration and geographical scope. The artist who wishes can define exactly the nature of the permitted publication. If possible, the artist should avoid selling all rights, (sometimes called exclusive world rights in perpetuity), which means the artist retains no rights to the work. Prior to 1978 magazines sometimes purchased all rights with the understanding that certain rights would be transferred back to the artist after publication. In such a case, the artist should have had a written contract setting forth precisely which rights the magazine would transfer back to the artist. Since 1978 this trust arrangement has become obsolete because contributions are protected by the magazine's copyright notice (although it is best to have copyright notice for the contribution in the artist's name).

The textile designer's contract leaves the limitation of rights to be filled in under special comments, but the approach to limiting rights is the same as in the other contracts.

It is important to state that *(only)* the specified usage is granted to the client. A more formal approach would be to recite, "All rights not hereby transferred are reserved to the Artist." Usage should also be limited to images actually purchased. Many photographers, for example, profit by using outtakes from assignments to create stock files for sale. This is an accepted practice as long as the photographer does not sell the outtakes to a company competitive with the original client.

Advances and expenses

Photographers and designers are paid for their expenses as a routine matter. An issue arises as to whether these expenses should be marked up. For example, should a 15 or 20 percent charge be added to the expenses when billing the client? The justification for such a charge is the bookkeeping cost involved, the overhead expense to make such outlays on behalf of the client and the cost (in lost interest) of paying money for the client and then having to wait to be reimbursed. There is no general rule, but a few photographers and virtually all designers mark-up expenses when billing the client.

Illustrators often do not bill for expenses because the expenses are minimal. If such expenses are not minimal, the illustrator is certainly justified in requesting a reimbursement (perhaps, for example, if the assignment requires hiring a model).

Sometimes an advance against expenses can be negotiated. Such an advance provides part or all of the money estimated for the expenses. When an advance is paid, the justification for marking up expenses is lessened. The artist is no longer in effect lending money to the client, although extra overhead costs are still incurred in keeping track of the expenses and billing them to the client.

Changes and reshoots

If changes are necessary, the artist should be given the first opportunity to make such changes. If the changes are due to a change in the assignment, of course, additional fees

should be payable. Likewise, a reshoot might be done on the basis of expenses plus half the regular fee when the client changes the assignment. Changes are covered by two articles of the Code of Fair Practice promulgated by the Joint Ethics Committee (see Articles 4 and 5, page 202.

Authorship credit and copyright notice

The contracts provide for such credit when the use of the art is editorial (such as for magazines or books). If the art is for corporate or advertising use, authorship credit is less common and would have to be added into the contract form.

Copyright notice does not accompany art unless the artist requires such notice. Often the name credit can simply be elaborated by adding the copyright symbol and the year date. A common mistake in magazines is a photograph with a copyright notice that lacks the year date. Such a notice would have been acceptable prior to 1978, but is no longer valid. Of course, the notice in the front of the magazine protects all contributions (except for advertisements which require their own notice), but the photographer who requires adjacent copyright notice should certainly include a date in the notice.

Return of originals and samples

Original art should be specified to remain the property of the artist. After the art has been used for reproduction, it should be returned to the artist. If clients expect to keep originals and are paying a sufficient fee, this should be stated. For photography, the client may expect to keep shots that are used but not outtakes. Stock sales for photographers and sales of originals for illustrators depend on the proper retention of ownership of rights and art. These can provide yet another source of residual income (in addition to reuses by the client beyond the usage originally agreed on and paid for). Also, if art is never used by the client, the contract may specify that after a certain amount of time passes, the original art and any rights granted will revert to the artist.

The artist will also want copies of the art in its reproduced form. So the contract should provide that a certain number of copies of the art as reproduced will be provided free of charge to the artist.

In addition, the textile designers' contract requires that the client provide insurance covering the fair market value of the art when it is being shipped.

Releases

If the client is supplying reference materials, the client should guarantee that use of these materials will neither violate anyone's right of privacy nor infringe any copyright. If this guarantee (called a warranty) is breached, the client should agree to pay any judgment as well as legal fees and court costs resulting from a lawsuit. Artists may also be asked to give warranties and indemnities for images they create, as is discussed with respect to book publication contracts on page 130.

Payment

The contract must state a time for payment, usually within 30 days of the submission of an invoice (although some clients take 60 or even 90 days to pay). Some artists include a contractual term charging interest for late payment. While rarely enforced by the artist due to the desire to keep the client's good will, such provisions may encourage timely payment. Some magazines pay on publication, rather than on acceptance of a contribution. This is not a desirable practice, since the artist is simply loaning money to the publisher. It also raises the risk that there will be no payment, since the magazine is under no obligation to publish the contribution. Payment on acceptance is best, but certainly payment should be required if publication does not occur with a reasonable time (such as six months after acceptance).

Estimates

If an estimate is given for an assignment, it should be specified whether or not the estimate is binding. For example, the designer's contract states than any estimate is a minimum only. However, the billing may not be increased more than 10 percent above the estimate without the client's approval. Any estimate must leave flexibility unless the scope of the work can be very precisely delineated.

Modifications

It would be ideal to have any modifications be written, but to keep work progressing smoothly oral modifications may be unavoidable. Such changes should be promptly confirmed in writing, especially if the fees or expenses will be increased due to the change.

The contracts require that the client object to terms either immediately on receipt or within 10 days of receipt. If the client complies with this, it will help to achieve a meeting of the minds.

Invoices

The forms for graphic designers and photographers are designed to serve as either an estimate, a confirmation or an invoice. On the other hand, the forms for illustrators and textile designers are only for use as confirmations. An invoice for illustrators has been included with the forms at the end of the chapter and can be used as a model for other artists as well.

An estimate is used in seeking an assignment, a confirmation after an assignment has been received and an invoice after the assignment has been completed. The invoice specifies the fee and includes most of the terms which appeared on the confirmation form, including the payment terms. It usually accompanies delivery of the finished assignment or is sent on acceptance of the assignment. If extra charges have been incurred that did not appear in the confirmation form, the invoice can include such charges. The invoice would also bill for the sales tax, if any were payable.

Collections and small claims court

Sending out an invoice is usually followed by payment. In some cases, however, the client either makes partial payment, places restrictions on the check used for payment or refuses to pay at all. In such a situation, the artist should first determine whether the client has a legitimate grievance. If the grievance is legitimate, the amount billed in the invoice might be reduced. If the grievance is not legitimate or if the client is simply refusing to pay, the artist will have to take steps to collect the invoiced amount.

A client may sometimes pay a partial amount and mark the check "paid in full." Or a client may write on the back of a check that the assignment was done as work for hire and signing the check is to serve as a signed contract for copyright purposes. The best course of action in such cases is to return the check and receive a check in full payment without any restrictive statements on it. If the artist is pressed for funds and reluctant to return the check, it would be wise to consult an attorney before crossing out anything or cashing the check. The client's refusal to pay properly is a breach of contract which can be the basis for a lawsuit.

Before suing, of course, the artist will try to collect the money owed by persuasion and persistence. Suing will involve time, energy and expense on the artist's part—not to mention the almost certain loss of the client. Collection procedures begin gently, often by sending a second invoice stamped "Past due" and then sending a pleasant letter directing the attention of the client to the overdue invoice. This may be followed by a phone call asking for an explanation of the failure to pay. If it seems the client does not plan to pay, the artist can build pressure through repeated letters and telephone calls, telegrams and mailgrams, registered letters, threats to report the client to a credit bureau and use a collection agency or attorney to collect and finally turning the claim over to a collection agency or attorney. By the way, a collection agency can't do more than write letters and make phone calls, so such agencies (which charge 25 to 50 percent of the amount collected) should only be used when the artist is unwilling to devote time and energy to collections.

Instead of turning the claim over to a lawyer, the artist may choose to sue in small claims court. Such courts provide an avenue for the inexpensive resolution of disputes, especially when the artist is seeking to collect amounts up to several thousand dollars. The amount that can be sued for in small claims court varies from locality to locality, but it will often be more than the amount in dispute. A call to the local bar association or courthouse will provide the relevant information as to the location of the small claims court, which in turn can advise as to local procedures.

If the artist decides to retain a lawyer to handle the case, pages 1–2 may be consulted with respect to how to find a lawyer.

Syndication agreements

A syndicate gathers marketable features for distribution on a regular basis to markets, such as newspapers. Cartoon strips are commonly syndicated. The Cartoonists Guild has collected six syndication contracts in their excellent *Syndicate Survival Kit,* which describes what the artist should look for in a syndication contract. The basic considerations are those of the book contract discussed in the next chapter, but the creation of unique characters can have some special implications. For example, the creators of Superman sold all their rights and benefitted hardly at all from the phenomenal success of Superman as a comic strip and as a character in numerous other commerical ventures.

The Guild states that the artist selling greater rights (such as "all rights" instead of only "first North American rights") should receive a greater payment. But the Guild strongly urges that the term be limited to no more than one or, at most, two years. This is to enable the artist either to negotiate a better contract, if the comic strip is a success, or to stop working on an unprofitable venture, if the comic strip is not popular. Since automatic renewal would defeat the purpose of a short term, the artist should refuse any such renewal provision.

The artist is normally paid in the form of a percentage of the receipts earned by the strip. But again, the artist should be careful that the percentage is taken against gross receipts, not net receipts (which might also be phrased as "gross receipts less expenses"). The Guild suggests 50 percent of gross receipts is usually fair payment to the artist, but indicates a minimum payment should always be specified. The Guild urges the artist to reserve a fair percentage of gross receipts—75 percent, perhaps—from all subsidiary rights, particularly since book, television, radio, periodical and novelty rights can be so valuable when cartoon characters are successful.

The Guild suggests that the artist retain copyright in the work, in which case copyright notice should appear in the artist's name. The artist should require powers of consultation and approval with regard to any changes to be made in submitted material. Also, the original art work should be returned to the artist.

The Guild stresses the importance of promotion for the success of a cartoon strip. The promotional plan should, ideally, be agreed upon in advance. The burden of promotional costs and the rights to use the work for promotion without additional payments should be resolved at this stage too.

The artist should have a right to periodic accountings showing the source of all receipts and the exact nature of any expenses. The artist should be able to inspect the books of the syndicate. Package deals, in which several features are sold together, should be forbidden. Each feature should stand on its own merit and be paid for individually. The Guild also suggests that legal fees and liabilities should be equally divided between the artist and the syndicate.

The artist must not relinquish the right to sell other creative work. The syndicate has received a license with regard to the comic strip at issue, so work too closely similar will infringe that license. But the artist should not agree even to refrain from marketing similar work because of the problem of defining what may be similar. Any option provision giving rights over future work of the artist to the syndicate should also be struck from the contract.

The Guild suggests that, in the event of the artist's death, controls be present in the contract which ensure that payments for the comic strip will continue to be made to the artist's estate. One possible way to do this would be to require minimum payments to the estate after the artist's death. Another way might be to have the estate pay for a replacement artist, who would continue the comic strip.

The syndication contract raises many of the same issues as the publication contract, but the artist who is negotiating a syndication contract should consult the *Syndicate Survival Kit* for advice on each of the provisions likely to appear in such contracts.

Commercial exploitation

Commercial exploitation through the reproduction of art work can take the form of jewelry, tee shirts, posters, prints and even useful household objects (such as lamps with decorative bases). The artist who is offered an opportunity to exploit copyrighted or patented work can limit the rights licensed with regard to use, duration and geographical scope. The artist will want to be certain that the entrepreneur seeking the license is financially stable, respected for honesty and capable of creating and distributing quality products.

The entrepreneur would normally bear the cost of reproducing the work, possibly under a binding schedule for production. The artist would want the right to approve the quality of the product at the various stages of manufacture. Promotional budgets and approaches might be specified in advance along with channels of distribution. Appropriate copyright or patent notice, the right to artistic credit, the artist's ownership of the original work, the artist's right to free copies and any warranties given by the artist would all be included in the contract.

The artist might be paid either a flat fee or a royalty. If a royalty is to be paid, the issue of gross and net receipts again becomes significant. The artist will want a stated percentage of the gross receipts, not the net receipts (or gross receipts less certain expenses). Nonetheless, the typical deal is to give the artist 5 to 12 1/2 percent of the net wholesale price received by the manufacturer from its distributors. The artist would want the right to both periodic accountings and inspection of the entrepreneur's books.

The entrepreneur might request that the artist either refrain from creating competing works or offer an option on the artist's next commercial creation to the entrepreneur. The artist should not agree to these provisions, however, for the same reasons discussed in the next chapter with regard to book contracts.

The contract should provide for termination in the event the entrepreneur fails to exploit the work or becomes bankrupt or insolvent. The rights would then revert to the artist who might be entitled to purchase stock on hand at the cost of the stock to the entrepreneur.

The commercial exploitation of art is merely a more general application of the principles which guide the artist in the specific exploitation of art involved in a publication contract. For the artist considering such a commercial venture, the principles discussed for the book contracts will be a helpful guide.

Model Contracts

The photographer's assignment agreement form is reproduced here by permission of Arie Kopelman from *Selling Your Photography: The Complete Marketing, Business and Legal Guide*. The illustrators' confirmation form, the graphic designers estimate/confirmation/invoice form, the textile designer's confirmation form and the illustrators' invoice are all reproduced here with permission of the Graphic Artists Guild. The Guild's contract forms were designed by Ross Design Associates, Inc.

Photographer's Model Assignment Form

(Photographer's letterhead)

ESTIMATE _____

CONFIRMATION _____

INVOICE _____

Client's name   Date:

Client's address   P.O./Job #

Job description

Usage: Category _____ Media _____ Title _____

Adjacent credit required: yes _____ no _____

BASIC FEE (Minimum guarantee and day or picture rate,
assignment rate or other) $ _____

OTHER FEES AS APPLICABLE
(Travel time, weather days, cancellation or postponements within 48 hours of shooting and reshoots due to client change, all are 50 percent of basic fee unless specified otherwise.)

$ _____

SPACE OR USE RATE (if applicable)   _____
EXPENSES
    Assistants   _____
    Find and processing (black-and- white, color, Polaroid) _____
    Liability insurance   _____
    Location/studio rental   _____
    Messengers and trucking   _____
    Models   _____
    Props   _____
    Sets (materials and labor)   _____
    Special equipment   _____

Special services
    Casting   —————
    Hair and makeup   —————
    Home economist   —————
    Location search   —————
    Styling   —————
    Other   —————
Transportation and travel
    Air and ground   —————
    Hotels and meals   —————
    Gratuities and miscellaneous   —————
Miscellaneous   —————
EXPENSE TOTALS $ ————— $ —————
    Subtotal   —————
    Sales tax (if applicable)   —————
    TOTAL   —————
Advance $ —————
    AMOUNT DUE $ —————*

(*Due within 30 days or subject to 1.5 percent per month service charge.)
    SUBJECT TO ALL TERMS AND CONDITIONS ABOVE AND ON REVERSE SIDE UNLESS OBJECTED TO IN WRITING BEFORE SHOOTING BEGINS.

(Photographer's Model Assignment Form/Reverse Side)

Terms and Conditions

1. USAGE: Rights granted depend upon payment and are limited solely to those stated under "usage". Editorial reproduction is limited to one-time North American use unless stated otherwise. All other rights reserved to photographer. "Category" of use means advertising, corporate or editorial, etc.; "media" means album, brochure, billboard, book (hard or soft cover), magazine (consumer, corporate or trade), point of purchase, poster slide show; "title" means product or publication name.
2. RETURN OF PHOTOGRAPHS: Unless all rights are granted, client agrees to return photographs safely and undamaged within 30 days of publication, by bonded messenger, air freight or registered mail.
3. CREDIT LINE AND COPYRIGHT: Adjacent credit line must accompany editorial use or fee is doubled.
4. RELEASES: Client will indemnify photographer against all claims and expenses due to uses for which no release was requested in writing or for uses that exceed authority granted by a release.
5. EXPENSES: Expense estimate is subject to normal trade variance of 10 percent and clients' oral authorizations for additional items.
6. ARBITRATION: Client and photographer agree to submit any disputes hereunder involving more than ($_____*) to arbitration in (photographer's city and state) under rules of the American Arbitration Association. An award therefrom may be entered for judgment in any Court having jurisdiction thereof.

Signed: _____   _____
      Client   Photographer
*Maximum amount photographer can sue on in small claims court (usually the quickest remedy).

Illustrator's Confirmation of Engagement

FRONT: ILLUSTRATOR'S LETTERHEAD

TO	DATE
	AUTHORIZED ART BUYER
	ILLUSTRATOR'S JOB NUMBER
	CLIENT'S JOB NUMBER

ASSIGNMENT DESCRIPTION

DELIVERY SCHEDULE

FEE (PAYMENT SCHEDULE)

ADDITIONAL ESTIMATED EXPENSES

CANCELLATION FEE (PERCENTAGE OF FEE)

BEFORE SKETCHES	
AFTER SKETCHES	
AFTER FINISH	

(more)

RIGHTS TRANSFERRED (ALL OTHER RIGHTS RESERVED BY THE ILLUSTRATOR)	
FOR USE IN MAGAZINES AND NEWSPAPERS, FIRST NORTH AMERICAN REPRODUCTION RIGHTS UNLESS SPECIFIED OTHERWISE HERE	
(remove all italics before using this form)	
FOR ALL OTHER USES, THE CLIENT ACQUIRES ONLY THE FOLLOWING RIGHTS	
TITLE OR PRODUCT	*(name)*
CATEGORY OF USE	*(advertising, corporate, promotional, editorial, etc.)*
MEDIUM OF USE	*(consumer or trade magazine, annual report, TV, book, etc.)*
GEOGRAPHIC AREA	*(if applicable)*
TIME PERIOD	*(if applicable)*
NUMBER OF USES	*(if applicable)*
OTHER	*(if applicable)*
ORIGINAL ARTWORK, INCLUDING SKETCHES AND ANY OTHER PRELIMINARY MATERIAL, REMAINS THE PROPERTY OF THE ILLUSTRATOR UNLESS PURCHASED BY A PAYMENT OF A SEPARATE FEE.	

Terms:

1. Time for Payment. Payment is due within thirty (30) days of receipt of invoice. A 1½% monthly service charge will be billed for late payment. Any advances or partial payments shall be indicated under Payment Schedule on front.

2. Default in Payment. The Client shall assume responsibility for all collection and legal fees necessitated by default in payment.

3. Grant of Rights. The grant of reproduction rights is conditioned on receipt of payment.

4. Expenses. The Client shall reimburse the Illustrator for all expenses arising from the assignment.

5. Sales Tax. The client shall be responsible for the payment of sales tax, if any such tax is due.

6. Cancellation. In the event of cancellation or breach by the Client, the Illustrator shall retain ownership of all rights of copyright and the original artwork, including sketches and any other preliminary materials.

7. Revisions. Revisions not due to the fault of the Illustrator shall be billed separately.

8. Credit Lines. On any contribution for magazine or book use, the Illustrator shall receive name credit in print. If name credit is to be given with other types of use, it must be specified here:

_____

_____

☐ If this box is checked by the Illustrator, the Illustrator shall receive copyright notice adjacent to the work in the form:
©_____198_____

9. Return of Artwork. Client assumes responsibility for the return of the artwork in undamaged condition within thirty (30) days of first reproduction.

10. Unauthorized Use. Client will indemnify Illustrator against all claims and expenses, including reasonable attorney's fees, arising from uses for which no release was requested in writing or for uses which exceed the authority granted by a release.

11. Arbitration. Any disputes in excess of $_____ (maximum limit for small claims court) arising out of this Agreement shall be submitted to binding arbitration before the Joint Ethics Committee as a mutually agreed upon arbitrator pursuant to the rules of the American Arbitration Association. The Arbitrator's award shall be final, and judgment may be entered upon it in any court having jursidiction thereof. The client shall pay all arbitration and court costs, reasonable attorney's fees and legal interest on any award or judgment in favor of the Illustrator.

12. Acceptance of Terms. If the terms of this confirmation are not objected to within ten (10) days of receipt, the terms shall be deemed accepted.

CONSENTED AND AGREED TO

_____
DATE

_____
ILLUSTRATOR'S SIGNATURE

_____
COMPANY NAME

_____
AUTHORIZED SIGNATURE

_____
NAME AND TITLE

MEMBER

Graphic Designer's Estimate/Confirmation/Invoice Form

☐ ESTIMATE	☐ ENGAGEMENT CONFIRMATION	☐ INVOICE
TO		DATE
		COMMISSIONED BY
		ASSIGNMENT NUMBER
		INVOICE NUMBER
		CLIENT'S PURCHASE ORDER NUMBER

ASSIGNMENT DESCRIPTION	DELIVERY DATE
	(PREDICATED ON RECEIPT OF ALL MATERIALS TO BE SUPPLIED BY CLIENT)
	MATERIALS SUPPLIED BY
	FEE

ITEMIZED EXPENSES. CLIENT SHALL REIMBURSE DESIGNER FOR ALL EXPENSES. IF THIS IS AN ESTIMATE OR ASSIGNMENT CONFIRMATION, ANY EXPENSE AMOUNTS ARE ESTIMATES ONLY. IF THIS IS AN INVOICE, EXPENSE AMOUNTS ARE FINAL.	
ILLUSTRATION PHOTOGRAPHY	
MATERIALS AND SUPPLIES	
MECHANICALS	
MESSENGERS	
PHOTOGRAPHIC REPRODUCTION	
PRINTING	
TOLL TELEPHONES	
TRANSPORTATION AND TRAVEL	
MODELS AND PROPS	
SHIPPING AND INSURANCE	
TYPE	
STATS	
OTHER	
	EXPENSES SUBTOTAL
	TOTAL
	SALES TAX
	TOTAL DUE

ANY USAGE RIGHTS NOT EXCLUSIVELY TRANSFERRED ARE RESERVED TO DESIGNER. USAGE BEYOND THAT GRANTED TO CLIENT HEREIN SHALL REQUIRE PAYMENT OF A MUTUALLY AGREED UPON ADDITIONAL FEE SUBJECT TO ALL TERMS ON REVERSE.

(more)

RIGHTS TRANSFERRED. DESIGNER TRANSFERS TO THE CLIENT THE FOLLOWING EXCLUSIVE RIGHTS OF USAGE.	
(remove all italics before using this form)	
TITLE OR PRODUCT	*(name)*
CATEGORY OF USE	*(advertising, corporate, promotional, editorial, etc.)*
MEDIUM OF USE	*(consumer or trade magazine, annual report, TV, book, etc.)*
EDITION (IF BOOK)	*(hardcover, mass market paperbook, quality paperback, etc.)*
GEOGRAPHIC AREA	*(if applicable)*
TIME PERIOD	*(if applicable)*

ANY USAGE RIGHTS NOT EXCLUSIVELY TRANSFERRED ARE RESERVED TO DESIGNER. USAGE BEYOND THAT GRANTED TO CLIENT HEREIN SHALL REQUIRE PAYMENT OF A MUTUALLY AGREED UPON ADDITIONAL FEE SUBJECT TO ALL TERMS ON REVERSE.

Terms:

1. Time for Payment. All invoices are payable within thirty (30) days of receipt. A 1½% monthly service charge is payable on all overdue balances. The grant of any license or right of copyright is conditioned on receipt of full payment.

2. Estimates. If this form is used for an estimate or assignment confirmation, the fees and expenses shown are minimum estimates only. Final fees and expenses shall be shown when invoice is rendered. Client's approval shall be obtained for any increases in fees or expenses that exceed the original estimate by 10% or more.

3. Changes. Client shall be responsible for making additional payments for changes requested by Client in original assignment. However, no additional payment shall be made for changes required to conform to the original assignment description. The Client shall offer the Designer the first opportunity to make any changes.

4. Expenses. Client shall reimburse Designer for all expenses arising from this assignment, including the payment of any sales taxes due on this assignment, and shall advance $_____ to the Designer for payment of said expenses.

5. Cancellation. In the event of cancellation of this assignment, ownership of all copyrights and the original artwork is retained by the Designer and a cancellation fee for work completed, based on the contract price and expenses already incurred, shall be paid by the Client.

6. Ownership of Artwork. The Designer retains ownership of all original artwork, whether preliminary or final, and the Client shall return such artwork within thirty (30) days of use.

7. Credit Lines. The Designer and any other creators shall receive a credit line with any editorial usage. If similar credit lines are to be given with other types of usage, it must be so indicated here:

_____

_____

8. Releases. Client will indemnify Designer against all claims and expenses, including reasonable attorney's fees, due to uses for which no release was requested in writing or for uses which exceed authority granted by a release.

9. Modifications. Modification of the agreement must be written, except that the invoice may include, and Client shall be obligated to pay, fees or expenses that were orally authorized in order to progress promptly with work.

10. Arbitration. Any disputes in excess of $_____ (maximum limit for small claims court) arising out of this Agreement shall be submitted to binding arbitration before the Joint Ethics Committee or a mutually agreed upon arbitrator pursuant to the rules of the American Arbitration Association. The Arbitrator's award shall be final and judgment may be entered upon it in any court having jurisdiction thereof. The Client shall pay all arbitration and court costs, reasonable attorney's fees, and legal interest on any award or judgment in favor of the Designer.

11. Acceptance of Terms. The above terms incorporate Article 2 of the Uniform Commercial Code. If not objected to within ten (10) days, these terms shall be deemed acceptable.

12. Code of Fair Practice. The Client and Designer agree to comply with the provisions of the Code of Fair Practice, a copy of which may be obtained from the Joint Ethics Committee, P.O. Box 179 Grand Central Station, New York, New York 10017.

CONSENTED AND AGREED TO

_____
DATE

_____
DESIGNER'S SIGNATURE

_____
COMPANY NAME

_____
AUTHORIZED SIGNATURE

_____
NAME AND TITLE

MEMBER

Textile Designer's Confirmation Form

FRONT: DESIGNER'S LETTERHEAD

TO	DATE
	PATTERN NUMBER
	DUE DATE

ESTIMATED PRICES	
SKETCH	
REPEAT	
COLORINGS	
CORNERS	
TRACINGS	
OTHER	

DESCRIPTION OF ARTWORK		
REPEAT SIZE		
COLORS		
TYPE OF PRINTING		
½ DROP	☐ YES	☐ NO

SPECIAL COMMENTS

(more)

Terms:

1. Time for Payment. Because the major portion of the above work represents labor, all invoices are payable fifteen (15) days net. A 1½% monthly service charge is payable on all unpaid balances after this period. The grant of textile usage rights is conditioned on receipt of payment.

2. Estimated Prices. Prices shown above are minimum estimates only. Final prices shall be shown in invoice.

3. Payment for Changes. Client shall be responsible for making additional payments for changes requested by Client in original assignment.

4. Expenses. Client shall be responsible for payment of all extra expenses arising from assignment, including but not limited to photostats, mailings, messengers, shipping charges, and shipping insurance.

5. Sales Tax. Client shall assume responsibility for all sales taxes due on this assignment.

6. Cancellation Fees. Work cancelled by the client while in progress shall be compensated for on the basis of work completed at the time of cancellation and assumes that the Designer retains the project whatever its stage of completion. Upon cancellation, all rights, publication and other, revert to the Designer. Where Designer creates corners which are not developed into purchased sketches, a labor fee will be charged, and ownership of all copyrights and artwork is retained by the Designer.

7. Insuring Artwork. The client agrees when shipping artwork to provide insurance covering the fair market value of the artwork.

8. Arbitration. Any disputes in excess of $_____ (maximum limit for small claims court) arising out of this agreement shall be submitted to binding arbitration before the Joint Ethics Committee or a mutually agreed upon arbitrator pursuant to the rules of the American Arbitration Association. The Arbitrator's award shall be final, and judgment may be entered upon it in any court having jurisdiction thereof. The Client shall pay all arbitration and court costs, reasonable attorney's fees, and legal interest on any award or judgment in favor of the Designer.

9. The above terms incorporate Article 2 of the Uniform Commercial Code.

_____
CONSENTED AND AGREED TO

_____
DATE

_____
DESIGNER'S SIGNATURE

_____
COMPANY NAME

_____
AUTHORIZED SIGNATURE

_____
NAME AND TITLE

MEMBER TEXTILE DESIGNERS GUILD
A DISCIPLINE OF THE GRAPHIC ARTISTS GUILD

124

Illustrator's Invoice

TO	DATE
	AUTHORIZED ART BUYER
	ILLUSTRATOR'S JOB NUMBER
	CLIENT'S JOB NUMBER

ASSIGNMENT DESCRIPTION

	FEE

ITEMIZED EXPENSES (OTHER BILLABLE ITEMS)

CLIENT'S ALTERATIONS	
SALE OF ORIGINAL ART	
MISCELLANEOUS	
	TOTAL
	SALES TAX
	PAYMENTS ON ACCOUNT
	BALANCE DUE

ORIGINAL ARTWORK, INCLUDING SKETCHES AND ANY OTHER PRELIMINARY MATERIALS, REMAIN THE PROPERTY OF THE ILLUS-TRATOR UNLESS PURCHASED BY PAYMENT OF A SEPARATE FEE SUBJECT TO TERMS APPEARING ON REVERSE SIDE.

(more)

RIGHTS TRANSFERRED (ALL OTHER RIGHTS RESERVED BY THE ILLUSTRATOR)	
FOR USE IN MAGAZINES AND NEWSPAPERS, FIRST NORTH AMERICAN REPRODUCTION RIGHTS UNLESS SPECIFIED OTHERWISE HERE	
	(remove all italics before using this form)
FOR ALL OTHER USES, THE CLIENT ACQUIRES ONLY THE FOLLOWING RIGHTS	
TITLE OR PRODUCT	*(name)*
CATEGORY OF USE	*(advertising, corporate, promotional, editorial, etc.)*
MEDIUM OF USE	*(consumer or trade magazine, annual report, TV, book, etc.)*
GEOGRAPHIC AREA	*(if applicable)*
TIME PERIOD	*(if applicable)*
NUMBER OF USES	*(if applicable)*
OTHER	*(if applicable)*

ORIGINAL ARTWORK, INCLUDING SKETCHES AND ANY OTHER PRELIMINARY MATERIAL, REMAINS THE PROPERTY OF THE ILLUSTRATOR UNLESS PURCHASED BY A PAYMENT OF A SEPARATE FEE.

Terms:

1. Time for Payment. Payment is due within thirty (30) days of receipt of invoice. A 1½ % monthly service charge will be billed for late payment.

2. Default in Payment. The client shall assume responsibility for all collection and legal fees necessitated by default in payment.

3. Grant of Rights. The grant of reproduction rights is conditioned on receipt of payment.

4. Credit Lines. On any contribution for magazine or book use, the Illustrator shall receive name credit in print. If name credit is to be given with other types of use, it must be specified here:

_____

☐ If this box is checked by the Illustrator, the Illustrator shall receive copyright notice adjacent to the work in the form
©_____ 198_____

5. Additional Limitations. If Illustrator and Client have agreed to additional limitations as to either the duration or geographical extent of the permitted use, specify here:

_____

6. Return of Artwork. Client assumes responsibility for the return of the artwork in undamaged condition within thirty (30) days of first reproduction.

7. Unauthorized Use. Client will indemnify Illustrator against all claims and expenses, including reasonable attorney's fees, arising from uses for which no release was requested in writing or for uses which exceed the authority granted by a release.

8. Arbitration. Any disputes in excess of $_____ (maximum limit for small claims court) arising out of this Agreement shall be submitted to binding arbitration before the Joint Ethics Committee or a mutually agreed upon arbitrator pursuant to the rules of the American Arbitration Association. The Arbitrator's award shall be final, and judgment upon it may be entered upon it in any court having jurisdiction thereof. The client shall pay all arbitration and court costs, reasonable attorney's fees, and legal interest on any award or judgment in favor of the Illustrator.

9. Acceptance of Terms. If the terms of this invoice are not objected to within ten (10) days of receipt, the terms shall be deemed accepted.

MEMBER

Chapter 15

Publishing contracts

One of the most sophisticated contracts for the sale of reproduction rights is the book publishing contract. A book of illustrations, photographs or any art will require the negotiation of the same type of contract offered to an author. Even if an artist and author collaborate, each will usually negotiate such a contract with the publisher. If the artist and author are co-authors, it is important to enter into a collaboration agreement to avoid misunderstandings as to rights, royalties and a myriad of other issues.

This chapter examines the standard clauses in the author's book contract to determine how each of the provisions should be negotiated. The Authors Guild, Inc., has published the Authors Guild Trade Book Contract and ASMP has published a Standard Photographers Book Agreement, both of which recommend terms the author or artist should seek. The provisions of a collaboration agreement are also examined.

A model contract appears at the end of the chapter and its terms are referred to in the discussion of the various provisions. Any professional publishing house will have its own contract, but the terms of the model contract may be used for comparison. Also, artists are sometimes asked by non-professional book publishers to illustrate a book. For example, a charity or chamber of commerce might want to do a book of special local interest. If neither party has any publishing background, the model contract could be adopted for this purpose. Certain clauses, such as the subsidiary rights clause, have been eliminated because they would not pertain to this kind of venture. However, the contract tries to cover all the areas that the artist and the other party might conceivably want to deal with in an agreement.

Many of the provisions will require negotiation and the terms that have been filled in are only suggestions. This agreement would be considered generally favorable to the artist. For artists who wish to delve more deeply into the subject of agreements with publishers, *The Writer's Legal Guide* by Tad Crawford is the most complete handbook on the subject.

The complexity of book contracts makes the advice of an agent or lawyer especially valuable.

Grants of rights

After setting out the names of the parties and the date, a book contract will detail the rights granted by the artist to the publisher (model agreement, Paragraph 1). "All rights" would be the transfer of all the rights possessed by the artist to the publisher. This would mean the publisher—and no one else—could exploit the work as a book or in any other medium without any limitation as to either territory or time. If, for example, the publisher wished to exploit the work on tee shirts, posters, jewelry or dolls, the artist would not have any right to prevent such uses. Artists who create designs for book covers frequently find that the design is subsequently used for advertising or paperbacks without the artist being entitled to additional payments.

The grant of rights can be limited as to uses which can be made of the art work, the time during which the work can be used in book form and the territory in which the book can be sold. The rights not conveyed in the grant of rights provision, however, might still be conveyed as subsidiary rights.

Subsidiary rights

Subsidiary rights cover many of the uses not permitted by the grants of rights, such as abridgments, anthologies, book clubs, reprints by another publisher, first and second serializations (which are magazine rights before and after book publication), syndication, advertising, novelty uses, translation and foreign language publications, motion pictures, dramatic, radio, television and mechancial rendition or recording uses. The definition of these rights can vary in different contracts.

The publisher often has the exclusive power to dispose of the subsidiary rights. The division of income between publisher and artist is specified as to each subsidiary right. Often the division of subsidiary rights income is shared equally by author and publisher. However, the Authors Guild makes the general distinction that only publishing rights should be granted in a publishing contract. Therefore, the Authors Guild would recommend against granting any control over, or benefits from, nonpublishing subsidiary rights, such as stage, record, radio, motion picture, television and audiovisual rights. The artist might particularly seek to reserve all rights to advertising and novelty uses. For each subsidiary right, the artist should consider demanding the power either to control the right or to veto exercises of the right by the publisher. At the least, however, the artist should receive copies of any licenses for subsidiary rights granted by the publisher.

Reservation of rights

The grant of rights and the subsidiary rights provisions will normally cover all the conceivable uses of the artist's work. However, the artist should anticipate unthought of, even uninvented, uses. This is done by insisting on a simple clause stating, "All rights not specifically granted to the publisher are reserved to the artist," (model agreement, Paragraph 2).

Delivery of manuscript

The contract will require the artist to deliver a manuscript on or before a specified date (model agreement, Paragraph 3). If the contract specifies that the manuscript be in "content and form satisfactory to the publisher," the artist should at least have the word "reasonably" inserted before "satisfactory." A less likely solution would be to allow the publisher to reject a manuscript deemed unsatisfactory, but not allow the publisher to demand back advances given to the artist (model agreement, Paragraph 20). If the publisher has seen either

completed work or work in progress, the provision should be modified to indicate such work as satisfactory. Also, the artist should have a grace period for illness and similar eventualities which may cause the work to be delivered late.

The contract may require the artist to deliver a manuscript consisting of more than just art work. The artist may be responsible for the title page, preface or foreword, table of contents, index, charts, all permissions (including payments for such permissions) and a bibliography (model agreement, Paragraphs 4 and 5). If the artist does not supply these materials, the publisher will normally have the right to pay for them and deduct the cost from the artist's royalties.

Royalties

The artist may sell art work for a flat fee, in which case no royalties would be payable. However, royalties permit the artist to share in the success of the book and usually are desirable. The artist receives a royalty for each copy sold, with the royalty rate often increasing with the number of copies sold (model agreement, Paragraph 7). If the artist has done both text and art for a hardcover trade book, the royalties might be 10 percent of retail price on the first 5,000 copies sold, 12 1/2 percent on the next 5,000 copies sold and 15 percent on all copies sold in excess of 10,000. If the artist has only contributed art to the book, an arrangement which divides the royalties between artist and author is fair. The precise sharing depends on the degree of work done by each party, who originated the concept for the book and whose name will make the book sell (if this is relevant). Because of the complexity of royalty rates and the fact these rates vary for different categories of books, the artist should really seek expert advice from more experienced artists or agents when trying to determine whether an offered royalty is fair. It is important to ascertain which copies sold are counted for purposes of reaching the 5,000 and 10,000 copy levels at which the royalty percentage escalates. While copies sold through bookstores at full price are generally counted, copies sold to book clubs or at high discounts are not counted.

Fairness, however, is not based only on the royalty percentages. The way in which the royalty is defined is very important. Basically, the royalty should always be a percentage based on the publisher's retail list price, the price at which the book will be sold to the public. If the royalty is based on net price—that is the price after discounts to wholesalers and book stores—the royalties will be far lower than if based on retail list price. The royalty should not be a specific amount, such as one dollar per copy, because the publisher invariably has the power to determine the selling price of the book.

Royalties will often be reduced on copies sold in digest form, in a foreign language edition, at higher than usual discounts, directly by the publisher due to the publisher's advertising and in other circumstances which are listed in each contract. The artist must consider whether each reduction is fair because of the significant effect reductions can have on royalties.

Advances

The advance is paid to the artist against royalties to be received in the future (model agreement, Paragraph 8). The artist might reasonably request an advance equal to 50 or 75 percent of the royalties anticipated during the first year of sale of the book. The advance may be paid in full at the time of signing the contract or may be paid in equal installments at the time of signing, delivery of the manuscript and publication. The artist should always request that the advance be nonreturnable except for failure to deliver the manuscript. Also, the artist should not permit a provision which would allow the advance under one contract to be deducted from royalties earned under a contract for a different book.

Payments, statements of account, inspection of books

Payment of royalties should be made on a periodic basis, usually quarterly or semiannually (model agreement, Paragraph 10). The right of the publisher to maintain a reserve against returns—that is to hold part of the royalties in case the books are re-turned by bookstores—should be limited to a small percentage of the royalties. There should also be a time period beyond which such reserved royalties cannot be held (model agreement, Paragraph 9).

The Authors Guild provision requires a statement of account showing the total sales to date and the number of copies sold for the period just ended, the list price, the rate for royalties, the amount of royalties, the amount of returns and information relating to licensing income (model agreement, Paragraph 9). The Authors Guild provides for the artist to examine the publisher's books and records at any time, upon the artist's written request, although most publishers will restrict this right of inspection (model agreement, Paragraph 11).

Duty to publish and keep work in print

The artist should ideally require the publisher to stipulate the date when the book will be published (model agreement, Paragraph 6). The Authors Guild provision requires publication within one year of delivery of the manuscript by the artist, while many other contracts specify a reasonable time or merely state that the date of publication will be at the publisher's discretion. The artist can request a provision expressly reverting all rights to the artist if the book is not published within the stipulated period of time, unless delays are of a nature which the publisher cannot avoid.

The artist should also seek to ensure that the book will be kept in print. If the publisher becomes bankrupt or insolvent or simply ceases to exploit the book by not printing copies for sale, the artist should no longer be obligated under the contract. In such an event, the artist should have the option within a certain time period (for example, sixty days) to purchase film, computer drive tapes, bound copies and sheet stock at or below the publisher's cost (model agreement, Paragraph 21). In order to seek a new publisher to promote the work more vigorously, the artist should receive back all rights, including any rights of copyright, which the publisher had in the work (model agreement, Paragraph 2). These provisions vary from contract to contract and often require that the artist either demand that the publisher reprint the work or give notice that the work is out-of-print, as defined in the contract.

Copyright and suits for infringement

The copyright should be secured in the artist's name by the publisher (model agreement, Paragraph 12). The publisher should be required to gain copyright protection by the use of appropriate notice whenever and wherever the work will be published. To assist in this, the artist should provide the publisher with a list of all previous publications of the work submitted for use in the book.

If the copyright is infringed, the publisher can sue the infringer but is not obliged to do so (model agreement, Paragraph 19). If the publisher or artist sues alone, the other party should have to cooperate. The party bringing suit would normally bear the costs and recoup them from any recovery. If both parties sue, the cost would be split as agreed in the contract. In either case, provision must be made for the division of amounts recovered in excess of costs. The artist should have exclusive power to sue for infringement of rights retained by the artist.

Warranty and indemnity

The contract will require the artist to give an express warranty to the effect that the work does not infringe any copyright, violate any property rights or contain any scandalous, libelous or unlawful matter (model agreement, Paragraph 13). The artist must agree to indemnify the publisher against all claims, costs, expenses and attorney's fees. This means the artist will pay for the publisher's expenditures caused by any breach or alleged breach. The publisher will have the right to withhold the artist's royalties until any suit or threatened suit is settled.

ASMP provides the exact opposite by requiring that the publisher indemnify the artist. The artist under the ASMP provision explicitly makes no warranty. More realistic is the Authors Guild provision in which the warranty is modified by the artist's stating that the work, "to his knowledge," is neither libelous nor violative of privacy rights. The artist's liability under the Author's Guild provision is limited to the lesser of a stated amount or a percentage of the sums due the artist under the contract. Such liability exists, however, only as to final judgments for damages after all appeals have been taken, so that alleged breaches of warranty which do not result in final judgments would not make the artist liable for any of the publisher's expenditures. If the artist defends the suit, then the artist is not liable to pay the fees of lawyers retained by the publisher. Also, the Author's Guild limits the amount of royalities which can be withheld by the publisher to a stated percentage, in no event more than the damages claimed in any suit.

Recently a number of leading publishers have extended their liability insurance to protect artists in the event of such lawsuits. Needless to say, this is an important advantage for the artist.

Artistic control

Since the contract requires the publisher's approval of or satisfaction with the work, artistic control resides in the publisher. Few publishers, if any, would agree to the ASMP provision requiring that the book be published in a form approved by the artist. The model agreement proposes consultation between publisher and artist as to title, price, promotion, production and similar important issues (model agreement, Paragraph 14). However, unless specified otherwise, the publisher is given the final decision-making power. But the artist should insist on the opportunity to make any necessary changes in the work and should certainly seek the right to approve any changes in the work done by other persons. If the artist chooses to change the work after the book is in production, he or she may be liable for part of the cost of such changes.

If an edition in the future is to be revised, the artist should have the opportunity to do any necessary revisions. If the artist cannot make such revisions, the cost of the revisions would be deducted from royalties due the artist (model agreement, Paragraph 17). But the artist should not permit any such payments to be deducted from royalties owed the artist under other contracts with the publisher. The artist can protect against losing royalties due to revisions by requiring that no revisions be made for a specified period after the signing of the contract.

The publisher will have the power to fix the book's retail price, title, form, type, paper and similar details. If the artist wishes to have a voice in any of these matters, an appropriate provision should be made in the contract.

Credits

The exact nature of the artist's credit should be specified, including size and placement, especially if a writer or editor has also worked on the book (model agreement, Paragraph 12). If another person may revise the book in the future, the credit to be given such a reviser should be specified. The artist should remember that, without a provision for credit, the artist's right to such credit may be in question and reside in the publisher's discretion.

Original materials

The publisher should be required to return the original art work to the artist (model agreement, Paragraph 15). The publisher will usually not agree to either insure the work or pay if the work is damaged, although the artist might demand this if the work is of great value. The publisher should agree to try and keep the original art work in good condition for return to the artist.

Competing works

The publisher may try to restrict the artist from creating competing works. Such a provision can prevent the artist from creating any work on the same subject as the work to be published. The artist may not be able to agree to such a provision, especially if all the artist's work is similar. The artist might, therefore, seek to have this provision limited to material

directly based on the work to be published. Another approach would be to limit the time during which the restrictions on competing works would remain in force. Ideally, the artist should seek to have this provision stricken from the contract.

Options

Another common provision gives the publisher the option to publish the artist's next work. Such a provision may well be unenforceable unless the terms of the future publication are made definite. In any case, the artist should insist that the option provision be deleted from the contract. If the artist and the publisher are satisfied with one another, they will want to contract for future books. If they are not satisfied, there is no reason why the artist should have to offer the next book to the publisher. If an option provision is agreed to, the artist should not give an option for more than one work and should require the publisher to make a determination with regard to that work within a reasonable time period after submission.

Another type of option clause gives the publisher the right to meet the terms offered by another publisher on a succeeding work. In any type of option clause, the publisher should be required to exercise the option based on submission of a proposal (with or without sample chapter) rather than on receipt of a full length manuscript or completed body of work.

Free copies

Most publication contracts will provide for the artist to receive five to ten free copies of the final book (model agreement, Paragraph 16). Additionally, provision is made for the artist to purchase unlimited copies at a substantial discount, such as 40 percent, from retail list price. The artist should be certain such a provision is contained in the contract. If the 40 percent discount provision requires the copies be used for personal purposes only, the artist should consider whether he or she might in fact want to sell the copies. And if the artist wants to buy hundreds or thousands of copies, it may very well be possible to negotiate a far higher discount than

40 percent. This is especially true if the artist places an order prior to the publisher's printing or reprinting of the book.

Assignment

ASMP provides that the artist may assign the contract without the publisher's consent, while the publisher can assign the contract only with the consent of the artist. A more common provision would require the written consent of either party to an assignment by the other. Presumably the publisher would not wish to have another artist substituted under the contract, but nothing should prevent the artist from assigning to another person money due or to become due under the contract (model agreement, Paragraph 18). The publisher may also require a provision permitting assignment to a new publisher which is taking over the publisher's business.

Agents

Book agents have traditionally received 10 percent of the monies due to an author, although some agents are now asking between 12 1/2 and 15 percent. The artist's contract with an agent may give the agent authority to act on behalf of the artist in all matters arising from the contract. If, in fact, the agent's powers are limited, it would be wise to strike this provision and append a copy of the artist-agent contract to the publishing contract. Also, the artist should always have the right to receive payment directly from the publisher for a minimum of 90 percent (or 85 percent if the fee is 15 percent) of sums due if the artist wants direct payment once the artist-agent contract has terminated. This can be accomplished by the use of a clause to the effect that "The authorization of the agent to act on behalf of the artist and to collect sums due the artist shall continue in effect until the publisher shall otherwise be instructed in writing, by the artist." The exact language of the agency clause will have to be negotiated in the artist-agent contract.

Advertising

Some artists who create books which are potentially very profitable to publishers may be able to require the designation of an advertising budget. If this is done, the budget should only be expendable for the single title, not group ads including other titles. A further breakdown into the categories of advertising is difficult prior to publication, although in special cases it may be possible to pinpoint markets in which advertising should later take place. The artist risks limiting the publisher's flexibility, however, and perhaps also having the publisher cease advertising once the stipulated amount has been expended. The more usual approach is to request the highest possible advance, and leave the publisher to its own ingenuity with respect to advertising and promotion.

Most contracts require that the artist allow the publisher to use the artist's name, likeness or photograph in advertising and promotion for the work. This clause is desirable, but the artist might want an assurance that a suitable decorum will be maintained.

Arbitration

The artist will generally benefit from an arbitration provision, because disputes under the contract can be quickly and easily resolved. Many contracts will provide for arbitration before the American Arbitration Association, but the artist should be satisfied as long as unbiased arbitrators will hear the dispute. The disadvantage of arbitration is that an arbitrator's adverse decision is very difficult to appeal to the courts, so the artist should feel certain the arbitration will be fairly conducted.

Other Provisions

The contract will require that modifications be in writing (model agreement, Paragraph 23). The state under the laws which the contract is governed will be specified. The contract will state their heirs, legal representatives, successors and assigns are bound by its terms (model agreement, Paragraph 18). Waivers or defaults under one provision will usually be restricted so as neither to permit future waivers or defaults nor to affect obligations under other provisions of the contract (model agreement, Paragraph 24).

Collaborators

The artist may collaborate with another artist, a writer, an editor, a technical expert or a well-known person. In some cases collaboration may be with someone the artist never meets, but who merely contributes material for the book. In any case, the artist and any collaborator must have a contract between them which divides up all the rights (especially the rights to control and receive income) contained in the publishing contract. In the absence of a provision giving control over uses of the work to one party, all collaborators will normally have the power to authorize nonexclusive licenses and the income will be shared among the collaborators. The contract must include a method for resolving disputes, such as a disagreement over

publishers to which the completed work will be submitted. Thought must be given to what will happen if one party became disabled or dies during the collaboration. Artistic control—and an orderly plan to progress the work—must be determined. Authorship credit will require elaboration. It must be decided who will own the copyright and what will be the form of copyright notice. If each collaborator can sell his or her interest in the work, the other parties may wish a right to have first opportunity to purchase the interest on the same terms being offered by outsiders. Consideration should also be given to whether the collaborators should have a separate or a joint contract with the publisher. For example, is the artist to be liable for breaches of a warranty by a collaborator? These and similar questions will depend on the contractual relationship of the collaborators to one another and the publisher. And if the collaboration fails to reach fruition, a determination must have been made as to the rights each collaborator will have in the incomplete work.

Model publishing agreement

Agreement, this _____ day of _____ , 19_____ , between _____
_____ residing at _____
_____ (hereinafter the Publisher), and, _____
_____ residing at _____

_____ (hereinafter the Artist).
WHEREAS, the Artist wishes to create a book on the subject of _____ ;
WHEREAS, the Publisher is familiar with the work of the Artist and wishes to distribute such a book; and
WHEREAS, the parties wish to have said distribution performed subject to the mutual obligations, covenants and conditions herein.
NOW, THEREFORE, in consideration of the foregoing premises and the mutual covenants hereinafter set forth and other valuable considerations, the parties hereto agree as follows:
1. GRANT OF RIGHTS. The Artist grants, conveys and transfers to the Publisher in that certain unpublished work titled _____ , the following rights: (Exclusive North American rights in hardcover book form in the English language for a period of five years would be one example of a possible—although unusually restrictive—grant of rights.)
2. RESERVATION AND REVERSION OF RIGHTS. All rights not specifically granted to the Publisher are reserved to the Artist. In the event of termination of the Agreement, the Publisher shall grant, convey and transfer all rights in the work back to the Artist.
3. DELIVERY OF MANUSCRIPT. On or before the _____ day of _____ , 19 _____ , the Artist shall deliver to the Publisher a complete manuscript of approximately _____ words and including the additional materials listed in Paragraph 4. If the Artist fails to deliver the complete manuscript within ninety days after receiving notice from the Publisher of failure to deliver on time, the Publisher shall have the right to terminate this Agreement and receive back from the artist all monies advanced to the Artist pursuant to Paragraphs 4, 5 and 8.

4. ADDITIONAL MATERIALS. The following materials shall be provided by the Artist: (photographs, drawings, maps, tables, charts, index, other illustrations, described more fully as follows _____ .) The cost of providing these additional materials shall be borne by the Artist, provided, however, that the Publisher at the time of signing this Agreement shall give a nonrefundable payment of $_____ to assist the Artist in defraying these costs.

5. PERMISSIONS. The Artist agrees to obtain all permissions that are necessary for the use of materials copyrighted by others. The cost of providing these permissions shall be borne by the Artist, provided, however, that the Publisher at the time of signing this Agreement shall give a nonrefundable payment of $_____ to assist the Artist in defraying these costs.

6. DUTY TO PUBLISH. The Publisher shall publish the book within twelve months of the delivery of the complete manuscript. Failure to so publish shall give the Artist the right to terminate this Agreement ninety days after giving written notice to the Publisher of the failure to make timely publication. In the event of such termination, the Artist shall have no obligation to return monies received pursuant to Paragraphs 4, 5 and 8.

7. ROYALTIES. The Publisher shall pay the Artist the following royalties: 10 percent of retail price on the first 5,000 copies sold; 12 1/2 percent of retail price on the next 5,000 copies sold; and 15 percent of retail price on all copies sold thereafter.

8. ADVANCES. The Publisher shall, at the time of signing this Agreement, pay to the Artist a nonrefundable advance of $_____ , which advance shall be recouped by the Publisher from payments due to the Artist pursuant to Paragraph 10 of this Agreement.

9. ACCOUNTINGS. The Publisher shall render quarterly reports to the Artist showing for that quarter and cumulatively to date the number of copies printed and bound, the number of copies sold, the number of copies returned, the number of copies distributed free for publicity purposes, the number of copies remaindered, destroyed, or lost, and the royalties paid to and owed to the Artist. If the Publisher sets up a reserve against returns of books, the reserve may only be set up for the four accounting periods following the first publication of the book and shall in no event exceed 15 percent of royalties due to the Artist in any period.

10. PAYMENTS. The Publisher shall pay the Artist all monies due Artist pursuant to Paragraph 9 within thirty days of the close of each quarterly period.

11. RIGHT OF INSPECTION. The Artist shall, upon the giving of written notice, have the right to inspect the Publisher's books of account to verify the quarterly accountings. If errors in any such accounting are found to be to the Artist's disadvantage and represent more than 5 percent of the payment to the Artist pursuant to the said accounting, the cost of inspection shall be paid by the Publisher.

12. COPYRIGHT AND AUTHORSHIP CREDIT. The Publisher shall, as an express condition of receiving the grant of rights specified in Paragraph 1, take the necessary steps to register the copyright on behalf of the Artist and in the Artist's name and shall place copyright notice in the Artist's name on all copies of the book. The Artist shall receive authorship credit as follows: _____ .

13. WARRANTY AND INDEMNITY. The Artist warrants and represents that he or she is the sole creator of the book and owns all rights granted under this Agreement, that the book is an original creation and has not previously been published (indicate any parts that have been previously published), that the book does not infringe any other person's copyrights or rights of literary property, nor, to his or her knowledge, does it violate the rights of privacy of, or libel, other persons. The Artist agrees to indemnify the Publisher against any final judgment for damages (after all appeals have been exhausted) in any lawsuit based on an actual breach of the foregoing warranties. In addition, the Artist shall pay the Publisher's reasonable costs and attorney's fees incurred in defending such a lawsuit, unless the Artist chooses to retain his or her own attorney to defend such lawsuit. The Artist makes no warranties and shall have no obligation to indemnify the Publisher with respect to materials inserted in the book at the Publisher's request. Notwithstanding any of the foregoing, in no event shall the Artist's liability under this Paragraph exceed $_____ or _____ percent of sums payable to Artist under this Agreement, whichever is the lesser. In the event a lawsuit is brought which may result in the Artist having breached his or her warranties under this Paragraph, the Publisher shall have the right to withhold and place in an escrow account _____ percent of sums payable to the Artist pursuant to Paragraph 10, but in no event may said withholding exceed the damages alleged in the complaint.

14. ARTISTIC CONTROL. The Artist and Publisher shall consult with one another with respect to the title of the book, the price of the book, the method and means of advertising and selling the book, the number and destination of free copies, the number of copies to be printed, the method of printing and other publishing processes, the exact date of publication, the form, style, size, type, paper to be used, and like details, how long the plates or type shall be preserved and when they shall be destroyed and when new print-

ings of the book shall be made. In the event of disagreement after consultation, the Publisher shall have final power of decision over all the foregoing matters except the following, which shall be controlled by the Artist: _____ .
No changes shall be made in the complete manuscript of the book by persons other than the Artist, unless the Artist consents to such changes.

15. ORIGINAL MATERIALS. Within thirty days after publication, the Publisher shall return the original manuscript and all additional materials to the Artist. The Publisher shall provide the Artist with a copy of the page proofs, if the Artist requests them prior to the date of publication.

16. FREE COPIES. The Artist shall receive ten free copies of the book, after which the Artist shall have the right to purchase additional copies at a 40 percent discount from the retail price.

17. REVISIONS. The Artist agrees to revise the book on request by the Publisher. If the Artist cannot revise the book or refuses to do so absent good cause, the Publisher shall have the right to have the book revised by a person competent to do so and shall charge the costs of said revision against payments due the Artist under Paragraph 10.

18. SUCCESSORS AND ASSIGNS. This Agreement may not be assigned by either party without the written consent of the other party hereto. The Artist, however, shall retain the right to assign payments due hereunder without obtaining the Publisher's consent. This Agreement shall be binding on the parties and their respective heirs, administrators, successors and assigns.

19. INFRINGEMENT. In the event of an infringement of the rights granted under this Agreement to the Publisher, the Publisher and Artist shall have the right to sue jointly for the infringement and, after deducting the expenses of bringing suit, to share equally in any recovery. If either party choses not to join in the suit, the other party may proceed and, after deducting all the expenses of bringing the suit, any recovery shall be shared equally between the parties.

20. TERMINATION. The Artist shall have the right to terminate this Agreement by written notice if: (1) the book goes out-of-print and the Publisher, within ninety days of receiving notice from the Artist that the book is out-of-print, does not place the book in print again; (2) if the Publisher fails to provide statements of account pursuant to Paragraph 9; (3) if the Publisher fails to make payments pursuant to Paragraph 10; or (4) if the Publisher fails to publish in a timely manner pursuant to Paragraph 6. The Publisher shall have the right to terminate this Agreement as follows: (1) as provided in Paragraph 3, if the Artist fails to deliver a complete manuscript; and (2) if the complete manuscript delivered pursuant to Paragraph 3 is unsatisfactory to the Publisher, but in the event of such termination the Publisher shall have no right to receive back monies paid to the Artist pursuant to Paragraphs 4, 5 and 8. This Agreement shall automatically terminate in the event of the Publisher's insolvency, bankruptcy or assignment of assets for the benefit of creditors.

21. PRODUCTION MATERIALS AND UNBOUND COPIES. Upon any termination, the Artist may, within sixty days of notification of such termination, purchase the plates, offset negatives or computer drive tapes (if any) at their scrap value and any remaining copies at cost.

22. NOTICE. Where written notice is required hereunder, it may be given by use of first class mail addressed to the Artist or Publisher at the addresses given at the beginning of this Agreement. Said addresses for notice may be changed by giving written notice of any new address to the other party.

23. MODIFICATIONS IN WRITING. All modifications of this Agreement must be in writing and signed by both parties.

24. WAIVERS AND DEFAULTS. Any waiver of a breach or default hereunder shall not be deemed a waiver of a subsequent breach or default of either the same provision or any other provision of this Agreement.

25. This Agreement shall be governed by the laws of _____ State.

_____
Artist

_____
Publisher

_____
By: (Signer's Name and Title)

Chapter 16

Video art works

The artist's ability to conceive works in new media offers a challenge for the lawyer who must innovate legally. Art on videotape, often combined with pictorial or sculptural elements, is becoming a medium used with regularity by artists. The legal problems of the video artist are for the most part the same as those of the artist using more traditional media. But the possiblity of both mass reproduction and public broadcasting of video works raises additional legal dimensions.

Artist-gallery agreement

The agreement on pages 142-143 is between an artist and a gallery for the sale and rental of a video work by the gallery. The video artist must consider all of the issues raised in Chapter 13 regarding artist-gallery relationships, and this agreement specifically deals with the nature and geographic scope of the agency (Article 1), the term (Article 2), the gallery's use of best efforts (Article 3), commissions for sale or rental (Article 4), statements of accounts and payment (Article 4), the quantity of work subject to the agreement (Article 5), prices (Article 7), promotion of work and the artist (Article 9), assignment (Article 10), termination (Article 11), the death of either party or cessation of business by the gallery (Article 12), arbitration (Article 13), modifications to be written (Article 14) and the laws of which state will govern the agreement (Article 15). The agreement also contains provisions not found when works in more traditional media are being sold or rented. The artist may create a video piece with several videotapes running simultaneously or with videotape to be used in conjunction with photographs, sculptures or paintings. The artist would not usually want the elements of such work to be exhibited separately. The agreement

provides that the sale or rental must be of the entire work (Article 1). Also, the ease of video reproduction makes copyright even more important for the artist working with video than for other artists. For this reason the agreement specifies that the agency is only to sell the physical videotape cassettes and requires the gallery to protect the copyright against infringement (Articles 1 and 3). The gallery must obtain the agreement of each person who purchases or rents a copy of the work not to make further copies (Article 8). The dealer can only replace copies of the work if the purchaser returns the defective or damaged copy originally purchased (Article 5). The gallery must also seek to prevent a purchaser's broadcasting the work or charging admission (Article 8).

The ease of reproduction also bears on another important issue—whether or not to make the video work a limited edition. This decision may turn on many factors, such as the extent of the market, the price enhancement created by limiting the edition and perhaps even the desire of the artist to maintain a tie to the traditional media in which work is usually either unique or original. The agreement provides that no more than fifty copies of the work shall be created, guaranteeing originality, and in this case reserves twenty-five copies to the artist for sale outside the scope of the agreement. The artist might wish to use a signed warranty of originality like that described for photographic works on page 67. This signature and assurance of the limited number of identical works or works derived from the entire work will reassure the collector as to value in this relatively new art medium.

The cost of creating copies from the master tape is the gallery's responsibility, but the artist keeps control of the master tape and has copyright notice on each copy in the artist's name (Article 6). This particular agreement does not reduce the adjusted gross proceeds specified in Article 4 by the gallery's cost of the copies, although the gallery might insist that such a reduction is only equitable.

If the gallery is to live up to the obligations contained in the agreement, the bill of sale or the rental agreement must conform to the terms restricting the purchaser's rights in the work. The bill of sale on page 144 therefore places many restrictions on the rights of the purchaser. The artist might also use this bill of sale with minor modifications when selling work directly to purchasers.

Broadcasting

The potentialities of videotape naturally open the possibility of far wider dissemination than art works have traditionally experienced. This potentiality has been recognized in an excellent article, "The Commissioning Contract for Video Artists," and in the contract draft with explanatory notes prepared for the American Council for the Arts by Harvey Horowitz, a member of the New York City law firm of Squadron, Ellenoff Plesent & Lehrer. The article and contract originally appeared in the *Arts Advocate* and are reprinted here by permission of the American Council for the Arts, © Advocates for the Arts 1975.

The commission contract for video artists by Harvery Horowitz

The commissioning contract is standard practice in publishing, film and commercial television, but it is relatively new for the creative video artist. It is therefore important for the video artists engaged in this field to be aware of the legal ramifications of a video commissioning contract.

In the legal sense a video artist is distinct from an employee for hire who is engaged to make a work for a fee where the finished product belongs to the employer. Video artists are those who conceive and produce their work and view the finished product as their own. They usually function simultaneously as producer, director, cameraman, technician, sound synchronizer and editor. There is often confusion over the rights to the product of video artists—who owns it and for how long?

The guiding principle the artist should understand is that the artist originally owns the work and all rights connected to it. From that premise on, what any contract does is to exchange part of those rights for certain benefits to both sides. What this contract tries to do is to keep the give and take on an even basis so that the quid is balanced with the quo equally for both parties. It is up to the artist to make sure he is not being short-weighted. Some commissioning stations, for example, begin negotiations with a pretty heavy finger on the scale, claiming that the large costs of production, advertising, etc., entitle them to most of the rights over the work. The argument may hold for the station's employees over whose work the station may have blanket rights, but not for the independent artist who already owns his package and barters rights in exchange for guarantees of how it is to be used, compensation and so on.

In television, including public broadcasting, contracts are commonplace. The following contract is not earthshaking, innovative, or novel in the law. It may, however, be innovative for the video artist. It is draftd in the traditional legal format and deals with the issues that matter. The artist should become familiar with the import of its language.

If we could win acceptance for a form contract tilted somewhat in favor of the artist who takes most of the risks, makes the most creative effort, and who, by rights, ought to be the one to propose "terms of agreement," we will have taken another small step forward for the economic rights of artists—a primary and continuing concern of Advocates for the Arts.

Model video broadcast contract

Dear _____

    This letter will confirm the agreement reached between A. Artist (herein "the Artist") and Broadcasting in Education (herein "BIE").

Par 1. BIE hereby commissions the Artist to create a video work having as a working title, "The High Tower" (herein "the Work"). In connection with the production of the Work, the Artist shall have the right to use the production facilities of BIE in accordance with Schedule A attached hereto. The Work shall be approximately fifty minutes in length and deal with the subject of high towers. The Artist agrees to consult with members of the staff of BIE at reasonable times although it is recognized that all artistic decisions with respect to the Work shall be made by the Artist.

Comment: The main thrust of the commissioning clause is to provide for the Work to be commissioned. Usually it will be unnecessary to describe the Work beyond the title and possibly the subject matter. The Artist should be able to use the facilities of the station, and, while he may be required to consult with station staff, it should be clear that artistic decisions will be made by the Artist. Schedule A to the agreement is intended to include the details of the Artist's permitted use of the station's production facilities including such items as, hours and days per week a facility will be available, equipment and supplies available to artist and personnel available to the Artist.

Sometimes the commissioning program involves the Artist serving as an artist-in-residence, or performing services in addition to producing the Work. Under such circumstances, the contract should be specific concerning the nature of the additional work to be performed by the Artist, the amount of time the Artist will be required to devote and additional compensation, if any. If the rendition of these additional services will possibly cause a time conflict for the Artist, the times and dates for the performance of these additional services should be subject to mutual agreement.

Par 2. In consideration for the rights to the Work granted to BIE hereunder, the Artist shall be paid the sum of three thousand dollars as a fee for the Artist's services payable as follows:

One thousand five hundred dollars upon execution of this agreement; and

One thousand five hundred dollars within 30 days of the completion of the Work or upon broadcast of the Work, whichever is earlier.*

The Work shall be deemed completed upon delivery of a finished master tape to BIE. In connection with the creation of the Work, BIE will reimburse the Artist for the expenses itemized on the expense schedule annexed hereto.

*Note: All money amounts and time periods given are, of course, arbitrary, included for the sake of continuity, and are not intended to suggest actual rates and conditions.

Comment: Aside from the obvious fact that the amount to be paid the Artist should be explicitly stated, some attention should be given to the language used to describe the method of payment. Care should be taken so that payments are related to objective events, such as selected date or delivery of a finished segment, rather than subjective criteria such as approval or acceptance of the Work. Additionally, if a payment is to be made upon the happening of an event under the control of the station, an outside date should be included in the schedule. Thus, if the last payment is to be made when the program is broadcast, the clause should read: "The final installment shall be paid the Artist when the Work is broadcast, but if the Work is not broadcast by November 30, 1986, then the final installment shall be paid the Artist on or before said date." If the station agrees to reimburse the Artist's expenses, the Artist should be prepared to conform to a station policy on expense vouchers. Some care should be taken in the preparation of the expense schedule so as to avoid disagreements over expenses after they have been incurred.

Par 3. All right, title and interest in and to the Work and all constituent creative and literary elements shall belong solely and exclusively to the Artist. It is understood that the Artist may copyright the Work in the Artist's name. The Artist grants BIE the right to have four releases of the Work on station WBIE for a period of two years commencing with the completion of the Work. A release is defined as unlimited broadcasts of the Work in a consecutive seven-day period; such consecutive seven-day period beginning with the first day the Work is broadcast. At the end of said two year period, the master tape and all copies of the Work in BIE's possession shall be delivered to the Artist by BIE. All rights not specifically granted to BIE are expressly reserved to the Artist.

Comment: The language suggested confirms the priciple that the Artist owns all rights to the resulting Work, including the copyright. The station can be expected to argue that the Artist is an employee for hire under the copyright law and the copyright should belong to the station. When the contract provides for the Artist to retain the copyright, the Artist should, as a matter of practice, register the copyright to the Work. The sentence describing the grant of release rights to the station is intended as an example rather than a suggestion. One major area of discussion will be the "rights" issue. In general, the commissioning station will seek to acquire rights to distribute or broadcast the Work in the noncommercial, educational, nonsponsored or public television markets. While most persons involved in the field have some general understanding of the meaning of the foregoing terms, working out wording for appropriate definitions would be useful.

When dealing with the "rights" question, two issues should be separated. First is the issue of who controls the rights, i.e. who can arrange for broadcasting, and the second is whether there will be a sharing of receipts from the following guidelines:

a) The Artist should not grant a license to the station to exploit or distribute the Work in a market in which the station does not actively participate. Thus, if a station has had no experience dealing with cable television, the station should not request a license in such a market. Certainly, if such a license is granted in a previously unexploited area, it should only be on a non-exclusive basis. Even though the grant of a non-exclusive license has some appeal as a compromise, the Artist should be aware that if the work has commercial value, a distributor may wish to have all the exclusive rights. Accordingly, the fact that there are non-exclusive licenses outstanding might affect the marketability of the Work. On the other hand, if the station is very active in a market, for example distribution to school systems, it might be in the interest of the Artist to have the station serve as a licensee for that market. Under such circumstances the second issue, sharing of revenues or royalties, becomes relevant.

b) All licenses granted by the Artist should be limited as to geographic area and as to time. There should be no reason to grant world wide rights in perpetuity to a station unless the artist views himself basically as creating the Work for the station rather than for him or herself.

c) If the Artist expects to realize a financial return from a grant of a license, the Artist should have the right to terminate the license if certain minimum levels of income are not reached. Thus, purely by the way of example, if the Artist grants the station a seven year license to exploit the Work in the educational market, and the Artist has not received at least $3,000 by the end of the third year of the license, he should have the right to terminate the license.

d) If the contract gives the Artist a percent of royalties received from the station's exploitation of the Work, at least three principles should be observed. First, percentages should be based on gross receipts rather than profits. From experience whenever the concept of net receipts or net profits is introduced, there is created an area of potential dispute as to what can be deducted from receipts to arrive at net profits. Second, the station should be obligated to remit the Artist's share of royalties at least semi-annually and such royalties should be accompanied by a royalty statement. Third, the Artist should have the right to inspect the books of the station at least annually for the purpose of verifying royalty statements. When royalties are involved, the Artist should at least consider requesting an advance against royalties.

e) Theatrical, sponsored television, commercial and subsidiary rights should be held exclusively by the Artist. Some or all of these rights, of course, can be granted to the station in return for a lump-sum payment or royalty participation.

f) All grant of rights or license clauses should end with this sentence: "All rights not specifically granted to the station are expressly reserved to the Artist."

The Artist should recognize that the fee payable under paragraph 2 and the rights granted to the station under paragraph 3 are very much negotiable matters. No general rule covering all artists can be formulated. For example, one artist might be willing to grant greater commercial rights to the station in return for a larger fee. To another artist, however, the amount of the fee could be less important compared with the rights desired to be retained.

Par 4. BIE shall not have the right to edit or excerpt from the Work except with the written consent of the Artist. Notwithstanding the foregoing, BIE shall have the right to excerpt up to sixty (60) seconds of running time from the Work solely for the purpose of advertising the telecast of the Work or publicizing the activities of BIE. On all broadcasts or showings of the Work (except the up to sixty (60) seconds publicity uses referred to above) the credit and copyright notice supplied by the Artist shall be included.

Comment: This clause limits the station's rights to edit or change the Artist's work and limits rights to excerpt except under stated circumstances. The language assumes that the Artist has included a credit and copyright notice in the Work. The station may request the Artist to include an acknowledgment among the credits recognizing the station's contributions to the creation of the Work.

Par 5. BIE will be provided with the Master Tape of the Work which it shall hold until termination of the license granted to it in paragraph 3 above (or if more than one license has been granted, the clause should refer to the lapse of the last license). BIE agrees to take due and proper care of the Master Tape in its possession and insure its loss or damage against all causes. All insurance proceeds received on account of loss or of damage to the Master Tape shall be the property of Artist and shall be promptly transmitted to Artist when received by BIE. Artist shall receive one copy of the tape of the Work in any tape format selected by the Artist. BIE agrees to use its best efforts to give the Artist reasonable notice of scheduled broadcast dates of the Work.

Comment: Custody of master tapes and duplicate tapes will largely depend on the nature and extent of rights to exploit the Work granted or reserved by the Artist. The Artist should understand that usually a station will attempt to disclaim responsibility for caring for the Master Tapes. In general, the law does not impose absolute responsibility on the station to take care of the tape. In the absence of language in the contract, the station will be held to what is described as a negligence standard; that it will be liable for loss of the Master Tape or damage to it if the station has been negligent. While the Artist through bargaining may not be able to improve upon this measure of responsibility, the Artist should not contractually relieve the station of this responsibility to adhere to the negligence standard.

Par 6. The Artist authorizes BIE to use the Artist's name, likeness and biographical material solely in connection with publicizing the broadcast of the Work or the activities of BIE. The Artist shall have the right to reasonably approve all written promotional material about the Artist or the Work.

Comment: Because of right of privacy law, the station must acquire the consent of the Artist to use the Artist's name, picture or likeness in connection with advertising or trade purposes. The Artist should limit this consent to use in connection with the Work or in connection with promotions for the station. It is of course desirable for the Artist to be able to approve all promotional material relating to the Artist or the Work. However, the station may not readily agree to this proposal. Under such circumstances, if the Artist wants specific material included in promotional pieces, the Artist should prepare this material beforehand and obtain the station's agreement to include this material in its promotional pieces.

Par 7. The Artist represents that he is authorized to enter into this agreement; that material included in the Work is original with the Artist or the Artist has obtained permission to include the material in the Work or such permission is not required; that the Work does not violate or infringe upon the rights of others, including but not limited to copyright and right of privacy; and that the Work is not defamatory. The Artist agrees to indemnify BIE against any damages, liabilities and expenses arising out of the Artist's breach of the foregoing representations.

Comment: The Artist should expect to represent to the station that the Work and material contained in the Work are not defamatory, do not infringe upon any copyrights and will in general not violate rights of others. The language of the indemnity or hold harmless clause should be examined closely. The Artist should not be liable to the station unless there has been an actual breach of the representations as distinguished from merely a "claimed" breach of the representations. Some hold harmless clauses are worded so that if someone claims the Work is, for example, defamatory, the station is permitted to settle the claim and charge the settlement to the Artist. It is this latter circumstance that is to be avoided. Consideration should also be given to obtaining insurance coverage for the Work against defamation, copyright and right to privacy claims. Stations usually have a form of this so-called "errors and omissions" insurance. Also, at least one artist has suggested that a station should be required as a preliminary matter to have its attorney view the Work to determine the probability of defamation or right of privacy claims. Based upon the advice of its attorney, the station would determine whether or not to broadcast the Work. If it elects to broadcast the Work, it would then assume the risk of such lawsuits. The rationale for such argument is that a station usually has an existing relationship with a lawyer and, as between the station and the Artist, is in a better position to evaluate the possibility of such litigation and be guided accordingly. This point is being raised for discussion purposes.

Par 8. In the event BIE files for bankruptcy or relief under any state or federal insolvency laws or laws providing for the relief of debtors, or if a petition under such law is filed against BIE, or if BIE ceases to actively engage in business, then this agreement shall automatically terminate and all rights theretofore granted to BIE shall revert to the Artist. Similarly, in the event the Work has not been broadcast within one year from the date the Work is completed (as the term completed is defined in paragraph 1), then this agreement shall terminate and all rights granted to BIE shall revert to the Artist. Upon termination of this agreement or expiration of the license granted to BIE under this agreement, all copies of the Work shall be delivered to the Artist.

Comment: This clause is intended to terminate the contract if the station should go bankrupt or cease business. Also, while a station usually will not agree to actually broadcast a Work, if it does not broadcast the Work by a given date, the agreement will terminate. Both of these clauses are intended to allow the Artist to find other means of exploiting the Work if the station goes out of business or, in essence, refuses or fails to broadcast the Work.

Par 9. This agreement contains the entire understanding of the parties and may not be modified, amended or changed except by a writing signed by the parties. Except as is expressly permitted under this agreement, neither party may assign this agreement or rights accruing under this agreement without the prior written consent of the other except either party may assign rights to receive money or compensation without the other party's consent. This agreement shall be interpreted under the laws of the State of New York.

Comment: This is the "boilerplate" or standard jargon usually included in written agreements, and should be self-explanatory. Also, as a miscellaneous matter, the Artist should be prepared to adhere to policy "taste" standards or rules adopted by the station. Most stations have some form of policy guidelines and the Artist should obtain a copy of these guidelines before signing the contract.

AGREED TO: BIE

_____   By: _____
Artist   Name and Title

Model artist-gallery video agreement

Agreement dated the _____ day of _____, 197___, between _____
_____ (the "Dealer"), residing at _____
_____ and _____
_____ (the "Artist"), residing at
_____ .

WHEREAS the Artist has produced and created a work of art titled _____
and described as a one-hour color videotape 3/4" cassette showing _____
_____
_____
_____(the "Work"); and

WHEREAS the Artist desires to have this Work distributed by the Dealer; and

WHEREAS the Dealer wishes to undertake the distribution of said Work; and

WHEREAS the parties wish to have said distribution performed subject to the mutual obligations, covenants, and conditions herein.

NOW, THEREFORE, in consideration of the foregoing premises and the mutual covenants hereinafter set forth and other valuable considerations, the parties hereto agree as follows:

1. Artist hereby grants to the Dealer the exclusive right to sell or lease the Work in the United States of America for the term of this agreement. The exclusive right granted hereby includes only the limited license to sell or lease the physical videotape cassettes representing single copies of the Work recorded thereon. In no event shall there be a sale or leasing consisting of less than the entirety of the Work as described above.

2. The term of this agreement shall be for a period of two (2) years, commencing as of the date set forth above.

3. Dealer agrees to give best efforts to promote the sale and leasing of the Work and to protect the Work from copyright infringement or illicit copying or distribution by others.

4. Dealer agrees to pay Artist for the rights granted hereby royalties in an amount equal to the following percentages of Dealer's adjusted gross proceeds from the Work:

(a) For the sale of copies of the Work by Dealer 50%
(b) For all leasing proceeds 50%

For the purpose of this provision, "Dealer's adjusted gross) proceeds from the Work" shall mean all revenues derived by Dealer from the sale or leasing of the Work after deducting only all taxes collected by the Dealer. Dealer shall furnish Artist quarterly reports during January, April, July and October of each year showing, for the preceding three months, and cumulatively from the commencement of this agreement, the number of copies of the Work sold by the Dealer, "Dealer's adjusted gross proceeds from the Work," and the royalties due Artist. Such report shall be accompanied by payment of all royalties to Artist for the period covered by such report.

5. It is understood that only fifty (50) copies of the Work shall be made, of which the Dealer shall have the right to sell twenty-five (25) of the said copies. The Dealer shall also have the right to request additional copies of the Work for leasing, subject to the consent of the Artist. Artist agrees that the Dealer may contract with purchasers or lessees of the Work to replace worn, defective or mutilated copies of the Work and, further, that the Artist shall be entitled to no royalty in the event of such replacement. Dealer agrees that no copy of the Work alleged to be worn, defective or mutilated will be replaced unless said copy is returned to the Dealer for destruction by the purchaser or lessee.

6. All copies of the Work shall be made at Dealer's cost from the master tape. It is understood that the master tape will remain the Artist's property and in his control, provided that it shall be used as necessary to make copies of the Work for sale or leasing under the terms of this agreement. All copyright and other literary property rights in the Work for the entire term of the copyright and any renewal thereof shall belong exclusively to the Artist. The master tape of the Work and each copy thereof shall bear a copyright notice in the Artist's name.

7. The retail selling price of each copy of the Work shall be _____ . It is agreed that Dealer may, in the exercise of reasonable business discretion, increase or reduce the price charged for any copy of the Work by ten percent (10%) in order to further the sales of the Work and the realization of returns from the exploitation of the Work. Dealer shall periodically consult with the Artist concerning Dealer's marketing program and pricing policies with respect to the Work.

8. Dealer shall not sell or lease any copy of the Work unless the purchaser or lessee agrees, in writing, that under no circumstance shall any further copies of the Work be made by the purchaser or lessee and that the purchaser or lessee shall neither broadcast their copy of the Work nor permit the charging of admission to view the Work.

9. The Artist agrees that Dealer shall have the right to list the Work, with appropriate descriptive material, in any catalog which Dealer publishes or maintains. The Artist further agrees that Dealer may use and authorize others to use the Artist's name, likeness and biographical material for the purpose of publicizing and promoting sales or leasing of the Work pursuant to this agreement.

10. Dealer agrees that neither this agreement nor any rights granted Dealer hereunder may be assigned without the prior written consent of the Artist. The Artist may freely assign this agreement, either in whole or in part.

11. This agreement shall automatically be renewed for successive periods of one year, each renewal commencing on the expiration date set forth above unless canceled by sixty (60) days written notice given by either party prior to the expiration of the term of this agreement or any renewal thereof.

12. This agreement shall be binding upon the parties and their respective heirs, successors and assigns.

13. Dealer and Artist agree to arbitrate any claim, dispute, or controversy arising out of or in connection with this agreement, or any breach thereof, before an agreed-upon arbitrator, or, if no arbitrator can be agreed upon, before the American Arbitration Association, under its rules.

14. The agreement constitutes the entire agreement of the parties and may not be changed except by an agreement in writing signed by both parties.

15. This agreement shall be construed under the laws of the State of New York applicable to agreements made and to be performed solely within such State.

IN WITNESS WHEREOF, the parties have signed this agreement as of the date set forth above.

_____   _____
Artist   Dealer

Model video bill of sale

Date:

Sold to: _____(Name)
         _____(Address)
         _____

Artist:
Title:
Medium:
Length:
Description:
Price:

It is hereby acknowledged and agreed that the copy of the videotape listed above is being purchased solely for noncommercial use and that acquisition of this copy is subject to the following conditions:

1. All copyrights and other rights of reproduction or commercial exploitation, including the right to make copies of the videotape, are reserved to the gallery.

2. The purchaser agrees not to make or permit others to make any copies of this videotape; not to broadcast or charge admission fees to any showings of the copy in any place; not to utilize the copy in advertisements in any media or utilize the copy commercially in any way; not to make photographs or reproductions from the copy.

3. The purchaser agrees not to show the videotape to others, other than in its entirety and with sound, if any.

4. The purchaser agrees not to sell or transfer this copy to anyone unless the person acquiring the copy agrees to be bound by the provisions of this agreement. The purchaser further agrees to notify the seller of any such transfer and to furnish the gallery with the name and address of the new owner.

5. The purchaser agrees not to rent or lend the copy to others or to permit others to use the copy in violation of the terms of this agreement.

6. The purchaser agrees that the rights given by this agreement shall also run in favor of the artist who is the author of the videotape and to the present and future holders of the copyrights thereon.

7. The gallery agrees to replace the copy of the videotape upon the purchaser's return of the copy purchased. The cost of replacement shall be the gallery's if the copy is defective and the purchaser's if the copy has been damaged in use.

The gallery acknowledges receipt of the purchase price set forth above and the purchaser acknowledges receipt of the copy of the videotape.

_____   _____

Purchaser   Gallery

Chapter 17

Studios and leases

Many artists find their work ideally requires a great deal of studio space. Such space is often only reasonably available in older structures such as rural barns or buildings in urban districts zoned for commerical or manufacturing use. If the space is unfinished, the artist may have to expend substantial sums to have necessary utilities and fixtures installed. On the other hand, if this installation has been made and paid for by a prior tenant, the artist may have to pay for fixtures which seem neither useful or aesthetically pleasing. Also, while the artist may wish to reside in the loft, zoning laws and regulations may impair the right of the artist to do this and, in some cases, create an occupancy which is illegal. Zoning laws may also affect artists who create studios in residential areas.

Practical considerations

The artist who is not an expert should find either a contractor or someone else with expertise to examine the building and space for a determination as to whether the structure and facilities will be adequate and safe for the artist's work and, if necessary, living quarters. An artist creating large and heavy works will have to be certain doorways, hallways, elevators and loading ramps can accomodate the completed work. An artist who needs power machinery must be certain the building is wired for such use. Heating, plumbing and gas lines must all be adequate for the artist's needs. Finally, if the building is considered sound, the artist can arrive at a figure—perhaps thousands of dollars—necessary to put the loft into the condition the artist desires.

Ownership of fixtures

The artist faced with such substantial fix-up costs, or perhaps a payment to a previous tenant for fixtures, is now offered a standard form lease by the landlord. A wise course is always to consult a lawyer when confronted with a legal document, and a lease is certainly no exception. The standard lease developed for commercial space by the Real Estate Board of New York provides, "Tenant shall make no changes in or to the demised premises without Landlord's prior written consent." If written consent is obtained and the changes are made, the lease then provides, "All fixtures and all paneling, partitions, railings, and like installations, installed in the premises at any time, either by Tenant or by Landlord in Tenant's behalf, shall become the propery of Landlord and shall remain upon and be surrendered with the demised premises . . . " The landlord's ownership of fixtures at the end of the lease term is a crucial factor with which the artist must contend when the lease is negotiated. The landlord may, in fact, permit the artist at the end of the lease term to sell the fixtures to the incoming tenant. But the landlord generally does not have to do this (except, for example, in New York City where lofts covered by Article 7-C of the Multiple Dwelling Law are subject to special rules regarding the tenant's right to sell fixtures). Also, if the market for commercial space is not good, there may be no incoming tenant and the artist may be forced to leave the space without receiving any payments at all.

The lease term

The fix-up costs bear on what the use of the space is truly costing over the lease term. The lease, for example, may provide for an annual rent of $7,200—that is, $600 per month. If the fix-up cost is $4,000, there is a substantial difference between the two-year and a five-year lease term on what can be called the "real rent"—the total monthly or yearly cost to the artist as a tenant. If the lease term is two years, the $4,000 of fix-up costs increase the rent by $2,000 each year. The real rent is $9,200 per year, not the $7,200 per year which appears in the lease. But if the lease term is five years, the $4,000 of fix-up costs only increase the rent by $800 each year, making the real rent $8,000. However, an artist may have to pay a higher rent for the additional security of a long lease term.

The artist benefits from a longer lease term because the fix-up costs can be enjoyed over a longer period. The artists may, therefore, seek a longer lease term, perhaps five years instead of two years. If the landlord agrees, the artist has the advantage of a rent fixed for a longer term, as well as a longer period to enjoy fix-up costs. The disadvantage is that the artist may wish to move before the end of the longer lease term without being responsible for rent to the end of the term.

Options to renew

A good alternative to requesting a longer lease is to request, in the lease, the option to renew (which must be definite as to term and rent). Thus, the initial lease term could be two years, but the artist might have the option to renew the lease for another three-year term at a specified rent. This gives the artist the advantage of five years to benefit from fix-up costs, but the opportunity to leave sooner if need be. A disadvantage of asking for an option to renew might occur if the landlord decides the option itself is valuable and insists that the rent during the renewal term be at an increased rate. Whether the option to renew is worth a certain rent increase is a decision the artist has to make on a case-by-case basis. It's also worth noting that when an artist moves into a building scheduled for destruction, renewal options to extend the lease term to the actual destruction date are a reasonable request and can be of great benefit if the destruction is delayed for any reason.

The right to terminate

An alternative, even more flexible than an option to renew, is the right to terminate. The artist might, for example, demand the right to terminate the lease upon one month's written notice to the landlord. Often this right can only be exercised after part of the lease term, perhaps six months or a year, has elapsed. In this way the artist can take a long lease term while retaining the power to leave at will without liability for the remaining rent.

Right to sublet or assign

A desirable lease clause, particularly important when a longer lease term is obtained, is the tenant's right to sublet. A typical lease provision reads, "Tenant . . . shall not . . . underlet, or suffer or permit the demised premises or any part thereof to be used by others, without the prior written consent of Landlord in each instance." This lease prohibition on underlets or sublets is absolute and the landlord need not justify his refusal to accept a proposed subtenant. The artist should negotiate for the right to sublet, since such a right will make the artist certain of being able to have the fix-up costs reimbursed as long as a new tenant can be found who desires the loft. A typical compromise sublet clause would require the landlord's consent for any sublet but provide that the landlord would not unreasonably withhold that consent. If the proposed subtenant is financially responsible and will pay the rent and use the loft properly, the landlord will not be able, arbitrarily, to refuse the subletting. When a loft is sublet, the subtenant pays the rent to the tenant, who in turns pays the landlord. A simpler method—with the landlord's consent—is to have the artist assign the lease to the new tenant. In contrast to a sublet, an assignment means the artist permanently gives up the lease and any right to return to the premises and the rent payments will go directly from the new tenant to the landlord. Nonetheless, the artist will still usually be liable for the rent if the new tenant defaults.

The limitation of a sublet or assignment clause is that the artist only has the right to find another tenant as a replacement. If another tenant can't be found, the artist will remain responsible for the rent. Where the lease has an option to renew, of course, the artist's responsibility for rent ends with the initial lease term and only continues for the renewal period if the artist exercises the option to renew the lease. The right to terminate would also protect the artist as to remaining rent. Ideally, in order to have maximum flexibility, the artist should seek either an option to renew or a right to terminate, as well as a right to sublet or assign.

Hidden lease costs

The artist should be aware that the lease may contain costs other than rent. For example, the artist in a loft will usually be responsible for making all nonstructural repairs. The artist must be certain who will pay for electricity, air conditioning and even water. The lease may provide for escalations of the artist's rent in proportion to increases in the landlord's real estate taxes or other expenses, such as that for heating fuel. Indeed, the lease may even contain a cost-of-living clause which increases the rent automatically to keep up with inflation. If the artist cannot negotiate these clauses out of the lease, a current cost for the landlord on each item should definitely be specified in the lease to establish an objective basis upon which future increases can be calculated. But the artist should try to include a maximum cost beyond which there can be no increases. In each of these cases the artist must attempt to approximate costs, perhaps by inquiring of the landlord and other tenants as to past increases or by relying on an expert's opinion, so these costs can be added into the calculation of real rent.

Zoning

Zoning governs the way in which buildings may be used. The development of a city or town may be guided through the use of zoning laws to control the density of buildings and population as well as the nature of activities in different areas. For example, zoning restrictions may limit the type of materials that an artist can use and store in the premises. Inflammable and volatile solvents may be prohibited in certain buildings.

If an area is zoned for residential use, questions may be raised to the legality of an art studio. Certainly an artist should be able to paint, draw or take photographs without worrying about the reaction of neighbors. Technically, however, if this is done in the pursuit of business, the zoning ordinance may be violated. If the business involves a lot of traffic to and from the premises, it is more likely that such a violation will be brought the attention of the zoning authorities.

Zoning ordinances and rulings vary from locality to locality. If the artist contemplates conducting a business in a residential space, he or she should find out whether or not a zoning ordinance forbids such business activity and what the penalties are if the zoning is violated. One likely penalty would be to have to stop doing the art business on the premises. To avoid this risk, the artist might prefer to seek appropriate administrative permission, usually obtained by a variance procedure, which would allow use of the premises for activities otherwise forbidden.

The reverse situation of living in commercial space also arises, especially in cities. In New York City, for example, artists often took up residence in areas zoned for manufacturing in order to benefit from the good floor space and high ceilings of these industrial lofts. Recognition of these illegal tenancies brought a liberalization of the zoning laws which, starting in 1964, allowed people to reside and work in up to two lofts in nonresidential buildings which met certain maximum size and safety requirements if the lofts were registered with the Building Department.

Many artists resisted this registration process and continued living as illegal loft tenants. In Soho, where there was a concentration of illegal loft tenancies, the Soho Artists Association led the campaign which resulted, in 1971, in the creation of legal loft zones in Soho, subject again to certain limitations such as maximum loft size. Artists must be certified as artists by the City's Cultural Affairs Department. Once certification is obtained by the artist, the building in which the loft is located has to conform to New York City's Building Code and Multiple Dwelling Law in order for a certificate of occupancy to be issued by the Building Department. This process is often difficult and expensive.

In 1976, legal loft zones were created in Noho and Tribeca. More recently, loft living was legalized in many other areas of the city. An artist facing a challenge over his or her status in a loft in New York City may contact the Lower Manhattan Loft Tenants Association (page 194) for advice and referral to an attorney. Outside New York City it would be wise to contact a local attorney who is knowledgeable regarding real estate law.

The use clause

An important lease clause is that specifying what use may be made of the loft by the artist. For example, this clause might provide, "Tenant shall use and occupy the demised premises for an artist's studio and for no other purpose." It is generally best for the artist to have as much latitude under this clause as possible. For example, a better clause for the artist would be, "Tenant shall use and occupy the demised premises for an artist's studio, residence and gallery."

But the artist who chooses to live illegally in a loft, perhaps even without the landlord's knowledge, cannot expect the landlord to agree to a lease clause permitting use as a residence. At the least, however, the artist should not accept a use clause specifying that no living in the loft will be permitted, such as "artist's studio, no living." Such a clause will place the artist clearly in breach of the lease and subject to eviction by the landlord unless state or local laws provide special protections for tenants.

Violations

The lease will also provide that the tenant must not use the loft in violation of the building's certificate of occupancy and that the tenant must act promptly to end any violations arising from the artist's use or occupancy of the loft. This sounds ominous but may in fact not create a problem.

If a violation is found, the artist at least has the opportunity under these lease provisions to correct the conditions causing the violations before the landlord can seek eviction. The artist should try to avoid any clauses which might provide for automatic termination of the lease if violations are not corrected within a limited time period, such as ten days.

Cooperative buildings

Some artists may be offered the opportunity to purchase space in a cooperative or condominium which owns the building. In such a case the determination by experts as to the adequacy of both the building and the loft for the artist is even more important than in the usual rental situation. Sponsors sometimes lure potential purchasers by concealing the extent of repairs an renovations which will be necessary after the building becomes a cooperative. Once the repairs are completed, the maintenance costs—basically the carrying costs of the building each individual owner must bear—take an upward bound and make ownership of the loft far less attractive than it originally appeared. In New York the attorney general seeks to prevent frauds by requiring extensive disclosures in the selling prospectus. The artist should be particularly cautious when considering the purchase of space, so consultation with an attorney is a necessity.

Chapter 18

Income taxation

The artist's professional income—for example, from sales of work, commissions, copyright royalties and wages—is taxed as ordinary income by the federal government and by the state and city where the artist lives, if such a state or city has an income tax. The business expenses of being an artist, however, are deductible and reduce the income which will be taxed. Both income—as gross receipts—and expenses are entered on Schedule C, Profit or (Loss) from Business or Profession, which is attached to Form 1040. A sample Schedule C is on page 156.

Although they are not the same as an income tax, the artist should also check whether any state and city sales taxes may have to be collected on art works. If such taxes must be collected, the artist may be entitled to a resale number which permits the purchase of materials and supplies without payment of any sales tax. The artist must also determine whether any other state or local taxes, such as New York City's unincorporated business tax and commercial rent for occupancy tax, must be paid in addition to the personal income tax. These taxes vary with each state and city, so guidance must be obtained in the artist's own locality.

General guides to federal taxation are IRS Publication 17, *Your Federal Income Tax,* for individuals and IRS Publication 334, *Tax Guide for Small Businesses,* for businesses. These and other IRS publications mentioned in the income tax chapters can all be obtained free of charge from any IRS office. The artist should keep in mind, however, that these publications represent the views of the IRS and are sometimes inconsistent with precedents already established by the courts. The artist may prefer to purchase a privately published guide, such as J.K. Lasser's *Your Income Tax* which is updated each year.

The tax laws are changed frequently. As this book goes to press, a major overhaul of the tax system has been proposed. Whether any—or all—of this revision will be enacted into law is impossible to know at this time. However, this annual addiction to tax-code tinkering requires artists to consult a tax guide which is updated annually. Nonetheless, the chapters on income and estate taxation in this book will provide a valuable overview of the area of taxation as it pertains to the artist. An excellent, annually updated tax guide for artists is *Fear of Filing* published by the Volunteer Lawyers for the Arts in New York City.

Record keeping

All income and expenses arising from the profession of being an artist should be promptly recorded in a ledger regularly used for the purpose. The entries should give specific information as to dates, sources, purposes and other relevant data, all supported by checks, bills and receipts whenever possible. It is advisable to maintain business checking and saving accounts through which all professional income and expenses are channeled separate from the artist's personal accounts. IRS Publications 552, *Recordkeeping for Individuals and a List of Tax Publications* and 583, *Recordkeeping, Information for Business Taxpayers—Business Taxes, Identification Numbers,* provide details as to the permanent, accurate and complete records required.

Accounting methods and periods

Like any other taxpayer, the artist may choose either of two methods of accounting: the cash method or the accrual method. The cash method includes all income actually received during the year and deducts all expenses actually paid during the tax year. The accrual method, on the other hand, includes as income all that income which the artist has earned and has a right to receive in the tax year, even if not actually received until a later tax year, and deducts expenses when they are incurred instead of when they are paid.

The Treasury regulations require accrual accounting for inventories "to reflect taxable income correctly . . . in every case in which the production, purchase or sale of merchandise is an income-producing factor." The artist who produces substantial quantities of identical works, such as 500 replicas of a statue, would be characterized as a manufacturer producing merchandise and should use accrual accounting for inventories. Some legal commentators even suggest that a sculptor might have to use accrual accounting for inventories if the sculptor's works required substantial costs in materials and the labor of others. However, Rubin L. Gorewitz, a New York C.P.A. who represents many artists, states that the income of artists, including sculptors, can only be correctly reflected by the use of cash basis accounting because of the obsolescence of art works as artists change styles, the possibility that even a completed work may be destroyed to use the materials in a newer work and the unknown sales potential of any work. Since most artists operate on the simpler cash method, the chapters on income taxes will assume that the cash method is being used.

Income taxes are calculated for annual accounting periods. The tax year for the vast majority of taxpayers is the calender year: January 1st through December 31st. However, a taxpayer could use any fiscal year (for example, July 1st through June 30th), although there must be a reason to change from a calendar to a fiscal year. Since most artists use the calendar year as their tax year, the income tax chapters will assume the use of a calendar year.

The cash method of accounting in a few cases, however, may include income not actually received by the artist, if the income has been credited or set apart so as to be subject to the artist's control. For example, income received by a gallery acting as agent for the artist will, when received by the gallery, be taxable to the artist unless substantial limitations or restrictions exist as to how or when the gallery will pay the artist.

One valuable tax-saving device for the cash basis, calendar year artist is to pay expenses in December while putting off receipt of income until the following January when a new tax year has begun. The expenses reduce income in the present year while the income is put off until the new tax year.

Further information on accounting methods and periods can be obtained in IRS Publication 538, *Accounting Periods and Methods.*

Types of income

The artist must be aware of the different types of income. The first distinction is between ordinary income and captial gains income. The artist realizes ordinary income from all income-producing activities of the artist's profession. Ordinary income is taxed at the regular income tax rates, which go up as high as 50 percent. Capital gains income is realized upon the sale of capital assets, such as stocks, real estate or silver bullion. Capital gains from assets owned more than six months are classified as long-term gains and receive preferential tax treatment (by basically being reduced by sixty percent before being taxed).

The substantial tax discrimination in favor of long-term captial gains as compared to ordinary income will cause the artist to wonder why an art work is not an asset which receives favorable capital gains treatment. Congress, when enacting the tax laws, specifically stated that "a copyright . . . or artistic composition . . . held by a taxpayer whose personal efforts created such property" cannot be an asset qualifying for capital gains treatment. And if the artist gives an art work to someone else, that person will own the work as the artist did—as ordinary income property rather than an asset qualifying for capital gains treatment. Unfair as it may seem, if the work is sold to a collector, the collector owns the work as a capital asset and may obtain the lower capital gains rate upon sale of the work, as discussed on page 186.

Another distinction to be kept in mind is between ordinary income which is earned and that which is unearned. The professional income of the artist is considered earned income, but income from stock dividends, interest, rent and capital gains, for example, is treated as unearned income. As a practical matter, most artists will be concerned about earned income in such areas as retirement (discussed on pages 158 - 159) and income earned abroad (discussed on pages 160 - 161).

Basis

The amount of profit to an artist on the sale of work is usually the sale price less the cost of materials in the work. The cost of materials is called the "basis" of the work for tax purposes. The cash-basis artist, who deducts the cost of art materials and supplies currently when purchased, must remember that such materials and supplies cannot be deducted again as the basis of the art works when sold. In other words, if the artist deducts materials and supplies currently, then the art works have a zero basis and the entire amount of the proceeds from the sales will be taxable. If the work is given to someone else, that person will have the same zero basis of the artist and, as mentioned earlier, realize ordinary income upon sale. The basis for a collector who purchases the work, however, will be the purchase price. The collector's gain on resale will be the difference between the price on resale and the basis. And the gain, as stated earlier, will be taxed at the favorable capital gains rates.

Grants

Grants to artists for scholarships or fellowships to further their education and training are excluded from gross income as long as the grants are not compensation for services and are not given primarily for the benefit of the grant-giving organization. Amounts given to cover expenses incurred in connection with such grants are excludable from income if they represent expenses specifically designated under the grant and are spent for the purpose of the grant. Such expense allowances do not use up the $300 per month limit mentioned below.

A degree candidate has no limit on the grant amounts which may be excluded as long as teaching, research or other employment under the grant is required for all candidates for the particular degree. An artist who is not a degree candidate may only exclude up to $300 times the number of months to which amounts received under the grant are attributable, but for no more than a total of thirty-six months, consecutive or otherwise, during the artist's lifetime. After the thirty-six months are exhausted, the full amount of any grants and related amounts for expenses are fully includable in income. An artist who is not a degree candidate can only exclude the grants at all if the grants are paid by certain governmental, nonprofit or international organizations. More information on the taxation of grants can be obtained in IRS Publication 17, *Your Federal Income Tax,* on pages 68-69.

Prizes and awards

Prizes and awards to artists are, in most cases, taxable, even if they are given in the form of goods or services. The sole area in which tax can be avoided is when prizes and awards are given in recognition of past achievements in the field of art without application or services on the part of the artist (for example, the Pulitzer Prize or Nobel Prize). Once the artist is selected as a candidate, however, filling out application forms or appearing for an interview will not cause the prize or award to be includable in gross income.

Valuation

Valuation is important when the artist realizes income in the form of goods or services. In such event, the amount included in gross income is the fair market value of the goods or services received, which is basically the price to which a buyer and a seller, dealing at arm's length, would agree. Valuation will be particularly important to the artist who gives art work in exchange for either the art work of friends or the services of professionals, such as lawyers, doctors and dentists. Such exchanges of art works for other works or services are considered sales. Since fair market value can be a factual issue, the artist should consider using the services of a professional appraiser. Such an appraisal will be helpful if the artist must make an insurance claim for work which has been damaged, lost or destroyed. Insurance proceeds are taxable as if a sale has occurred.

Professional expenses

Deductible business expenses are all the ordinary and necessary expenditures which the artist must make professionally. Such expenses, which are recorded on Schedule C, include, for example, art materials and supplies, work space, office equipment, certain books and magazines, repairs, travel for business purposes, promotional expenses, telephone, postage, premiums for art insurance, commissions of agents and legal and accounting fees.

Art supplies and other deductions

Art materials and supplies are generally current) expenses, deductible in full in the year purchased. These include all items with a useful life of less than one year, such as canvas, film, brushes, paints, paper, ink, pens, erasers, typewriter rentals, mailing envelopes, photocopying, file folders, stationery, paper clips and similar items. Moreover, the sales tax on these and other business purchases is a deductible expense and can simply be included in the cost of the item. Postage is similarly deductible as soon as the expense is incurred. The cost of professional journals is deductible, as is the cost for books used in preparation for specific works. Dues for membership in the artist's professional organizations are deductible, as are fees to attend workshops sponsored by such organizations. Telephone bills and an answering service are deductible in full for a business telephone. If, however, use of the telephone is divided between personal and business calls, then records should be kept itemizing both long-distance and local message units expended for business purposes and the cost of any answering service should also be prorated. Educational expenses are generally deductible for the artist who can establish that such expenses were in-

curred to maintain or improve skills required as an artist (but not to learn or qualify in a new profession). IRS Publication 508, *Educational Expenses,* can be consulted here.

Repairs to professional equipment are deductible in full the year incurred. If the artist moves to a new house, the pro rata share of moving expenses attributable to professional equipment is deductible as a business expense.

Work space

If the artist rents work space at a location different from where the artist lives, all of the rent and expenses in connection with the work space are deductible. However, the tax law places limitations on business deductions which are attributable to an office or studio at home. Such deductions will be allowed if the artist uses a part of the home exclusively, and on a regular basis, as the artist's principal place of business. Even though the artist may have another profession, if the studio at home is the principal place of the business of being an artist, the business deductions may be taken. Also, the artist who maintains a separate structure used exclusively, and on a regular basis, in connection with the business of being an artist is entitled to the deductions attributable to the separate structure. Provisions less likely to apply to artists allow deductions when a portion of the home is used exclusively, and on a regular basis, as the normal place to meet with clients and customers or when the artist's business is selling art at retail and the portion of the home, even though not used on an exclusive basis, is the sole, fixed location of that business.

For employees, the home office deduction is available only if the exclusive use if for the convenience of the employer—in addition to the criteria listed above. In a case involving employee-musicians who practiced at home, the United States Court of Appeals decided their home practice studios were the principal place of business—not the concert hall where they performed. The court wrote:

Rather, we find this the rare situation in which an employee's principal place of business is not that of his employer. Both in time and in importance, home practice was the "focal point" of the appellant musicians' employment-related activities. (*Drucker v. Commissioner*), 715 F.2d 67)

Might this discussion apply as well to artists whose home studio work is crucial to their employment—for example, as teachers?

To determine what expenses are attributable to an office or studio, the artist must calculate how much of the total space in the home is used as work space or what number of rooms out of the total number of rooms are used as work space. If a fifth of the area is used as work space, 20 percent of the rent is deductible. A homeowner makes the same calculation as to the work space use. However, capital assets, those having a useful life of more than one year, must be depreciated. A house has a basis for depreciation (only the house, land is not depreciated), which is usually its cost. Depending on whether the house was acquired before the end of 1980 or after 1980, different systems are used to determine the number of years over which depreciation is taken and the percentage of basis taken each year. Thereafter, the percentage of the house used professionally is applied to the annual depreciation figure to reach the amount of the depreciation which is deductible for the current year. IRS Publication 529, *Miscellaneous Deductions*, and 534, *Tax Information on Depreciation*, are of aid in the determination of basis and the calculation of depreciation. IRS Publication 587, *Business Use of Your Home*, can also be consulted with regard to deductions for or related to work space.

The portion of expenses for utilities, insurance and cleaning costs allocable to the work space are deductible. Repairs to maintain the house or apartment are also deductible on this pro rata basis. Property taxes and mortgage interest are deductible in full regardless of whether or not the artist's home is used for work purposes, provided the artist itemizes personal deductions on Schedule A of Form 1040. If personal deductions are not itemized on Schedule A, the portions of property taxes and mortgage interest deductible as business expenses would be entered on Schedule C.

The tax law also limits the amount of expenses which may be deducted when attributable to a home office or studio. Assuming the artist qualifies to take the deductions under one of the tests described above, the deductions for work space cannot exceed the artist's gross income from art minus deductions which would be allowed whether or not connected with a business or trade (such as real estate taxes and mortgage interest, which can be itemized and deducted on Schedule A). For example, an artist earns income of $1,500 in a year from art, while exclusively, and on a regular basis, using one-quarter of the artist's home as the principal place of the business of being an artist. The artist owns the home, and mortgage interest is $2,000 while real estate taxes are $1,600, for a total of $3,600 of deductions which could be taken on Schedule A regardless of whether incurred in connection with a business. Other expenses, such as electricity, heat, cleaning and depreciation, total $8,800. A one-quarter allocation would attribute $900 of the mortgage interest and real estate taxes and $2,200 of the other expenses to the artist's business. The artist's gross income of $1,500 is reduced by the $900 allocable to the mortgage interest and real estate taxes, leaving $600 as the maximum amount of expenses relating to work space which may be deducted. Since the remaining expenses, in fact, total $2,200, the artist will lose the opportunity to deduct $1,600 because the income from art was not large enough to match against the expenses. An artist who rents will make a simpler calculation, since the expenses attributable to a home office or studio will simply be subtracted from gross income from art and any excess expenses will not be deductible. This provision works a hardship on the many artists who sacrifice to pursue their art despite not earning large incomes.

Professional equipment

Traditionally, the cost of professional equipment having a useful life of more than one year could not be fully deducted in the year of purchase but had to be depreciated. However, the constant changes in the tax laws have made an exception to this rule and changed the method by which depreciation is determined. Again, IRS Publication 534, *Depreciation,* will aid in the computation of depreciation. Form 4562, *Depreciation and Amortization,* is used for all types of depreciation discussed here.

Almost all equipment placed in use after 1980 must have depreciation computed under the Accelerated Cost Recovery System (called ACRS). ACRS provides different categories for depreciation which depend on the nature of the equipment acquired. Most equipment is 5-year property. The basis (usually the cost of the equipment) is depreciated 15 percent in the first year, 22 percent in the second year and 21 percent in each of the third through fifth years. No determination need be made of either useful life or salvage value (since salvage value is not deducted from basis prior to application of the yearly percentages). Cars are 3-year property while house are 18-year property.

Instead of using the ACRS percentages, it is possible to choose an alternate ACRS method which allows basis simply to be divided out over a specified number of years. For 5-year property, this recovery period could be 5, 12, or 25 years. If 5 years were chosen, 20 percent of the basis would be deducted as depreciation in each year. Again salvage value would not be relevant. This alternate ACRS allows greater flexibility in tax planning.

A new feature allows a certain dollar amount of professional equipment to be deducted in full in the year of purchase. This treatment of such equipment as a current expense is limited to total amounts of $5,000 in each of 1983 through 1987, $7,500 in each 1988 and 1989 and $10,000 for 1990 and thereafter. If an artist choses to treat some purchases of equipment as a current expense, an election must be made on Form 4562 for the tax year in which the equipment was acquired and the items of equipment must be specified along with the amount of the cost to be treated as a deduction for the year of purchase. Neither depreciation nor the investment credit discussed on page 159 may be taken with respect to that part of the cost of equipment which is

deducted under these provisions in the year of purchase. A careful computation must be made to determine whether a larger current deduction is worth losing the investment tax credit on that portion of the basis.

The tax law restricts the use of ACRS, current expensing of equipment and the investment credit for cars (and other personal transportation vehicles), entertainment or recreational property (such as a television or record player) and computers unless these types of equipment are used more than 50 percent for business purposes. If they are used less than 50% for business purposes, special rules apply. In any case, deductions can only be taken for that portion of use which is business use—not for nonbusiness use of equipment. For the listed types of property, adequate records must be kept to document how much of the use is business use or there must be sufficient evidence to corroborate an owner's statements as to whether use is for business. This is true regardless of when the property was acquired. Also, expensive cars used predominantly for business will nonetheless be restricted as to the amounts of the ACRS deductions and the investment credit which may be taken each year. A standard mileage rate may be used for cars instead of calculating depreciation and actual operating and fixed expenses for the car. Publication 534 details the interplay of these provisions, but it will often be advantageous to calculate depreciate and *not* use the standard mileage rate (which is adjusted periodically).

The computation of depreciation for equipment placed in use during 1980 or earlier tax years will be done differently from the systems just discussed for equipment placed in use after 1980. The useful life of the pre-1981 equipment has to have been determined. The useful life of such professional equipment varied, but a good faith estimate based on the personal knowledge and experience of the artist (or upon the guidelines of the more complex Class Life Asset Depreciation Range System described in Publication 534) was acceptable. The salvage value of an asset (other than a house) having a useful life of three years or more could be reduced by 10 percent of the asset's original cost for depreciation calculations, and thus a salvage value of less than 10 percent did not affect the depreciation computation at all. Bonus depreciation of 20 percent of original cost could be added to the first year depreciation of an asset (other than a house) having a useful life of at least six years—as computed in Publication 534. If an asset became worthless before expiration of its estimated useful life, the remaining basis was claimed as depreciation in the year of worthlessness. Knowledge of the rule for pre-1981 acquisitions is important since depreciation on such equipment may be continuing now.

Travel, transportation and entertainment

Travel, transportation and entertainment expenses for business purposes are deductible, but must meet strict record-keeping requirements. Travel expenses are the ordinary and necessary expenses, including meals, lodging and transporatation, incurred for travel overnight away from home in pursuit of professional activities. Such expenses would be deductible, for example, if the artist traveled to another city to hang a gallery show and stayed several days to complete the work. If the artist is not required to sleep or rest while away from home, transportation expenses are limited to the cost of travel (but commuting expenses are not deductible as transportation expenses). Entertainment expenses, whether business luncheons or parties or similar items, are deductible as long as the expense is incurred for the purpose of the developing business. Business gifts may be made to individuals, but no deductions will be allowed for gifts to any one individual in excess of $25 during the tax year.

Accurate and contemporaneous records detailing business purpose (and the business relationship to any person entertained or receiving a gift),
date, place and cost are particularly important for all these deductions. The artist should also get into the habit of writing these details on copies of bills or credit card charge receipts, particularly since this documentation is required for charges of $25 or more. IRS Publication 463, *Travel, Entertainment, and Gift Expenses,* gives more details, including the current mileage charge should the artist own and use a car. Also, self-promotional items, such as advertising, printing business cards or sending Christmas greetings to professional associates, are deductible expenses.

Commissions, fees and salaries

Commissions paid to agents and fees paid to lawyers or accountants for business purposes are tax deductible, as are the salaries paid to typists, researchers and others. However, the artist should try to hire people as independent contractors rather than employees, in order to avoid liability for social security, disability and withholding tax payments. This can be done by hiring on a job-for-job basis, with each job to be completed by a deadline, preferably at a place chosen by the person hired. Record-keeping expenses and taxes will be saved, although Form 1099-MISC, *Statement for Recipients of Miscellaneous Income,* must be filed for each independent contractor paid more than $600 in one year by the artist.

Schedule C

The completion of Schedule C—by use of the guidelines in this chapter—finishes much, but not all, of the artist's tax preparations. The next chapter discusses other important tax provisions—not reflected on Schedule C—which can aid the artist or which the artist must observe. A sample Schedule C appears on page 156.

| SCHEDULE C
(Form 1040)

Department of the Treasury
Internal Revenue Service (O) | **Profit or (Loss) From Business or Profession**
(Sole Proprietorship)
Partnerships, Joint Ventures, etc., Must File Form 1065.
▶ Attach to Form 1040 or Form 1041. ▶ See Instructions for Schedule C (Form 1040). | OMB No. 1545-0074

1984
09 |

Name of proprietor	Social security number
Jane Artist	000 : 00 : 0000

A Main business activity (see Instructions) ▶ Artist   Product or Service ▶ Paintings

B Business name and address ▶ 125 Main Street, Indian Rock, Idaho   **C** Employer ID number

D Method(s) used to value closing inventory: N/A
   (1) ☐ Cost   (2) ☒ Lower of cost or market   (3) ☐ Other (attach explanation)

		Yes	No
E Accounting method: (1) ☒ Cash (2) ☐ Accrual (3) ☐ Other (specify) ▶			
F Was there any change in determining quantities, costs, or valuations between opening and closing inventory? N/A If "Yes," attach explanation.			
G Did you deduct expenses for an office in your home?			X

Part I Income

1 a	Gross receipts or sales	1a	25,592
b	Less: Returns and allowances	1b	0
c	Subtract line 1b from line 1a and enter the balance here	1c	25,592
2	Cost of goods sold and/or operations (from Part III, line 8)	2	2,727
3	Subtract line 2 from line 1c and enter the **gross profit** here	3	22,865
4 a	Windfall Profit Tax Credit or Refund received in 1984 (see Instructions)	4a	
b	Other income	4b	
5	Add lines 3, 4a, and 4b. This is the **gross income** ▶	5	22,865

Part II Deductions

6	Advertising	75	23	Repairs	523
7	Bad debts from sales or services (Cash		24	Supplies (not included in Part III below)	
	method taxpayers, see Instructions)		25	Taxes (Do not include Windfall	
8	Bank service charges			Profit Tax here. See line 29.)	
9	Car and truck expenses		26	Travel and entertainment	239
10	Commissions	2,250	27	Utilities and telephone	820
11	Depletion		28 a	Wages	
12	Depreciation and Section 179 deduction		b	Jobs credit	
	from Form 4562 (not included in Part		c	Subtract line 28b from 28a	
	III below)	1,420	29	Windfall Profit Tax withheld in 1984	
13	Dues and publications	158	30	Other expenses (specify).	
14	Employee benefit programs		a	Miscellaneous	323
15	Freight (not included in Part III below)		b		
16	Insurance	326	c		
17	Interest on business indebtedness	178	d		
18	Laundry and cleaning		e		
19	Legal and professional services	556	f		
20	Office expense	241	g		
21	Pension and profit-sharing plans		h		
22	Rent on business property	2,400	i		

31	Add amounts in columns for lines 6 through 30i. These are the **total deductions** ▶	31	9,509
32	**Net profit or (loss).** Subtract line 31 from line 5 and enter the result. If a profit, enter on Form 1040, line 12, and on Schedule SE, Part I, line 2 (or Form 1041, line 6). If a loss, you **MUST** go on to line 33	32	13,356

33 If you have a loss, you **MUST** answer this question: "Do you have amounts for which you are not at risk in this business (see Instructions)?" ☐ Yes ☐ No
If "Yes," you **MUST** attach **Form 6198.** If "No," enter the loss on Form 1040, line 12, and on Schedule SE, Part I, line 2 (or Form 1041, line 6).

Part III Cost of Goods Sold and/or Operations (See Schedule C Instructions for Part III)

1	Inventory at beginning of year (if different from last year's closing inventory, attach explanation)	1	
2	Purchases less cost of items withdrawn for personal use	2	
3	Cost of labor (do not include salary paid to yourself)	3	756
4	Materials and supplies	4	1,971
5	Other costs	5	
6	Add lines 1 through 5	6	2,727
7	Less: Inventory at end of year	7	
8	**Cost of goods sold and/or operations.** Subtract line 7 from line 6. Enter here and in Part I, line 2, above	8	2,727

For Paperwork Reduction Act Notice, see Form 1040 Instructions.   ☆U.S. Government Printing Office: 1984—423-087 23-0918750   Schedule C (Form 1040) 1984

Chapter 19

Income taxation: II

The artist must also be aware of a number of other tax benefits and obligations in order to be able to make rational choices and to seek professional advice when necessary. These provisions, while not gathered neatly in one place as income and expenses are on Schedule C, are of great signifcance to the artist.

Income averaging

Income averaging might be a valuable tax-saving device for the artist if there is a large increase in the artist's taxable income for one tax year as compared to the previous years. The effect of averaging, which is computed on Schedule G of Form 1040, is to treat a certain amount of the extra income realized in the current tax year as if it had actually been received over the preceding three years. Substantial savings result because of the progressive nature of the tax structure. IRS Publication 506, *Income Averaging,* should be consulted for details.

Self-employment tax

The social security system of the United States creates numerous benefits for those who have contributed from their earnings to the federal social security system. It provides benefits for a person's family in the event of death or disablement as well as providing a pension and certain medical insurance. Artists, whether employees or self-employed, are covered by the system. Since the payments for social security are not automatically withheld for a self-employed artist, as they are for one who is an employee, the self-employed artist must file with Form 1040 a Schedule SE, *Computation of Social Security Self-Employment Tax,* and pay the self-employ-

ment tax shown on the Schedule SE. Self-employment income is basically the net income of the artist reported on Schedule C, subject to certain adjustments. If an artist and spouse both earn self-employment income, each must file a separate Schedule SE. If an artist has more than one business, the combined business earnings should be totaled on Schedule SE for purposes of calculating the self-employment tax.

Social security coverage to gain the various benefits is created by having a certain number of years during which a worker makes payments for social security. A self-employed artist must, in any case, make social security payments for each year when net self-employment income is more than $400, but, when the artist does so, a year of work credit is recorded for social security benefits. If a minimum number of years of work credit is established, the artist qualifies for benefits. The amount of benefits is based on average yearly earnings covered by social security. Therefore, the artist benefits by paying self-employment tax each year on the maximum permissible amount of self-employment income. The maximum amount of income on which tax must be paid has been increasing constantly over the years; for example, from $14,000 in 1975 to $37,800 in 1984.

Calculation of the self-employment tax is done by first taking all income from employers from which the social security tax has already been withheld and subtracting that from the maximum amount of income on which tax must be paid to determine how much tax must be paid on the remaining self-employment income. In 1984 the social security tax rate was 11.3 percent for the self-employed. For 1984, the maximum self-employment tax was $4,271.40 payable if the income to be taxed, as shown on Schedule SE, was $37,800 or more.

Further information as to the computation of the self-employment tax can be found in IRS Publication 533, *Self-Employment Tax.* Additional information as to the benefits available under social security to either the artist or the artist's family is available from the local office of the Social Security Administration, including pamphlets titled "Your Social Security" and "If You're Self-Employed . . . Reporting Your Income for Social Security."

Estimated tax

Employers withhold income and social security taxes from the wages of their employees. However, the self-employed artist must pay income and social security taxes in quarterly installments computed on Form 1040-ES, *Estimated Tax for Individuals,* and mailed on or before April 15, June 15, September 15 and January 15. In most cases, Form 1040-ES is required if the artist estimates that the total of income and self-employment taxes for the next year will exceed any withheld taxes by $500 or more. IRS Publication 505, *Tax Withholding and Estimated Tax,* gives more detailed information regarding the estimated tax.

Retirement plans

Keogh plans permit a self-employed person like an artist to contribute to a retirement fund and to deduct the amount of the contribution from gross income when computing income taxes. However, the deduction is allowed in any year only if the artist places the amount to be deducted in one of the following retirement funds: a trust, annuity contracts from an insurance company, a custodial account with a bank or another person, special U.S. Government retirement bonds or certain face-amount certificates purchased from investment companies. Even if the artist is employed by a company with a retirement program, the artist may still have a Keogh plan for self-employment income from the career in art.

There are several ways to determine the amount of contributions to be made to a Keogh plan. The artist is most likely to use the defined contribution plan which allows as a deduction a contribution up to the lesser of either 20 percent of net self-employment income or $30,000. If an artist has employees, it is quite likely that a plan to benefit the artist will also require contributions for the benefit of the employees.

A contribution to a Keogh plan can be made before the filing date of the tax return, which is usually the following April l5th, or any extensions of the filing date, as long as the Keogh plan was in existence during the tax year for which the deduction is to be taken. Because the money contributed to a Keogh plan is deductible, there are penalties for withdrawal of monies from a plan prior to age 59 1/2 unless the artist becomes permanently disabled. No taxes are levied on the growth of a Keogh fund until the funds are withdrawn. Distributions are taxed when made, and must begin no later than age 70 1/2 (or, in some cases, the year of retirement if the person is older than 70 1/2 on retiring). The artist's tax bracket then, however, may be much lower than when the contributions were made and the funds have had tax-free growth. If a trust is created, it is possible for the artist to act as trustee and administer the investments. More information about Keogh plans can be obtained from the institutions, such as the local bank or insurance company, which administer them. Also helpful are IRS Publication 560, *Self-Employed Retirement Plans,* and 566, *Questions and Answers on Retirement Plans for Self-Employed.*

Separate from the Keogh plan, the artist may begin an Individual Retirement Account. By creation of such an account, the artist may contribute into a retirement fund up to $2,000 per year (assuming wages and professional fees amount to at least that much). A married artist with a non-working spouse may be able to contribute $2,250 to benefit both spouses, while two working spouses could contribute $2,000 each for a maximum of $4,000 deduction.

The amount of the contribution is a deduction from gross income. Again the funds contributed must be taken out of the artist's hands and placed in a trust, a custodial account with a bank or other person, annuity contracts with a life insurance company or special U.S. Government retirement bonds. The payment, to be deductible, must be made by April 15th of the year following the tax year for which the deduction will be taken. More information may be obtained from the institutions administering Individual Retirement Accounts, as well as IRS Publication 590, *Individual Retirement Arrangements (IRA's).*

Keogh plan contributions are claimed on Form 1040, line 27, and Individual Retirement Account contributions are claimed on Form 1040, line 26a. The artist should consult with the Keogh plan or Individual Retirement Account administrator to determine what additional forms may have to be filed. Also, the custodial fees charged by a plan administrator may be deducted as investment expenses on Schedule A if these fees are separately billed and paid for. Commissions paid on transactions in the retirement fund do not qualify as deductible.

Investment credit

Apart from depreciation, another significant tax consideration for the artist's equipment (but not applicable to buildings) is the investment tax credit. This gives a tax reduction equal to 10 percent of the investment in new or used 5-year depreciable property (if used, only to the amount of $125,000 through 1987 and $150,000 thereafter). The amount of credit is reduced to 60 percent if the asset is 3-year property under the ACRS categories. The basis for depreciation is reduced by 50 percent of the amount of the investment credit (or, alternatively, the taxpayer may choose to reduce the investment credit by two points and not reduce the asset's basis at all). Form 3468, *Computation of Investment Credit,* is used for the computation and sets forth some limitations on such credit. Early disposition of the asset causes recapture of part of the investment credit on Form 4255, *Recapture of Investment Credit.*

A tax credit is subtracted directly from the tax owed, so it is more beneficial than a deduction of the same amount which merely reduces income prior to application of the tax rates. This is why the investment tax credit serves as an incentive to the improvement and expansion of plant. IRS Publication 572, *Investment Credit,* contains additional information regarding the investment credit. This publication also discusses credits for certain investments in energy-producing property and for the rehabilitation of older buildings.

Child and disabled dependent care

Child or disabled dependent care may also create a tax credit. The amount of the credit is 30 percent (or lesser percentages for incomes over $10,000) of the employment-related expenses which an artist pays in order to be gainfully employed. Basically, this credit is available to the artist who maintains a household including either a child under age fifteen or a disabled dependent or spouse for the care of whom it is necessary to hire someone so the artist can gainfully pursue employment, self-employment or the search for employment. The maximum credit is $720 per year for one qualifying dependent or $1,440 for two or more qualifying dependents. IRS Publication 503, *Child and Dependent Care Credit, and Employment Taxes for Household Employers,* describes in greater detail the availability of and limitations on this credit.

Contributions

Contributions to qualified organizations are deductible if personal deductions are itemized on Schedule A. Since the artist's own art works, and any gifts of works by other artists, have a tax basis of zero (if the artist is on a cash basis) or the cost of materials (if the artist is on an accural basis), the artist's deduction is limited to such basis. Numerous bills have been proposed to rectify this inequitable treatment, and perhaps the artist will someday be able to deduct either part or all of the fair market value of contributed works. The rule, of course, is otherwise for the collector—an artist, for example, who purchases work which increases in value. The deductions for a collector's contributions are discussed on page 186. A number of states have enacted laws giving artists the right to deduct their own contributed art on the basis of fair market value for the purpose of state taxes. These states include Arkansas, California, Kansas, Maryland, Michigan, Oregon and South Carolina.

159

Bad debts

A common error is the belief that if an artist (on the cash basis) sells a work for $1,000 and the purchaser never pays, the artist can take a bad debt deduction. The artist cannot, since the $1,000 purchase price has never been received and included in income. As stated in Publication 334, Tax Guide for Small Businesses, "Worthless debts arising from sales, professional services rendered . . . and similar items of income will not be allowed as bad debt deductions unless the income from those items has been included in gross income in the return for the year which the deduction is claimed or for the previous year."

A cash basis taxpayer can, however, gain a tax benefit from either business or nonbusiness bad debts of the proper kind. In almost all cases, the artist's bad debts will be nonbusiness. For example, if the artist makes a loan to a friend who never repays the loan, the amount of the loan will be a nonbusiness bad debt. The loan cannot be a gift, however, and must be legally enforceable against the borrower. The nonbusiness bad debt deduction is taken in the year in which the debt becomes worthless. It is reported as a short-term capital loss on Schedule D.

Net operating losses

The artist who experiences a business loss as determined on Schedule C will carry the loss to Form 1040, where it is eventually subtracted from gross income in the calculations to reach taxable income. However, if the loss is large enough to wipe out other taxable income for the year, the excess loss can first be carried back to reduce taxable income in three prior years and then carried forward for fifteen future taxable years. This type of loss is likely to arise when a professional artist is changing over from being employed to devoting all working time to art. The result is that the artist will be entitled to a tax refund (if taxable income in previous years is reduced) or will save on taxes in future years. IRS Publication 536, *Net Operating Losses and the At-Risk Limits,* describes the net operating loss,

but the artist will probably need an accountant's help for the computation of a net operating loss.

American artists living abroad

American citizens, whether or not they live in the United States, are taxable by the United States government on all of their income from anywhere in the world. However, a tax benefit for many American citizens living abroad is the exclusion from American taxable income of $80,000 of earned income from foreign sources. The $80,000 figure will apply though 1987, after which the amount will increase. This exclusion can result in substantial tax benefits when the tax rates of the foreign country—such as Ireland, where a qualified artist can live tax free—are lower than the tax rates in the United States.

Publication 54, *Tax Guide for U.S. Citizens Abroad,* generally explains the guidelines for eligibility for these exclusions. The basic requirements are either a one-year residence or a physical presence in a foreign country and earned income created from work done in the foreign country. Residence is a flexible concept based on the circumstances of each individual. While the residence must be uninterrupted (for example, by owning or renting a home continually), remaining abroad for all the taxable year in question is not necessary. Brief trips to the United States do not affect the tax status as a resident abroad. However, the length of each visit and the total time spent in the United States must be watched carefully. Physical presence requires the taxpayer to be present in a foreign country or countries for at least 330 days (about 11 months) during a period of twelve consecutive months. Regardless of which test is met, the income to be excluded must be received no later than the year after the year in which the work was performed which generated the income. Certain foreign housing costs may also be excludable or deductible from income.

Assuming the artist met either the residence or physical presence test, the requirement that the income to be excluded had to be earned income often proved fatal to the artist's attempt to benefit from the exclusion. The reason for this was the definition, once found in Publication 54, of most of the income of an artist as unearned.

This unjust situation was rectified, however, in a case involving the painter, Mark Tobey, while he was a resident of Switzerland. In *Tobey v. Commissioner* the issue before the tax court was whether Mark Tobey, all of whose "works were executed . . . without prior commission, contract, order, or any such prior arrangement," had earned income such that he could avail himself of the exclusion from United States taxable income. The court, noting that earned generally implies a product of one's own work, reasoned:

> The concept of the artist as not "earning" his income for the purposes of Section 911 would place him in an unfavorable light. For the most part, the present day artist is a hard-working, trained, career-oriented individual. His education, whether acquired formally or through personal practice, growth and experience, is often costly and exacting. He has keen competition from many other artists who must create and sell their works to survive. To avoid discriminatory treatment, we perceive no sound reasons for treating income earned by the personal efforts, skill and creativity of a Tobey or a Picasso any differently from the income earned by a confidence man, a brain surgeon, a movie star or, for that matter, a tax attorney. (*Tobey v. Commissioner,* 60 T.C. 227)

This rationale necessarily led to the conclusion that Tobey's income was earned. Publication 54 now reflects this by stating, "Income of an artist. Income you receive from the sale of art paintings is earned income if you painted the pictures yourself."

Each artist hoping to benefit from the exclusion for income earned abroad must, of course, consult with a lawyer or an accountant to determine the effect of the foregoing legal provisions on each unique situation. Artists already living abroad should also inquire at their American consulate to determine whether any treaty regarding taxation between the United States and the country in which they live might affect their tax status.

The artist living abroad should also consider whether any income taxes paid to a foreign government may be taken as either a deduction or a tax credit. No such credit or deduction will be allowed on foreign income taxes paid on earned income excluded from the United States taxation. IRS Publication 514, *Foreign Tax Credit for U.S. Citizens and Resident Aliens,* explains these provisions further.

Foreign artists in the United States

Foreign artists who are residents of the United States are generally taxed in the same way as United States citizens. Foreign artists who are not residents in the United States are taxed on income from sources in the United States under special rules. A foreigner who is merely visiting or whose stay is limited by immigration laws will usually be considered a non-resident. A foreigner who intends, at least temporarily, to establish a home in the United States and has a visa permitting permanent residence will probably be considered a resident. IRS Publication 519, *United States Tax Guide for Aliens,* should be consulted by foreign artists for a more extensive discussion of their tax status.

Forms of doing business

Depending on the success of the artist, various forms of doing business might be considered. There may be both business and tax advantages to conducting the artist's business in the form of a corporation or partnership, but there may be disadvantages as well.

Generally, the nontax advantages of incorporation are limited liability for the stockholders, centralized management, access to capital, transferability of ownership and continuity of the business. For the artist, the most important of these nontax advantages will probably be limited liability. This means that a judgement in a lawsuit will affect only the assets of the corporation, not the personal assets of the artist. Limited liability is quite significant when the work locale, machinery, chemicals or even art work are potentially hazardous. The attribute of limited liability applies to all corporations—the regular corporation and the Subchapter S corporation. The tax treatment, however, differs significantly between the two types of corporations.

For regular corporations, net corporate income is taxed at 15 percent to $25,000, 18 percent from $25,000 to $50,000, 30 percent from $50,000 to $75,000, 40 percent from $75,000 to $100,000 and 46 percent over $100,000. Usually the tax on the corporation can be substantially avoided by the payment of a salary to the artist, which creates a deduction for the corporation. Such an arrangment can effectively average the artist's income from year to year. The Subchapter S corporation is not taxed at all, but the income is credited directly to the accounts of the stockholders and they are taxed as individuals. Both types of corporations are less likely to be audited than an individual proprietor. It may also be easier to choose a fiscal year (any tax year other than the calendar year) and, particularly in the case of a regular corporation, shift some of the artist's income into the next tax year. Some of the disadvantages of incorporation are additional recordkeeping, meetings and paper work, as well as significant expenses both for the initial incorporation and for any ultimate dissolution.

A partnership is an agreement between two or more persons to join together as co-owners of a business in pursuit of profit. Partnerships are not subject to the income tax, but the individual partners are taxable on their share of the partnership income. Partners are personally liable for obligations incurred on behalf of the partnership by any of the partners. A partnership offers to the artist an opportunity to combine with investors under an agreement in which the investors may gain tax advantages by being allocated a greater share of partnership losses. A variation of the usual partnership is the "limited partnership," in which passive investors have limited liability (but the artist, running the business actively, is still personally liable). Another variation is the "joint venture," which can be described simply as a partnership created for a single business venture.

The artist contemplating doing business as either a corporation or partnership should consult a lawyer for advice based on the artist's unique needs.

Gifts

The artist can avoid paying income taxes by giving away the artist's creations. Both art works and copyrights can be transferred by gift to family members or others whom the artist may wish to benefit. The art work and copyright on the work can be transferred separately from one another if the artist chooses. The artist could keep the work and transfer the copyright, transfer the copyright and keep the work, or transfer both the work and the copyright. If the person who receives the gift is in a lower tax bracket than the artist, tax savings will result upon sale by the person who received the gift. Gifts over certain amounts, however, are subject to the gift tax. The making of gifts and the gift tax are discussed on pages 175-178, but careful planning is a necessity if gifts are to play an effective role in tax planning.

Chapter 20

The hobby loss challenge

Often the artist sufficiently dedicated to pursue an art career despite year after year of losses on Schedule C will face a curious challenge from the IRS: that the losses incurred by the artist cannot be deducted for tax purposes because the artist was only pursuing a hobby and did not have the profit motive necessary to qualify the art career as a business or trade. A hobbyist in any field may deduct the expenses of the hobby only up to the amount of income produced by the hobby. For example, if a hobbyist makes $500 in a year on the sale of art, only up to $500 in expenses can be deducted. On the other hand, an artist actively engaged in the business or trade of being an artist—one who pursues art with a profit motive—may deduct all ordinary and necessary business expenses, even if such expenses far exceed income from art activities for the year.

A test: two years out of five

But how can an artist determine whether the requisite profit motive is present to avoid being characterized as a hobbyist by the IRS? At the outset, there is an important threshold test in favor of the taxpayer. This test, which was introduced in the Tax Reform Act of 1969, provides a presumption that an artist is engaged in a business or trade—and hence is not a hobbyist—if a net profit is created by the activity in question during two of five consecutive years ending with the taxable year at issue. Thus, many artists who have good and bad years need not fear a hobby loss challenge to a loss in one of the bad years.

If a hobby loss problem is anticipated, artists on the cash basis may be able to create profitable years by regulating the time of receipt of income and the time of incurrence of expenses. For example, instead of

having five years of small losses, an artist is far better off having two years in which a small profit is earned and three years in which larger than usual losses are incurred. Another way to create a profitable year is to sell art to a friend and buy some of the friend's art. In essence a trade, this will lose some deductions but gain a profitable year (and also entitle the artist to hold the purchased art as a collector which may have favorable tax consequences). If the artist has an art-related job, some daring accountants enter the wages from the job as income on Schedule C from the business of being an artist. While this is not recommended, an artist might wish to discuss this with his or her own professional advisors.

Profit motive: the nine factors

But even if an artist does not have two profitable years in the last five years of art activity, the contention by the IRS that the artist is a hobbyist can still be overcome if the artist can show a profit motive. The Regulations to the Internal Revenue Code specifically provide for an objective standard to determine profit motive based on all the facts and circumstances surrounding the activity. Therefore, statements by the artist as to profit motive are given little weight. But the chance of making a profit can be quite unlikely, as long as the artist actually intends to be profitable.

The regulations set forth nine factors used to determine profit motive. Since every artist is capable, in varying degrees, of pursuing art in a manner which will be considered a trade or business, these factors can create an instructive model. The objective factors are considered in their totality, so that all the circumstances surrounding the activity will determine the result in a given case. Although most of the factors are important, no single factor will determine the result of a case. The nine factors follow.

1. Manner in which the taxpayer carries on the activity. The artist should keep accurate records of all business activities, especially receipts and expenses.

2. The expertise of the taxpayer or his advisors. Study is one indication of expertise, but equally important is professional acceptance as shown by gallery exhibitions, encouragement by agents or dealers, the winning of prizes, professional memberships, or critical recognition in articles or books. Use of professional equipment and technqiues can also be important. The appointment to a teaching position, if the appointment is based at least in part on professional art ability, further demonstrates expertise.

3. The time and effort expended by the taxpayer in carrying on the activity. The activity doesn't have to absorb all of the artist's time, but a failure to work at all is not consistent with having a profit motive. Exactly what is sufficient time has never been spelled out, but on one occasion the court found four hours a day acceptable. It is helpful if the art activity is the only occupation of the artist, but employment in another field does not negate the presence of a profit motive with respect to art.

4. Expectation that assets used in activity may appreciate in value. This factor has yet to be applied to the arts, although artists, of course, expect that their art will increase in value.

5. The success of the taxpayer in carrying on the other similar or dissimilar activities. Previous critical or financial success in art, despite an intervening slack period, is helpful.

6. The taxpayer's history of income or losses with respect to the activity. Increasing income each year from the art activity is very positive. On the other hand, losses don't imply a lack of a profit motive, unless such losses continue over a lengthy time period during which income is being received from nonart sources and a large imbalance exists between art-related income and expenses. Ironically, the change of profession to a nonart activity after an unprofitable art career would also show that a profit motive had existed in the pursuit of the art activity.

7. The amount of occasional profits, if any, which are earned. Here the amount of profits is compared to the amount of expenses, but this factor is only important where the taxpayer is sufficiently wealthy to gain tax benefits from disproportionate expenses without feeling any financial strain from the amount of the expenses.

8. The financial status of the taxpayer. Wealth and independent income are unfavorable to having a profit motive, while the need for income from the art activity and the lack of funds to support a hobby would tend to indicate the presence of a profit motive.

9. Elements of personal pleasure or recreation. This has little application, since the pursuit of an art career is as painstaking and rigorous as any occupation. However, where travel is involved, the artist should be fully prepared to justify the necessity of such travel in furtherance of the art activity.

To give perspective to these nine factors, a look at two hobby loss cases will be helpful. In the first case, the tax court found the artist a hobbyist; in the second case, a professional artist. These cases should serve as models for the artist, as well as illustrating the approach of the tax court to hobby loss cases.

Case 1: the hobbyist

Johanna K.W. Hailman was a prominent social leader in Pittsburgh, Pennsylvania. Born in 1870, she had painted from an early age—mainly portraits and flowers—and by the time of her death in 1958 had completed 500 to 600 paintings. She owned a large estate and received substantial income from investments and a trust established by her deceased husband. On her estate she had a fully equipped and heated four-room studio located about 150 feet from her main house. During her winters in Florida, she maintained a room in her residence for her studio. She was recognized as a leading artist in western Pennsylvania and had good standing throughout the United States. She had shown her work in the First International Exhibition at Carnegie Institute in 1896 and, apparently, exhibited at all the subsequent International Exhibitions at Carnegie through 1955.

Betweeen 1920 and 1949 she sold about 50 paintings, but made no sales from 1949 to 1954. She did not use a dealer or agent, but offered her paintings for sales at various exhibitions in Pittsburgh and other places. In the 1950s the prices for her paintings were in a range between $700 and $1,500, and she refused to accept offers she felt would be inadequate to maintain her prestige as an artist. From 1936 to 1954 her income from painting amounted to $7,200 while her expenses incidental to making and selling paintings came to $131,140. The IRS did not allow all of these expenses, but instead adopted the practice through 1951 of permitting as a deduction the amount of $3,000 per year.

The cessation of sales in 1949 did not correspond to a cessation of expenses, which totaled $9,654 in 1952, $7,718 in 1953, and $6,457 in 1954. The IRS determined that none of the expenses in these three years should be allowed as deductions because Mrs. Hailman was not engaged in the business of being an artist.

The tax court agreed with the IRS. The court concluded that where—over a lengthy period such as 1936 to 1954—expenses are eighteen times as great as receipts from an activity; and only independent wealth permits the continuance of the activity, including the setting of high prices and the retention of most of the art works, then the activity must be determined to be pursued for the pleasurable diversion provided by a hobby without the necessary profit motive to be engaged in a business or trade. The result was that no deductions for her art activities were allowed Mrs. Hailman for the years 1952, 1953 and 1954.

Case 2: the professional

Anna Maria de Grazia, who painted under the name of Anna Maria d'Annunzio, was born in Switzerland. The granddaughter of Gabriele d'Annunzio, the famous Italian writer and military hero, she was raised in Italy where, in 1940, she became interested in painting. During World War II, she served as a guide for the Allied forces but continued her painting until 1944, when polio forced her to learn how to paint with her left hand rather than her right. In 1942 she won first prize in an exhibition by young painters in Florence and in the same year placed third in a contest open to all Italians. She did not paint from 1943 to 1947 but did paint and exhibit from 1948 to 1951. During this period she was admitted to the Italian painters' union upon the attestation of three professional artists that she was also a professional artist. In 1952 she moved to the United States, married Sebastian de Grazia and neither painted nor exhibited until 1955, when she also became a naturalized citizen of the United States. By 1957, she had studied with artists Annigoni, Carena and Kokoschka and had been recognized by having her self-portrait and biographical background appear in a book on Italian painting from 1850 to 1950.

She resumed her painting in 1956 and 1957, supported by the modest income of her husband, who was a visiting professor at Princeton University. In 1957 she worked at Princeton in a rented house she felt had inadequate facilities for a studio. Finally, in May, she left to paint at the Piazza Donatello Studios in Florence, Italy, which had been built for artists and had excellent light. Her decision to go to Florence was prompted by her familiarity with the Italian art world, although she had also made several unsuccessful visits to New York in 1957 in an attempt to find an art gallery for her work there. She painted four hours a day in 1957, devoting additional time to stretching and preparing her canvases and transacting business with art dealers and her framemaker. She had been told that a prestigious gallery in New York would require numerous paintings for an exhibition, and by the end of 1957 she had completed twelve or fifteen paintings with ten more in progress. After 1957 she did exhibit successfully, having a number of solo shows in Italy as well as having her work exhibited in Princeton and New York City. In 1957 she had no receipts from her painting, while her expenses were $5,769; in 1958 she had $500 in receipts, while her expenses were $6,854; in 1959 she had $575 in receipts, while her expenses were $5,360; and in 1960 she had $710 in receipts, while her expenses were $4,968. She did not keep formal business books, but did have records relating to her receipts and expenses as an artist. The IRS challenged her deduction of $5,769 in 1957 on the ground that she had been merely pursuing a hobby or preparing to enter a business or trade, but had not been engaged in the business or trade of being an artist in that year.

The tax court, in an excellent opinion, disagreed with the IRS and concluded that she had indeed been in the business or trade of being an artist in the year 1957. The tax court considered the following as significant proof of her profit motive: She began painting in her youth and won prizes for her work; she struggled to overcome the handicap imposed by polio; she studied with recognized artists; she received recognition from the Italian painters' union and in critical publications; she had exhibited both prior and subsequent to 1957; she worked continually and unstintingly at her painting and necessary incidental tasks; she had no other sources of income so that the losses were a financial strain; and she had constantly increasing receipts in the years after 1957. Also, the tax court rejected explicitly the argument that she had merely been preparing to enter a trade or profession, stating that the history of her art activities after 1940 rebutted any such contention. In a notable section of the decision, the court wrote:

It is well recognized that profits may not be immediately forthcoming in the creative art field. Examples are legion of the increase in value of a painter's works after he receives public acclaim. Many artists have to struggle in their early years. This does not mean that serious artists do not intend to profit from their activities. It only means that their lot is a difficult one. (*Sebastian de Grazia,* 21 T.C.M. 1572)

In another case favorable to artists, a woman who had painted for twenty years without making a profit was found to have a profit motive. For the three years in which the IRS tried to deny her deductions, she had only one sale for $250. The tax court noted that she had made extensive efforts to market her work, including running a gallery for a year, keeping a mailing list, seeking other galleries and making different efforts—such as doing posters and writing books—to enhance the likelihood of sales. She kept a journal for sales and kept all her receipts. Also, she had studied and taught art. Her work did appear at least once a year in commercial galleries and she had been written up in newspapers and magazines. She had also received a grant to do a film. She devoted a substantial amount of time to her artistic activities.

In holding that the artist had a profit motive, the court wrote:

It is abundantly clear from her testimony and from objective evidence that petitioner is a most dedicated artist, craves personal recognition as an artist, and believes that selling her work for a profit represents the attainment of such recognition. Therefore, petitioner intends and expects to make a profit. For section 183 purposes, it seems to us irrelevant whether petitioner intends to make a profit because it symbolizes success in her chosen career or because it is the pathway to material wealth. In either case, the essential fact remains that petitioner does intend to make a profit from her artwork and she sincerely believes that if she continues to paint she will do so. (*Churchman v. Commissioner,* 68 T.C. 696)

An overview

Artists with wealth and independent incomes, whose art activity expenses are large relative to their receipts over a lengthy period, are most likely to be found to be pursuing a hobby. Artists who devote much time to their art, who have the expertise to receive some recognition and for whom the expenses of art are burdensome will probably be found to be engaged in a business or trade rather than a hobby. Especially younger artists, who are making financial sacrifices so common to the beginning of an art career, should be considered to have a profit motive even if other employment is necessary for survival during this difficult early period.

Each case in which an artist is challenged as a hobbyist requires a determination on its own facts, but an awareness on the part of the artist as to what factors are relevant should aid in preventing or, if necessary, meeting such a challenge. It is advisable to have the professional assistance of an accountant or lawyer as soon as a hobby loss issue arises on an audit. Such professional advisors can be par- ticularly helpful in effectively present- ing the factors favorable to the artist. The presence of a lawyer or accoun- tant at the earliest conferences with the IRS can aid in bringing a hobby loss challenge to a quick and satisfac- tory resolution.

Chapter 21

The artist's estate

Estate planning should begin during the artist's lifetime with the assistance of a lawyer and, if necessary, a life insurance agent and an officer of a bank's trusts and estates department. Artists, like other taxpayers, seek to dispose of their assets to the people and institutions of their choice, while reducing the amounts of income taxes during life and estate taxes at death. But artists must take special care with their estate planning because of the unique nature of art works and the manner of valuing art works at death for the purposes of determining the value of the estate on which the appropriate estate tax rate will be levied. This chapter cannot substitute for consultation and careful planning with the professional advisors mentioned above, but it can at least alert the artist to matters of importance which will make the artist a more effective participant in the process of planning the estate.

The art works are unique because they are the creation of the artist and possess aesthetic qualities not found in other goods which pass through an estate. The artist may wish to control the completion, repairs, reproductions, exhibitions and sales of the works even after death.

Integrity of the art

David Smith, for example, during his life condemned a purchaser of one of Smith's painted metal sculptures who removed the paint from the sculpture after purchase. Smith branded this willful vandalism and considered the work a ruin which he repudiated as "60 lbs. of scrap steel."

Smith, in his will, had carefully selected as his executors the critic Clement Greenberg, the painter Robert Motherwell and the attorney Ira Lowe. Yet after Smith's death, these executors permitted important changes in some of the works remaining in the estate. *Circle and Box,* a work originally painted white, was stripped and apparently varnished. *Primo Piano III,* also white, was repainted brown. Another work, *Rebecca's Circle,* was permitted to deteriorate and rust.

Unauthorized reproductions

Another important aesthetic control is that exercised by the executors (or beneficiaries, if the copyrights are bequeathed with the works, once distribution occurs) over reproductions of the artist's work. If a painter usually authorized the sale of photographic reproductions of paintings, the executors may confidently continue to do so. Serious questions arise, however, as commercial offers to reproduce and profit from the art reach into areas where the artist never authorized reproductions. If the painter permitted photographic reproductions, would reproductions on tee shirts, jewelry, plates or potholders be permissible? The executors are bound to conserve the assets of the estate, so these offers are tempting. Indeed, a failure to accept a lucrative offer might even be argued to be a wasting of the assets of the estate. But the executors must deal as well with the intangible factors of the artist's wishes and reputation.

A not uncommon event is the authorization of reproductions by the beneficiares who receive the work. For example, the heirs of sculptor Julio Gonzalez allowed posthumous bronze replicas of the sculptures to be cast and sold. Not only had Gonzalez always used iron as the material for his sculptures, but in some cases the bronze replicas were sold without any indication of their being made posthumously. An even more egregious example involved lithographs supposedly executed by Renoir. The entrepreneur exploiting Renoir's name advertised "authentic Renoir lithographs." The prospectus for purchasers advised:

You have been selected as one of a very limited number of

collectors in the United States, South America, and Japan to receive notice of this unique opportunity to possess a Renoir . . . Starting with the original lithograph stones left by his grandfather, Paul Renoir . . . personally supervised every step in the creation of each lithograph (from mixing the colors, to finally embossing the only official Renoir signature and Atelier Renoir Seal.)

Each lithograph, priced at $375, was stated to be part of a limited, numbered edition of 250. The United States Attorney intervened, however, and the entrepreneur agreed in a court stipulation to send a letter to all purchasers of the lithographs telling a very different story:

> The lithograph you purchased is part of a limited edition of 250 and was authorized by Paul Renoir, grandson of the French Impressionist painter Pierre Auguste Renoir. However, the master himself had nothing to do with its creation. The lithographs are reproductions of oil paintings done by Pierre Auguste Renoir. They were executed in 1972.

The lithographs did not start with original lithograph stones left by Renoir, but rather with paintings never made into lithographs during Renoir's lifetime. Surely an artist has a right to more respectful treatment by those who posthumously wield power over the artist's creations.

To prevent situations such as these from arising, the will of Jacques Lipchitz, for example, provided, "These terra-cotta and plaster models are the prime of my inspiration, my only true original work, and are the most precious property I possess. It is my desire that no reproductions of any sort except photographs be made from said terra-cotta and plaster models."

Exhibitions

Executors must also stand in for the artist by objecting to any exhibition of work which the artist would

have sought to prevent. Mark Rothko, for example, had strong preferences as to the manner in which his paintings were displayed. Considering both atmosphere and the placement of paintings important, he cancelled a commission to paint murals for the Seagram Building when he learned they were to hang in the Four Seasons Restaurant.

The artist while alive can prevent such inappropriate exhibitions or, at least, object to them if the work is owned by another party. Carl Andre, the Minimalist sculptor, objected to the way the Whitney Museum displayed (near an exit door and a fire extinguisher) work lent by him for its "Two Hundred Years of American Sculpture" show. Andre withdrew the piece, although he could not prevent the museum from exhibiting another work, this one owned by the Whitney, in an equally objectionable way (that is, with rubber backing added to the small copper floor discs which comprise the sculpture). But for executors to act as the artist would have in objecting to inappropriate exhibitions of work requires an unusual joining of sensitivity and determination.

Artists and collectors often bequeath art to museums. The reasons for this vary widely: to benefit a worthy institution, to perpetuate the donor's name and to gain a federal estate tax deduction. If such a bequest is of large magnitude, the museum may accept it despite restrictions which require a certain manner or frequency of exhibition. Thus, the Lehman Collection in The Metropolitan Museum of Art in New York is housed in rooms like those which held the art in the collector's own home, and the collection is always on display.

Others who have given substantial quantities of art haven't been as fortunate in having their restrictions observed. Adelaide deGroot, a collector who died in 1967, donated much of her art to The Metropolitan with the express request that any art not kept by The Metropolitan be given to other museums. Correctly interpreting this restriction as merely a wish which is not legally binding, The Metropolitan in the early 1970s began selling and trading paintings from the deGroot bequest instead of giving such paintings to other museums. The Metropolitan considered its collection improved by these actions, but the moral issue of violating the intent of the bequest remains.

Museums have even ignored or evaded restrictions which were intended to be legally binding. Another collector, Benjamin Altman, required in his will that The Metropolitan exhibit his bequest in two rooms of suitable size, one room for his Chinese porcelains and the other room for his paintings (which would hang in a single row on the wall, not one above another). No other art would be exhibited in the rooms. Altman stated in his will that the bequest would be forfeited if the restrictions were violated and the art would go to an Altman Museum of Art, for which funds had been set aside. After his death, however, the agreed-upon two rooms gave way to an arrangement of Altman's art through several galleries. Altman's executors failed to prevent this. So too did the executors of the Michael Friedsam estate. They agreed to permit The Metropolitan to disperse his collection throughout the entire museum although the bequest was conditioned on the collection being kept separate and intact.

While in these cases the wishes of collectors were disregarded, the artist bequeathing work to a museum or similar cultural institution is in the same position as the collector. Unless the artist's executors possess both the sensitivity and volition to resist abuse of the artist's intentions, the artist can expect no better treatment than these collectors received. This concern prompted the agreement discussed on pages 180-181 between Hans Hofmann and the University of California regarding the exhibition and disposition of Hofmann's work to be received by the university. Less prominent artists might seek similar understandings with local universities and cultural institutions.

Precipitous sale of works

An artist's reputation is often built through a carefully designed program of sales, with both prices and the prestige of the purchasers orchestrated to rise ever higher. Litigation over the Mark Rothko estate revealed that the painter had been extremely concerned with his reputation as an artist.

When he died, Rothko owned 798 paintings, many from his early Surrealist period. His choice to own these paintings and sell them gradually, if at all, was a decision of great importance to his reputation. To continue this course, like David Smith, he had carefully chosen his executors to achieve a balancing of backgrounds and talents: Bernard Reis, an accountant, Theodoros Stamos, a painter, and Morton Levine, an anthropologist.

Yet these executors entered into highly controversial contracts to sell outright to the Marlborough Galleries 100 paintings for $1,800,000 to be paid over 12 years and to consign to the Marlborough Galleries another 698 paintings at a commission rate of 50 percent, which many people considered too high for works by an artist of Rothko's reputation. Both these contracts were executed only three months after Rothko's death. Not only could this bulk transaction have been interpreted as the executors lacking confidence in Rothko's future reputation and sales potential, but the contracts were also made at very unfavorable terms. A complex, bitter and costly legal struggle was begun by Rothko's heirs and joined by the New York Attorney General because a substantial part of the estate had been left to the Mark Rothko Foundation. The court rescinded the contracts and awarded damages of $9,252,000 against the executors, Marlborough Galleries and the owner of Marlborough Galleries (one of the executors was liable only for the lesser amounts of $6,464,880).

These examples could be multiplied, but their import for the artist is that lifetime planning is a necessity if the artist has concern for the posthumous artistic and financial treatment to which the work passing through the estate will be subject.

The will

A properly drafted will is crucial to any estate plan. A will is a written document, signed and witnessed under strictly observed formalities, which provides for the disposition of the property belonging to the maker of the will on his or her death. If the maker wishes to change the will, this can be done either by adding a codicil to the will or by drafting and signing a completely new will. If no will is made, property passes at death by the laws of intestacy. These laws vary from state to state, but generally provide for the property to pass to the artist's spouse and other relatives. An administrator, often a relative but sometimes not, is appointed by the court to manage the estate. The artist's failure to make a will concedes that the artist will not attempt to govern either the distribution, aesthetic standards or financial exploitation of the work after death.

A will offers the opportunity to distribute property to specific persons. For art works, this usually is done by bequest either to specific individuals or to a class. A bequest means a transfer of property under a will, while a gift is used to mean a transfer of property during the life of the person who gives the property. An example of a bequest to a specific individual would be:

I give and bequeath to my son, JOHN ARTIST, who resides at _____ , the oil painting created by me, titled _____ and dated _____ , if he should survive me. An example of a bequest to a class would be: I give and bequeath to my son, JOHN, and my daughter JUNE, and my daughter MARY or the survivors or survivor of them if any shall predecease me, all my paintings, sculptures and other art works, except such articles specifically disposed of by Paragraphs _____ of this Will. If they shall be unable to agree upon a division of the said property, my son, JOHN shall have the first choice, my daughter JUNE shall have the second choice, and my daughter MARY shall have the third choice, the said choices to continue in that order so long as any of them desire to make a selection.

Copyrights, of course, can also be willed. For example:

I give and bequeath all my right, title, and interest in and to my copyrights (describe which copyrights) and any royalties therefrom and the right to a renewal and extension of the said copyrights in such works to my daughter JUNE.

But the renewal right granted under the Copyright Act of 1909 cannot be willed if the artist's spouse or children are surviving, since in that case the renewal right would automatically pass to the spouse or children. And the right of termination under the copyright law effective in 1978 provides that the artist's copyrights passing by his or her own will cannot be terminated. Also, the right of termination cannot be passed by will but automatically goes to the artist's surviving spouse, children and grandchildren.

Use of a will permits: (1) the payment of estate taxes in such a way that each recipient will not have any taxes assessed against the work received, (2) the uninterrupted maintenance of insurance policies for the works and (3) the payment of storage and shipping costs so the recipient need not pay to receive the work. The estate taxes are usually paid from the residuary of the estate, the residuary being all the property not specifically distributed elsewhere in the will.

Choosing executors

The will allows an artist to choose the executor of an estate. Since decisions of the executors were the focal points of the controversies as to the alterations of David Smith's work and the sale of Mark Rothko's work, the importance of choosing suitable executors cannot be emphasized too strongly. Yet both Smith and Rothko had chosen as executors men whom the artists knew and trusted and chose in part to achieve a diversity of backgrounds. Smith chose a critic, an artist and a lawyer. Rothko chose an anthropologist, an artist and an accountant. Each estate had, at least in theory, the benefit of both artistic and financial insights and concerns. Yet the failure of the executors to continue dealing with the art works as the artists would have intended is a warning to every artist, regardless of the size of the estate, who seeks to plan what will become of work after death.

The College Art Association, a national organization with a membership of diverse art professionals, has issued guidelines, applicable to unethical bronze castings, which can be given a wider scope. "Sculptors should leave clear and complete written instructions or put into their wills their desires with respect to the future of their works after their death or in the event of their incapacity to continue working." All artists, as well as sculptors, should take such precautions. If necessary, the artist's wishes can be written into a will to specify how the art works are to be repaired, reproduced, exhibited and sold. This may conflict, however, with the usually desirable practice of giving to the executor the maximum powers for management of the estate. Each estate, whether large or small, will require a decision by the artist as to executors and their powers, based on the unique facts of the artist's own situation. At the least, however, the College Art Association states, "All heirs and executors of the sculptor's estate should be scrupulous in discharging their responsibilities and when necessary consult with experts on such questions as those of new castings," or, it can be added, artistic questions generally.

The executor, especially for a small estate, will often be a spouse or close relative. It is important, however, to be certain that such a person will be capable of making the necessary artistic and financial decisions for the estate. Joint executors, particularly when one is an art expert and the other a financial expert, would seem well suited to run the estate. For example, the determination to sell bronze castings of an iron sculpture is a decision with both artistic and financial implications. The extent to which the artist may safely restrict the discretion of the executors as to artistic matters may depend upon other aspects of the estate, such as whether sufficient funds are available to pay estate taxes and meet the immediate needs of the estate. Only by resolving problems such as these can the artist be certain the executors will act as the artist would have wished.

Estate taxes

The will also provides the opportunity to anticipate and control the amount of taxes to be levied by the state and, more importantly, federal governments. Reforms in the tax laws have benefitted the artist by removing the tax burden from many estates.

If art works are scattered among a number of states—for example, on long-term museum loans or perhaps long-term gallery consignments—the estate plan can avoid the vexing problem of numerous state estate proceedings by gathering such works in the state where the artist permanently resides. An artist who lives in more than one state may risk having a so-called double domicile and being taxed by more than one state, but careful planning can parry such a danger.

The artist will also wish to benefit from a number of deductions, discussed below, which can substantially reduce the estate if planned for properly. But tax planning is especially necessary for the artist because art works are valued at fair market value in computing the artist's gross estate.

Trusts

Trusts are a valuable estate-planning device in which title to property is given to a trustee to use the property or income from the property for the benefit of certain named beneficiaries. Trusts can be created by the artist during life or, at death, by will. Trusts can also be revocable—subject, that is, to dissolution by the creator of the trust—or irrevocable, in which case the creator cannot dissolve the trust. Trusts are frequently used to skip a generation of taxes, for example, by giving the income of a trust to children for their lives and having the grandchildren receive the principal. In such case the principal would not be included in the estates of the children for purposes of estate taxation. The tax law, however, severely restricts the effectiveness of generation-skipping trusts and other transfers for a similar purpose.

If the artist is concerned that the recipients, perhaps minor children, won't be in a position to make decisions regarding the art, trusts can be created in order to let the trustees fill this decision-making role. If the artist creates a trust (or foundation, as Mark Rothko did in his will), it is possible to do this while the artist is alive so the capacity of the trustees can be evaluated.

The gross estate

The gross estate includes the value of all the property in which the artist had an ownership interest at the time of death. Complex rules, depending on the specific circumstances of each case, cover the inclusion in the gross estate of such items as life insurance proceeds, property which the artist transferred within three years of death and in which the artist retained some interest, property over which the artist possessed a general power to appoint an owner, annuities, jointly held interests and the value of property in trusts.

Valuation

The property included in the artist's gross estate is valued at fair market value as of the date of death or, if so chosen on the estate tax return, as of an alternate date six months after death. Fair market value is the price at which the property would change hands between a willing buyer and a willing seller, if both had reasonable knowledge of relevant facts and were under no compulsion to buy or sell.

Expert appraisers are used to determine fair market value of art works. But whether an estate is large or small, the opinions of experts can exhibit surprising variations. Because of this, the Internal Revenue Service in 1968 created an Art Advisory Panel, composed of ten art experts representing museums, universities and dealers, to determine for income, estate and gift tax purposes whether or not privately obtained appraisals of fair market value were realistic.

Estate of David Smith is an example of the extremes which are possible in appraisals of fair market value. When David Smith died at age fifty-nine in an automobile accident, he still owned 425 of his metal sculptures— many of substantial size and weight and located at Bolton Landing, New York. Smith had never had great success financially during his life. He sold only 75 works during the entire period from 1940 to his death in 1965. He in-

sisted on maintaining high prices and the size of much of the work also limited possible buyers. In the two years after his death, sales soared and 68 works were sold for nearly $1,000,000.

Smith's executors, in attempting to determine fair market value, first estimated the retail price of each piece individually if sold on the date of death. The total for the 425 works was $4,284,000, which the executors then discounted by 75 percent because any sale made immediately would have to be in bulk at a substantial discount. This figure was further reduced by one-third to cover commissions which would be paid to the Marlborough Galleries. The executors concluded that the fair market value of the 425 sculptures was therefore $714,000. The Internal Revenue Service, however, disagreed that any discounting should be allowed and simply placed a fair market value of $4,284,000 on the works.

The tax court considered numerous factors related to fair market value, such as the market effect of a bulk sale, Smith's growing reputation, the lack of general market acceptance of nonrepresentational sculpture, the quality of the works, sales, prices immediately before and after death and the inaccessibility of the 291 works located at Bolton Landing. Terming its decision "Solomon-like," the tax court found the fair market value of the 425 sculptures to be $2,700,000 as of the date of Smith's death. (*Estate of David Smith*, 57 T.C. 650, acquiesced in, I.R.B. 1974-27) This is approximately the figure which would result if the values argued for by the executors and the Internal Revenue Service were added together and then divided in half. This is certainly not scientific, but the artist must prepare for these possible variations in the valuation of the gross estate when attempting to gauge what will be the amount of the estate taxes.

Taxable estate

The gross estate is reduced by a number of important deductions to reach the taxable estate. The deductions include funeral expenses, certain administrative expenses, casualty or theft losses during administration, debts and enforceable claims against the estate, mortgages and liens, the value of property passing to a surviving spouse subject to certain limitations and the value of property qualifying for a charitable deduction because of the nature of the institution to which the property is given.

Proper estate planning offers the opportunity to be as certain as possible that expenses, particularly selling commissions for art works, will be deductible as administration expenses.

The marital deduction provides an important tax saving. The deduction equals the value of property left to the surviving spouse (provided that the value of the property has also been included in the gross estate). A spouse, especially a wife, is entitled in any case to a share of the deceased spouse's estate by law in most states. In New York, for example, a surviving spouse has a right to one-half of the deceased spouse's estate, but the right is reduced to one-third if there are also surviving children. The value of property used for the marital deduction must basically pass in such a way that it will eventually be taxable in the estate of the surviving spouse. The marital deduction thus postpones estate taxes but does not completely avoid them.

The charitable deduction is of particular interest to the artist, since this provides the opportunity to give art works to institutions such as museums or schools which the artist may wish to benefit. The fair market value of such donated works is deducted from the artist's gross estate. A will clause is used stating that if the institution is not of the type to which a bequest qualifying for a charitable deduction can be made, the bequest will be made to a suitable institution at the choice of the executor.

The tax effect of willing a work to a charity is identical to the artist's destroying of the work prior to death. If the work is willed to charity, fair market value is included in the gross estate, but the same fair market value is then subtracted as a charitable deduction in determining the taxable estate. But even if the estate tax rate were as high as 55 percent, keeping the work would still pass 45 percent of the value to the recipients under the will. However, if the estate does not have cash available to pay the estate taxes, charitable bequests may be an excellent way to reduce the amount of the estate taxes. Also, the intangible benefits, including perpetuating the artist's reputation, may well outweigh considerations of the precise saving or loss resulting from such bequests. Once the gross estate has been reduced by the deductions discussed above, what is left is the taxable estate.

Unified estate and gift tax

A progressive tax applies to the artist's cumulated total of taxable gifts and the taxable estate. In 1986 the progressive rates rise from 18 percent if the cumulated total of taxable gifts and taxable estate is under $10,000, to 55 percent if the cumulated total is over $3,000,000. The amount of tax on the cumulated total the taxable gifts and taxable estate is reduced by a tax credit. The credit increases from 1984 to 1987, the applicable amount of the credit depending on the year in which the artist dies:

Year	Tax Credit
1984	$96,300
1985	$121,800
1986	$155,800
1987 and thereafter	$192,800

A single artist who made taxable gifts of $70,000 and left a taxable estate of $80,000 would owe, according to the rate schedule, a unified gift and estate tax of $38,800. If the artist died in 1984, the $96,300 tax credit would cause no tax to be payable. If an artist who died in 1987 had made taxable gifts of $475,000 and had a taxable estate of $525,000, the unified tax would be $345,800. This would be reduced by a credit of $192,800, so that the tax payable would be $153,000. An artist who dies in 1987 or thereafter will only pay a tax if the cumulated total of taxable gifts and the taxable estate is greater than $600,000. It should be noted that the federal estate tax is reduced by either a state death tax credit or the actual state death tax, whichever is lesser.

Liquidity

The tax court in *Estate of David Smith* found a fair market value of $2,700,000 for the 425 art works. As of the date of death, cash available to the estate other than from sales of sculptures amounted to only $210,647. The discrepancy between estate taxes owed—which normally must be paid within nine months of death at the time the estate return is filed—and available cash can plague estates composed largely of art works.

One of the best ways to have cash available to pay estate taxes is to maintain insurance policies on the life of the artist. The proceeds of life insurance payable to the estate are included in the gross estate. So are the proceeds of policies payable, for example, to a spouse or children if the insured artist keeps any ownership or control over the policies. But policies payable to a spouse or children and not owned or controlled by the artist will not be included in the artist's gross estate. If a spouse or children are the beneficiaries under both insurance policies and the will, they will naturally want to provide funds to the estate to pay estate taxes so that the art works do not have to be sold immediately at lower prices. The funds can be lent to the estate or used to purchase art work from the estate at reasonable prices. Such policies should probably be whole life insurance, rather than the less expensive term insurance which may be nonrenewable after a certain age or under certain health conditions. Also, such life insurance may sometimes best be maintained in a life insurance trust, especially if a trustee may have greater ability than the beneficiaries to manage the proceeds. This stage of estate planning requires consultation with the artist's insurance agent to determine the most advisable course with regard to maintaining such life insurance.

Another method for easing estate liquidity problems may be available to an artist's estate. Upon a showing of reasonable cause (as opposed to the pre-1977 undue hardship standard), the district director may extend the time for payment up to ten years. The interest on such unpaid taxes is adjusted to reflect the current prime interest rate.

Tax deferral may also be achieved under a different provision of the tax law. If more than 35 percent of the adjusted gross estate consists of an interest in a closely held business (such as being the sole proprietor engaged in the business of making and selling art), the tax can be paid in ten equal yearly installments. And, if the executor so elects, the first installment need not be paid for five years. Interest payable on the estate tax attributable to the value of the business property (up to $1,000,000) receives a special rate of 4 percent.

Gifts

After seeing the tax computations, the artist may decide that it would be advisable to own fewer art works at death. If the artist makes gifts of art works while alive, the value of the gross estate at death could be reduced. The incentive for making gifts is a yearly exclusion of $10,000 applicable to each gift recipient. If an unmarried artist in one year gave paintings with a fair market value of $11,000 each to each of three children and two friends, there would be total gifts of $55,000. This gift to each person, however, would be subject to the $10,000 exclusion applied each year to each person to whom a gift is given—one person or a hundred. Thus, the $11,000 gifts to each person would be taxable only to the extent of $1,000. The total taxable amount would, therefore, be $5,000. The artist who can afford gifts should usually take advantage of the yearly exclusions.

If the artist were married rather than single, the artist and spouse could elect to treat all gifts as being made one-half from each. This has the effect of increasing to $20,000 the yearly exclusion for each gift recipient. Also, an artist may generally make unlimited gifts to a spouse without payment of any gift tax.

Gifts must be complete and irrevocable transfers, including transfers in trust, for the benefit of another person or group. Especially if the gift of an art work is to a family member, every effort should be taken to show a gift has truly been given. This can be done by delivery of the work and execution of a deed of gift. After the gift, the artist must completely cease to exercise control over the work. If, for example, the work is exhibited, the name of the owner should be that of the family member who has received the work, not of the artist. If the artist retains rights, there will not be a valid gift for tax purposes and the value of the work given will be included in the artist's gross estate. The artist also should not serve as custodian of gifts given to minor children, since such custodianship will again cause the value of the gift property to be included in the artist's gross estate.

Gift tax returns must be filed on an annual basis. The failure to file a gift tax return can result in assessments of interest, penalties and, in some cases, even criminal charges.

A factor which might make the artist wary of giving too many art works as gifts is the elusiveness of financial security and the possibility that an artist's earlier work may be more valuable than later work. Work from the critical period which forged the artist's sensibility and perhaps contributed to the definition of an art movement may prove far more valuable than work done when other new movements have become predominant or the artist has developed a different style. Giorgio de Chirico was acclaimed as a leader in the development of surrealistic art, but his later work never met with as favorable a reception. While early work he no longer owned sold for higher and higher prices, his later style was so unrewarding that he occasionally resorted to imitating his earlier work and misdating the results to his earlier period, creating what were truly self-forgeries.

The artist can also make gifts to charities without having to pay a gift tax. Such gifts may give the artist the opportunity to see if the charities will put the art works to suitable uses. But charitable gifts have no advantage over charitable bequests under the will in terms of saving estate taxes. After the gift of a work, the artist of course would not own the work at death and its value could not be included in the gross estate. While the value of the same work would be part of the gross estate if owned at death, a charitable bequest would reduce the gross estate by the value of the work. The taxable estate would be the same in either case. After 1981, both a work of art and its copyright will be considered separate properties for estate and gift tax charitable deductions. So a charitable deduction would be allowed for a work of art given or bequested to a charity even if the copyright were not also transferred to the charity.

Deed of gift

I, _____, residing at _____being the absolute owner of an art work titled _____created by _____and described as _____ do hereby give, assign and transfer _____to residing _____at all of my right, title and interest in and to said art work, absolutely and forever. It is my intention that this transfer of the above described art work shall constitute a gift of the same by me to _____. IN WITNESS WHEREOF, I have hereunto set my hand and seal with this _____ day of _____198____.

_____
Donor

_____
Notary public

Basis

The recipient of an art work as a gift holds the work as ordinary income property and takes the basis of the artist who gave the gift. But a beneficiary who receives an art work under a will holds the work as a capital asset with a stepped-up basis of the work's fair market value as included in the gross estate. For example, an artist in 1985 created an art work with a zero basis. If the art work were given to a daughter, the daughter would have a zero basis and receive ordinary income when she sold the work. If the sale price were $5,000, she would receive $5,000 of ordinary income. On the other hand, if the artist died in 1988 and the work were valued in the estate at $5,000, the daughter who received the work under the will would have a basis of $5,000. So if she sold the work for $5,000, she would not have to pay any tax at all. If she sold the work for $7,500, the tax would be on $2,500 at the favorable capital gains rates. This difference in treatment may be an important factor in determining whether to make gifts or bequests.

The estate plan

The planning of an artist's estate is a complex task often requiring the expertise of accountants, insurance agents and bank officers, as well as that of a lawyer. But an informed artist can be a valuable initiator and contributor in creating a plan which meets both the artistic and financial estate planning needs of the artist.

Chapter 22

Artists and museums

Museums in the United States are usually controlled privately by a board of trustees and supported by tax-exempt gifts and endowments. The development of museums coincided with the growth of large industrial fortunes. The patronage of the wealthy has often been critical to the creation and continued vitality of museums. Because of this, many artists feel alienated from the power structures controlling the museums. One of the goals of Artists for Economic Action, for example, is to have artists serve as museum trustees. This position is consistent with the broader interests of artists in the cultural institutions which preserve art and make it available to the public. Museums must make difficult decisions, such as whether to acquire art obtained illegally in foreign countries or whether to exhibit controversial art, and the advice of artists might be invaluable. But since the wider spectrum of issues confronting museums has been considered in other sources, this chapter will focus on the artist's specific concerns when either loaning or giving art to museums.

Loans to museums

The concerns of the artist in lending work are quite similar to the concerns when consigning work (discussed on pages 99 - 106). The most important assurance is that the work will be returned promptly and in good condition or, if this is not possible, that the artist will be reimbursed for any damage to the work or for the cost of replacement.

If the artist simply lends work to a museum or similar exhibitor without a contract, the museum or borrower will hold the work under a bailment and will have to exercise reasonable care in keeping the work. But since neither the museum nor the artist normally will be satisfied with such an arrangement, the best method of guaranteeing satisfaction to both parties is insurance. The museum should provide wall-to-wall insurance in the amount specified by the artist as value of the work. Wall-to-wall insurance take effect when the work leaves the hands of the artist and lasts until the work is returned to the artist. The lending contract will usually specify that the museum will not be liable for any amount greater than the stated insurance value, which is likely to be less than the artist's value of the work.

If the museum or other borrower refuses to provide insurance, the artist should either not lend the work or should insist upon a provision making the borrower absolutely liable regardless of fault in the event of loss, damage or theft to the work.

But even wall-to-wall insurance or absolute liability may be insufficient to protect an irreplaceable work. Attacks on works in museums—Picasso's *Guernica* and Rembrandt's *Night Watch*, for example—are becoming a more frequent occurence, despite laws penalizing such vandalism. The artist might wish to have certain minimum security precautions specified in the lending contract, regardless of who would have to pay for the work if damaged.

Of course, the lending contract should also specify receipt of specific works described by title, size (and weight for sculpture) and medium. The duration of the loan—and the exact location where the works will be shown—should be included. If work can be sold from the exhibition, as is often the case, the commission rate and other relevant provisions—such as price, time of payment to the artist and risks with regard to the purchaser's credit—should be set forth. Shipment, storage, framing, photography, restoration and similar costs will need detailing.

Artistic control is also an important consideration. The artist's work will be exhibited—but in what manner? Publicity about the artist may accompany the exhibition. Reproductions of the works may be used in catalogs, or even sold as postcards or jewelry. The artist will wish to control all of the aesthetic aspects of lending work. Even if the copyright for the work is in the public domain, the artist can fairly demand payments for any commerical exploitation of the work by the museum. Certainly, the artist will want to make an express condition of any right to reproduce the art be that copyright notice in the artist's name appear on the reproductions. Some remaining uncertainty as to whether a loan to a museum will be a publication suggests that copyright notice should be placed on the work prior to any loan. Also, since the copyright encompasses the right of display (except that the owner of a work may also display it to viewers who are present where the work is), a museum taking art on loan will need the artist's permission to display the art.

Before sending work on loan to other states, the artist should consider whether any creditors in that state might seize the work. The United States has enacted a statute exempting from seizure works loaned from foreign countries into the United States, provided certain requirements are met. Following this lead, New York State has enacted a similar provision for works loaned by out-of-state exhibitors to non-profit exhibitions in New York State. But the artist with creditors should beware when loaning work in other states without such a statute.

Lastly, the artist might well demand an assurance from the museum that work in fact will be exhibited for the time specified in the loan contract. This provision, like the others, will be subject to negotiation based on the needs of both the artist and the museum.

Gifts or bequests to museums

The artist, either while alive or at death, may wish to transfer works to museums and similar cultural institutions. If, however, the artist thought the museum would either deaccession (that is, sell) or never exhibit the work, the artist would hesitate. Museums, on the other hand, are reluctant to restrict their flexibility by accepting works with requirements as to

exhibition or restrictions against deaccessioning. The moral issues, particularly when a will asks for but does not legally require a certain course of action with regard to a collection, can be difficult for the museum. If the museum has accepted legal restrictions, in changed circumstances it may go to court to request a different use for the works than the restrictions specify.

A collection of immense value, like that now housed in the Lehman Pavilion at the Metropolitan Museum of Art in New York City, can be used to gain legal guarantees of highly favorable treatment from the museum. Most artists, of course, do not have collections rivaling that in the Lehman Pavilion. However, their collections well might be given intact to a smaller museum or cultural institution which would be willing to make concessions in order to receive the work. In this connection, the agreement between Hans Hofmann and the regents of the University of California makes an interesting study.

The Hans Hofmann agreement

In 1963, Hans Hofmann made an agreement with the regents of the University of California whereby he would donate certain works to the University of California as a permanent Hofmann Collection to be kept in a separate wing or gallery as a memorial to Hofmann and his wife, Maria.

Hofmann initially transferred an undivided one-half interest in twenty works to the university, and agreed to transfer the same interest in another twenty works of his choosing before December 1, 1968. An agent of Hofmann's selection was appointed with the power to sell those works and raise $250,000 for the university before that date. If, by December 1, 1968, or Hofmann's death, whichever occurred later, $250,000 had not been raised for the university from the sale of forty paintings, Hofmann's estate would pay the balance.

The university in return agreed to expend $250,000 to build and complete the separate wing or gallery for the Hofmann Collection by December 1, 1968. If the wing or gallery were destroyed, the university would be obliged to rebuild it only to the extent of insurance proceeds.

The Hofmann Collection was then specified to consist of thirty-five additional paintings, ten of which were listed in the agreement and twenty-five of which were to be transferred or bequeathed by Hofmann. The university had the power to accept works transferred and to select from all Hofmann's paintings if the balance of the paintings were bequeathed.

The university agreed to substantial restrictions over what could be done with the works composing the Hofmann Collection. The Hofmann Collection, or a part of the collection, along with other works by Hofmann the university might have, would be primarily exhibited in a separate wing or gallery. Until December 1, 1993, work by persons other than Hofmann could be shown only if the Hofmann Collection were temporarily exhibited at another museum or gallery. After December 1, 1993, the university could retain the entire Hofmann Collection but would only have to exhibit the collection exclusively thirty days during each year. Alternatively, after December 1, 1993, the university could sell or exchange twenty paintings from the Hofmann Collection and use the proceeds to purchase modern art considered *avant garde* at that time. The remaining fifteen paintings of the Hofmann Collection would have to be exhibited primarily in the wing or gallery. Primarily is defined as exhibition during a major portion of the calendar year—and not being exhibited only when loaned temporarily to another museum or gallery. Thus a balance is struck which guarantees either the collection of thirty-five paintings will be exhibited one month per year or the collection of at least fifteen paintings will be exhibited during most of the year.

The agreement between Hans Hofmann and the regents of the University of California is a good example of balancing the needs of each party. Hofmann received guarantees that the collection would be exhibited and would not be deaccessioned. The university received the paintings, a new wing or gallery, and the power eventually either to sell part of the collection or to exhibit the entire collection less often. These considerations are typical and the artist giving work to any museum or cultural institution should certainly try to negotiate restrictions similar to those obtained by Hans Hofmann.

Rights of the artist in the museum-owned works

The artist who gives or sells work to a museum should treat the museum like any other purchaser. If the artist wishes to retain rights in the work—such as the power to control the manner of exhibition or to repair the work—the contract of sale should so specify. Similarly, if the artist sells the work to any purchaser, these rights must be retained at the time of sale. Otherwise, when a purchaser gives a work to a museum, the museum will own the work without restrictions. In such a situation the museum may exhibit the work with little fear of the artist being able to take successful legal action.

In the 1976 exhibition, "200 Years of American Sculpture," at the Whitney Museum in New York City, for example, both Robert Morris and Carl Andre sought to prevent the Whitney from showing certain works. Morris contended the Whitney was showing a damaged work from its own collection—rather than any work submitted for the exhibiton. Andre withdrew the work he had submitted on the ground that it was placed next to a bay window and a fire exit. He then sought to purchase for $25,000 the work which the Whitney substituted from its own collection for the exhibition. Andre contended that the substitute piece had been misinstalled by placing rubber under copper floor pieces. If the artists had retained rights over their works, these controversies would not have arisen.

Also, the museum will have power of commercial exploitation over works which the museum owns unless the artist retains the copyright. There is no reason for an artist to sell a copyright to a museum, although the artist might be willing to sell certain rights to make reproductions. Museums will, in any case, often pay royalties or fees for commercial exploitation, although exact payments vary and will be completely within the discretion of the museum if the artist fails to retain the copyright.

Chapter 23

The artist as a collector

The artist often becomes—through trades, gifts and purchases—a collector of work by other artists. While the collector will often have to know the legal and practical considerations relevant to artists, certain problems are unique to collectors. The following discussion highlights some of the unique areas so that the artists who collect will know when legal advice may be helpful.

The value of art

Most collectors own art for the sake of enjoyment, but the value of art as a commodity cannot be ignored. The concept of art as an investment has been closely associated with the activities of auction houses such as Christie's of London and Sotheby Parke-Bernet of New York. Auctions often show the public art which has increased fantastically in value. The speculative gains to be made have brought art investment companies like Artemis into being. Much of this investment art is kept in storage and remains out of the public view until resold by the company.

The prices for art are so high that art thefts and forgeries have become a fact of life in the art world. The illicit trade in art is international and extends to antiquities which are illegally excavated and exported from the countries where ancient cultures flourished. To prevent this illegal antiquities trade, the United States has signed a treaty with Mexico, passed a law affecting numerous Latin American countries and passed the enabling legislation for the UNESCO Convention on the Means of Prohibiting and Preventing the Illicit Import, Export, and Transfer of Cultural Property. Many of the large cities of Europe now have specialized art crime squads—as does New York City. Interpol, with the assistance of the International Council of Museums, has even gone so far as to create wanted posters of the world's Most Wanted Works of Art.

The response of collectors to this art crime has been varied. Some insure their collections, a definitive but often expensive solution. Others have fakes created which are then substituted for the real works. French collectors can avail themselves of a tower 240 feet high and 180 feet in diameter which is hidden behind the facade of a former bank and can be seen only from the top of the Eiffel Tower. The security includes cameras, special keys, electronic devices and a tunnel which fills with water and lethal gas.

Art thieves will often offer back the stolen works to the owner and demand a ransom. For example, a collector of rare Russian enamels entrusted them to a New York City storage company before leaving for Europe. When he returned he found the storage company had, without checking for identification, given the enamels to another person who claimed to be a messenger for the collector. The enamels were valued at $731,000, which the storage company was liable to pay the collector if the enamels couldn't be recovered. The collector advertised that a ransom would be paid and, by paying $71,000, received back almost the entire collection. He then sued the storage company for the $71,000, having saved the company from paying the $731,000. The storage company, however, argued that perhaps no ransom had been paid since the collector refused to disclose the persons through whom he had recovered the enamels. The collector refused such disclosure because he said he had been threatened with death. The New York Court of Appeals upheld a jury verdict for the collector despite this refusal, although the dissenters on the court argued strongly that the payment of such a ransom should be against public policy.

The crime problem is not limited to theft. Today, sophisticated forgers create art to appear to be the work of another artist. Sometimes art of another period may be attributed to an artist rather than the school which surrounded the artist or the period generally in which the artist worked—far more subtle issues. Authentication requires statements by experts who are often reluctant to give opinions because of the risk of being sued for defamation of the art work should they be incorrect. The most modern techniques of science are brought to bear on solving authenticity problems, but, similarly, some forgers rely upon science as well. The collector must be vigilant if art crime is to be avoided.

Purchasing art

The collector will wish to consult pages 66–67 to determine what warranties may be created upon the purchase of an art work. The purchaser can certainly rely on the fact that the seller has title or the right to convey title in the art work. For example, in 1932, a couple living in Belgium purchased a work by Marc Chagall for about $150. Forced to flee the German invasion of 1940, the couple found, when they returned six years later, that the painting had disappeared. In 1962 they noticed a reproduction of the painting in an art book indicating the name of the collector who had innocently purchased the work in 1955 for $4,000 from a New York City gallery. The couple sued the collector for the value of the work in 1962—$22,500—or the return of the work. Not only did the couple win, but the collector also successfully sued the gallery for his loss. The gallery, which had received only $4,000 on sale, became liable for $22,500 which could only be recouped, if at all, by bringing suit against a gallery in Paris.

Auctions have become a major force in the art market. Auctions are a process of offer and acceptance through public bidding. If the auctioneer sells art with a reserve price, no offers by purchasers will be accepted which are less than the reserve price. This protects the person who has consigned art to the auctioneer from receiving too low a price. The auctioneer can, therefore, withdraw the art from the bidding at any time if the price is not satisfactory. On the other hand, if the auction is without a reserve price the auctioneer must ac-

cept the highest bid made. The art cannot be withdrawn once the bidding has begun. The purchaser, regardless of whether the auction is with or without reserve, may withdraw a bid at any time prior to the fall of the hammer or other customary completion of the sale.

The collector may be inclined to rely upon the representations made in an auctioneer's catalog. But the Uniform Commerical Code warranties may not be fully effective to protect the collector, particularly since most catalogs contain warranty disclaimers. Also, certain of the representations made in the catalog can be construed merely as puffing—touting a saleable item in a way which the purchaser should know not to accept at face value.

In 1962 a doctor paid $3,347.50 to Parke-Bernet for a painting stated in the catalog to be the work of Raoul Dufy, but which was, in fact, a forgery. However, the catalog stated that Parke-Bernet disclaimed all warranties and sold any property "as is." The New York Supreme Court held for the doctor, who sought to recover what he had paid. The Appellate Term reversed and held for Parke-Bernet on the rationale that authenticity was a factor in the sale price and the purchaser had the burden to satisfy himself with regard to authenticity.

The New York attorney general recommended legislation to rectify this ruling. In 1968 a law passed regulating the "Creation and Negotiation of Express Warranties in the Sale of Works of Fine Art." This law covers any sale by an art merchant, which includes an auctioneer, to a purchaser who is not an art merchant, if a written instrument such as a catalog or prospectus makes representations as to authorship. Such statements as to authorship, even if not stated to be warranties, shall be considered express warranties and a basis upon which the purchaser made a purchase. For example: (1) a work stated to be by a named artist must be by such artist; (2) a work attributed to a named artist means a work of the period but not necessarily by the artist; and (3) a work of the school of the artist means work of a pupil or close follower of the artist, but not by the artist.

An art merchant can disclaim warranties created by this law, but only if the disclaimer satisfies certain conditions. The disclaimer must be conspicuous and written separate from any statements as to authorship. It must not be general, such as a negation at the beginning of a catalog that all warranties are disclaimed, but must be specific as to the particular work. If a work is counterfeit, defined as fine art made or altered to appear to be by a certain artist when it is not, the fact of the counterfeiting must be conspicuously disclosed. Also, if a work is unqualifiedly stated to be by a given artist, such a statement cannot be disclaimed.

The effect of this New York law is to create valuable protections beyond those contained in the Uniform Commerical Code for purchasers from art merchants. Another New York law enacted in 1969 makes the falsification of a certificate of authenticity, such certificate being a written statement as to authorship by a person apparently having an expert's knowledge, punishable as a misdemeanor.

The New York laws are important safeguards for collectors who may be prone to rely too much on statements contained in catalogs or certificates of authenticity. But the absence of such laws in other states, where only the Uniform Commerical Code would govern transactions, is a warning to collectors to exercise caution in the purchase of art. Also, while auctions are subject to some legal regulation, the news media do report irregular practices such as collusive bidding from time to time. The auction house rules have often become complex as well, so expert advice may be a necessity for the collector entering the auction market.

Purchasing art abroad

The collector who purchases art abroad should be aware that many countries have enacted laws to protect artistic and archeological objects. Italy's law, for example, regulates such objects, but does not apply either to works of living artists or to works created within the last fifty years. Collectors must obtain an export license from the Office of Exportation for items which come within the law. The export license will not be issued if exportation would cause great injury to the national patrimony. The collector

must declare the market price of each item, which the Ministry of Education has the power to purchase at that price within two months of the application for an export license. The result is that the collector either may not be allowed to export art from Italy or may find the Ministry of Education intends to purchase the art for the stated market price. The collector must be aware that these laws, however erratically enforced, exist in most of the nations which possess an abundance of art.

If the art can legally be exported from the nation where purchased, the collector must next consider whether United States custom duties will be payable on the work to be imported. Generally, however, no duties are payable on original works of art, such as paintings, drawings, fine prints (which must be printed by hand from hand-etched, hand drawn, or hand-engraved plates, stones or blocks), sculptures (the original and up to ten replicas), mosaics and works of the fine arts not fitting into the other categories (such as collages). The artist who has created work while living temporarily abroad may bring such work back to the United States without paying duties.

Tax status of the collector

A collector may fall into three categories for treatment: a dealer, an investor or a hobbyist. Each category has distinctly different tax consequences.

One who very frequently buys and sells art works will be taxed as a dealer and will receive ordinary income from art sales, rather than the more favorable capital gains. A dealer will be able to deduct all the ordinary and necessary expenses of doing business.

On the other hand, the collector may be an investor in art works, similar to person who invests in stocks and bonds. An investor will have capital gains and losses. Ordinary and necessary expenses will be deductible if incurred for the management and preservation of the works, such as insurance and storage costs. However, the investor must own the art works primarily for profit. In one case, collectors, who kept their collection in their homes and derived personal use and pleasure from the collection, were found not to own the collection primarily for profit. But the alternative of storing art will hardly satisfy the collector.

The third category, the hobbyist, includes the collector who buys and keeps art works mainly for pleasure. Gains on sale will be taxed as captial gains, not ordinary income. But if a capital loss is incurred upon the sale of an art work, there must be a profit motive for the loss to be deductible. A limited exception to this allows the hobbyist to deduct captial losses up to the amount of capital gains, when the losses and gains result from the same activity (the sale of art works) during the tax year. Similarly, the expenses of keeping up the collection can be deducted up to the amount of income generated by the collection.

Charitable Contributions

The collector also has an advantage over the artist in the area of charitable contributions because the collector can deduct either all or part of the fair market value of contributed works of art (fair market value is defined on page 151). However, the tax laws have complex limitations designed to prevent tax abuses of charitable deductions. Taxpayers may only receive a charitable deduction for donations up to a percentage of their contribution base (which is their adjusted gross income with some modifications). The deduction limit is 50 percent of the contribution base for most charities, including a church,

hospital, school, museum, publicly supported religious, charitable or similar organization, or certain limited private foundations. The collector must verify whether the organization is exempt and, if so, whether it is a 50 percent organization. The purpose of these limitations is to prevent reducing taxable income to zero through the use of charitable contributions.

If cash is being donated, the full amount is a deduction. If, however, art works which have increased in value are being donated, complicated rules regarding the contribution of appreciated property come into play. Basically, these rules reduce the amount which can be taken as a charitable deduction when appreciated work is contributed. Also, the amount of the deduction will be reduced if the art work which has appreciated in value will not be used for a purpose related to the exempt purpose or function of the organization which receives the donation. A lawyer or an accountant should be consulted to aid in determining the best strategy for charitable contributions when art works which have appreciated in value are involved. For any art work valued at more than $5,000, an appraisal must be obtained and attached to the tax form. It must be made within 60 days of the donation and cannot be done by the person giving the donation, the person who sold the art work originally or the institution receiving the work. IRS Publications 526, *Income Tax Deductions for Contributions* and 561, *Determining the Value of Donated Property*, will aid the collector who can take advantage of the deduction for contributions.

Chapter 24

Grants and public support for the arts

The important role of the artist in society raises the issue of what assistance society should appropriately offer to the artist. The legislation creating the National Endowment for the Arts (the "NEA") in 1965 stated:

> [T]hat the encouragement and support of national progress and scholarship in the humanities and the arts, while primarily a matter for private and local initiative, is also an appropriate matter of concern for the Federal Government . . . [and] that the practice of art and the study of the humanities requires constant dedication and devotion and that, while no government can call a great artist or scholar into existence, it is necessary and appropriate for the Federal Government to help create and sustain not only a climate encouraging freedom of thought, imagination, and inquiry, but also the material conditions facilitating the release of this creative talent.

Whether the NEA has created such material conditions remains a matter of debate, since most supporters of the arts contend that far more must be done to aid artists than the NEA has achieved.

NEA funding

The budget for the NEA in 1966, the first year of operation, was $2,500,000. Over the next two decades the budget continually increased to reach the level of $162,224,000 for the fiscal year beginning in October 1984. These budgets, however, had to be allocated among all the arts.

Also, the amount allocated to the visual arts does not simply go to individual artists. Grants are available to individuals (for further information see page 00), but grants are also given to the offical arts agencies of the states and territories as well as to tax-exempt, non-profit organizations.

In the 1984 fiscal year, for example, $6,553,000 was spent on the Visual Arts Program, which provides funding for individual artists directly. Visual artists are defined as those artists who work in painting, sculpture, crafts, photography, printmaking, drawing, artists' books, conceptual art, video art and new genres. Grants also aid visual artists organizations—those started by or for artists, that exhibit contemporary art, provide working facilities for the creation of art or provide a variety of service activities for individual artists. These grants also support the commissioning and placement of art works in public spaces and visiting artists forums to encourage interactions between artist and the public. Examples of this include visiting artists lecture series at colleges and universities, conferences and symposiums and non-profit critical art journals.

Other funds would filter down to individual visual artists through allocations for programs such as the State Programs, which received $24,300,000 to stimulate the arts in the states. The Museum Program, which includes among various purposes the "purchase of works by living American artists," received $11,842,352 for fiscal 1984.

In fiscal 1985 $6,300,000 will be allocated among the various parts of the Visual Arts Program as shown on the following chart.

FISCAL 1985
VISUAL ARTS PROGRAM
OF THE NEA

Visual Artists Fellowships	$3,200,000
Visual Artists Organizations	1,950,000
Visual Artists Forums	450,000
Art in Public Places	500,000
Special Projects	200,000
	$6,300,000

State and local support

The first state arts council was created in 1902, but by 1960 only six councils were in existence. However, the period since 1960, when the New York State Council on the Arts was created, has seen the creation of an arts council in every state and territory, as the list of such councils on pages 195-199 indicates.

According to the National Assembly of State Arts Agencies, the total state arts council appropriation from 1975 to 1985 is $1,076,140,744 (but these expenditures are not limited to the visual arts). And, according to the National Association for Local Arts Agencies, an estimated $300,000,000 is generated annually by local community arts agencies for the visual arts alone. While the latter figure is an approximation due to the difficulty in gathering data on the local level, it emphasizes the magnitude of local arts support.

One innovative step has been supplied by localities requiring a percentage—usually 1 percent or 2 percent—of construction funds for government buildings to be used for art. Philadelphia initiated the first "1 percent for art" program in 1959. Baltimore followed this lead in 1964. San Francisco in 1965 enacted even more comprehensive legislation giving its arts commission control over design for all public buildings—whether or not publicly financed. Both Miami and Miami Beach became beneficiaries of a similar program under legislation enacted by Dade County, Florida, in 1974.

By 1984, 20 states had enacted similar programs, and six others had introduced legislation to the same effect. In 1972, the federal General Services Administration reinstated a policy of spending .5 percent of estimated construction budgets on art.

The artist in the Great Depression

One model for public support of artists was created in the 1930's when the Great Depression made the precarious profession of the artist even more untenable. The federal govern-ment, as part of the overall effort to create work, funded a number of extensive art projects. The first program, created under the Treasury Department, was the Public Works of Art Project which lasted from December 1933 to June 1934 and employed about 3,700 artists without a rigid relief test. The cost was $1,312,000. The next program, also under the Treasury Department, was the Section of Painting and Sculpture which obtained art work by competitions for new federal buildings. It began in October 1934 and lasted until 1943, awarding approximately 1,400 contracts and costing about $2,571,000. The third program, the Treasury Relief Art Project under the Treasury Department, started in July 1935, and lasted until 1939. The cost was $833,784 and 446 people were employed—about 75 percent of whom had been on relief.

The final and most important project was the Works Progress Administration's Federal Art Project (WPA) which began in August 1935, and lasted until June 1943. The WPA employed more than 5,000 artists at one point, subject to the WPA rules for relief, and had a total cost of $35,000,000. Some of the results of the WPA were: (1) Over 2,250 murals for public buildings were painted; (2) 13,000 pieces of sculpture were completed; (3) 85,000 paintings—of more than 100,000 produced—went on permanent loan to public institutions; (4) 239,727 prints were created from 12,581 original designs; (5) 500,000 photographs were made; and (6) art centers were organized in 103 communities.

The nearly $40,000,000 of federal support spent in the 1930's on the visual arts is of different magnitude from the support the NEA can now generate. But the WPA suffered from political turmoil, mainly challenges of Communist domination, which even caused some to doubt the artist accomplishments and importance of the WPA. The NEA has never experienced similiar political criticism, and perhaps with increased funding could use the WPA "as a model for the years ahead, for the artists and the public of tomorrow . . . for never in the history of any land has so much cultural progress been achieved in so brief at time as in the New Deal years." (Audrey McMahon, "A General View of the

WPA Federal Art Project in New York City and State." *The New Deal Art Projects: An Anthology of Memoirs,* pages 75-76)

The need for a model suggests the value of looking abroad to other countries which have created their own systems to support and encourage the arts and the artist. Some of these countries—the Netherlands, Ireland and Japan—are presented as examples. Comparisons of the actual costs of supporting the arts between countries would have little value, but the nature and variety of the programs as possible models are certainly of interest.

The Netherlands

The Netherlands has a scheme which is typical of many European countries. A Ministry of Cultural Affairs, Recreation and Social Welfare deals with matters relating to the visual arts and architecture. The ministry actually purchases and commissions art works in order to encourage artists and increase public ownership of representative works.

The ministry is aided by advisory committees in sculpture, graphic arts, drawing, the applied arts and architecture. Works acquired by the government are placed in the Registry of State-Owned Works of Art, not in state museums and art galleries. This national institution is a repository used in the dissemination of these works to museums and galleries to supplement exhibitions or collections as well as for display by the ministry in public or other buildings. The works in the registry are available for display not only in the Netherlands, but also abroad. The registry creates a unique cultural heritage in the hands of the government rather than museums.

The ministry regularly commissions artists to do woodcuts, etchings or lithographs which are distributed free of charge to schools in the Netherlands. Similarly, on the Delta Project, artists are commissioned to work in relationship to industrial projects which are going on under government sponsorship in the Netherlands. The works created go to schools, museums and galleries.

A system of subsidized art sales has operated since 1960 at public exhibitions having a minimum of forty art works by at least ten artists, subject to approval by the ministry. The subsidy gives a private buyer a 25 percent reduction—which the ministry pays to the exhibitor—on the price of the art work. Restrictions are a requirement that the buyer be of Dutch nationality, that the sales prices be within a specific range, and that the buyer agrees to keep the work for at least five years.

The ministry does not subsidize exhibitions in the Netherlands, but provides subsidies for other organizations which would subsidize exhibitions. Museums and galleries, of course, have additional budgets independent of such subsidies. The ministry does arrange certain international exhibitions abroad and chooses appropriate works by use of a special commissioner.

Individual artists are eligible for grants to pursue their art. Travel grants are also available for artists to encourage innovation. Those artists over sixty-five who have devoted valuable services to the arts in the Netherlands are eligible for a state stipend.

The Government Buildings Department uses 1 1/2 percent of the costs of new government buildings for murals, stained-glass windows, mural sculptures, wall hangings, graffiti, mosaics and the like. A similar 1 percent provision applies to schools and other educational buildings funded in part or in whole by the state.

A Provident Fund exists under the Ministry of Social Affairs and Public Health and provides that unemployed artists are entitled to as much as six times the artist's contribution to the fund—but for no more than thirteen weeks in any year. Contributions are made through artists' associations affiliated with the fund, so the result is a form of voluntary unemployment insurance. Each contribution is matched 310 percent by the government and 200 percent by the municipalities in which the member artist resides.

Also, the municipalities will—upon finding financial need on the part of an artist who is over twenty-five years of age—either seek suitable work for the artist or purchase one or more of the artist's works. The municipality provides 25 percent of the funding and the Ministry of Social Affairs and Public Health provides the rest. The works of art are divided between municipalities and the government on that prorated basis. Works passing to the ministry go into the Registry of State-Owned Works of Art and works passing to the municipalities go to local museums or galleries.

Ireland

In 1960 the government of Ireland enacted an unprecedented law designed to give tax relief to artists, composers and writers within the boundaries of Ireland. The minister of finance, in presenting the legislation to the Dail Eireann, stated:

> The purpose of this relief is . . . to help create a sympathetic envirnoment here in which the arts can flourish by encouraging artists and writers to live and work in this country. This is something completely new in this country and, indeed, so far as I am aware, in the world . . . I am convinced that we are right in making this attempt to improve our cultural and artistic environment and I am encouraged by the welcome given from all sides both at home and abroad to the principle of the scheme. I am hopeful that it will achieve its purpose.

The legislation completely frees the artist, regardless of nationality, from any tax obligation to Ireland with respect to income dervied from art. The main requirement for application is that artist be resident in Ireland for tax purposes. Simply explained, this requires the artist to rent or purchase a home in Ireland and work at that home during a substantial part of the year. However, while the residence must be uninterrupted, an artist does not necessarily have to be in Ireland for the entire year. Brief trips back to the United States, for example, would not affect an artist's tax status as a resident of Ireland. Every United States artist should remember, however, that the United States reserves the right to tax its citizens anywhere in the world. Pages 160 - 161 should be consulted for the United States tax law applicable to artists who live abroad.

Once the artist is resident in Ireland, there are two methods to qualify for tax relief. An established artist, who has produced "a work or works generally recognized as having cultural or artistic merit," would use Artists Application Form 1. A less established artist would use Artists Application Form 2 for the exemption of a particular work "having cultural or artistic merit." In both cases the determination of "cultural or artistic merit" is made by the Irish revenue commissioners after consultation, if necessary, with experts in the field. Once an artist qualifies under either Artists Application Form 1 or Form 2, all future works by the artist in the same category will be exempt from Irish tax. The offices of the Revenue Commissioners are in Room 5, Cross Block, Dublin Castle, Dublin 2, Ireland. For the artist exempt from Irish tax, the sole Irish tax requirement is that a tax return showing no tax due be prepared and filed with the Revenue Commissioners in Dublin.

By early 1985, however, only about 1,200 people had qualified to live tax free in Ireland. This was true despite the ease of application, absence of excessive tax paper work and high percentage of applicants approved by the revenue commissioners. Of those qualified, about 33 percent were painters and sculptors, while 61 percent were writers and 6 percent composers. The assistance to the individual artist who comes to Ireland is certainly valuable, but Ireland's hope to create a new Byzantium has yet to be realized.

Japan

Japan has a unique approach under which an organization or individual artist can be registered as a "Living National Treasure." Legislation in 1955 created the National Commission for Protection of Cultural Properties, which, by 1967, had designated fifty-seven persons and seven organizations as living national treasures for their role in aiding and continuing the culture and arts of Japan. Fields where living national treasures have been designated include ceramic art, dyeing and weaving, lacquered ware, metalwork, special dolls, Noh and Kabuki acting, Bunraku puppets, music, dance, singing and so on. The living national treasures receive a stipend in order to be able to improve their special artistic talent while training students to perpetuate their art form.

Grants

For the visual artist who considers seeking a grant there are several funding sources: The National Endowment for the Arts, individual state agencies, private foundations and prizes and awards.

The NEA, as previously described, has a variety of funding disciplines, each with program guidelines which can be obtained from the National Endowment for the Arts, Nancy Hanks Center, 1100 Pennsylvania Avenue, N.W., Washington, D.C. 20506. The Visual Artists Fellowships Program booklet includes applications in the following areas: new genres (formerly "Conceptual/Performance/New Genres" and "Video"), painting, printmaking/drawing/artists books, photography, sculpture and crafts. Fellowships are available to practicing professionals and can amount to $15,000 with a very limited number of $25,000 fellowships awarded at the Panel's discretion.

On the state level, all fifty states, as well as the District of Columbia, Puerto Rico and the Virgin Islands, have agencies. (Their addresses can be found on pages 195-199.) The programs and application procedures differ state to state. Since many state agencies give most of their grants to organizations, individuals seeking grants often must be affiliated with an eligible organization.

Of the 22,000 private foundations, 950 are currently offering support to individual projects. Application procedures vary with each foundation or grant-giving agency. It is important that applicants pinpoint the organization best matched to their qualifications, so careful preliminary research is necessary.

An excellent source of reference for grant seekers is The Foundation Center Network, an independent national service organization which provides authoritative sources of information on private philanthropic giving. There are Foundation Centers in New York City, Washington, D.C., Cleveland and San Francisco with over 100 cooperating library collections. Toll-free information at 1-800-424-9836 will provide locations.

The Foundation Center publishes a number of invaluable books, including *The Foundation Directory* and *Supplement* which contains over 4,000 listings of grantmakers giving interests, addresses, telephone numbers, financial data, grant amounts, gifts received, plus full application information. *Foundation Grants to Individuals* is the only publication devoted entirely to foundation grant opportunities for individual applicants. The listings include awards of $2,000 or more.

Though limited, corporations can be a funding source for the individual. The American Council for the Arts, 570 Seventh Avenue, New York, N.Y. 10018, publishes a number of useful reference books including *Guide to Corporate Giving 3* most recently updated in 1983. It provides information on corporate sources of support, focused primarily on giving to organizations, but with a section on the approximately 40 companies which have offered commissions to individual artists. Again, as with state agency grantmakers, artists should try to affiliate themselves with organizations that are eligible for corporate funding.

Awards and prizes for artists can range from trophies to $10,000 fellowships and are sponsored by a variety of arts organizations and universities. *Awards, Honors, and Prizes* (published by Gale Research Company in Detroit) is a directory of awards for many disciplines, including the visual arts. It describes 5,000 different programs and lists the trophies, medals, scrolls and monetary awards. An easy-to-use volume on the subject is *Money Business: Grants and Awards for Creative Artists,* published by The Artists Foundation, Inc., 110 Broad Street, Boston, MA 02110.

Another organization that provides information concerning grants and fellowships is the Grantsmanship Center, 1015 W. Olympic Boulevard, Los Angeles, CA 90015, an organization which conducts proposal-writing workshops, publishes a bimonthly newsletter and has library resources.

The Appendix of Artists Groups and Organizations for the Arts should also be consulted with respect to organizations which give grants or provide information about obtaining grants.

Appendices

Artists groups and organizations for the arts

Advertising Photographers of America, Inc. (APA), 45 East 20th Street, New York, New York 10003. A professional trade association, APA was begun in 1981 to promote the highest standards of business practice within the industry. Benefits are: APA/SPAR Estimate/Invoice Form and Stock Delivery Memo, four annual meetings, *APA Newsletter*, APA Hotline, free legal consultation, group medical insurance, group disability income, rental car discount, seminars and *Assistants Directory*.

American Council for the Arts (ACA), 570 Seventh Avenue, New York, New York 10018. ACA addresses significant issues in the arts by promoting communications, management improvement and problem solving among those who shape and implement policy. ACA accomplishes this by: fostering communication and cooperation among arts groups and leaders in the public and private sector; promoting advocacy on behalf of all the arts; sponsoring research, analysis studies and publishing books, manuals and ACA Update for leaders and managers in the arts.

American Craft Council (ACC), 401 Park Avenue South, New York, New York 10016. The ACC, founded in 1943, is a national non-profit organization devoted exclusively to the support and encouragement of crafts. The Council, under guidance of a national Board of Trustees, maintains the following: the American Craft Museum, the magazine *American Craft*, American Craft Enterprises, American Craft Library and Information Services, and Your Portable Library.

The American Institute of Graphic Arts (AIGA), 1059 Third Avenue, New York, New York 10021. Founded in 1914, AIGA conducts a nationwide program to promote excellence in, and the advancement of, the graphic design profession. AIGA sponsors competitions, exhibitions, publications (including an Annual, a quarterly Journal, a Code of Ethics, professional practice guidelines, and a sales tax document), educational activities and projects in the public interest. Chapters of AIGA are active in eight cities.

American Society of Magazine Photographers (ASMP), 205 Lexington Avenue, New York, New York 10016. The organization, with 26 Chapters throughout the country, promotes the photographic profession through consistent action and information exchange on rights, ethics, standards and technical subjects. Its services include publications, insurance, surveys and member support with publishers, advertising agencies and corporate/industrial clients.

Art Dealers Association of America, Inc., 575 Madison Avenue, New York, New York 10022. Representing over 100 established galleries, its general purposes are to promote the interests of individuals and firms dealing in works of fine art and to enhance the confidence of the public and of government in responsible fine arts dealers. Any dealer who fails to observe the generally accepted standards of fair and honest business conduct will have his or her membership terminated.

Art Dealers Association of California, 3091 Wilshire Boulevard, Los Angeles, California 90010. The association was created in 1970 to establish public awareness of the role and function of fine arts dealers, to improve the status of the fine arts business, to secure the confidence of the public and to elevate the position of art dealer to that of a fully recognized profession.

Art Directors Club, Inc., 250 Park Avenue South, New York, New York 10003. Founded in 1920, "to promote and elevate the profession of Art Directing." Provides professional services, conducts educational programs, publishes, exhibits and seeks to elevate professional standards through active participation in the Joint Ethics Committee.

Artists Equity Association, Inc. (AEA), P.O. Box 28068 Central Station, Washington, D.C. 20005. A non-profit, aesthetically and politically nonpartisan organization which lobbies before the U.S. Congress and provides representation for agencies that have responsibilities in forming arts policies and programs. Membership offers: Newsletter, book discounts, fine art and health insurance, debt collection service, legal referral, model contracts, publications and information.

Artists Equity Association of New York, Inc., 225 West 34 Street, New York, New York 10018. Newsletter, code of ethics, contracts, insurance.

Artists for Economic Action (AFEA), 842 South Ogden, Los Angeles, California 90049. AFEA is dedicated to: furthering the economic, social, and cultural needs of the visual artist; educating the community at large to recognize the artist's contribution to society; promoting understanding and appreciation of the visual artist; encouraging collection and utilization of art work in all areas of life and maintaining an emergency fund to assist artists in crisis.

The Artists Foundation, Inc., 110 Broad Street, Boston, Massachusetts 02110. Incorporated in 1973, the foundation works to enhance the careers of creative artists with a major emphasis on those working in the Commonwealth of Massachusetts. It offers: The Artists Fellowship Program, Artist-in-Residence and Artists Abroad Programs, Artists Services Program and Research and Development.

Association of Artist-Run Galleries, 152 Wooster Street, New York, New York 10013. A service organization dedicated to the expansion of the alternative art world, its services include: information about artist-run cooperative gallery maintenance; distribution of books, catalogs, newsletters, video tapes, etc. and educational events.

Boston Visual Artists Union (BVAU), 77 North Washington Street, Boston, Massachusetts 02114. The BVAU is an organization of over 900 professional artists and individuals who work in and appreciate the visual arts. The Union aims to make closer connections between artists and the public. The BVAU offers Wednesday night programs, a monthly newsletter, Saturday workshops and serves as a resource center for artists.

The Business Committe for the Arts, Inc., 1775 Broadway, New York, New York 10019. It is the first and only national not-for-profit organization of business leaders committed to supporting the arts and to encouraging new and increased support to the arts from the American business community.

Cartoonists Guild, Inc. (CG), a division of the Graphic Artists Guild, 30 East 20th Street, New York, New York 10003. Founded in 1967 as a national organization of professional cartoonists, the CG affiliated with the Graphic Artists Guild in February, 1984. The CG works to upgrade business practices and standards in the field. Benefits are: publications, newsletters, confidential market information and bulletins, workshops and seminars on the industry. CG members are eligible also for all benefits of membership in the Graphic Artist Guild.

Center for Arts Information, 625 Broadway, New York, New York 10012. The Center serves as an information clearinghouse for and about the arts. Its information and referral services are available to members of the arts community and the general public. It is equipped with a library of over 5,000 reference books, pamphlets and directories and subscribes to over 325 arts periodicals. It also has 400 files on service organizations and funding agencies and publishes a bulletin.

Chicago Artists' Coalition (CAC), 5 West Grand Avenue, Chicago, Illinois 60610. The Coalition is an artist-run, service organization for visual artists. Services include a newsletter, slide registry, job referral service, health insurance, free lectures, discounts at art supply stores, annual tax and record-keeping workshop, business of art conferences, a resource center and publications.

The Foundation Center, 79 Fifth Avenue, New York, New York 10003. The Foundation Center Network is an independent national service organization which provides authoritative sources of information on private philanthropic giving. There are Foundation Centers in New York City, Washington, D.C., Cleveland and San Francisco with over 100 cooperating library collections. Toll-free information at 1-800-424-9836 will provide locations.

The Foundation for the Community of Artists, 280 Broadway, Room 412, New York, New York 10007. A 15-year-old, multi-discipline, service organization with emphasis on visual arts, it provides group health insurance, Fall and Spring Seminar/Workshop Series, tax filing and consultation service and general information and referral services. It publishes the *Artist Update* (monthly listing of competitions, grants, services and resources for artists) and *Art & Artist,* a bimonthly newspaper on issues affecting artists.

Foundation for Independent Video and Film, Inc. (FIVF), 625 Broadway, New York, New York 10012. Formerly Association of Independent Video and Filmmakers, it works through the combined effort of the membership to provide practical information and moral support for independent video and filmmakers.

Grantsmanship Center, 1015 West Olympic Boulevard, Los Angeles, California 90015. A compendium of sources and resources for managers and staffs of non-profit organizations, the center conducts proposal-writing workshops, publishes a bimonthly newsletter, has library resources and numerous publications.

Graphic Artists Guild (GAG), 30 East 20th Street, New York, New York 10003. This national organization represents 5,000 professional artists active in illustration, graphic design, textile and needleart design, computer graphics and cartooning. Its purposes include: to establish and promote ethical and financial standards, to gain recognition for the graphic arts as a profession, to educate members in business skills and lobby for artists' rights legislation. Programs include: group health insurance, monthly newsletters, publication of the *Pricing & Ethical Guidelines,* legal and accounting referrals, artist-to-artist networking and information sharing.

International Sculpture Center, 1050 Potomac Street, N.W., Washington, D.C. 20007. Devoted exclusively to contemporary sculpture, the Center offers a bimonthly magazine, International Sculpture Biennials, symposia and workshops, ISC publication, audio cassettes and insurance plans.

Lower Manhattan Loft Tenants Association, P.O. Box 887, Bowling Green Station, New York, New York 10004. A volunteer organization which provides a clearinghouse for information about the loft situation, periodicals, public meetings, housing clinic and legal referrals.

New York Artists Equity Association, 32 Union Square East, Suite 1103, New York, New York 10003. This service organization representing professional visual artists was formed to further economic, cultural and legislative interests of artists. Services available include: health insurance and dental plan, fine art insurance and term life insurance, newsletter, contract forms, legal information, legislative advocacy and cultural programs.

The Organization of Independent Artists (OIA), 201 Varick Street, New York, New York 10014. Founded in 1976 as a grassroots movement among artists, OIA turned a federal mandate encouraging the use of government buildings for cultural and educational activities into an innovative resource for visual artists' exhibitions. It has sponsored more than 200 exhibitions in federal, state and municipal buildings, corporate lobbies and on the grounds of local universities and public parks.

Picture Agency Council of America, Inc. (PACA), c/o Henry Scanlon, Comstock, 32 East 31st Street, New York, New York 10016. PACA's goal is to develop uniform business practices within the stock photo industry based upon ethical standards established by the Council. Through improved channels of communication with sister agencies and other professional groups, the Council hopes to make available information necessary to improve and protect the business of its members. Annual directory available.

Society of Illustrators (SI), 128 East 63rd Street, New York, New York 10021. Begun in 1901 and dedicated to the advancement of the art of illustration and the welfare of persons in the field. Included in programs: Museum of American Illustration, welfare fund to help indigent members, U.S. Air Force program—yearly exhibit and tours, annual scholarship program, annual exhibition of American illustration, annual books, lecture series. SI also serves as an official archive of illustration.

Society of Photographer and Artist Representatives, Inc. (SPAR), P.O. Box 845, FDR Station, New York, New York 10022. Formed in 1965, with the continuing purpose of establishing and maintaining high ethical standards in the business conduct of representatives and the creative talent they represent, and fostering productive cooperation between talent and client. This organization runs speakers' panels and seminars with buyers of talent from all fields; just completed "Standards" relations statement to clarify urgent problems and abuses; works with new reps to orient them on business, contracts, the Joint Ethics Committee and free legal advice. Members: regular (agents), associates, out-of-town. Publishes a newsletter.

Society of Publication Designers (SPD), 23 Park Avenue, New York, New York 10017. Began in 1964. Main purposes: to encourage and help publication designers in ways which will advance the level and efficiency of their endeavors; to increase the exposure given to the contributions of these designers and to achieve professional recognition. Concerned with consumer publications, newspapers, business and company publications. Activities include: annual exhibition, monthly newsletter, monthly special programs or lectures.

State arts agencies, regional groups, national arts service organizations, & NEA regional representatives

Alabama State Council on the Arts & Humanities
Mr. Albert B. Head, Executive Director
114 North Hull Street
Montgomery, Alabama 36130-5801
(205) 261-4076

Alaska State Council on the Arts
Ms. Christine D'Arcy, Executive Director
619 Warehouse Avenue, Suite 220
Anchorage, Alaska 99501
(907) 279-1558

American Samoa Council on Culture, Arts & Humanities
Ms. Matilda Lolotai, Executive Director
Office of the Governor
P.O. Box 1540
Pago Pago, American Samoa 96799
9-011-684-633-5613
9-011-684-633-2059

Arizona Commission on the Arts
Ms. Shelley Cohn, Executive Director
417 West Roosevelt
Phoenix, Arizona 85003
(602) 255-5882 or 255-5884

Arkansas Arts Council
Ms. Amy Aspell, Director
The Heritage Center
225 East Markham Street, Suite 200
Little Rock, Arkansas 72201
(501) 371-2539

California Arts Council
Mrs. Marilyn Ryan, Executive Director
1901 Broadway, Suite A
Sacramento, California 95818
(916) 445-1530
(916) 322-8911 (Office)

Colorado Council on the Arts & Humanities
Ms. Ellen Sollod, Executive Director
Grant-Humphreys Mansion
770 Pennsylvania Street
Denver, Colorado 80203
(303) 866-2617 or 866-2618

Connecticut Commission on the Arts
Mr. Gary M. Young, Executive Director
190 Trumbull Street
Hartford, Connecticut 06103
(203) 566-4770

Delaware State Arts Council
Ms. Cecelia Fitzgibbon, Administrator
State Office Building
820 North French Street
Wilmington, Delaware 19801
(302) 571-3540

District of Columbia Commission on the Arts & Humanities
Mr. James Backas, Executive Director
420 Seventh Street, N.W., 2nd Floor
Washington, D.C. 20004
(202) 724-5613 or 727-9332

Arts Council of Florida
Mr. Chris Doolin, Director
Division of Cultural Affairs
Department of State
The Capitol
Tallahassee, Florida 32301
(904) 487-5780 or 487-2980

Georgia Council for the Arts & Humanities
Mr. Frank Ratka, Executive Director
2082 East Exchange Place, Suite 100
Tucker, Georgia 30084
(404) 493-5780

Guam Council on the Arts & Humanities
Ms. Annie Benavente Stone, Executive
Director
Office of the Governor
P.O. Box 2950
Agana, Guam 96910
(011-671) 477-9845 or 477-7413

Congressman Ben Blaz, Local Representative
1729 Longworth House Office Building
Washington, D.C. 20515
(202) 225-1188

State Foundation on Culture & the Arts
Mrs. Sarah M. Richards, Executive Director
335 Merchant Street, Room 202
Honolulu, Hawaii 96813
(808) 548-4145

Idaho Commission on the Arts
Ms. Joan Lolmaugh, Executive Director
304 West State Street
c/o STATEHOUSE MAIL
Boise, Idaho 83720
(208) 334-2119 (Office)
(208) 343-3155 (Home)

Illinois Arts Council
Mrs. Adrienne N. Hirsch, Executive Director
111 North Wabash Avenue, Room 720
Chicago, Illinois 60602
(312) 793-6750

Indiana Arts Commission
Mr. Thomas B. Schorgl, Executive Director
32 East Washington Street, 6th Floor
Indianapolis, Indiana 46204
(317) 232-1268

Iowa Arts Council
Mr. Doug True, Acting Executive Director
State Capitol Building
Des Moines, Iowa 50319
(515) 281-4451

Kansas Arts Commission
Mr. John A. Reed, Executive Director
112 West 6th Street
Topeka, Kansas 66603
(913) 296-3335

Kentucky Arts Council
Ms. Nash Cox, Director
Berry Hill
Louisville Road
Frankfort, Kentucky 40601
(502) 564-3757

Department of Culture, Recreation & Tourism
Division of the Arts
Mr. Eddy Martin, Acting Executive Director
P.O. Box 44247
Baton Rouge, Louisiana 70804
(504) 925-3930 or 925-3934

Maine State Commission on the Arts & the
Humanities
Mr. Alden C. Wilson (Denny), Executive
Director
55 Capitol Street
State House Station 25
Augusta, Maine 04333
(207) 289-2724

Maryland State Arts Council
Mr. Hank Johnson, Executive Director
15 West Mulberry Street
Baltimore, Maryland 21201
(301) 685-6740

Massachusetts Council on the Arts &
Humanities
Ms. Anne Hawley, Executive Director
1 Ashburton Place, #1305
Boston, Massachusetts 02108
(617) 727-3668

Michigan Council for the Arts
Mr. E. Ray Scott, Executive Director
1200 Sixth Avenue
Executive Plaza
Detroit, Michigan 48226
(313) 256-3735

Minnesota State Arts Board
Dr. Sam W. Grabarski, Executive Director
432 Summit Avenue
St. Paul, Minnesota 55102
(612) 297-2603
(800) 652-9747—Toll Free Within MN

Mississippi Arts Commission
Ms. Lida Rogers, Executive Director
P.O. Box 1341
Jackson, Mississippi 39205
(601) 354-7336

Missouri State Council on the Arts
Mr. Rick Simoncelli, Executive Director
Wainwright Office Complex
111 North Seventh Street, Suite 105
St. Louis, Missouri 63101
(314) 444-6845

Montana Arts Council
Mr. David E. Nelson, Executive Director
35 South Last Chance Gulch
Helena, Montana 59620
(406) 444-6430

Nebraska Arts Council
Ms. Robin Tryloff, Executive Director
1313 Farnam-on-the-Mall
Omaha, Nebraska 68102-1873
(402) 554-2122

Nevada State Council on the Arts
Mr. William L. Fox, Executive Director
329 Flint Street
Reno, Nevada 89501
(702) 789-0225

New Hampshire Commission on the Arts
Mr. Robert Hankins, Executive Director
Phenix Hall
40 North Main Street
Concord, New Hampshire 03301
(603) 271-2789

New Jersey State Council on the Arts
Mr. Jeffrey A. Kesper, Executive Director
109 West State Street
Trenton, New Jersey 08625
(609) 292-6130

New Mexico Arts Division
Mr. Bernard Blas Lopez, Executive Director
224 East Palace Avenue
Santa Fe, New Mexico 87501
(505) 827-6490

New York State Council on the Arts
Ms. Mary Hays, Executive Director
915 Broadway
New York, New York 10010
(212) 614-2900

North Carolina Arts Council
Miss Mary B. Regan, Executive Director
Department of Cultural Resources
Raleigh, North Carolina 27611
(919) 733-2821

North Dakota Council on the Arts
Ms. Donna M. Evenson, Executive Director
Black Building, Suite 811
Fargo, North Dakota 58102
(701) 237-8962

Commonwealth Council for Arts & Culture
(Northern Mariana Islands)
Ms. Ana Teregeyo, Executive Director
CNMI Convention Center
(use Mariana Islands address)
Capitol Hill, Saipan
P.O. Box 553, CHRB
Commonwealth of the Northern Mariana
Islands 96950
Telephone 9982/83

Ohio Arts Council
Dr. Wayne P. Lawson, Executive Director
727 East Main Street
Columbus, Ohio 43205
(614) 466-2613

State Arts Council of Oklahoma
Mrs. Betty Price, Executive Director
Jim Thorpe Building, Room 640
2101 North Lincoln Boulevard
Oklahoma City, Oklahoma 73105
(405) 521-2931 (State)
(405) 525-8153 (Private)

Oregon Arts Commission
Mr. Peter deC. Hero, Executive Director
835 Summer Street, N.E.
Salem, Oregon 97301
(503) 378-3625

Commonwealth of Pennsylvania Council on the
Arts
Ms. June Batten Arey, Executive Director
Room 216, Finance Building
Harrisburg, Pennsylvania 17120
(717) 787-6883

Institute of Puerto Rican Culture
Mr. Miguel Angel Nieves,
Acting Executive Director
Apartado Postal 4184
San Juan, Puerto Rico 00905
(809) 723-2115

Rhode Island State Council on the Arts
Ms. Iona Dobbins, Executive Director
312 Wickenden Street
Providence, Rhode Island 02903-4494
(401) 277-3880

South Carolina Arts Commission
Ms. Scott Sanders, Executive Director
1800 Gervais Street
Columbia, South Carolina 29201
(803) 758-3442

South Dakota Arts Council
Mrs. Charlotte Carver, Executive Director
108 West 11th Street
Sioux Falls, South Dakota 57102
(605) 339-6646

Tennessee Arts Commission
Mr. Bennett Tarleton, Jr., Executive Director
505 Deaderick Street, Suite 1700
Nashville, Tennessee 37219
(615) 741-1701 (Switchboard)
(615) 741-6395 (Office)

Texas Commission on the Arts
Mr. Richard Huff, Executive Director
P.O. Box 13406, Capitol Station
Austin, Texas 78711
(512) 475-6593

Utah Arts Council
Mrs. Ruth R. Draper, Executive Director
617 East South Temple Street
Salt Lake City, Utah 84102
(801) 533-5895/5896

Vermont Council on the Arts, Inc.
Mr. Alan L. Erdossy, Executive Director
136 State Street
Montpelier, Vermont 05602
(802) 828-3291

Virginia Commission for the Arts
Ms. Peggy Baggett, Executive Director
James Monroe Building
101 North 14th Street, 17th Floor
Richmond, Virginia 23219
(804) 225-3132

Virgin Islands Council on the Arts
Mr. John Jowers, Executive Director
P.O. Box 6732
St. Thomas
U.S. Virgin Islands 00801
(809) 774-5984

Washington State Arts Commission
Mr. Michael A. Croman, Executive Director
9th & Columbia Building
Mail Stop GH-11
Olympia, Washington 98504
(206) 753-3860 (Office)
(206) 357-9589 (Home)

Arts & Humanities Division, West Virginia
Department of Culture & History
Mr. James B. Andrews, Executive Director
Capitol Complex
Charleston, West Virginia 25305
(304) 348-0240

Wisconsin Arts Board
Mr. Arley G. Curtz, Director
107 S. Butler Street
Madison, Wisconsin 53703
(608) 266-0190

Wyoming Council on the Arts
Ms. Joy E. Thompson, Executive Director
Equality State Bank Building, 2nd Floor
Cheyenne, Wyoming 82002
(307) 777-7742

Regional organizations

Affiliated State Arts Agencies
of the Upper Midwest (ASAAUM)

Iowa, North Dakota, Minnesota, South
Dakota, Wisconsin

Mr. David Fraher, Executive Director
Dr. Sam W. Grabarski, President
Hennepin Center for the Arts
528 Hennepin Avenue, Suite 302
Minneapolis, Minnesota 55403
(612) 341-0755

Consortium for Pacific Arts & Cultures
(CPAC)

American Samoa, Guam, Northern Marianas

Ms. Annie B. Stone, Interim Program
Administrator
Ms. Ana Teregeyo, Chairman
P.O. Box #4502
Agana, Guam 96910
(671) 477-7413

Great Lakes Arts Alliance (GLAA)

Illinois, Indiana, Michigan, Ohio

Mr. Gregory G. Gibson, Executive Director
Mrs. Judith Ann Rapanos, Chairman
11424 Bellflower Road
Cleveland, Ohio 44106
(216) 229-1098

Mid-America Arts Alliance (MAAA)

Arkansas, Kansas, Missouri, Nebraska,
Oklahoma, Texas*

*Associate Member

Mr. Henry Moran, Executive Director
Mr. Harry P. Seward, Chairman
20 West 9th Street, Suite #550
Kansas City, Missouri 64105
(816) 421-1388

Mid-Atlantic States Arts Consortium (MASAC)

Delaware, District of Columbia, Maryland,
New Jersey, New York, Pennsylvania,
Virginia, West Virginia

Ms. Sandra Lorentzen, Executive Director
Mrs. Kay Goodwin, Chairman
11 East Chase Street, Suite 7-B
Baltimore, Maryland 21202
(301) 685-1400

New England Foundation for the Arts, Inc.
(NEFA)

Connecticut, Maine, Massachusetts, New
Hampshire, Rhode Island, Vermont

Ms. Marcia Erickson Noebels, Executive
Director
Ms. Marcia Alcorn, President
25 Mount Auburn Street
Cambridge, Massachusetts 02138
(617) 492-2914

Southern Arts Federation (SAF)

Alabama, Florida, Georgia, Kentucky,
Louisiana, Mississippi, North Carolina, South
Carolina, Tennessee

Ms. Sharon Donahue, Executive Director
Mr. Al Head, Chairman
1401 Peachtree Street, N.E.
Suite 122
Atlanta, Georgia 30309
(404) 874-7244

Western States Arts Foundation (WSAF)

Alaska, Arizona, Colorado, Hawaii, Idaho,
Montana, Nevada, New Mexico, Oregon,
Utah, Washington, Wyoming

Mr. Terry Melton, Executive Director
Mr. Peter Hero, Chairman
141 East Palace Avenue
Santa Fe, New Mexico 87501
(505) 988-1166

National organizations

National Assembly of Local Arts Agencies
(NALAA)

Mr. Robert L. Lynch, Executive Director
1785 Massachusetts Avenue, N.W.
Suite 413
Washington, D.C. 20036
(202) 483-8670

National Assembly of State Arts Agencies
(NASAA)

Mr. Jonathan Katz, Executive Director
1010 Vermont Avenue, N.W., Suite 920
Washington, D.C. 20005
(202) 347-6352

Regional Representatives of the National Endowment for the Arts

Northeast States and Caribbean

Connecticut, Maine, Massachusetts, New
Hampshire, New York, Puerto Rico, Rhode
Island, U.S. Virgin Islands, Vermont

Ms. Ellen Thurston
2 Columbus Circle
New York, New York 10019
(212) 957-9760

Mid-Atlantic and Mid-South States

Delaware, District of Columbia, Kentucky,
Maryland, New Jersey, North Carolina,
Pennsylvania, South Carolina, Tennessee,
Virginia, West Virginia

Mr. Adrian King
P.O. Box 15141
Washington, D.C. 20003
(202) 737-5268

Southern and Gulf States

Alabama, Florida, Georgia, Louisiana,
Mississippi, Texas

Mr. E. Henry Willett III
310 North Hull Street
Montgomery, Alabama 36104
(205) 264-3797

Great Lakes States

Illinois, Indiana, Michigan, Ohio, Wisconsin

Ms. Bertha Masor
4200 Marine Drive
Chicago, Illinois 60613
(312) 935-9530 or
Answering Service (312) 782-7858

Plains States

Arkansas, Iowa, Kansas, Minnesota, Missouri,
Nebraska, North Dakota, Oklahoma, South
Dakota

Ms. Romalyn Tilghman
P.O. Box 22489
Kansas City, Missouri 64113
(816) 523-0001

Western States

Arizona, Colorado, Idaho, Montana, Nevada,
New Mexico, Oregon, Utah, Washington,
Wyoming

Cynthia Schultz
Interim Information Service
P.O. Box 45010
Seattle, Washington 98145
(206) 322-7465

California, Alaska and Pacific Islands

Alaska, American Samoa, California, Guam,
Hawaii, Northern Mariana Islands

NOTE: All calls and inquiries are to be
forwarded to the Regional Representative
Coordinator at 682-5759, Room 528

Code of Fair Practice

for the Graphics Communications Industry
The Joint Ethics Committee
Formulated in 1948,
revised in 1978

I Introduction

II Personnel

III Code of Fair Practice

IV Action

V Mediation

VI Arbitration

VII Committee Scope

VIII Committee Limitations

IX Committee Maintenance

I Introduction

In 1945 a group of artists and art directors in the City of New York, concerned with the growing abuses, misunderstandings and disregard of uniform standards of conduct in their field, met to consider possibilities for improvement. They reached the conclusion that any effort, to be successful, must start with the most widespread backing, and further that it must be a continuing, not a temporary, activity. On their recommendation, three leading New York art organizations together established and financed a committee known as the Joint Ethics Committee.

In 1978 the expanded committee representing six organizations revised the code to include the new communications industries. This booklet is published in response to the many requests for information concerning the operation and scope of the Committee.

II Personnel

The Joint Ethics Committee is composed of four members with three votes from each of the following organizations: Society of Illustrators, Inc., The Art Directors Club, Inc., American Society of Magazine Photographers, Inc., Society of Photographer and Artist Representatives, Inc., and the Graphic Artists Guild, Inc. appointed by the directing bodies of each organization, but serving jointly in furtherance of the purposes for which the Committee was founded.

Members of the Joint Ethics Committee are selected with great care by their respective organizations. Their selection is based upon their experience in the profession, their proven mature thinking and temperament, and their reputation for impartiality.

III Code of Fair Practice

The Code of Fair Practice, as established by the Joint Ethics Committee, was conceived with the idea of equity for those engaged in the various aspects of creating, selling, buying and using graphic arts.

The Code is reproduced later in this booklet. The Committee zealously upholds the ethical standards set forth in the Code and invites with equal readiness any and all reports of violations.

IV Action

The Committee meets one or more times a month to read and act upon complaints, requests for guidance, and reports of Code violations. The proceedings and records of the Committee are held in strict confidence. In the interest of the profession typical cases are published periodically without identification of the parties involved. All communications to the Committee must be made in writing. When complaint justifies action, a copy of the complainant's letter may be sent, with the plaintiff's permission, to the alleged offender. In the exchange of correspondence which follows, matters are frequently settled by a mere clarification of the issues. Further action by the Committee becomes unnecessary, and in many instances both sides resume friendly and profitable relationships. When, however, a continued exchange of correspondence indicates that a ready adjustment of differences is improbable, the Committee may suggest mediation or offer its facilities for arbitration.

In the case of flagrant violation, the Committee may, at its discretion, cite the alleged offender to the governing bodies of the parent organizations and recommend that they publicize the fact of these citations when (a) the Committee after a reasonable length of time and adequate notice recieves no response from the alleged offender or (b) when the Committee receives a response which it deems unacceptable.

V Mediation

Both parties meet informally under the auspices of a panel of mediators composed of three members of the Committee. If the dispute requires guidances in a field not represented in the Committee's membership, a specially qualified mediator with the required experience may be included. The names of members of the panel are submitted to both parties for their acceptance.

The conduct of a panel of mediators is friendly and informal. The function of the panel members is to guide, not to render any verdict. The panel's purpose is to direct the discussion along such lines and in such a manner as to bring about a meeting of minds on the questions involved. If mediation fails, or seems unlikely to bring about satisfactory settlement, arbitration may be suggested.

VI Arbitration

A panel of five arbitrators is appointed. One or more is selected from the Committee, and the remainder are chosen by virtue of their particular experience and understanding of the problems presented by the dispute. Names of the panel members are submitted to both parties for their approval. Both parties involved sign an agreement and take oath to abide by the decision of the panel. The panel itself is sworn in and the proceedings are held in compliance with the Arbitration Law of the State of New York. After both sides are heard, the panel deliberates in private and renders its decision, opinion, and award. These are duly formulated by the Committee's counsel for service on the parties and, if the losing side should balk, for entry of judgment according to law.

So far, every award has been fully honored. The decisions and opinions of this Committee are rapidly becoming precedent for guidance in similar situations. The Committee's Code has been cited as legal-precedent.

VII Committee Scope

The Committee acts upon matters which can be defined by them as involving a violation of the code or a need for its enforcement.

Upon occasion, the Committee has been asked to aid in settling questions not specifically covered by the Code of Fair Practice. The Committee gladly renders such aid, providing it does not exceed the limitations of its authority.

VIII Committee limitations

The Committee offers no legal advice on contracts, copyrights, bill collecting, or similar matters. But its judgment and decisions as to what is fair and ethical in any given situation, are backed by the support of the entire profession represented by the Committee.

The Committee's influence is derived from widespread moral support, and while it has neither judicial nor police powers, and cannot punish offenders, nor summon alleged violators to its presence, still, its growing prestige and dignity of operation have made it a highly respected tribunal to which few have ever failed to respond when invited to settle their differences.

IX Committee maintenance

The Committee's facilities are not limited to members of its supporting groups. They are available to any individual, business, or professional organization in the field of communications.

The operating expenses of the Committee are defrayed by the sponsoring organizations represented. The time and services of the members are voluntarily contributed without any form of personal gain.

Articles of the Code of Fair Practice

Relations
Between Artist & Buyer

1. Dealings between an artist* or the artist's agent and a client should be conducted only through an authorized buyer.

2. Orders to an artist or agent should be in writing and should include the specific rights which are being transferred, the price, delivery date, and a summarized description of the work. In the case of publications, the acceptance of a manuscript by the artist constitutes an order.

3. All changes or additions not due to the fault of the artist or agent should be billed to the purchaser as an additional and separate charge.

4. There should be no charges to the purchaser, other than those authorized expenses, for revisions or retakes made necessary by errors on the part of the artist or the artist's agent.

5. Alterations should not be made without consulting the artist. Where alterations or retakes are necessary and time permits and where the artist's usual standard of quality has been maintained, the artist should be given the opportunity of making such changes.

6. The artist should notify the buyer of an anticipated delay in delivery. Should the artist fail to keep his contract through unreasonable delay in delivery, or nonconformance with agreed specifications, it should be considered a breach of contract by the artist and should release the buyer from responsiblity.

7. Work stopped by a buyer after it has been started should be delivered immediately and billed on the basis of the time and effort expended and expenses incurred.

8. An artist should not be asked to work on speculation. However, work originating with the artist may be marketed on its merit. Such work remains the property of the artist unless purchased and paid for.

9. Art contests for commercial purposes are not approved because of their speculative and exploitative character.

10. There should be no secret rebates, discounts, gifts, or bonuses requested by or given to buyers by the artist or the artist's agent.

11. Artwork ownership and copyright ownership is initially vested in the hands of the artist.

12. Original artwork remains the property of the artist unless it is specifically purchased and paid for as distinct from the purchase of any reproduction rights.**

13. In cases of copyright transfers, only specified rights are transferred in any transaction, all unspecified rights remaining vested in the artist.**

14. If the purchase price of artwork is based specifically upon limited use and later this material is used more extensively than originally planned, the artist is to receive adequate additional renumeration.

15. Commissioned artwork is not to be considered as "done for hire."

16. If comprehensives, preliminary work, exploratory work, or additional photographs from an assignment are subsequently published as finished art the price should be increased to the satisfaction of artist and buyer.

17. If exploratory work, comprehensives, or photographs are bought from an artist with the intention or possibility that another artist will be assigned to do the finished work, this should be made clear at the time of placing the order.

18. The publisher of any reproduction of artwork shall publish the artist's copyright notice if the artist so requests and has not executed a written and signed transfer of copyright ownership.**

19. The right to place the artist's signature upon artwork is subject to agreement between artist and buyer.

20. There should be no plagiarism of any creative artwork.

21. If an artist is specifically requested to produce any artwork during unreasonable working hours, fair additional remuneration should be allowed.

22. An artist entering into an agreement with an agent or studio for exclusive representation should not accept an order from, nor permit his work to be shown by any other agent or studio. Any agreement which is not intended to be exclusive should set forth in writing the exact restrictions agreed upon between the two parties.

23. All artwork or photography submitted as samples to a buyer by artists' agents or studio representatives should bear the name of the artist or artists responsible for the creation.

24. No agent, studio, or production company should continue to show the work of an artist as samples after the termination of the association.

25. After termination of an association between artist and agent, the agent should be entitled to a commission on accounts which the agent has secured, for a period of time not exceeding six months (unless otherwise specified by contract).

26. Examples of an artist's work furnished to an agent or submitted to a prospective purchaser shall remain the property of the artist, should not be duplicated without the artist's consent, and should be returned to the artist promptly in good condition.

27. Interpretation of the Code shall be in the hands of the Joint Ethics Committee and is subject to changes and additions at the discretion of the parent organizations through their appointed representatives on the Committee.

Sponsored by Society of Illustrators, Inc., The Directors Club, Inc., American Society of Magazine Photographers, Inc., Society of Photographer and Artist Representatives, Inc., The Graphic Artist Guild, Inc.

* The word artist should be understood to include creative people in the field of visual communications such as graphics, photography, film, and television.
**Artwork ownership, copyright ownership, and ownership and rights transfers after January 1, 1978 are to be in compliance with the Federal Copyright Revision Act of 1976.
Copyright 1954 by The Joint Ethics Committee, Post Office Box Number 179, Grand Central Station, New York, New York 10017.

Selected bibliography

ASMP—The American Society of Magazine Photographers. *ASMP Guide: Business Practices in Photography: 1982*. New York: ASMP—The American Society of Magazine Photographers, 1982.

ASMP—The American Society of Magazine Photographers. *ASMP Stock Photography Handbook*. New York: ASMP—The American Society of Magazine Photographers, 1984.

Associated Councils of the Arts, The Association of the Bar of the City of New York, and Volunteer Lawyers for the Arts. *The Visual Artist and the Law*. 1st Revised ed. New York: Praeger Publishers, 1974.

Baumgarten, Paul A., and Farber, Donald C. *Producing, Financing and Distributing Film*. New York: Drama Book Specialists, 1973.

Bay Area Lawyers for the Arts. *The Art of Deduction*. San Francisco: Bay Area Lawyers for the Arts, 1985.

Bay Area Lawyers for the Arts. *Legislative Masterpieces: A Guide to California Arts*. San Francisco: Bay Area Lawyers for the Arts, 1985.

Bunnin, Brad, and Beren, Peter. *Author Law & Strategies: A Legal Guide for the Working Writer*. San Francisco: Bay Area Lawyers for the Arts.

Caplin, Lee Evan. *The Business of Art*. Englewood Cliffs, N.J.: Prentice-Hall, Inc., 1982.

Cartoonists Guild. *Syndicate Survival Kit*. New York: Cartoonists Guild, a division of the Graphic Artists Guild, 1975.

Cavallo, Robert M., and Kahan, Stuart. *Photography, What's the Law?* Revised ed. New York: Crown Publishers, Inc., 1980.

Cochrane, Diane. *This Business of Art*. New York: Watson-Guptill, 1978.

Crawford, Tad. *The Writer's Legal Guide*. New York: Hawthorn/Dutton, 1977.

Crawford, Tad, and Kopelman, Arie. *Selling Your Graphic Design and Illustration*. New York: St. Martin's Press, 1981.

Crawford, Tad, and Kopelman, Arie. *Selling Your Photography*. New York: St. Martin's press, 1980.

Crawford, Tad, and Mellon, Susan. *The Artist-Gallery Partnership*. New York: American Council for the Arts, 1981.

Davidson, Marion, and Blue, Martha. *Making It Legal: A Law Primer for the Craftsmaker, Visual Artist, and Writer*. New York: McGraw-Hill, 1979.

DuBoff, Leonard D. *The Deskbook of Art Law*. Washington: Federal Publications Inc., 1977, Supp. 1984.

DuBoff, Leonard D. *Art Law: Domestic and International*. Littleton, Colorado: Fred B. Rothman & Co., 1975.

Duffy, Robert E. *Art Law: Representing Artists, Dealers, and Collectors*. New York: Practicing Law Institute, 1977.

Feldman, Franklin, and Weil, Stephen E. *Art Works: Law, Policy, Practice*. New York: Practicing Law Institute, 1974.

Goldberg, Morton David. *Current Developments in Copyright Law 1985*. New York: Practicing Law Institute, 1985.

Graphic Artists Guild. *Pricing and Ethical Guidelines*. 5th ed. New York: Graphic Artists Guild, 1984.

Holcomb, Bill, and Striggles, Ted. *Fear of Filing*. New York: Volunteer Lawyers for the Arts, 1984, Supp. 1985.

Hollander, Barnett. *The International Law of Art*. London: Bowes & Bowes, 1959.

Klayman, Toby, and Steinberg, Cobett. *The Artist's Survival Manual*. New York: Scribner's.

Knoll, Alfred P. *Museums—a Gunslinger's Dream*. Legal Rights Guide Number 3. San Francisco: Bay Area Lawyers for the Arts, 1975.

Lindley, Alexander. *Entertainment, Publishing and the Arts*. 4 vols. New York: Clark Boardman Co., Ltd., 1980, Supp. 1984.

Merryman, John Henry, and Elsen, Albert E. *Law, Ethics and Visual Arts*. New York: Matthew Bender, 1979, pages 5–134—5–188.

Nimmer, Melville. *Nimmer on Copyright*. 2 vols. New York: Matthew Bender, 1963, Supp. 1984.

Norwick, Kenneth P., Chasen, Jerry Simon with Kaufman, Henry R. *The Rights of Authors and Artists*. New York: Bantam Books, 1983.

Roosevelt, Rita K., Granoff, Anita M., and Kennedy, Karen P.K. *Money Business: Grants and Awards for Creative Artists*. Revised ed. Boston: The Artists Foundation, Inc., 1982.

Stone, Norman H. *An Introduction to Contracts for Visual Artists*. San Francisco: Bay Area Lawyers for the Arts.

Volunteer Lawyers for the Arts. *Artists' Housing Manual*. New York: Volunteer Lawyers for the Arts, 1985.

Volunteer Lawyers for the Arts. *To Be or Not To Be: An Artist's Guide to Not-For-Profit Incorporation*. New York: Volunteer Lawyers for the Arts, 1982.

Advertising, 38
Advertising Photographers of America (APA), 193
Agents, 101–102, 108–110
A.I.R. lofts, 147
American Arbitration Association, 132
American Council for the Arts (ACA), 193
American Craft Council (ACC), 193
American Institute of Graphic Artists (AIGA), 193
American Society of Magazine Photographers (ASMP), 193
Andre, Carl, 34, 170
Arbitration, 105, 132
Arizona consignment statute, 99
Arkansas statutes
    charitable contributions, 159
    consignment, 99
    print law, 93
Arrington, Clarence, 55–56
Art Advisory Panel, 174
Art Dealers Association of America, Inc., 193
Art Dealers Association of California, 193
Art Directors Club, Inc., 193
Art law, 1
Artemis, 183
Artists Equity Association (AEA), 193
Artists Equity Association of New York, 193
Artists for Economic Action (AFEA), 193
Artists Foundation, Inc., 193
Artists groups, 1
Artist's Reserved Rights and Transfer Sale Agreement. See Projansky contract
ASMP, 193
ASMP Standard Photographers Book Agreement. See Publishing Associated Councils of the Arts. See American Council for the Arts
Association of Artist-Run Galleries (AARG), 193
Auctions, 183, 184
Authenticity
    expert opinions, 184–185
    New York statute, 184–185
Authors Guild Trade Book Contract. See Publishing.

Bailments, 87
Bay Area Lawyers for the Arts, 2
Berne Copyright Convention, 33
Bonnard, 36
Boston Visual Artists Union (BVAU), 193
Brancusi, Constantin, 92
Buenos Aires Convention, 45
Buffet, Bernard, 34
Buildings, photographing, 57
Business Committee for the Arts, Inc., 194
Business names, 40

California statutes
    charitable contributions, 159
    consignment, 99
    moral rights, 38–39
    print law, 93–94
    reproduction rights and ownership of original art, 85–86
    resale proceeds right, 89–90
Camoin, 36
Cartoonists Guild, Inc., 115–116, 194
Cartoonists Guild Syndicate Survival Kit, 115–116
Center for Arts Information, 194
Chagall, Marc, 184
Charitable bequests and contributions, 159, 175, 186
Checks, cashing if restricted, 114–115

Chicago Artists' Coalition (CAC), 194
Child models, 58
Christie's, 183
Code of Fair Practice, 201–205
Coins, images of, 59–60
Collecting money owed, 114–115
Collectors
    auctions, 183, 184
    authenticity, 184–185
    charitable contributions, 186
    customs, 105
    forgeries, 183
    income taxation, 185–186
    museums, 170–171
    purchases abroad, 185
    thefts, 183–184
    warranties, 184–185
College Art Association, 173
Colorado consignment statute, 99
Commercial licensing, 116–117
Commercial rent tax, 149
Commissioned works
    commission agreement for fine art, 78–81
    video broadcast contract, 138–143 (See also Contracts and Reproduction rights)
Connecticut consignment statute, 99
Consignment. See Contracts and Galleries.
Consumer Product Safety Act, 61
Consumer Product Safety Commission, 61
Contracts
    acceptance, 64
    artist-agent agreement, 101–102, 108–110
    artist-gallery consignment agreement model forms, 100, 106–107
    artist-gallery model print agreement, 96
    artist-gallery model video agreement, 137–138, 142–143
    assignment of, 67
    bailments. See Bailments
    bill of sale, 73–74
    bill of sale, video works, 144
    breach of, 68
    commission agreement for fine art, 78–81
    consideration, 64–65
    consignment agreement, 100–107
    counteroffer, 64
    defined, 63
    goods, sale of, 64
    graphic designers' estimate/confirmation/invoice form, 121–122
    idea, protection of, 69–70
    idea, submission letter, 69
    illustrators' confirmation form, 119–120
    illustrators' invoice, 125–126
    insurance, 86–87
    installment payments, 73–74
    leases. See Leases
    lectures, contracts for, 70–72
    legality, 65
    liquidated damages, 87–88
    minors, 65
    negotiation, 63
    nonperformance excused, 67–68
    offer, 64
    oral, 65–66
    partial performance, 68
    parties as competent, 65
    photographers' assignment form, 117–118
    prints, 94–96
    Projansky contract, 74–78, 90
    public policy, 65
    publishing. See Publishing
    rental agreement, 82–84
    reproduction rights. See Reproduction rights
    revocation of offer, 64
    risk of loss, 73

services, 64, 68
specific performance, 68
statutes of limitation, 68–69
substantial compliance, 68
textile designers' confirmation form, 123–124
Uniform Commercial Code, 64, 65–66, 69
video broadcast contract, 138–142
warranties, 66–67, 92–93, 130
warranty, model form, 67
written, 65–66
Contributions. *See* Charitable contributions.
Cooperative buildings, 148
Cooperative galleries, 108
Copyright
  artwork, ownership of, 5–6
  assignment form, 8
  Berne Copyright Convention, 4–5, 33
  Buenos Aires Convention, 4–5
  California statute, 5–6, 7
  common law, 3, 7
  compulsory licensing, 30
  Constitution, 13
  contributions to collective works, 8–9
  copyright information kit, 3
  copyrightability, 3–4
  damages, 27–28
  defective notice, 11–12
  deposit of copies
    alternate, 17–18
    Library of Congress, for, 18
    requirements, 16–17
  duration, 6–7
  exclusive rights, 5–6
  fair use, 28–29
  fees, 15
  foreign, 4–5
  forms
    Form CA, 15
    Form GR/CP, 16, 19, 22
    Form IS, 5
    Form PA, 15, 19
    Form RE, 6
    Form TX, 5
    Form VA, 5, 15, 16, 18–19, 20–21
    obtaining forms, 3
  galleries, 104
  history, 12–13
  ideas, 4, 69–70
  infringement, 27–28, 31
  international, 4–5
  Library of Congress, 18
  manufacturing requirement, 5
  New York statute, 56, 7
  nonexclusive licenses, 6
  notice of, 4, 9–12
  permissions, 29–30, 73
  permission form, 30
  persons entitled to, 4–5
  pseudonyms, 6
  public domain, 3–4
  publication, 9
  reference files, 27
  registration
    advantages, 15
    alternate deposit, 17–18
    deposit of copies, 16–17
    forms, filing out, 18–21
    group, 15–16
  renewal, 6
  term, 6
  termination of grant, 7–8
  titles, protection of, 4, 39–40
  transfer of, 7–8
  Universal Copyright Convention, 4–5
  unpublished works, 3
  work for hire, 23–26

Copyright Revision Act of 1976. *See* Copyright
Corporations. *See* Income taxation and
  Incorporation
Crafts, product liability, 61
Crimi, Alfred, 35, 43–47
Criticism, 41
Cropping, 38
Currency, 59–60
Customs, 105

Damages
  breach of contract, 68
  copyright infringement, 27–28
  liquidated, 87–88
Dangerous art, 60–61
Dealers. *See* Galleries
de Chirico, Giorgio, 34
Defamation
  art works, 53–54
  artist committing, 53–54
  artist protected against, 41
  criticism, 41
  public figures, 54
de Grazia, Anna Maria, 165–166
Depression art projects, 188–189
Destruction of art. *See* Moral rights
Dibbets, Jan, 92
Droit de suite, 89
Dubuffet, Jean, 35
Duchamp, Marcel, 91
Dufy, Raoul, 184

Estate planning
  copyrights, 172
  executors, 172–173
  exhibitions, 170–171
  gifts, 162, 176–177
  Gonzalez, Julio, 169
  Hofmann, Hans—University of California
    agreement, 180–181
  repairs, 169
  reproductions, 169–170
  Rothko, Mark, 170–174
  sales, 171
  situs of art works, 173
  Smith, David, 169, 171, 174
  taxable estate, 174–175
  trusts, 173–174
  will, use of, 171–172
Estate taxation
  basis, 178
  charitable deduction, 175
  double domicile, 173
  extended time for payment, 176
  gifts, 162, 176–177
  gross estate, 174
  insurance, 174
  I.R.S. Art Advisory Panel, 174
  liquidity, 176
  marital deduction, 175
  situs of art works, 173
  Smith, David, 169, 171, 174
  tax credit, 175
  tax rates, 175
  valuation, 174
Exhibitions, 102

Federal Trade Commission, 61
Fine prints. *See* Prints
First Amendment, 53–61
Fish, use in art, 61
Flag desecration, 59
Flammable Fabrics Act, 61
Flavin, Dan, 91, 92
Forain, 89
Forgeries of art, 183
Foundation Center, 194

Foundation for the Community of Artists, 194
Foundation for Independent Video and Film,
    Inc. (FIVF), 194
Galella, Ronald, 55
Galleries
    accountings, 103
    arbitration, 105
    Arizona statute, 99
    Arkansas statute, 99
    artist-gallery consignment agreement model
        forms, 100, 106–107
    artist-gallery model print agreement, 94–96
    artist-gallery model video agreement,
        142–143
    artistic control, 102
    artist's biographical data, 102
    bankruptcy, 104
    California statute, 99
    Colorado statute, 99
    commissions, 102–103
    Connecticut statute, 99
    consignment, 99–100
    cooperative, 108
    copyright, 104
    creditors of, 104
    customs, 105
    damage to art, 105
    death of artist, 105
    exhibitions, 102
    fiduciary obligations, 99, 101
    foreign currency, 103–104
    inspection of books and records, 106
    location, 101
    loss of art, 105
    Maryland statute, 99
    Massachusetts statute, 99
    Michigan statute, 99
    Minnesota statute, 99
    New Mexico statute, 99
    New York statute, 99
    Oregon statute, 99
    payments to artist, 103–104
    personnel, 101
    prices, 103
    prints, 94–96
    scope of agency, 101
    statement of account, 103
    stipends, 104
    Texas statute, 99
    theft, 105
    video works, 137–138, 142–143
    Washington statute, 99
    Wisconsin statute, 99
Gemini G.E.L., 95, 97–98
Gifts, 162, 170–171, 175, 176–178
Gonzalez, Julio, 169
Governmental symbols, images of, 59
Grants
    income taxation of, 151
    National Endowment for the Arts, 187–188,
        191
    sources of, 191
    state arts agencies, 195–199
Grantsmanship Center, 194
Graphic Artists Guild (GAG), 194
Greenberg, Clement, 169
Guille, 34

Hailman, Johanna K.W., 164–165
Hawaii print statute, 93
Hofmann, Hans, 180–181
Holding form, 87–88
Hutchinson, Peter, 92

Ideas, protection of, 4, 69–70
Illinois print statute, 93

Income taxation
    accounting methods and years, 149–150
    appraisals, insurance, 151–152
    bad debts, 160
    basis, 151
    child and disabled dependent care, 159
    collectors, 186
    cooperative galleries, 108
    contributions, 159, 187
    de Grazia, Anna Maria, 165–166
    estates, 178
    estimated tax, 158
    expenses
        art supplies, 152
        business gifts, 155
        commissions, 155
        depreciation, 153–155
        dues, 152
        educational expenses, 152
        entertainment, 155
        equipment, 153–155
        fair market value, 151
        fees, 155
        moving expenses, 152
        rent, 152–153
        repairs, 152
        salaries, 155
        studio, 152–153
        transportation, 155
        travel, 155
        working space, 152–153
    foreign artists, 161
    foreign residence or presence, 160–161
    foreign taxes, 160–161
    Hailman, Johanna K.W., 164–165
    heirs, 178
    hobby losses, 163–167
    income
        awards, 151
        capital gains income, 150
        earned income, 150
        grants, 151
        ordinary income, 150
        prizes, 151
        valuation, 151–152
    income averaging, 157
    incorporation, 161–162
    Individual Retirement Accounts, 158–159
    insurance proceeds, 152
    investment credit, 159
    Ireland, artists' tax relief, 190
    joint ventures, 162
    Keogh plans, 158–159
    net operating losses, 160
    partnership, 161–162
    profit motive, 163–164
    record keeping, 149
    retirement plans, 158–159
    Schedule C form, 149, 155, 156
    Schedule G, 157
    Schedule SE, 157
    self-employment tax, 157
    Social Security, 157
    tax-exempt organizations, 108
    Tobey, Mark, 161
Incorporation, 161–162
Insurance
    accidents, 86–87
    art consigned, 105
    art in studio, 86–87
    estate taxation, 176
    income taxation, 152
    museum loans, 179
    product liability, 61
    risk of loss, 73, 86–87
International Council of Museums, 183

International Sculpture Center, 194
Interpol, 183
Ireland, artists' tax relief, 190
Italy, laws regulating export of art, 185

Japan, Living National Treasures, 190–191
Jewelry, 10, 116
Joint Ethics Committee, 1, 201–204
Juley, Paul, 86

Kansas statute, 159
Kinstler, Everett Raymond, 86
Kramer, Hilton, 92

Labeling, 61
Lawyers for the arts, 1–2
Lawyers for the Creative Arts, 2
Leases
    assignment, 146
    fixtures, ownership of, 145
    hidden costs, 147
    renewal options, 146
    rent, 145–146
    subletting, 146
    term, 145–146
    termination, 146
    uses of premises, 147, 148
    zoning, 147
Lectures, contracts for, 70–72
LeWitt, Sol, 92
Libel. See Defamation
Lipchitz, Jacques, 170
Lofts. See Studios
Lowe, Ira, 169
Lower Manhattan Loft Tenants Association,
    194

Magazines. See Publishing
Manufacturing, 116–117
Marlborough Galleries, 171
Maryland statutes
    charitable contributions, 159
    consignment, 99
    print, 93
Massachusetts statutes
    consignment, 99
    moral rights, 33, 37–38
Michigan statutes
    charitable contributions, 159
    consignment, 99
Minnesota consignment statute, 99
Minors
    contracts, 65
    models, 58
    releases, 57
Models, see Privacy and Child models
Money, images of, 59–60
Moral rights
    Berne Copyright Convention, 33
    California, 33, 37–38
    Crimi, Alfred, 35, 43–47
    disclosure, 35–36
    enforcement of, 36
    integrity, 34
    Massachusetts, 33, 37–38
    New York, 38–39
    paternity, 33
    Projansky contract, 74–78, 90
    United States legislation, 33–37
    Vargas, Alberto, 33–34, 47–52
Morrel, Mark, 59
Motherwell, Robert, 169
Museums
    artist's rights in museum's works, 181
    bequests to, 180
    commercial exploitation, 181
    gifts to, 180

Hofmann, Hans—University of California
    agreement, 180–181
    loans to, 179–180
    seizure of loaned works, 180

Namath, Joe, 41
Names, business, 40
National Endowment for the Arts, 187–188,
    191
National organizations, 199
Negatives, ownership of, 86
Negotiation, 63
Netherlands, public support programs,
    189–190
New Mexico consignment statute, 99
New York Artists Equity Association, 194
New York statutes
    Art, ownership of, 85–86
    authenticity, 184–185
    child models, 58
    gallery consignments, 99
    moral rights, 38–39
    print law, 94
    privacy, 55–56
    reproduction rights, 85–86
    seizure of loaned works, 180
Noho, 147

Obscenity, 58–59
Onassis, Jaqueline, 55
Oppenheim, Dennis, 91
Oregon statutes
    charitable contributions, 159
    consignment, 99
    reproduction rights and ownership of art,
        85–86
Organization of Independent Artists (OIA), 194
Ownership
    art, 85–86
    negatives, 86

Patents, 41–42
Photographic negatives, ownership of, 86
Posters, 116–117
Picture Agency Council of America, Inc.
    (PACA), 194
Price, and scarcity, 91
Prints
    Arkansas statute, 93
    artist-gallery model print agreement, 96
    California statute, 93–94
    contracts, 94–96, 116–117
    documentation, 95, 97–98
    Gemini G.E.L. form of documentation, 95,
        97–98
    Hawaii statute, 93
    Illinois statute, 93
    Maryland statute, 93
    New York statute, 94
    printers, contracts with, 94
Privacy, right of
    artists protected by, 40–41
    buildings, 57
    child models, 57, 58
    invasion by artist, 54–56
    New York statute, 55–56
    newsworthy event, 55
    public figure, 55
    public interest, 55–56
    release form, 56
    releases, 56–57
    retouching, 57
Projansky, Bob, 74, 78
Projansky contract, 74–78, 90
Public support
    Depression art projects, 188–189
    Ireland, 190

Japan, 190–191
local, 188
National Endowment for the Arts, 187–188,
    191
Netherlands, 189–190
percent for art, 188
state, 188
state arts agencies, 195–198
Works Progress Administration's
    Federal Art Project, 188–189
Publicity, right to, 41
Publishing
    accountings, 129
    advances, 129
    advertising, 132
    agent's fees, 132
    arbitration, 132
    artistic control, 130–131
    ASMP Standard Photographers Book
        Agreement, 127, 130
    assignment, 132
    Authors Guild Trade Book Contract, 127,
        128, 129, 130, 132
    competing works, 131
    collaborators, 133
    contract, model form, 133–135
    copyright, 130
    credits, 131
    delivery of manuscript, 128
    duty to publish, 129
    free copies, 131–132
    grant of rights, 127
    infringement, 130
    inspection of books and records, 129
    options, 131
    original materials, 131
    out-of-print, 129–130
    payments, 129
    permission form, 30
    permissions, 29–30, 128
    reproduction rights. See Reproduction rights.
    reservation of rights, 128
    return of art work, 131
    revisions, 130–131
    rights granted, 127
    royalties, 128–129
    subsidiary rights, 127
    warranty and indemnity, 130
    Writer's Legal Guide, The, 127

Radich Gallery, 59
Rauschenberg, Robert, 91
Reasonable care of art. See Bailments
Reference files, 27
Regional organizations, 198
Regional representatives of The National
    Endowment for the Arts, 199
Renoir, Paul, 170
Renoir, Pierre Auguste, 169–170
Rental of art, 82–84
Reproduction rights
    advances, 113
    assignment description, 111
    California statute, 85–86
    cancellation, 112
    changes, 113, 114
    collections, 114–115
    commercial products, 116–117
    contract forms, conflicts in, 111
    copyright notice, 113
    credit as creator, 113
    due date, 111
    estimates, 114
    expenses, 113
    fee, 111
    graphic designers' estimate/confirmation/
        invoice form, 121–122

illustrators' confirmation form, 119–120
illustrators' invoice, 125–126
invoices, 114
New York statute, 85–86
Oregon statute, 85–86
originals, return of, 113
payment, 114
photographers' assignment form, 117–118
preparation time, 111
releases, 114
reshoots, 113
samples, return of, 113
small claims court, 114–115
syndication, 115–116
textile designers' confirmation form, 123–124
travel time, 111
usage, 112–113
weather days, 111. (See also Publishing)
Resale proceeds right
    California statute, 89–90
    droit de suite, 89
    Projansky contract, 74–78, 90
Retirement, 158–159
Retouching, 57
Rothko, Mark, 170–174
Rouault, 36

Sales
    bill of sale, 74
    bill of sale, video works, 144
    commission agreement for fine art, 78–81
    prints, 93–95
    Projansky contract, 74–78, 90
    reproduction rights. See Reproduction rights
    video works. See Video works
Sales taxes, 149
Security interest, 74
Slander. See Defamation
Small claims court, 114–115
Smith, David, 169, 171, 174
Smokey Bear, 59
Social Security, 157
Society of Illustrators (SI), 194
Society of Photographer and Artist
    Representatives, Inc. (SPAR), 195
Society of Photographers in Communications.
    See American Society of Magazine
    Photographers
Society of Publication Designers (SPD), 195
Soho, 147
South Carolina charitable contributions statute,
    159
Sotheby Parke-Bernet, 183
S.P.A.D.E.M., 89
Specific performance, 68
Stamps, images of, 59–60
State arts agencies, 195–198
Studios
    cooperative buildings, 148
    fixtures, ownership of, 145
    fix-up costs, 145
    suitability for artists, 145
    uses of premises, 148
    zoning, 147
    (See also Leases)
Submission form, 87–88
Swiss Confederation coat of arms, 59
Syndication, 115–116

Taxes
    commercial rent, 149
    sales, 149
    unincorporated business, 149 (See also
        Income taxation)
Tax-exempt organizations, 108
Texas consignment statute, 99
Textile design, 101–102, 112–113

Thefts of art, 183–184
Titles, protection of, 4, 39–40
Tobey, Mark, 161
Trade, 38
Trademarks, 40–41
Tradenames, 40–41
Travel time, 112
Tribeca, 147

UNESCO Convention on the Means of
    Prohibiting and Preventing the Illegal
    Import, Export, and Transfer of Cultural
    Property, 183
Unfair competition, 39–40
Unincorporated business tax, 149
Uniform Commercial Code
    creditors, 99, 104
    financing statements, 99
    Form 1, 74, 104
    risk of loss, 105
    sales of goods, 64
    security interest, 74
    time in which to sue, 65–66
    warranties, 66–67, 184
    written evidence required, 65–66
United States Fish and Wildlife Service, 61
Uniqueness of art, 91–93
Universal Copyright Convention, 4

Vargas, Alberto, 33–34, 47–52
Video works
    artist-gallery video agreement, 137–138,
        142–143
    bill of sale, 144
    broadcast contract, 138–142
    originality, 137
    reproduction, 137
Volunteer Lawyers for the Arts, 2

Warhol, Andy, 91
Warranties. See Contracts
Washington consignment statute, 99
Weather days, 112
Weiner, Lawrence, 91, 92
Whistler, 35–36
Wildlife, use in art, 61
Wilson, Ian, 91
Wisconsin consignment statute, 99
Woodsy Owl, 59
Work for hire, 23–26
Works Progress Administration's Federal Art
    Project, 188–189

Zoning, 147

Photo: Toby Titus

Tad Crawford, attorney and author, has lobbied for artists' rights on the state and federal level. A graduate of Columbia Law School and former General Counsel to the Graphic Artists Guild, he teaches art law at the School of Visual Arts in New York City. A columnist for *Communication Arts Magazine,* he frequently lectures to artists' groups and students around the nation. His other books include *Selling Your Photography* (Arie Kopelman, co-author), *Selling Your Graphic Design and Illustration* (Arie Kopelman, co-author) and *The Writer's Legal Guide.*